Problems and Opportunities in U.S.-Quebec Relations

Also of Interest

Wilderness of Mirrors: Images of Canada in the World, edited by Don Munton and Denis Stairs

†*Natural Resources in U.S.-Canadian Relations: Volume 1—The Evolution of Policies and Issues,* edited by Carl E. Beigie and Alfred O. Hero, Jr.

†*Natural Resources in U.S.-Canadian Relations: Volume 2—Patterns and Trends in Resource Supplies and Policies,* edited by Carl E. Beigie and Alfred O. Hero, Jr.

†*Change in the International System,* edited by Ole R. Holsti, Randolph M. Siverson, and Alexander L. George

†*Nations and States: An Enquiry into the Origins of Nations and the Politics of Nationalism,* Hugh Seton-Watson

†Available in hardcover and paperback.

Westview Special Studies in International Relations

Problems and Opportunities in U.S.-Quebec Relations
edited by Alfred O. Hero, Jr., and Marcel Daneau

The failure of the May 1980 Quebec referendum on sovereignty and the ratification in 1982 of a Canadian constitution, over Quebec's vehement objection but with the acquiescence of all other provinces, would appear to indicate that the likelihood of Quebec's independence has been sharply reduced, if not eliminated. Not so, is the considered judgment of the editors of this first serious empirical study to be published on the complex network of linkages between the United States and Canada's French-speaking province. Far from having settled the fundamental issues of Quebec nationalism, they conclude, the developments of the past few years have served to exacerbate the dispute. Unless and until the federal leadership and English-speaking Canadians generally become willing to make significant concessions toward de facto special status for Quebec, allowing local control over linguistic, cultural, and related economic policies, a majority of Quebeckers will support the Lévesque Parti Québécois (PQ) or successor political movements devoted to achieving the above minimum objectives and, failing that, to taking Quebec out of the federation.

This volume is the first to consider authoritatively the implications for the United States of a more autonomous, if not independent, Quebec. The authors—half from Canada, half from the United States—address relations in the areas of trade, investment, labor, the environment, migration, cultural and communications linkages, and the organization of government and private institutions for maximizing opportunities for advantage. Emphasizing trends and problems that need to be addressed on both sides of the frontier, irrespective of the eventual outcome of the continuing controversy between Quebec, Ottawa, and anglophone Canada, the authors also devote particular attention to how Quebec's interests and actions that are of concern to the United States differ from those of the rest of Canada. In the final chapter the editors consider some likely implications, for U.S.-Quebec relations, of alternative outcomes of the Quebec-Ottawa constitutional dispute.

Alfred Olivier Hero, Jr., is Claude T. Bissell Professor of Canadian-American Relations, University of Toronto. **Marcel Daneau** is director of the Centre Québécois des Relations Internationales and professor of economics at Université Laval.

Problems and Opportunities in U.S.-Quebec Relations

edited by Alfred O. Hero, Jr.,
and Marcel Daneau

Westview Press / Boulder and London

Westview Special Studies in International Relations

Published in 1984 in the United States of America by Westview Press, Inc., 5500 Central Avenue, Boulder, Colorado 80301; Frederick A. Praeger, President and Publisher

Library of Congress Cataloging in Publication Data
Main entry under title:
Problems and opportunities in U.S.-Quebec relations.
  (Westview special studies in international relations)
  Includes index.
    1. United States—Relations—Québec (Province)—
Addresses, essays, lectures. 2. Québec (Province)—
Relations—United States—Addresses, essays, lectures.
3. United States—Foreign economic relations—Québec
(Province)—Addresses, essays, lectures. 4. Québec
(Province)—Foreign economic relations—United States—
Addresses, essays, lectures. I. Hero, Alfred O.
II. Daneau, Marcel. III. Title: Problems and
opportunities in US-Quebec relations. IV. Series.
E183.8.C2P76 1984   327.730714   83-16900
ISBN 0-86531-634-1

45,224

Printed and bound in the United States of America

Contents

Illustrations

Foreword

This book is in part an update of a comparable multi-authored volume by Canadians and Americans a decade ago, *Le nationalisme québécois à la croisée des chemins.*[1] That earlier book analyzed evolving Quebec nationalism in the context of the network of interests and linkages of the majority-French-speaking province with both the rest of Canada and the United States. The endeavor was cosponsored by the Quebec Center for International Affairs at Laval University in Quebec City, the McGill University Center for French-Canadian Studies in Montreal, and the World Peace Foundation in Boston. It considered impacts of dynamic post–World War II communication, cultural, economic, and political factors on Quebec nationalism and its objectives, and implications of these factors for English Canada and, particularly, the United States.

The studies for the earlier book were undertaken in 1972–1973, drafted into discussion papers in early 1974, and rewritten after a three-day meeting in May 1974 of the authors, editors, and perceptive participant observers in the pertinent processes in the respective governments, private sectors, and institutions. The meeting took place at an authentically Québécois country inn on the Richelieu River near where British forces defeated the Patriots' insurrection in 1838—a movement that sought to create an independent, French-speaking, democratic Quebec. The volume that was subsequently published was directed primarily at Quebeckers,[2] and was, therefore, published in Quebec in the language spoken by over four-fifths of its population.

Since that volume appeared, the federalist Provincial Liberal (PLQ) Bourassa government was replaced in 1976 by the independentist Lévesque Parti Québécois (PQ) government. Nearly three-fifths of the Quebec population, including a small majority of French-speakers, voted in a 1980 referendum against that government attempting to negotiate sovereignty, paired with continued economic association in a common market or customs union and a common currency with the rest of Canada. However, that PQ government was reelected in

1981. Subsequent to defeat of the referendum, the Trudeau government has further centralized the federation and patriated (as Canada's own) the constitution created by the British North America Act of 1867, which otherwise could theoretically have been changed by the British Parliament like any other legislation. The Trudeau government took this action with the acquiescence of all the English-speaking provinces. However, it was done over Quebec's vociferous opposition and without its rights of veto over amendments—rights that both the PQ government and a majority of its PLQ opposition regard as crucial, the sine qua non of Quebec's acceptance of federation over a century ago, and customary thereafter.

Quebec's network of relationships with the United States has also developed significantly since the earlier volume went to press in late 1974. Notwithstanding the worst and most prolonged economic recession on both sides of the frontier since the Great Depression—more severe in Canada than in the United States and particularly so in Quebec— economic interdependence between Quebec and the United States, especially the latter's northeastern and Great Lakes regions, has grown in complexity and intensity. Balance of payments in favor of Quebec in trade in merchandise has grown as well, while the balance in tourism favorable to Quebec a decade ago has rather sharply reversed, not- withstanding decline in the value of the Canadian dollar[3] relative to the American dollar. Transborder contacts and collaboration between provincial and state officials, private and public enterprise, media, and other walks of life have grown significantly, as have U.S. cultural and media influences in Quebec society.

The first electoral victory of the more social-democratic PQ, em- phasizing state roles in economic development over private enterprise as favored by the PLQ, followed by only a few days U.S. election of Democrat Jimmy Carter to the White House and Democratic majorities to both houses of Congress, over the more business-biased Republicans. However, replacement of the more decentralizing, pro-business Clark minority government in Canada by an increasingly centralist and interventionist Trudeau majority regime in early 1980 was succeeded in the United States late that year by election of a conservative, decentralizing, private enterprise–dominated Reagan Republican ad- ministration, a conservative Republican-controlled Senate, and a less Democratic House. In Quebec the PQ was reelected several months thereafter. Confronted with its loss of the referendum and especially with widespread unemployment and general economic malaise, the second Lévesque government shifted appreciably from its earlier em- phasis on political sovereignty and public investment and intervention toward encouragement of private enterprise and foreign, particularly U.S., direct investment.

The World Peace Foundation and the Quebec Center for International Affairs, in the interim between the appearance of the 1974 volume and this one, sponsored together with others and separately a variety of programs on relations of Canada as a whole and Quebec in particular with the United States, and on topics of mutual interest regarding other countries, areas, and issues. After reelection of the Lévesque government, these two cosponsors decided to enlist the most able talent in both societies to reexamine systematically the relationships between the United States and Quebec across the relevant spectrum of economic, cultural, and political domains, with a view toward drawing out opportunities for the future and policy issues related to achieving them.

The outcomes of the continuing debates and active struggles between the Lévesque government and its PLQ opposition, and between both and the federal and other provincial authorities over Quebec's future political and constitutional roles vis-à-vis the patriated constitution or a considerably amended federal system, will inevitably affect the politics, locales of decision making, mechanisms, and overall tones of coping with this complex network of relationships. However, the eventual constitutional and political jurisdictions of Quebec and the emphases, politics, and other pertinent qualities of the governments that will implement them cannot be predicted. The cosponsors, therefore, decided to focus primarily on basic phenomena and issues that will face whatever constitutional system might emerge and whatever governments may be empowered to deal with them. Except for brief observations directly pertinent to how U.S.-Quebec relations might evolve, in the chapter on Quebec policies toward the United States, the authors do not deal with the various complicated speculative scenarios and subscenarios for Quebec vis-à-vis Canada. The editors will hazard in their conclusions some brief general hypotheses about the potential implications for Quebec's relations with the United States of several alternatives short of either complete independence for Quebec or its membership in a considerably more centralized Canadian federation, both considered unlikely.

With generous financial support from the Quebec Ministry of Intergovernmental Affairs, the Quebec Center involved the talents and energies of leading Québécois experts on economic, cultural, and political domains, and the World Peace Foundation engaged their nonfrancophone counterparts in the United States and, in one case, Anglo-Canada. The draft research manuscripts prepared by these selected experts provided the agenda for thoroughgoing, off-the-record discussion by the authors among themselves and with others actively involved in both public and private sectors in the phenomena being analyzed, at the Harvard Faculty Club in Cambridge, Massachusetts, in September 1982. This volume is composed of revisions of some of those manuscripts plus two others later prepared by participants in light of those discussions. Two authors were unable to divert sufficient time from other commitments to accomplish the further research that appropriate revisions would require. A number of the authors were obliged to reduce sharply the original detail and length of their contributions to meet stringent space limitations. The quality of the analysis that follows in this volume is due primarily to the seriousness and wisdom that the authors applied to their respective contributions, and to their willingness to deal so constructively with the many criticisms and suggestions of their colleagues and, particularly, the rather demanding editors.

This volume, like the research and the participation by Quebec authors in the meeting in Cambridge, would not have been possible but for further generous financial assistance of the Quebec government. Its Ministry of Intergovernmental Affairs provided a substantial part of the expense of the senior editor's eight months as visiting scholar during the academic year 1982–1983 at the University Consortium for Research on North America, located at the Center for International Affairs at Harvard University. The editor devoted part of this time to working with the authors and with his coeditor, who at that time was on sabbatical leave in France from Laval University, to refine their manuscripts for publication. The ministry also financed other editorial expenses and part of the expense of manufacture of this book.

The editors profited extensively from the thoughtful and efficient labors of the staffs of their respective organizations, the Quebec Center for International Affairs, the World Peace Foundation until September 3, 1982, and thereafter the University Consortium for Research on North America at Harvard University. In particular, Lily Réhel, Elizabeth Ferber, Victoria Bolles, Margaret Blake, and Melissa Haussman must be acknowledged for their assistance.

The interpretations and judgments in this volume are, of course, those of the authors after considering detailed suggestions from the editors and others as earlier noted. Neither the sponsoring organizations—which are precluded as nonprofit educational institutions from arguing particular policies in the public domain—nor the Quebec government have acted to influence any author, nor are they responsible for any errors of fact or interpretation.

Although this volume is published in English in the United States primarily to reach U.S. readers, we trust it will be of equal interest not only to Québécois but to other Canadians as well.

Alfred O. Hero, Jr.
Cambridge, Massachusetts

Marcel Daneau
Montpellier, France

Notes

1. Albert Legault and Alfred O. Hero, Jr., eds., *Le nationalisme québécois à la croisée des chemins* (Quebec: Centre Québécois des Relations Internationales, *Choix* 7, 1975).

2. By the 1970s, most native French-speakers in Quebec had come to consider themselves Québécois rather than French-Canadians. That term will be used in this volume interchangeably with francophone, or French-speaking Quebeckers. The use of Quebeckers without limiting adjectives will denote all citizens and landed immigrants residing in Quebec province. (Connotations of this term among nonfrancophone Quebeckers are briefly discussed in Chapter 11.)

3. Data in dollars in this volume are in Canadian dollars unless otherwise indicated.

1
Introduction

Alfred O. Hero, Jr.
Marcel Daneau

The United States—its economy and society—is the most important overall influence on Quebec outside Canada. In some respects, the long-term significance of the United States for Quebec may well be greater than that of the rest of Canada.

For the United States, Quebec represents nearly a fifth of its largest foreign market for merchandise (a twentieth of its world market) and a still larger share of its foreign income from tourists and services. Quebec is the United States' principal international source of the controversial mineral asbestos and of paper and pulp. Quebec is also one of several major U.S. sources of copper, zinc, and increasingly, gold. The U.S. aerospace industry has important links with that of Quebec— half the aerospace industry of all Canada. And Quebec will probably become a growing source of hydroelectric power for the most densely populated region of the United States, its northeast, where electricity is dear. Of vacation lands with different languages and associated cultures, Mexico and Quebec are the least costly to reach. Americans of French-speaking Canadian ancestry comprise one of the United States' largest non–Anglo-Saxon ethnic groups.

Even more significant to Americans will probably be the eventual outcome of the enduring, deeply rooted, shearing, and far-from-resolved political and constitutional issues posed by Québécois nationalism, because Canada is the state with which the United States has by far the greatest network of political, cultural, economic, and collective-security linkages and interests. The nationalism controversy has been more exacerbated than alleviated by patriation of the constitution from Britain in 1981 after years of controversy with Quebec. The PQ government and most of the PLQ opposition had vehemently opposed the move, although all the other provincial governments had acquiesced. Most members of francophone elites in Quebec feel that the new

1

constitution's amendment procedures are designed at least in part to override Quebec's opposition with anglophone majorities and that the charter of rights as interpreted by federal courts will threaten Quebec's language and culture.

Canadians need eventually to resolve this divisive dispute among themselves, but until they do, it will divert the attention, energies, and priorities of talented Québécois and other Canadians from other critical issues of concern to Americans and will affect the actions of governments in both Quebec and Ottawa with respect to these issues. Any likely U.S. government is apt to continue to avoid behavior that might be construed by either the Ottawa or Quebec governments as intervention in their quarrel. Nevertheless, by inadvertence, ignorance, or systematic biases toward one side in the dispute, Americans, especially in the private sector, may find themselves implicated to the perceived advantage of that side. Finally, the specifics of the arrangement finally worked out between Quebec and the rest of Canada may significantly impinge on U.S. interests and concerns.

The Bilateral Economic, Cultural, and Political Context

If Quebec's economy is to evolve out of its persisting economic malaise of consistently higher unemployment, lower overall productivity, and major dependence on traditional, obsolescent, labor-intensive manufactures of textiles, clothing, footwear, leather goods, and furniture—saleable almost exclusively behind highly protectionist tariffs, quotas, and other trade barriers—it must develop higher-technology, internationally competitive, export-oriented industries commensurate with its potential comparative advantage. Most of the markets for newer products, whether electronic goods, office and communications equipment, computer softwear, biomedicals and pharmaceuticals, or more fabricated forms of Quebec's natural resources, must be developed in the United States. Such industries are unlikely to evolve in Quebec on the scale required without major U.S. participation through expanded private investment, joint ventures, transfers of technology, continent-wide marketing systems, and injections of technical and other expertise. Quebec's comparative export of greatest long-term potential in growth and leverage is probably inexpensive hydropower, the most lucrative natural market for which is the U.S. northeast.

The United States is Quebec's potentially most profitable source of tourists, as well as the principal vacationland for its own population outside the province. The United States is also Quebec's primary outside source of sophisticated business and professional services and of advanced graduate school and professional education for its most talented youth.

Quebec vitally needs its recurring favorable balances in trade in tangible goods with the United States to offset its negative balances in trade in tourism and services with the United States and in all trade combined with the rest of the world, including Canada itself. And the United States will long remain Quebec's principal source of both direct and indirect foreign investment for both private and public economic enterprises.

Mutually fruitful economic cooperation with the United States should be especially important for the 18 to 35 percent of Québécois who, since the 1976 election, have preferred an independent Quebec even if a common market, free-trade area, or customs union, along with common currency with Canada, could not be negotiated. Such cooperation should be almost as important to the 32 to 54 percent of Québécois who have preferred political sovereignty only with the noted economic association.[1] Growing majorities of Québécois expressing opinions in polls since the mid-1960s have either favored independence (with or without economic association) or a dualistic approach to Canadian federalism that recognizes their province as the homeland of one of two founding peoples whose language and culture are inherently different from and equal to those of the Canadian majority. Most Québécois favor further devolution from the Canadian to the Quebec government of jurisdictions they regard as significant in preserving and developing their unique culture— including related economic domains. They prefer such decentralizations over the status quo and especially over what they generally regard as increasing centralization under successive Liberal federal governments headed by Pierre Eliot Trudeau.[2]

Most Québécois, including elites, would probably accept as a viable long-term compromise a solution along the general lines of the January 1979 recommendations of the Pépin-Robarts Task Force on Canadian Unity. Those recommendations were explicit in recognizing Quebec's "distinctive culture and heritage" and would permit devolution of powers bearing on such distinctive aspects to all provinces. Only Quebec would likely avail itself of this privilege, so that the recommendations amounted to de facto special status for Quebec. But these recommendations were never seriously considered by the Trudeau government, although it set up the prestigious and knowledgeable commission that urged them; the government's actions since then have been largely in the reverse direction.

Unwillingness of the Canadian government to negotiate such a compromise undoubtedly accounts for a considerable fraction of the large Québécois minority who favor independence with or without economic association. Yet persistence of those who favor a Pépin-Robarts type resolution partly hinders more francophones from supporting the PQ alternative, and concerns about economic consequences have probably been an even more potent deterrent.

Many Québécois have doubted, in light of the contrary economic interests of most provinces other than Ontario,[3] that the rest of Canada would accept an economic association that would assure protected markets for Quebec's soft goods across the country and the flow of prairie oil and gas to a Quebec no longer part of Canada—or that the association would be effectively implemented or long endure even if negotiated. A majority is unlikely to go along with assuming those economic risks so long as the Quebec economy is dependent on exports across Canada of its internationally uncompetitive traditional products, which still account for more than a quarter of its manufacturing jobs. Thus, development of a modernized, export-based economy linked primarily with the giant market to Quebec's south is a top objective of the "progressiste" PQ government and the growing francophone business community of federalist, private-enterprise persuasions alike.

Quebec francophones, moreover, have been at least as favorable as other Canadians to expansion of trade with, and to most types of investment from, the United States.[4] Indeed, from the 1930s until the mid-1970s, Québécois held generally more favorable attitudes toward the United States and its citizens than did anglophone Canadians—a pattern that seems to have reappeared since 1980.[5] Anglo-Canadian nationalism has been directed primarily against U.S. economic penetration and influence and related cultural impacts on Canadian identity. On the other hand, Québécois nationalism, with the exception of the small anticapitalist, anti-American left—of little practical influence beyond intellectuals, their students, and a minority of trade union activists, mainly in the public sector—has been much more directed against influences of anglophone Canada (especially Quebec's own Montreal minority and Ontario) and a federal government apt to be increasingly controlled by anglophones perceived as little sensitive to or interested in francophone priorities. Québécois nationalists have been mainly concerned about preserving and developing their language and their integrally interdependent culture, perceiving themselves as inherently North American but clearly different from Americans, and feeling relatively insulated from U.S. cultural influence by their different traditions and language. Thus they have felt less threatened and more at ease with the United States than with the rest of Canada. Québécois who have preferred independence or sovereignty-association and voted for the PQ have not differed in these respects from those of federalist persuasion and PLQ partisan preferences.[6]

Unlike many nationalist anglophones, especially in Ontario, most Québécois nationalists interested in the United States consider Americans unduly indifferent but friendly neighbors. A number of the more sophisticated and politically active Québécois regard Americans as potential counterweights, even levers, for coping with Ottawa, Toronto, and Anglo-Canadian influences and pressures.

The Québécois general public, moreover, harbors more favorable opinions about the United States and its people and accords higher priority to relations with them than to France and the French.[7] Most of those with favorable feelings about France are positively inclined toward the United States as well.[8] France is regarded primarily as a cultural counterweight to the surrounding anglophone continent; French investment and trade is, and will remain, very modest. Americans consider this well documented pattern surprising, particularly given that most of the international news read by Québécois, including developments in the United States and U.S. relations with Europe and the rest of the world, comes from *Agence France Presse* or the publications *Le Monde, Nouvel Observateur, Le Point, L'Express,* and other French sources to which Québécois are exposed, and is written by French journalists primarily for European rather than Canadian audiences.

The underpinnings of those proclivities favoring the United States and its people are multiple and mutually reinforcing. U.S. society, people, and ways of life are the milieu outside Quebec with which Québécois are most familiar and feel the most affinity. They like to deal with, visit, and retire to this atmosphere of life. Most of the growing francophone business, managerial, technical, and professional class has been trained in U.S. methods and is most "at home" with U.S. counterparts, business practices, products, customers, and consultants. Winter respites in Florida and other warm locales and a summer week or more on the New England shore have become habitual for the masses and elites alike, virtually regardless of political and ideological persuasion. The vast majority of Québécois are much more North American in their values, aspirations, and tastes than they are like Europeans, French-speaking or otherwise. And even the university-educated cosmopolitan elite outside business who appreciate French literature, theater, philosophy, arts, food and drink, and culture in general are usually equally open to counterparts from the United States. They, like many other Québécois, often feel more at ease with Americans than with English-speaking Canadians in Anglo-Canada.

This cultural, social, economic, and attitudinal reality poses opportunities for the people of both the United States and Quebec for more effective cooperation in their mutual interests, to which very few Americans and only a limited minority of Quebeckers seem to have devoted much consideration. But it also suggests growing problems, dilemmas, and policy issues in both the public and private sectors for the majority of thoughtful Québécois elites—notwithstanding their constitutional and political preferences—who want to develop a lively, attractive, French-speaking North American culture different from that of France on the one hand, the United States and Anglo-Canada on the other, and thus unique to francophone Quebec.

A unique Quebec francophone culture and identity were effectively preserved for two centuries after cession of New France to Britain in 1763 until the Quiet Revolution, which surfaced under the Liberal government of former federal MP and cabinet member Jean Lesage in the early 1960s. The conditions and means that had assured the uniqueness—a culturally insulated French-speaking people whose educational, social service, and other significant private institutions were controlled by an ultramontane, isolationist, Catholic church; a traditional agrarian economy and social system; a francophone elite that left industry and commerce beyond the local economy to anglophones; and minimalist governments, hostile to state intervention and sympathetic to private enterprise and foreign investment—no longer pertain. The combination of massive urbanization, industrialization, secularization, modernized education, modern electronic communication, travel outside Quebec (especially in the United States), expanded learning of English as a second language, and escalating exposure to Anglo-Canadian and particularly U.S. ideas, tastes, media, direct contacts, and cultural products has resulted in accelerating penetration of this small society of less than 6,000,000 francophones surrounded and outnumbered forty to one by North American anglophones and separated by 3,000 miles from the nearest major concentration of French-speaking people. Québécois' North American experience and mentality and that of their overwhelmingly anglophone superpower neighbor are partly in common. A widespread preference for much that is American over other alternatives, their affinities for American ways and people, the growth of available choices of American over other cultural products due to cable television, satellite communications, and other developing communications technologies, and expanded direct investment by U.S. enterprises in Quebec, with attendant U.S. methods and contacts with U.S. consultants and their ideas, will continue to expand American cultural penetration.

Some cultural and intellectual elites are increasingly concerned about the apparent preferences of so many Québécois, especially the young, for mass U.S. culture over more sophisticated alternatives indigenous to Quebec or related to European and other francophone societies. However, analyses of the U.S. impacts and serious consideration of how to cope with them over the next several decades have been surprisingly infrequent among social scientists, communications specialists, journalists, government officials, and other elites. Most of these groups have been much more concerned about arresting cultural influences of anglophone Canada, particularly the economically powerful Quebec minority, and reinforcement of the anglophone culture through its assimilation of immigrants and their descendants and, to a lesser extent, of native francophones as well.

In the longer run, however, the more pervasive U.S. cultural penetration, both directly and through Anglo-Canada, will probably become regarded as a growing threat. Resources and vehicles for countervailing it, and for providing indigenous alternatives to it, will, however, remain quite limited. Although the development of communications technologies will permit making French and other foreign francophone ideas and cultural products more widely available across Quebec, their impacts at the mass level, outside the more cosmopolitan, culturally interested minority, will remain modest beyond those cultural aspects integral to the French language itself.

Quebec's problems of communicating valid images of its cultural, economic, and political interests and objectives to Americans, particularly those apt to influence decisions and actions pertinent to Quebec, are enormous. Its material and human resources and available instruments for this communication are, of course, quite modest. So far, Quebec's particular cultural, economic, and other interests and arguments have reached only small minorities, most of them atypical even among the more cosmopolitan, culturally aware, and internationally alert people of English-speaking America.

Few people of the United States have much direct experience with Quebec except as non-French-speaking tourists, businessmen, professional people, and others with practical reasons for going there, or except when dealing with Quebeckers in the United States or by telephone or mail. U.S. contacts are predominantly with Canadians whose native tongue is English, including within Quebec where they constitute only 10 percent or so of the population (10.9 percent in 1981).[9] Americans' perceptions and interpretations of Quebec come from anglophones they have met, Canadian English-language media written by anglophones, and U.S. media derived from anglophones. The relatively few people of the United States who communicate with Quebec francophones do so primarily with bilingual ones whose views on Quebec and its relations with Ottawa, the rest of Canada, and the United States most nearly approach those of their Canadian anglophone equivalents. These observations also generally apply, albeit to a somewhat attenuated degree, to most of the non–French-speaking U.S. foreign-policy community and to many others with significant interests in Canada.

The resulting biases in favor of anglophone arguments in the fundamental Canadian cultural and linguistic controversy are reinforced by natural affinities of the English-speaking U.S. citizens for English-speaking Canadians and their culture. Anglo-Canadian culture and history are more like U.S. culture and history in experience and tradition. The melting-pot myth, loss of ethnic languages and assimilation of most children of immigrants, the bloodiest war in U.S. history over secession of its most different culture and region, recent concerns over coping with Hispanics concentrated in the U.S. southwest, and the often prickly U.S. relations with France, all encourage proclivities within the United States for Anglo-Canada over Quebec.

Cultural and informational efforts made in the United States by successive Quebec governments have understandably been limited, and similar efforts actively involving private Quebec institutions have been very few. The most focused endeavors have been for U.S. minorities of francophone Canadian descent, particularly in Louisiana and, to a lesser extent, in areas of the U.S. northeast near Quebec.

The language and related cultural differences that filter American cultural impacts on Quebec as contrasted to those on English-speaking Canada conversely limit Quebec's cultural influence in the United States beyond the relatively small minorities whose ancestors came from Canadian or other French-speaking societies, or who, for one reason or another, can read or speak French. But efforts to reach even these people have been frustrating, and endeavors designed to reach wider publics with English translations of Quebec drama, novels, poetry, and other cultural products have usually been disappointing. The images of Quebec obtained in the United States, as described above, and the paucity of exposure to more interesting aspects of Quebec culture are interrelated, particularly among the politically and culturally alert U.S. minority who are influential both on the opinions of others and on public and private decisions of interest to Quebec.

Better-developed political and public-policy aspects of current and potential relationships will be crucial to the development of all other aspects of U.S.-Quebec interactions. To what extent are the Quebec body politic, and particularly its elites and politically active and in-fluential minorities, aware of longer-term Quebec interests vis-à-vis the United States and apt to accord priorities and develop sustained policies to advance those interests? How broadly based among PQ activists and supporters, and in the body politic at large, are the apparent shifts in emphases and in organization by the Lévesque government toward developing more pragmatic, mutually rewarding economic relations, and to a lesser degree, cultural and informational relations with the United States? Would an alternative government behave differently, and would its base support it if it did? Or are preoccupations with Quebec's internal politics and economic problems, and with the continuing struggle with the federal government and Anglo-Canada over greater Quebec autonomy, apt to continue so to monopolize the priorities, attention, and energies of able personalities in and out of government as to render more systematic thought and action unlikely toward developing relations of long-term significance with the United States?

Finally, priorities and perceptions in the United States as they pertain to Quebec, to Canada, and to the international scene in general—especially at the decision-making and decision-influencing levels—will be critical to most future relationships. Priorities and perceptions in the private sector in particular, as they bear on direct and indirect investment, media coverage, and political uncertainties regarding Quebec's future relationships with the rest of Canada, will be particularly significant. The perceptions of the foreign-policy community in and out of Washington, much influenced by elements in the private sector, will bear more directly on the content and more subtle tones of U.S. governmental thinking, utterances, and actions, especially if the conflict between Quebec and Ottawa intensifies and significant U.S. interests appear threatened thereby.

Objectives and Limitations of This Volume

No brief volume can cope systematically with all the factors impinging on so many significant issues. Moreover, systematic research on critical aspects of most of the factors, particularly outside the economic domain, is often nonexistent or rudimentary, or at best devoted to limited parts of such broad questions. Few Americans, even among those concerned with Canada generally, have been sufficiently interested or informed about Quebec, have ascribed enough importance to it, or have had requisite command of the French language to examine authoritatively the developments there, even from primarily U.S. frames of reference.

Most Québécois who have expertise appropriate to such research, again with the partial exception of economists, have been preoccupied with internal Quebec developments and their significance for Quebec's relations with anglophone Canada. There has been no multidisciplinary francophone center for systematic attention to the United States and either Quebec's or Canada's relationships with it. There is only a relative handful of Québécois specialists on the United States outside the Canadian government, the School of Advanced Commercial Studies in Montreal, one or two other major business schools with graduate programs, a few consultants and other executives of U.S.-involved corporate enterprises, and a few teachers of individual courses in comparative literature, history, or two or three other domains. Faculty members and courses in francophone universities dealing systematically with Quebec's or Canada's relations with the United States are fewer still, and those in U.S. foreign policy no more than one or two.

Thus, the limited body of prior research and knowledgeable talent on which this volume can draw in either Canada or the United States renders it only an initial effort to assess and interpret some of the pertinent facts and to consider alternative lines of action to deal with the implications of those facts. Chapters focused on particular issue areas, groups, and determinants in U.S.-Quebec relationships are necessarily limited to a few of the more significant topics for which appropriate talent could be secured. The editors in their conclusions attempt to deal briefly with some other important considerations, in some domains derived from their own and others' investigations but involving many of their own impressions, hypotheses, and speculations. Inevitably some of the latter will prove incorrect or in need of serious modification as events unfold, or as other researchers examine these aspects in depth.[10]

The editors hope that this volume will stimulate social scientists, other scholars, their graduate students, journalists, governmental officials, and other individuals to examine the speculations suggested and the many gaps apparent in knowledge of phenomena that are of critical long-term significance. Most of the impetus and the ensuing research should come from Québécois as those most affected. Relations with the United States will be much more vital in almost every respect to them than to the U.S. people.

A handful of qualified Americans will at best devote significant blocs of their careers to one or another aspect of these linkages, most likely as part of broader theoretical, substantive, or policy interests or concerns about Quebec's relevance to wider issues of U.S.-Canadian relations. A larger number and diversity of able Americans may be persuaded to provide some of their U.S. experience and expertise where relevant to analyses in process or in draft by imaginative and otherwise qualified Québécois or other Canadians.

The Chapters in Brief

Although economic, cultural, and communicational and political relations are usually closely interrelated, for analytical feasibility the chapters in this volume are organized in three successive sections in that general order. However, the authors consider factors across these domains insofar as they bear on their particular topics.

Chapter 2, by Bernard Bonin, professor of economics at the National School of Public Administration and visiting scholar at the Center for International Business Studies at the School of Advanced Commercial

Studies, associated with the University of Montreal, considers linkages among trade, investment, and other broad economic aspects. The author previously served as assistant deputy minister of intergovernmental affairs charged with research on Quebec's economic relationships with the rest of Canada, the United States, Europe, and other countries. He held this position during the first Lévesque administration; still earlier he was deputy minister of immigration under both PQ and PLQ ministers and a professor of economics at the School of Advanced Commercial Studies.

Chapter 3, by Alexander C. Tomlinson, president of the National Planning Association since January 1982, discusses perceptions of Quebec in U.S. corporate communities, and how those perceptions pertain to private investment in Quebec. Mr. Tomlinson was with Morgan Stanley and Co. from 1950 until 1976 and was a partner after 1958. He was president, Morgan Stanley Canada Ltd., in Montreal, from 1972 to 1976. In 1976 he became chairman of the Executive Committee and Director of the First Boston Corporation and Chairman of First Boston (Canada) Ltd. He retired from investment banking in 1982 but continues as a First Boston director.

Chapter 4, by Jean Boivin, professor of collective bargaining and labor union history in the Department of Industrial Relations at Laval University in Quebec City, examines the role of Quebec in the evolution of Canadian trade unions toward greater autonomy from U.S. international unions and their U.S. federations, and the implications of trade union developments in Quebec for U.S. international unions and U.S. investment and other interests.

Chapter 5, by Réjean Lachapelle, director of research, Quebec Ministry of Cultural Communities and Immigration, considers migrations of Americans to Quebec and vice versa in the contexts of Quebec's economic needs, needs for talent, overall receipt of immigrants from other Canadian provinces and other countries, and loss of emigrants to other provinces and countries.

Chapter 6, by John E. Carroll, associate professor of environmental conservation at the University of New Hampshire, closes the analyses of economic linkages with an examination of transborder environmental issues and the efforts and potentialities of the Quebec government to cope with them in collaboration with governments of nearby states.

The cultural discussion begins with the Chapter 7, by Yvan Lamonde, director and associate professor of history, French-Canadian Studies Program, McGill University, and research associate at the Quebec Institute of Research in Culture. Mr. Lamonde puts into historical perspective two centuries of American cultural influence and analyzes available data on its growing recent impacts.

Chapters 8 and 9 consider Quebec linkages with U.S. minorities of francophone ancestry, particularly in Louisiana and New England. The first of these chapters, by Gerald L. Gold, associate professor of anthropology and coordinator of the ethnic research program, York University, and formerly of Laval University, is derived from extensive field research conducted during four years (ending in 1980) among Louisiana Acadians, Creoles, and other Louisianians of French extraction by a team of social scientists associated with Laval, McGill, and York Universities. Mr. Gold was chief organizer of the investigative team. The second chapter, by Armand B. Chartier, associate professor of French and head of the section of French studies at the University of Rhode Island in Kingston—and himself a New Englander of Quebec ancestry active in that minority's efforts to preserve and develop its heritage—describes the evolution of his ethnic group, its linkages with Quebec since the initial immigration to the United States in the 1840s, prospects and potentially fruitful programs for effective containment and reversal of assimilation since World War II, and useful roles of Quebec toward achieving that end.

Chapter 10, by Stephen Banker, a U.S. journalist who for twenty years has been a regular contributor to the Canadian Broadcasting Corporation (CBC), whose writings have appeared in *Smithsonian, The New York Times, The Washington Post,* and *TV Guide,* and who publishes the audio-cassette series *Tapes for Readers,* examines the content, thrust, and tone of coverage of Quebec in U.S. media and the sources and processes that result in biases in this coverage. Mr. Banker himself has frequently covered Washington, D.C., and broad U.S. developments for CBC's English-language network.

Chapter 11 notes the images and attitudes that prevail about Quebec in the 18 percent of the Quebec population that is either native anglophone or nonfrancophone immigrants and their offspring, then discusses how those images influence the images of Quebec in the United States. The chapter also devotes brief attention to impacts of the United States on nonfrancophone Quebec attitudes and behavior. These phenomena deserve systematic analysis, although very little has so far been done. In Quebec, nonfrancophones have been too preoccupied with their changing status in the province and especially with language legislation and its enforcement (first under Law 22 in 1974 under the Liberal Bourassa government, but especially under Law 101 in 1977 under the first Lévesque PQ regime) to divert serious attention to their relations with the United States and the implications thereof for both themselves and the U.S. people. This chapter by Martin Lubin, associate professor of political science and fellow of the Center for the Study of Canada at the State University of New York in Plattsburgh, is based primarily on experiences of the author as a Montreal native and of others brought to his attention, plus his own pilot study of transborder relations of ethnic group organizations.

Political and related public-policy considerations are examined in Chapters 12 and 13. In the first of these chapters, Louis Balthazar, professor of political science at Laval University, discusses long-term political interests of Quebec with respect to its superpower neighbor and the projected trends within Quebec's society and body politic as they might impinge upon policies apt to achieve objectives in line with these interests. The chapter makes a relatively optimistic prognosis.

Charles Doran's and Brian Job's chapter on priorities and perceptions of U.S. policymakers in Washington, the influential U.S. foreign-policy community (for the moment outside government), and other elites notes quite different concerns, policy objectives, and emphases relating to Quebec than those among their Quebec counterparts in the priorities noted by Balthazar. These differences may result in frictions, tensions, and important conflicts, particularly should Quebec gain control over its foreign policy. Mr. Doran is director of the Center for Canadian Studies and professor of political science at the School of Advanced International Studies of The Johns Hopkins University, and Mr. Job is associate professor of political science at the University of Minnesota.

The editors' concluding views will integrate the findings of the individual chapters with other research, experience, and impressions to derive observations and suggestions of broader long-run implications pertaining to the domains that were considered separately. The editors will also offer hypotheses about implications of some alternative future developments in Quebec, between it and the rest of Canada, and in the United States, for the interests of both Quebec and the United States and for relations between them. Finally the editors will advance some recommendations toward achieving more mutually fruitful relations, for consideration by governments, private institutions, and individuals on both sides of the border.

Notes

1. See Richard Hamilton and Maurice Pinard, "Quebec Public Opinion and Constitutional Reform," in Calvin J. Veltman, ed., *Contemporary Quebec* (Montreal: University of Quebec, 1981), Tables 1 and 2, pp. 124–126, for summaries of pertinent surveys in Quebec, 1962–1981; and see *Le Devoir*, March 25, 1982, for summaries of further surveys through January 1982. Percentages favoring independence and sovereignty with association differed as indicated over this period and also differed depending on the precise wording of the questions.

2. For example, 49 percent of Quebec francophones in May 1980 favored so changing the federal constitution, contrasted with 29 percent who preferred the status quo (Joel Smith and David K. Jackson, "Restructuring the Canadian State: Prospects for Three Political Scenarios," unpublished paper, Duke University, 1980, Table 2). A year before, 56 percent favored increased provincial powers by constitutional change and 36 percent did not (Canadian Broadcasting Company [CBC] survey of March 1979). In 1977, substantially more than half of Quebec francophones favored redistribution of powers in favor of provincial governments; only a tenth favored increased powers in Ottawa (Michael D. Ornstein and H. Michael Stevenson, "Cracks in the Mosaic: Elite and Public Opinion on the Future of Canada," unpublished paper, Quality of Life Project, Institute for Behavioral Research, York University, Downsview, Ontario, 1979, p. 17). In May 1980, 57 percent favored renewed federalism, but 52 percent a special status for Quebec (Jon H. Pammett et al., "Political Support and Voting Behavior in the Quebec Referendum," unpublished paper, Duke University, 1980). Three months after the 1980 referendum, 61 percent of francophones felt their PQ government was "right" in pressing Ottawa for change in the status of their province (survey sponsored by the Quebec Ministry of Intergovernmental Affairs).

A series of surveys sponsored by the federal government between April 1979 and June 1980 discovered two-thirds of all Quebeckers (including nonfrancophones) favored major constitutional changes toward provincial autonomy. Eighty percent preferred that their provincial government should have more control over provincial economic development; 58 percent felt that a constitutional compromise toward more provincial powers could ultimately be achieved between sovereignty-association proposed by the PQ government and the then prevailing federal system (reprinted in *Le Devoir*, October 16, 1980). In March 1979, 47 percent of Québécois anticipated either no federated Canada with Quebec still in it or a considerably more decentralized Canada within ten years (CBC survey). Just before the 1981 Quebec election, 47 percent of Quebec francophones expressed more confidence that a PQ rather than a PLQ government would achieve such renewed, devolved federation—certainly a major reason for the PQ's victory (reported in *Le Devoir*, April 6, 1981). A Québécois majority in 1980 felt that their linguistic and cultural identities were threatened by even the less centralized, pre-patriation federal-provincial system (Smith and Jackson, p. 38). Diversely worded surveys since 1965 have documented growing fractions of Québécois in favor of greater autonomy and special status for Quebec. See Maurice Pinard, "La dualité des loyautés et les options constitutionelles des Québécois francophones," in Albert Legault and Alfred O Hero, Jr., eds., *Le nationalisme québécois à la croisée des chemins*, (Quebec: Centre Québécois des Relations Internationales, *Choix* 7, 1975), pp. 75–80.

3. Economic interests contrary to entering a customs union with an independent Quebec, other than in Ontario, are discussed in Alfred O. Hero, Jr., and Louis Balthazar, *The United States, Quebec, and Canada*, forthcoming, Chapter 11.

4. Successive opinion polls between the early 1960s and the mid-1970s found Quebeckers less opposed than Canadians generally to U.S. direct investment, and more favorable to that direct investment than Canadians other than residents of the economically still less developed Atlantic Provinces. See also Stuart Rothenberg, "The Impact of Affluence: Restrictions on Foreign Investment in Canada," *American Review of Canadian Studies* 9(2), Autumn 1979, p. 79. A survey of governmental, business, and other elites in 1973 revealed that 73 percent in Quebec—more than in any other province—agreed that "having allowed foreign corporations to invest . . . almost without restriction . . . as a whole (had) been good for Canada." See Garth Stevenson, "Foreign Direct Investment and the Provinces: A Study of Elite Attitudes," *Canadian Journal of Political Science* 7(4), December 1974, p. 640. These opinion differences between Quebec and the rest of Canada declined or disappeared beginning around 1975, due more to the decline of anglophone Canadian opposition to U.S. investment in a stagnating economy (to Quebec levels) than to any increase in Quebec opposition. However, by mid-1980, the ratio of Québécois who believed U.S. investment "good" versus those who felt it "bad" for Canada was again significantly higher than in other regions (J. Alex Murray and Lawrence LaDuc, "Attitudes of Canadians Toward Foreign Policy and Trade Issues," Institute for Canadian-American Studies, University of Windsor, 1980, p. 2, Table 1). By May 1982, 43 percent of Québécois, as compared to 37 percent of other Canadians, wanted closer economic relations with the United States; 77 percent as compared to 66 percent of other Canadians felt U.S. investment had been advantageous to Canada; and 63 percent as compared to 45 percent of other Canadians wanted their federal government to stimulate the growth of U.S. investments (CROP survey reported in Canada West Foundation, *Opinion Update*, Report No. 13, July 14, 1982).

5. Mildred Schwartz, *Public Opinion and Canadian National Identity* (Berkeley, CA: University of California Press, 1967), pp. 65–73; J. Alex Murray and Mary C. Gerace, "Canadian Attitudes Toward the U.S. Presence," *Public Opinion Quarterly* 36(3), Fall 1972, pp. 388–397; John H. Sigler and Dennis Goresky, "Public Opinion on United States-Canadian Relations," *International Organization* 28(4), Autumn 1974, p. 667; Terrence Keenleyside, Lawrence LeDuc, and J. Alex Murray, "Public Opinion and Canada-United States Economic Relations," *Behind the Headlines* 35(4), 1976; Lawrence LeDuc and J. Alex Murray, "Canadian Nationalism: Pause or Decline?" unpublished paper for the Conference of the World Association of Public Opinion Research, Oslo, Norway, August 27–28, 1976; Albert A. Kinney, "Canadian Collective Consciousness: A Theoretical Framework and Some Empirical Evidence," unpublished M.A. thesis, Carleton University, Ottawa, 1977; and David K Jackson, "Anti-Americanism Among French Québécois, Young and Old," paper presented at the 42nd Annual Meeting of the Southern Sociological Society, April 4–7, 1979, pp. 25–29.

6. Jackson, p. 40.

7. Ibid., p. 32.

8. Ibid., p. 33.

9. 1981 census.

10. A forthcoming volume by Alfred O. Hero, Jr., and Louis Balthazar of Laval University will focus primarily on implications of Quebec developments for the United States. It will also consider alternative constitutional and political roles of Quebec vis-à-vis Canada in terms of likely impacts on U.S. interests both within Quebec and in Canada in general.

U.S.-Quebec Economic Relations: Some Interactions Between Trade and Investment

Bernard Bonin

This chapter will focus on the more significant linkages between trade and investment flows in U.S.-Quebec economic relations. Such linkages seem fruitful from the policymaking standpoint. Indeed, the quickest and surest way to an extensive "international" trade between the United States and the Province of Quebec appears to be through the presence of subsidiaries of U.S. multinationals in Quebec and/or the presence of subsidiaries of Quebec-based multinational firms in the United States.

Trade flows will be reviewed first. Then, in the second part of the chapter, attention will focus on investment flows and particularly on the extent of U.S. direct investment in Quebec. When seen from the host country standpoint, foreign direct investment (FDI) is never an unmixed blessing. There are benefits deriving from FDI, but there are also costs and tensions. Some attention will be devoted to the results of public opinion surveys over the years, which tend to show that attitudes in Quebec vis-à-vis foreign direct investment are not fundamentally different than in the rest of Canada. On that point at least, Quebec seems to be *une province comme les autres* (a province like the others). In the third section, behavioral differences of four types of bourgeoisies will be noted regarding the ownership of industries, foreign investment policies, sales of enterprises between members of the business community, origin of managers, and promotion of the elites. These differences are one of the reasons why recent Quebec governments have called for better integration of foreign-owned firms into the Quebec economy and have concentrated their efforts on encouraging smaller and medium-sized firms. Finally, based on important policy documents that were published in 1979 and in 1982, the Quebec government seems determined to follow a modern industrial policy, even if such an approach

Table 2.1.   Value of Quebec's Exports to the United States (Can$)

Year	Exports to U.S. ($000)	Total Exports ($000)	U.S. Share of Total Exports (%)
1974	3,308,035	5,240,875	63
1975	3,376,546	5,593,474	60
1976	3,925,060	6,257,166	63
1977	4,862,726	7,487,432	65
1978	6,134,187	9,420,189	65
1979	7,780,700	12,196,591	64
1980[a]	8,911,773	15,241,738	58

[a]Preliminary.

Source: Bureau de la Statistique du Québec, Exportations Internationales du Québec, annual, various issues.

seems unlikely to constitute a primrose path. That industrial policy will, however, have some bearing on policies toward foreign direct investment and, as such, is of interest to the United States.

Trade Flows: The Global Picture

Although the volume of world trade has increased rather slowly in recent years (when it has not in fact fallen) and the United States has been a slow-growth economy for almost a decade now, the share of Quebec in total Canadian imports and exports has gained some ground.[1] Quebec has been hurt by a lagging economy in the United States, as the annual rate of increase of its exports clearly shows. Standing at a 30 percent annual increase in 1978, this rate dropped to a mere 14.5 percent in 1980 over 1979, that is, just slightly over the rate of Canadian inflation. But in the process, Quebec fared better than the rest of Canada. Quebec's share of total Canadian exports to the United States has increased from 16.4 percent in 1978 to 18.5 percent in 1980. Quebec's share of total Canadian imports from the United States has also been increasing from 12.7 percent in 1978 to 14.5 percent in 1980.[2]

Thus, one major point must be emphasized. It is true that the Quebec economy relies relatively more on trade with Europe than Canada as a whole does. Still, trade flows with the United States remain the dominating force by an overwhelming margin, in that about 60 percent of exports abroad from Quebec go to the U.S. market (Table 2.1) and one half of total Quebec imports come from the United States.

This global picture conveys a clear message. The U.S. economy has become increasingly open to foreign trade over the last three decades, and given the extensive trade relations that exist between it and Quebec,

Table 2.2. Distribution of Quebec's Exports to the United States by
U.S. Census Region, 1979

U.S. Region	% of Quebec's Exports to U.S.	U.S. Region	% of Quebec's Exports to U.S.
New England	12	Southeastern Central	3
Mid-Atlantic	35	Southwestern Central	4
Northeast Central	28	Mountain	1
Northwest Central	4	Pacific	3
Southeastern Seaboard	10		

Source: Bureau de la Statistique du Québec, Exportations Internationales du Québec 1979   (3e trimestre 1980).

an economic policy regarding the United States must indeed be a priority
for Quebec. However, efforts by Quebec to diversify trade relations to
other countries also make sense, for if it were to tie its policy more to
the United States, it would run the risk of becoming a satellite of an
economy that has not been among the more dynamic ones since 1973.

Trade Flows: Main Features

It is appropriate to go beyond the global picture just drawn and pay
some attention to the main features of Quebec's import-export trade.
First, of total Quebec exports, raw materials and semiprocessed goods
account for about two-thirds and finished (fully manufactured) products
for only one-third. By comparison, finished products constitute about
two-thirds of Ontario's exports, the auto trade with the United States
being the most significant factor in that structural difference. Second,
exports are rather heavily concentrated on a few countries of destination.
Besides the United States with some 64 percent in 1979, another quarter
goes to seven countries (the United Kingdom, the German Federal
Republic, Japan, the Netherlands, France, Italy, and Belgium by de-
creasing order of importance). The total for the European Economic
Community is roughly 20 percent

Third, the distribution of Quebec's exports to various regional markets
in the United States is also a point of interest, as Table 2.2 shows.

Hence, the Mid-Atlantic Region and the Northeast Central Region
alone absorb 63 percent of Quebec's exports to the United States. New
England accounts for another 12 percent. By comparison, the same three
regions take about 62 percent of total Canadian exports to the United
States. Ontario's exports to the United States also go for the most part
(almost 60 percent) to the Northeast Central Region and to the Mid-
Atlantic Region (about 20 percent). The Southeastern Seaboard takes 5
percent in the case of Ontario, with the rest widely dispersed among

all other regions. So geographical proximity of markets being served appears to be a significant factor. There is some competition between the two central Canadian provinces (Ontario and Quebec), but probably not as much as could have been anticipated. More disaggregated data would confirm this view, in that products exported by these two provinces to the same U.S. region are seldom similar.

Fourth, there is also a high concentration of Quebec's exports on a few goods, although this concentration appears to be diminishing somewhat. In the mid-1970s, six products made up more than half the total exports. In order by value, they are pulp and paper (particularly newsprint); ores, concentrates, and waste metal; automobiles; asbestos (unmanufactured); copper; and aluminium. In 1979, nine products amounted to 54 percent of total exports (the preceding six plus aircraft engines and parts, lumber, and precious metals). This lack of diversification may be at least a partial explanation for the instability of Quebec's exports. Indeed, exports to the United States fluctuate a great deal from year to year and are quite sensitive to upswings and downswings in the U.S. economy. These exports are also more highly concentrated than Quebec exports as a whole, in that roughly 62 percent are based on the ten principal products exported in 1981. As could be expected, Quebec's imports from the United States are much more diversified than its exports to that country and do not lend themselves as easily to detailed analysis.

Summarizing, about 60 percent of Quebec's international exports go to the United States and more than half of Quebec's imports come from that country. In turn, three-quarters of Quebec's total exports to the United States go to three regional U.S. markets, so that there is certainly some complementarity between the U.S. northeast and Quebec. Quebec's economy is a very open one and is particularly sensitive to downturns in the U.S. economy, especially in the demand for raw materials. Eighty percent of the asbestos imported by the United States, 70 percent of its imported aluminium, 45 percent of its imported newsprint, 40 percent of its imported iron ore and concentrates, and about one-third of its imported aircraft engines and parts, copper, and zinc come from Quebec.

The Quebec economy is relatively well endowed in natural resources and must face a very high unemployment rate in spite of a respectable rate of job creation over the years. Quebec has an industrial structure problem that has been documented ad nauseam. Traditional industries, or so-called soft sectors, are still heavily concentrated in Quebec. And these industries, which account for close to one half of manufacturing jobs in Quebec, are in turn highly dependent on protected Canadian markets. Indeed, with less than a quarter of the Canadian population,

Quebec produces one-half of the goods protected by tariffs of 10 percent or more. And yet, with the tariff reductions that resulted from the Tokyo Round (the full impact of which will be felt a few years from now), closer economic integration between U.S. and Quebec economies is almost a certainty. These protected industries will very likely become endangered species in Quebec, even though any elimination or reduction of protection will likely push unemployment still higher in the short run, unless many thousands of jobs can be created in industries with more promising futures.

Markets broader than Canada, especially in the United States, will be a sine qua non for most of the future industries. Such export industries might very well be the principal long-term hope for Quebec of gradually phasing out the industries that have been facing growing difficulties for quite a few years.

Energy Exports

As a transition before moving to the foreign investment question, brief mention should be made of the existing possibilities of energy exports. Energy sales to the United States are of course part of the trade flows just discussed. Besides, they are nothing new. They go back to the beginning of the present century. However, it is only recently that they became really significant, and the future seems even more promising. Exports of electricity to the United States have gone from under 50 million kilowatt-hours per year in 1970 to 68 million in 1971, 95 million in 1972, 270 million in 1976, 1,406 million in 1978, and 7,500 million in 1979. This is impressive growth.

Furthermore, until the present time only surplus electricity has been involved in these exports. It is expected that such surpluses will be available up until 1988 (some are even talking now in terms of 1995). There have been high-level talks about what would be a significant evolution of Quebec's usual policy with regard to energy exports. Until recently, Quebec was in favor of building energy interconnections with the United States because they made economic sense, especially in view of the anticipated surpluses. Although the concern here is not with direct investments, interactions between trade and investment similar to those that will be discussed below have been obvious in electricity sales to the United States. Hydro-Quebec has traditionally been a heavy borrower on the U.S. financial market. Funds thus obtained were subsequently used to build major power-generating dam projects, the last one being that of James Bay. In turn, part of the hydroelectricity produced was sold to U.S. customers as "exportable surpluses," facilitating debt servicing in the process.

But recently the Quebec energy minister, apparently encouraged by statements made by the governors of some of the United States (particularly Governor Snelling of Vermont), has been quoted to the effect that he was now willing to consider hydro-developments that could lead to firm export contracts for base energy (not just surpluses) with New York and New England. This is a significant change in Quebec's traditional position in several ways. Quebec's long-lasting reluctance to consider that option was based on fear of losing her main comparative advantage and the ability to attract energy-consuming industries. That fear has apparently been overcome. Also, Canada (and Quebec) would thereby get a step closer to a continental energy policy with the United States, a subject that has been nearly taboo north of the border. However, even if the significance of politicians' statements on both sides of the border is not underestimated, subsequent progress appears to be at a snail's pace.

Intrafirm trade

But it is through intrafirm trade that the types of interactions previously mentioned emerge in the clearest possible way. Such trade is becoming an important feature of world trade. In the mid-1970s, more than half of total U.S. external trade, 30 percent of United Kingdom exports, and 29 percent of Swedish exports fitted that description. But Canada-U.S. commerce certainly represents a unique example of the importance of intrafirm trade for a developed country. Some 60 percent of total Canadian exports to the United States are in fact intrafirm trade. Similarly, 72 percent of Canadian imports in 1978 were credited to subsidiaries of foreign-owned firms, although not necessarily intrafirm trade strictly speaking. This type of "international" trade is not via arm's-length transactions; indeed, they are not even market transactions. They are the results of links through direct investments (or international production as it has also been called). A private organization is, in fact, trading with itself, whether it is a parent company dealing with its affiliates around the world or is one of various subsidiaries of a particular parent company exchanging goods and services with the parent company or other subsidiaries across national frontiers. Economic observers are faced with a sort of trade the policy implications of which are not yet altogether clear, but might very well be far-reaching.

What about Quebec? Comparative figures are not available. However, based on experience and judging from the list of major exports, it is likely that the percentage of intrafirm trade involving Quebec does not significantly differ from that of Canada as a whole, even if probably inferior to Ontario's. It is also a little known fact that Quebec's exports are highly concentrated on a few firms, 70 percent on roughly two dozen firms. Among these, U.S.-owned firms undoubtedly play a major role, which brings up the second part of this paper: the examination of foreign direct investments in Quebec.

U.S. Direct Investments in Quebec

The quality of the data on foreign investment in Canada is excellent. However, data on the regional and provincial distributions of foreign investment are not nearly as complete. Yet, data are available from the Corporations and Labor Unions Returns Act (CALURA) annual report on (1) regional allocation of corporate taxable income by industrial division and by country of ownership, (2) the number of establishments, (3) shipments of goods of own manufacture, (4) value added by manufacturing activity, (5) number of employees, and (6) employees' salaries and wages.[3] From these one can get a fairly good view of foreign direct investment (FDI) in Quebec. Comparison with Ontario is interesting in that the gap that has existed between the two provinces as host to foreign investments seems to be narrowing somewhat, at least on the basis of what could be anticipated from earlier studies:

1.   In 1978, foreign direct investment was virtually nonexistent in Quebec in the agricultural, forestry, and fisheries sectors, but was present in these sectors to a significant extent in Ontario (16 percent of corporate taxable income). In mining, however, the role of foreign direct investment was dominant in Quebec (about 80 percent of taxable income), but was considerably less in Ontario, 34 percent.
2.   In the manufacturing sector, Ontario still attracts more capital from abroad than Quebec (66 percent of taxable income in Ontario compared to 53 percent in Quebec). According to earlier surveys the difference between the two provinces was much larger. More disaggregated data is now available from these sources. The role of foreign direct investment in the construction industry is about the same in the two provinces (11–12 percent of corporate taxable income). Percentages of foreign investment in utilities are also approximately the same.
3.   In trade (wholesale and retail), the proportion of taxable income originating from foreign-owned firms is lower in Quebec than in Ontario. Few significant differences exist in services industries (except in the financial sector, for which comparable data are not available).

4. In all sectors of activity where foreign direct investment is significant in the Quebec economy, U.S. direct investment is overwhelmingly the dominant force, as it is in Canada generally. Only in manufacturing would foreign capital other than U.S. capital seem to be of significance. Hence, Quebec has attracted less foreign direct investment than Ontario, but within this direct investment, U.S. capital comes out on top in Quebec just as much as anywhere else in Canada. Other indicators (number of employees, number of establishments, value added, wage-bill, etc.) provide a similar picture.

Benefits and Costs Deriving from Foreign Direct Investment

Empirical studies of the impacts of U.S. direct investment in Quebec, should they exist, would certainly provide results of a different magnitude than what has been obtained for other countries. However, there is no reason, a priori, why analysis of direct investment should not fit into the framework that has been noted time and again in the relevant literature elsewhere in the world. This literature clearly shows that there are benefits stemming from foreign direct investments and the activities of multinational corporations (MNCs). But given the nature of the two institutions involved, i.e., nation-states and multinational corporations, tensions or costs will also result for the host countries. Consequently, these countries are concerned with maximizing the net benefits that they can derive from foreign direct investment, which, in turn, explains widespread government intervention in this field.[4]

Major benefits are in relation to economic growth. Foreign direct investment is an international movement of corporations. Hence, it is more than a simple movement of capital. It is rather a package of capital, technology, management and marketing skills, and access to foreign markets through corporations whose parent companies retain control of affiliates abroad. At least some of the major decisions concerning these affiliates will be made outside of the host countries and tensions will be, to some extent, inherent in the organizational structure of multinational corporations.

The major contribution of foreign direct investment to the economic growth of host economies is not necessarily with regard to domestic capital formation. On the contrary, one may even conceive of FDI in which there would be no international transfer of financial capital. Funds to finance investments can be obtained on financial markets of the world outside of that of the host country or transferred from the parent company to affiliates. But they can also be obtained on the financial market of the host country (through borrowings or share issues) or can be internally generated (reinvestment of profits and of depreciation allowances). In these cases, they are in fact largely financed from local savings. In Canada, the Gray Report has shown that from 1946 to 1967 some 70 percent of the funds used to finance foreign direct investment were indeed funds generated from local savings, so that the contribution from abroad should not be exaggerated.

But the major contribution might very well be technology transfers. Technology is often the barrier to entry into an industry that is most difficult to overcome. To the extent that it has transferred its technology abroad, the multinational corporation has played a major role in the international diffusion of innovations. But this type of transaction is not the only possible channel for international transfer of technology. Circumstances vary from one country to the other, from one industry to the other, and even from one corporation to another within an industrial sector. Besides, the interest of host countries does not always correspond to that of the multinational corporation as to important aspects of the transfer—cost, availability, adaptation to host country economic conditions, or speed of diffusion. Host countries have often tried to divide the package provided by the MNC and have sought to get technology from abroad without the foreign control inherent in the international transfer through a multinational corporation. But overall, these efforts have been at best moderately successful (with the notable exception of Japan), and the multinational corporation has been a major channel, if not *the* major channel, for international transfers of technology.

Brief mention must also be made of two other elements of the package. Host countries generally value more the importation of management skills or methods than the importation of managers. But it is not always possible to distinguish one from the other, so that many countries have been led to the conclusion that management methods are more fully and more easily obtained through a relationship between a parent company and a wholly-owned subsidiary. Overall, the point would appear to be valid with the possible qualification that, since learning-by-doing is particularly important for management, factors like mobility of personnel, recruitment and promotion of elites, and integration of the foreign-owned subsidiary within the host economy will impact on the net result, as will be shown below.

Access to foreign markets clearly applies in the case of resource-based industries, for instance, when a raw material is exported to be processed in another country. Examples in Quebec could be found for most of the ten main exports previously mentioned. But this benefit can also exist in the manufacturing sector if a subsidiary is fully integrated into the world activities of a multinational corporation, rather than being of the branch plant variety. As previously mentioned, intrafirm trade will provide a satisfactory measure of the extent to which access to foreign markets can be deemed a benefit resulting from foreign direct investment. Again, based on experience, intrafirm trade certainly exists to some extent even for Quebec's exports that fall into the manufactured goods category.

In addition to these benefits related to economic growth, and to by-products like contributions to local employment and taxes, other more questionable benefits have also been identified in various empirical studies. One has to do with the contribution that foreign direct investment might bring to regional development in host countries where it is government policy to try to get a better balance in the distribution of economic activities between regions. But in Canada this has hardly been the case; overall it can safely be said that foreign direct investment (or the lack thereof) has probably intensified rather than alleviated regional disparities in Canada. Another possible benefit has to do with the strengthening of internal competition that entry of new firms might bring about, with the resulting effects on prices, innovations, productivity, quality of service, and so forth. Even if these results are admittedly a possibility, or a certainty in some sectors in Canada, overall the evidence for all sectors appears inconclusive. Finally, a third possible benefit has to do with the contribution that FDI can make to the balance of payments of host countries. Again this benefit is questionable for several reasons. First, for it to be a real benefit, a host country's balance of payments must be in need of being redressed (shortages of major currencies, for instance). Second, the net result will depend on the destination of the investments (protected industries or not), and in all cases heroic assumptions have to be made as to what would have happened in the absence of these foreign investments. Third, with foreign direct investment, a whole corporation is moving from one country to another, so that the effect is likely to be different when the initial investment is undertaken than when the affiliates abroad are fully operating. In the latter case, there will be imports of goods as well as exports, dividends will be paid on capital invested, royalties will be paid for technology, fees will be paid for management services, and so forth. There might also be some import substitutions. It is even possible that the use of transfer prices that have very little to do with arm's-length transactions will significantly impact on the balance of payments of host countries. In the end, it is not at all unlikely that what was seen as a benefit when the investment was undertaken turns out later to be a net "cost" from the balance of payments standpoint.

It is important to note that even if one considers these benefits to be real, they are not obtained free of charge. Interest payments or dividends will have to be paid on the capital invested by the foreign owners. "Free" access to the technology of parent companies does not mean access without cost, since specific payments like royalties, or unspecific payments like additional dividends, will result from the international flow of factors of production. But in addition to these financial, out-of-pocket costs, there are often other economic or political costs for host countries. These costs will be examined next.

Potential risks exist with regard to efficiency (increasing concentration of economic activity, restrictive practices like international market-sharing, excess capacity, distortion of economic development potential, etc.), with regard to equity (between factors of production within a host country as well as between countries), and with regard to sovereignty (or what could more appropriately be called autonomy in policy formulation or room to maneuver). Since tensions or costs have been more frequently and more spontaneously stated in terms of the sovereignty question, most costs have come to be regarded as political, and most benefits are considered to be of an economic nature.

Some tensions are inherent in the organizational nature of multi-national corporations. The degree of centralization of the decision-making process at the headquarters varies, but from various empirical studies some generalizations seem valid. The centralization of financial and control decisions is entirely consistent with a multinational corporation status. Yet host countries are not likely to be very happy with such centralization. Decisions relating to research and development efforts are not readily decentralized. The same applies to some marketing decisions. On the other hand, personnel and labor relations are more likely to be decentralized. Policies of the multinational corporation and the host country will also clash occasionally. The parent company will often show a strong preference for wholly-owned affiliates; not so for host country governments. It is not illogical for multinational corporations to set up some sort of market-sharing arrangement within the organization, whereby some affiliates will be confined to serving some markets, and others will be allowed to export everywhere possible. Host countries are always anxious to see firms on their territory export as freely and as much as possible. Again, it might be advantageous for MNCs to centralize buying orders for the whole organization or most of it; host countries usually want affiliates to buy as much as possible from local sources. Host countries want to get as much research and development as possible done locally, while multinational corporations generally want to keep this function close to the headquarters and marketing people, that is, in the country of origin of the MNC. Transfer prices are often a source of considerable friction. Tensions like these are inevitable as long as host countries want the benefits brought about by multinational corporations, for the two entities do not have the same "space horizon."

In addition to these tensions inherent to the organizational structure of multinational enterprises and the essence of nation-states, other tensions stem from the fear of industrial domination either through the sheer size of U.S. multinational corporations, their strong concentration in key sectors or high-growth industries, or their aggressive behavior in the competitive struggle. News of takeovers usually fuel this fear of industrial domination from abroad. What has been called the oligopolistic reaction of firms is also likely to feed this type of fear. That is, one company of an oligopolistic industry sets foot abroad, and others are likely to follow within a few years, giving rise to cluster investments.[5]

A fear of technological dependence (preventing the technological gap that exists between nations from being narrowed with time) can affect host countries. The possibility must also be faced that the host country's policies will lose effectiveness and scope in the presence of a substantial number of multinational enterprises (stabilization policy in general and monetary policy in particular; exchange-rate policy complicated by transfer prices, leads and lags, and tax havens; trade policy given the considerable number of options that MNCs have in this respect; and competition policy). And for some countries the darkest shadow is the possibility that the MNC might act as a Trojan horse carrying cultural penetration. All these fears have been the focus of considerable attention in the technical literature. Last but not least, the extraterritorial application of U.S. laws and policies, particularly with respect to antitrust, exports control, and balance of payments policies in the 1960s and the 1970s, has also been the object of a great deal of criticism around the world.

This overview of harmonies as well as tensions between multinational corporations and nation-states is relevant to U.S.-Quebec relations as much as it is elsewhere in the world. The role of MNCs in Quebec is so extensive that their contributions to whatever economic growth there is cannot be negligible. Their role in molding trade relations with the United States is important, to say the least. They are major producers in so many sectors of economic activity that potential risks have to be considered seriously, whether in regard to efficiency, equity, or sovereignty. The tensions that stem from the organization of the MNCs must be just as real in Quebec as they are elsewhere. Fear of industrial domination, of technological dependence, of ineffective national policies—whether the fears are based on perceptions or on facts—should be expected just as much in Quebec as elsewhere. The risk of cultural penetration (again supposing that such a risk is real) would be just as great in Quebec, since that country has a unique culture in North America. (See Chapter 7). Some Quebec-based firms have felt the impact of the extraterritorial application of U.S. laws and policies. Given such experiences and fears, what are the prevailing attitudes in Quebec toward foreign direct investment?

Attitudes Toward Foreign Direct Investment in Quebec

Public opinion surveys tend to show that attitudes in Quebec vis-à-vis foreign direct investment are not fundamentally different than in the rest of Canada. In 1967, Stephen Clarkson undertook for the Watkins Task Force a study of the content of major Canadian newspapers as an indicator of public opinion with regard to foreign investment.[6] Five years later, John Fayerweather polled Canadian opinion on the same subject.[7] Since then, two researchers from the University of Windsor have done public opinion surveys annually to provide a reasonably good view of the way public opinion has evolved about foreign investment in Canada.[8]

In 1972, Fayerweather noted that reactions in Quebec and in the Atlantic Provinces were clearly more favorable than in Ontario. Clarkson, five years before, obtained a similar result for the Atlantic Provinces but he was led to believe that the debate was clearly more radical in Quebec than everywhere else in Canada. More recent surveys tend to show that the concern expressed by the public in general appears to have peaked in 1973, leveled off for some years, and then declined drastically beginning in 1977. That year, the number of Canadians stating that incoming foreign investment is fundamentally a "good thing" was, for the first time since 1969, higher than those expressing concern. As Table 2.3 shows, although Quebec was in 1976–1977 the province where the largest percentage felt that foreign investment was a "bad thing," the margin is very slight. Moreover, Quebec is also the province where public opinion seems to be most volatile.

Leaving surveys of public opinion in general to deal more specifically with elite attitudes, Quebec elites seem to follow closely the rest of Canada; that is, businessmen are the most favorable to U.S. direct investment and union leaders the least favorable. In between are politicians, civil servants, and intellectuals (academics as well as others). Young people are more likely to be unfavorable. Low-income people are also more likely to be unfavorable; this attitude changes toward more favorable as one moves up the income scale. Not only would these results seem to hold quite well for all Canadian regions, but the pattern appears to have been fairly consistent for the past two decades or so. Interpreting these results as general hostility toward U.S. multinational corporations would certainly represent a giant leap.

Table 2.3. Canadian Opinion by Region on U.S. Investment in Canada, 1976-1977 and 1975-1976 (% of responses)

	Atlantic Provinces	Quebec	Ontario	Prairie Provinces	B.C.	Canada
"Good thing"						
1976-1977	44	46	51	47	48	48
1975-1976	38	35	43	40	41	39
"Bad thing"						
1976-1977	41	40	39	38	41	39
1975-1976	41	46	40	44	41	42
Qualified						
1976-1977	4	7	5	5	6	6
1975-1976	7	8	7	6	9	9
No opinion						
1976-1977	11	7	5	10	5	7
1975-1976	14	11	10	10	9	10
Number sampled in 1976-1977	384	1090	1418	668	429	3989

Source: J. Alex Murray and Lawrence Le Duc, "Changing Attitudes Toward Foreign Investment in Canada," in John Fayerweather, ed., Host National Attitudes Toward Multinational Corporations (New York: Praeger, 1982) p. 222.

From the Two Solitudes to the Four Solitudes

Readers are aware of the existence of two solitudes in Canada. But with regard to the business sector and the question of foreign ownership in Quebec, it is more appropriate to discuss four solitudes. Whether in relation to the ownership of manufacturing industries, foreign investment policies, sales of enterprises between members of the business community, or origin of managers and promotion of elites, a group of researchers at the University of Montreal under the directorship of Professor Arnaud Sales[9] has found few common patterns of behavior among four groups: first, the "comprador bourgeoisie" working for foreign-owned firms, and second, third, and fourth, the internal Canadian bourgeoisie subdivided into its Anglo-Saxon, Jewish, and French-speaking components. In fact, these four groups act like many solitudes, with relatively few relations between them.

Insofar as the ownership of manufacturing industries is concerned, there is a considerable underrepresentation of French-speaking Canadians, a slight overrepresentation of the Anglo-Saxon Canadian bourgeoisie, and a very strong overrepresentation of the Jewish Canadian bourgeoisie. Moreover, a clear pattern of specialization has developed over the years that contrasts these groups. First, there is a very heavy concentration of French-speaking and Jewish owners in small and medium-sized firms, but much less for the Anglo-Saxon Canadian bourgeoisie, and less still for foreign ownership. Overall, this pattern holds for consumer, intermediary, and investment goods industries (less than 200 employees for consumer goods, less than 500 for the others). Second, in the foreign-owned firms, Anglo-Saxons are a near majority among senior executives. They are followed by Canadians recently arrived (some expatriates from headquarters) and by French-speaking Canadians, who are again grossly underrepresented. Jewish Canadians are virtually absent among the senior executives of foreign-owned firms.

A totally different picture emerges in the firms belonging to the internal bourgeoisie: French-Canadians clearly predominate there, followed by the Jewish-Canadian bourgeoisie; the Anglo-Saxons are a distant third. These data are in relation to the total number of senior executives, not in relation to the total Quebec population. In the latter case, French-speaking executives are still grossly underrepresented.

Third, there is a very strong correlation between the origin of ownership and the ethnic origin of senior executives. French-Canadian and Jewish firms managed by persons of a different origin are almost nonexistent. French-Canadians do not hire Jews or Anglo-Saxons. Jews hire practically no French-Canadians or Anglo-Saxons. Anglo-Saxon owners hire close to one-third of their managers among the French-speaking population, but surprisingly few Jews, given the linguistic affinity between these two groups.

Fourth, foreign-controlled firms are dominant in petroleum and coal, tobacco, machinery, chemicals, nonmetallic minerals, precision instruments, rubber, electrical appliances, transportation equipment, primary metals, and miscellaneous industries. Canadian Anglo-Saxons are dominant in printing and publishing, pulp and paper, furniture, and lumber. French-Canadians are dominant in the metal products and food and beverages, and they have a strong presence also—although not a dominating one—in transportation equipment. But the so-called soft sectors are certainly interesting cases, in that Jewish owners are dominant in all of them (clothing, footwear and other leather goods, hosiery and knitting, and textiles).

With regard to foreign-ownership policies, based on opinions expressed in 1974, close to 80 percent of business executives surveyed were in favor of some form of control. The vast majority of them were not in favor of the key sector approach whereby some industries are closed to foreign investment, but for those (some 20 percent) who were in favor of such an approach, resource industries were the most likely candidates for such restrictions, followed by transportation, communications, energy, cultural industries, and defense production industries. As to the way such control should be exercised, some 40 percent were in favor of a case-by-case review à la the Foreign Investment Review Act (see pp. 33–34), but more than half were in favor of majority-owned Canadian equity and a Canadian majority on the boards. Potential antagonism exists in this regard between the internal bourgeoisie and the foreign-owned firms, in that the latter still had (at least a decade ago) strong preference for wholly-owned affiliates.

Given the large majority in favor of some form of control, the comprador bourgeoisie was in a rather uncomfortable position. It felt compelled to accept such controls, but favored (much more than the internal bourgeoisie) the case-by-case screening mechanism because of the possibility for bargaining and pressures such a mechanism entailed. This finding is interesting in view of the recent opposition of foreign and especially U.S.-owned firms to the Foreign Investment Review Act. Another interesting finding is that the French-speaking business bourgeoisie did not like this solution, opting instead in favor of a much stricter form of control.

There are strikingly few bridges between these various business bourgeoisies. French-Canadians buy firms almost exclusively from other French-Canadians. Because it is difficult for a small firm to buy a bigger one, French-Canadians are seldom in a position to buy a firm from either the internal Anglo-Saxon bourgeoisie or the nonresident bourgeoisie. However, French-Canadian owners sell mostly to Canadians of Anglo-Saxon descent and to other French-Canadians, and seldom to nonresidents, who are generally the most frequent buyers. Anglo-Saxon Canadian firms are rarely able to buy U.S.-owned firms, but they will buy French-Canadian firms almost as frequently as Anglo-Saxon firms. As sellers, half their sales are to nonresidents and half to Anglo-Saxons— none to French-Canadians. Similarly, according to Sales' study, the Jewish group does not sell firms to, or buy them from, French-Canadians.

When asked about "the main obstacle" that firms encounter, close to one half of the firms in which the major equity holder was French-Canadian mentioned lack of financing, which did not seem to bother the Anglo-Saxons a great deal. They were much more concerned, as were the Jews, with the lack of manpower. Nonresident-owned firms mentioned competition by a 2-to-1 margin over lack of manpower, and by a 3-to-2 margin over lack of financing.

Overall, senior executives acceded to their positions through entrepreneurship (creations or acquisitions) in approximately half the cases. Inheritance and nepotism explained another 15 percent, formal training and education less than one-third, and training on the job, some 10 percent. But it is only for large foreign-owned firms that formal training and education is clearly the privileged route to a senior executive's job (over 75 percent of the time). The somewhat paradoxical result is that the comprador bourgeoisie, working in "truncated" firms, is indeed the better educated group.

These observations can hardly lead one to conclude that the Quebec bourgeoisie is a well-integrated, tightly-knit group. The divisons within it are one of the reasons why the Tetley Report[10] prepared by the Liberal Bourassa government in 1974 called for better integration of foreign-owned firms into the Quebec economy (notably through a more wide-spread diffusion of information and know-how), in addition to closer liaison between government and business to facilitate the emergence of leading firms and indigenous innovation among the French-speaking bourgeoisie. The existence of four solitudes within the business sector and their lack of integration into the Quebec economy are also important reasons why the post-1976 (PQ) government appears to have focused so much on small and medium-sized business firms.

Recent Quebec Policies Toward Foreign Direct Investment

Quebec's policies must be consistent with the Foreign Investment Review Act (FIRA) passed by the Canadian Parliament (1973–74, c.46, amended by 1976–77, c.52). This act established the Foreign Investment Review Agency (also called FIRA) for the review and assessment of acquisitions of control of Canadian business enterprises by certain persons, and for the review and assessment of the establishment of new businesses in Canada (but not of additional investments by already existing concerns except when such investments would be unrelated to the businesses already being carried on in Canada by those firms). The reviewing process is based on the assessment of some criteria seen as proxies for the Canadian interest:

1. the effect of the acquisition or establishment on the level and nature of economic activity in Canada, including, without limiting the generality of the foregoing, the effect on employment, on resource processing, on the utilization of parts, components, and services produced in Canada, and on exports from Canada;
2. the degree and significance of participation by Canadians in the business enterprise or new business and in any industry or industries in Canada of which the business enterprise or new business would be a part;
3. the effect of the acquisition or establishment on productivity, industrial efficiency, technological development, product inno-vation, and product variety in Canada;

4. the effect of the acquisition or establishment on competition within an industry or industries in Canada; and
5. the compatibility of the acquisition or establishment with national industrial and economic policies, taking into consideration industrial and economic policy objectives enunciated by the government or legislature of any province likely to be significantly affected by the acquisition or establishment.

At the time the FIRA was passed, the government of Quebec was Liberal (PLQ), but it opposed the federal initiative, stating that Quebec had different priorities in that it needed more foreign capital, not less. Occasional similar criticisms are still forthcoming from various provincial governments. Yet FIRA, which was also strongly criticized by businessmen for being an undue restriction of foreign investment, did not really result in serious limitations, as figures would show. The annual rate of growth of the book value of U.S. direct investment in Canada was higher in 1973, 1974, 1975, and 1976 (that is, for the last two years after the act came into force) than in any year previous to the act, from 1966 to 1972. The rate of foreign investment increase appears to have slackened somewhat since, but even more recently the percentages of applications approved among total applications were 91, 86, 86, and 76 percent for 1977, 1978, 1979, and 1980 respectively.

Moreover, at least from 1974 to mid-1977 there were few disagreements between FIRA and a similar bureau in Quebec. Although the federal agency does not have to follow recommendations made by provinces, consultation is usual when a particular application is of some concern to one or more provinces. From 1974–1975, when the act came into force, to June 30, 1977, more than 250 applications (251) were referred to the Quebec government for consultation and recommendation. Only 13 percent of takeover applications were refused by Quebec. Of the applications for takeovers, 52 percent were from U.S. investors and 41 percent from European firms. There was no significant difference in rejection rate between the two groups. For new establishments, results were similar: 75 percent of applications were accepted, only 9 percent turned down, and 16 percent were withdrawn by the applicants.[11] So, rhetoric aside, if Quebec policies were different from federal policies for the first four years of the act, they had to be marginally rather than fundamentally different.

What about the PQ government? In 1979 and later in 1982, the government published statements on economic policy in which its industrial strategy was enunciated.[12] Natural resources and hydroelectricity are the two main assets on which the industrial strategy would rest. For natural resources, but only for natural resources, the PQ government has stated quite clearly its intention to favor an increased presence of "Quebec interests" in the ownership structure of the operating firms.

Some industries have been mentioned as likely to receive specific attention from the government: food and agriculture, fisheries, forestry, pulp and paper (and particularly newsprint), minerals, and tourism. Others will be the focus of governmental attention because they rest basically on the quality of human resources: heavy electrical machinery and other types of machinery, urban transportation equipment, aircraft and parts, "cultural" products (books, magazines, records, films, cassettes, handicrafts, etc.), consulting engineering, and company headquarters. Finally, some other industries are considered as being so basic as to be in need of development (chemical products, petrochemicals, steel, information industries, and transportation), and others, at present labor-intensive and less competitive, are in need of adaptation (textiles, clothing, knitting, and footwear).

This list adds up to quite a program, but in the 1982 document several more industrial sectors were added in relation to so-called megaprojects: in particular, shipbuilding and offshore equipment. Significant encouragements are also contemplated for the business services sector. And last, new technologies must be developed according to the Quebec government: electronic technologies, especially microprocessors (production as well as utilization in plants and offices), and biotechnologies and their industrial applications.

In spite of some ill-conceived criticism of the federal policy toward foreign investment in the 1979 Quebec document, overall this statement on economic policy has to be seen as one of the most comprehensive documents to be published so far in Canada. The panoply of government measures to be implemented before 1986 is impressive indeed. Yet the Lévesque government can be criticized in several respects:

1. The government intends to encourage local entrepreneurship as much as possible and nowhere has made clear that this emphasis would be to the exclusion of foreign investors. Also, even if industries have been stated as priorities, this must not be interpreted as an intention to shut foreign investors off from some sectors, except natural resources where there would be some restrictions as to the structure of ownership. However, it is probably not unfair to say that the government missed a golden opportunity to link its industrial policy with its foreign policy. Foreign-owned firms play an important role in the Quebec economy, as noted earlier. But nowhere in Quebec's industrial policy has the contribution expected from the foreign-owned firms or from foreign

relations in general been clearly stated. The absence of an international perspective is noticeable in both documents. Whatever comments exist in this respect are rather negative, because the fact that the Quebec economy is indeed a very open one is seen as domination from abroad.

2. The government can also be faulted for not being selective enough. Some industries must be helped because they are strong, others because they are weak, still others because they do not exist but should. As a result, probably well over half the private sector is mentioned as being in need of some form of government intervention.

3. The cost of this industrial policy has not been stated in either of the documents. However, the cost was mentioned by the minister responsible for the preparation of these documents at a news conference: Can$ 1 billion a year up to 1986, which is probably a conservative estimate. Coming from a government that claims to be financially so limited that it had to renege on labor contracts with its civil servants, teachers, and social affairs employees, the proposed cost leads observers to wonder where the necessary financing is going to be raised.

4. Insufficient attention was paid to training of human resources. Language Law 22 enacted in 1974 and more stringent Law 101 enacted in 1977 (see Chapter 11) have had the effect of restricting immigration of needed technicians (especially those who are English-speaking) and has caused a significant exodus of the English-speaking population from Quebec, as the 1981 Census for the half-decade and the decade preceding has shown. (See also Chapters 5 and 11.) Consequently, the necessary human resources will have to be generated locally to a greater extent. Should the critical human resources be unavailable, then putting considerable sums of money into biotechnologies, electronics, and other high-technology industries would not produce significant results.

Conclusion

Although it would be inappropriate for Quebec to tie its economy exclusively to that of the United States, the fact remains that the United States is Quebec's main economic partner by a considerable margin. Interactions between trade and foreign direct investment seem to point to FDI as the surest way to more extensive and mutually beneficial trade relations. Yet Quebec's official position vis-à-vis foreign direct investment has been and remains ambivalent. The official discourse has not really been hostile, especially when foreign investment offered Quebec an opportunity to oppose Ottawa's policies. On the other hand, the role of FDI in the Quebec economy is an issue that politicians appear reluctant to tackle publicly for fear of adverse reactions. From the corporations' standpoint, Quebec offers opportunities that benefited them in the past and are likely to benefit them in the future. But the long-standing *dirigiste* attitudes of Quebec governments, particularly the PQ government, also bring the corporations some misgivings. The relations between mutlinational corporations and nation-states have been characterized by some analysts as a type of love-hate relationship. The expression is not inappropriate for Quebec vis-à-vis the United States.

Notes

1. The transshipment problem in Quebec's trade data must be noted. Data on exports and imports are collected at port of entry or exit. Hence, products may exit from a province where they were not produced and products imported may not stay in the province by which they enter Canada. Statistics Canada does not correct these data. However, the Bureau de la Statistique du Québec usually does, and, where possible, its data will be used. Comparisons with the rest of Canada remain nevertheless complicated by the transshipment problem.

2. Imports from the United States stood at more than Can$ 7 billion in 1980. Consequently, for 1980, Quebec has had a substantial surplus in its U.S. trade balance of nearly Can$ 2 billion.

3. See also the Foreign Investment Review Agency, "Indicators of Foreign Control of Non-Financial Industries by Province," paper no. 3, May 1978, Government of Canada, Ottawa; and Foreign Investment Review Agency, "Compendium of Statistics on Foreign Investments," paper no. 4, May 1978, Government of Canada, Ottawa.

4. The analytical framework used here can be found, totally or partially, in many major works on foreign investment and multinational corporations: J. N. Behrman, *National Interests and the Multinational Enterprise* (Englewood Cliffs, NJ: Prentice-Hall, 1970); Herb Gray, *Investissements étrangers directs au Canada* (Ottawa: Information Canada, 1972); Gilles Y. Bertin, *Les sociétés multinationales* (Paris: Presses Universitaires de France, 1975); Raymond Vernon, *Storm Over the Multinationals: The Real Issues* (Cambridge, MA: Harvard University Press, 1979); N. Hood and S. Young, *The Economics of the Multinational Enterprise* (New York and London: Longman, 1979); J. H. Dunning, *International Production and the Multinational Enterprise* (London: George Allen and Unwin, 1981).

5. F. T. Knickerbocker, *Oligopolistic Reaction and Multinational Enterprise* (Boston: Graduate School of Business Administration, Harvard University, 1973).

6. Stephen Clarkson, *The Politics of Economic Dependence* (Ottawa: Privy Council Office, 1967).

38   *Bernard Bonin*

7. John Fayerweather, *Foreign Investment in Canada* (White Plains, NY: International Arts and Sciences Press, Inc., 1973).

8. J. Alex Murray and Lawrence Le Duc, "Changing Attitudes toward Foreign Investment in Canada," in John Fayerweather, ed., *Host National Attitudes toward Multinational Corporations* (New York: Praeger, 1982).

9. Le groupe de recherche sur les élites industrielles au Québec (directeur: Arnaud Sales), *Les industriels au Québec et leur rôle dans le développement économique* (Quebec: Ministère de l'Industrie et du Commerce du Québec, August and December 1977).

10. William Tetley, for Comité interministériel sur les investissements étrangers, *Le cadre et les moyens d'une politique québécoise concernant les investissements étrangers* (Quebec: Conseil Exécutif, 1974).

11. Bernard Bonin and Mario Polèse, *A propos de l'association économique Canada-Québec* (Montreal: École Nationale d'Administration Publique, January 1980).

12. *Bâtir le Québec*, 1979, and *Le virage technologique*, 1982 (Quebec: Ministère du Conseil Exécutif).

3
U.S. Perceptions of Investment Opportunities and Risks in Quebec

Alexander C. Tomlinson

It is important that a distinction be made between portfolio investment in Quebec securities, real estate, etc., by U.S. investors, on the one hand, and direct investment in business enterprises or new private sector resource projects and joint ventures in Quebec by U.S. entities (usually corporations or entrepreneurs), on the other. Perhaps surprising to some, for many years the major portion of U.S. private investment in Quebec has taken the form of bond purchases or long-term loans to crown corporations and well-established private sector Canadian companies. This flow of funds reflects a basic perception in the United States that Quebec is a safe place for this kind of investment, and interest rates are correspondingly favorable. This regular flow has become an important favorable element in the international balance of payments to Quebec (and Canada). Interest and dividend payments to U.S. institutions and individuals have, of course, become a significant negative factor.

Portfolio Investment

As to portfolio investment, Hydro-Quebec is the largest Quebec borrower, primarily for the James Bay Hydroelectric Project. Total U.S. dollar–denominated securities of Hydro-Quebec outstanding on December 31, 1982, aggregated $7,848,437,000. Approximately $6.1 billion of this total was sold in the United States and currently earns $637 million per year for its holders. A total of Can$ 3 billion has been expended annually in recent years on the James Bay Project alone. Of this figure, approximately Can$ 2 billion has been financed from outside Hydro-Quebec, the remainder being internally generated. To put these financing needs in perspective, 1973 estimates of the total cost of the project at Can$ 9 billion made it the largest project in history. The previous record-size project financed through private sector funds was Churchill

Falls, in Labrador, at a cost of a little under Can$ 2 billion. The basic credit that made feasible the financing of that project was the obligation of Hydro-Quebec to take the power produced.

Against such amounts, the latest estimate of Can$ 16 billion for completion of James Bay is indeed a challenging figure. To date, however, the necessary funds have been obtained without difficulty. The scale of Hydro-Quebec borrowing that the U.S. market has absorbed is impressive. At the time the James Bay Project was being launched I argued that it should not be undertaken unless commitments with respect to the total funds required could be negotiated in advance. There is hardly a greater financial disaster than a half-finished, totally useless project when the funds to complete it cannot be obtained. However, the management of Hydro-Quebec decided that the financing could be handled as part of the ordinary course of its regular financing activities. The First Boston Corporation accepted this challenge and has played a significant role in assuring the success of the program. There were, however, some anxious moments.

After the victory of the Parti Québécois in the 1976 election and particularly as a result of Premier Lévesque's speech in New York in early 1977, it became impossible to raise funds for Hydro-Quebec in the United States and relatively difficult in Canada. Pursuant to a continuing policy, Hydro-Quebec had wisely prefinanced about Can$ 1 billion—approximately the requirements for the project for the remainder of the year 1977. The inability to finance reflected the concerns of investors, who dislike uncertainty more than anything else and are not prepared to take significant risks. However, as the months passed, it became apparent that Quebec was, in fact, unlikely to leave the Canadian federation. More important, investors recognized that, even if Quebec were to become independent, any adverse effect on the quality of Hydro-Quebec's credit would be negligible.

In late 1977, Hydro-Quebec was able to reenter the U.S. market and sell bonds at an interest rate only about 1 percent (100 basis points) higher than the rate at which Ontario could have financed its hydro needs at that time. Traditionally, this investment quality differential between the two central Canadian provinces had been only some 25 to 30 basis points. In the ensuing months the interest differential narrowed, and Hydro-Quebec was able to raise increasing amounts of funds in 1978 and 1979. The interest differential rose slightly in 1981, probably reflecting the general level of interest rates, but the differential prevailing in early 1983 has not been much larger than that which was customary before the PQ came to power. In the last several years Hydro-Quebec has raised about Can$ 2 billion per year, more than half of this total typically in the United States. Excluding the U.S. government, Hydro-

Quebec in 1982 was one of the three largest borrowers in the U.S. capital market, along with Citicorp and General Motors Acceptance Corporation. The conclusion has to be that the U.S. market is very receptive to this large Quebec credit. The recent reduction in the credit rating for Hydro-Quebec bonds, which was based primarily on the financial problems of the Quebec government, will have little effect on further access to the U.S. market, except for a very marginal increase in interest costs. Investors attach little significance to the province's guarantee of Hydro-Quebec obligations.

Direct Investment: Some Deterrents

U.S. direct investment is currently (1983) down all across Canada. One perhaps should be surprised that it is down more in Quebec than elsewhere in Canada, since at least half the reasons for decline in Quebec are applicable to the rest of Canada. In my opinion, there are ten or more deterrents to investment in Quebec perceived by U.S. businessmen and investors:

1. The most important deterrent has been, of course, the operation of the Foreign Investment Review Act (FIRA). It is often argued that the impact of FIRA is negligible, inasmuch as so few applications are rejected. However, applications are time consuming and involve a great deal of nuisance, negotiations, uncertainty, and delay. Terms imposed, to assure "significant benefit to Canada," are often unrealistic and make the investment unattractive to boot. Potential investors often simply look elsewhere instead and their applications are never made. In late 1983 the Ottawa government and the FIRA board adopted a more positive (and realistic) attitude toward foreign investment, a reminder that in its operation FIRA has deterred U.S. investors all across Canada, though probably less so in Quebec. Contrary to the impression of Bernard Bonin, I believe Quebec is perceived in the U.S. business community as relatively more hospitable to U.S. investment than some other parts of Canada. While important elements of public opinion may be passively hostile to foreign investment in Quebec, the Parti Québécois and previous governments have been, by and large, receptive to foreign investments outside of certain narrowly defined areas. This receptivity undoubtedly stems from government recognition of the relatively greater need of Quebec for outside investment to assure economic growth—a triumph of the practical over the doctrinaire and the popular. Quebec leaders have frequently condemned FIRA, and

in 1982 all provincial premiers together attacked it, an encouraging move for the pace of Canadian development in the absence (or misdirection to oil company purchases) of adequate internal resources.

2. In order of significance, the second most important deterrent has been the general economic situation in both the United States and Canada.

3. Relatively high labor costs in Canada are a third significant deterrent, leading as they do to low productivity. This labor cost deterrent applies all across Canada, although perhaps slightly more so for Quebec.

4. Concern over possible separation of Quebec from Canada is significant but it should not be overemphasized as a deterrent. It must be recognized as a two-edged sword, inasmuch as there have been a number of instances where companies have made the decision to make two investments in Canada, one of them in Quebec. Without the concern over possible Quebec independence, there might have been only one investment, probably outside Quebec. The straddle assures that the investor would be positioned on both sides of any new frontier, with or without economic association. On balance, I think it is fair to say that anxiety over the possible adverse business impact of separation constitutes a net deterrent to investment. In fact, there are many potential U.S. investors, particularly but not exclusively looking toward direct investment, who have abstained from investing in Quebec because they feared they might be facilitating the move toward separation, which is generally disapproved across the U.S. business community as it is in the United States as a whole.

5. Another deterrent to investment is the concern that arises out of the provincial expropriations that have taken place across Canada. The record of Quebec in this regard is a relatively good one. In the case of the asbestos takeover, which represented a modest portion of the whole industry, the government leaned over backward to allow time to reach an acceptable settlement. It worked to reassure investors that the expropriation approach was a very limited one and not a forerunner of attacks on other industries. This favorably influenced potential investors. However, the pattern established by Premier Blakeney with regard to potash in Saskatchewan, and more recent moves by Newfoundland and Nova Scotia, tend to discourage direct investment anywhere in Canada.

6. The next deterrent is strikes. The amount of labor unrest in Canada is, to say the least, unreasonable. It is obviously costly. It tends to be three to four times greater than in the United States, and although it may not compare so unfavorably with

certain alternative places for foreign investment, i.e., Australia, it nevertheless looks unattractive to U.S. investors compared to the recent experience in the states. One should remember that in a sense Canada is frequently regarded by U.S. investors as simply an extension of their own industrial environment; thus a decision not to invest in Canada may not mean funds are diverted to other parts of the world.

7. A potential if not actual deterrent is the language requirements in Quebec. I do not want to overemphasize this point, because these requirements may be of little concern to U.S. corporations accustomed to operating abroad. However, I am sure they are an element in certain decisions, particularly where the alternative is elsewhere in Canada.

8. An obvious deterrent is the provincial restrictions on foreign ownership, even though they are limited to relatively small segments of the economy. These restrictions reflect a point of view of successive Quebec governments that suggests to wary potential investors that there may be future problems. To be sure, similar such deterrents exist in a number of other Canadian provinces.

9. The list of deterrents has to include the effects of the relative decline of Montreal as a corporate and financial center. Investment in Quebec has clearly suffered, despite the current commercial building activity in Montreal that would seem to belie it. Primarily because of the actions of the PQ, the power and dynamism have gone out of Montreal as a center, and it simply cannot attract certain types of businesses that in earlier years would have seen it as a good location. Much of the infrastructure that is essential to the operation of headquarters staffs of corporations is in the process of disintegration. Financial and other services, for example, are less available.

10. A deterrent so common to Canada that it is often taken for granted is the severe winters, which increase a variety of industrial costs.

11. My final negative element is something I see as a threat down the road. This arises from the dispute between Quebec and Newfoundland over Churchill Falls, where Hydro-Quebec is the target of a legal challenge by Newfoundland questioning the validity of the contract on the basis of which the Churchill Falls project was financed. Regardless of the possible merits, if Newfoundland were to be successful in this lawsuit and demonstrate to the world that a Canadian province can renege on a firm contract for a major financing, the impact would be to the detriment of all the provinces. And Quebec, being one of the larger importers of capital, would suffer considerably.

The foregoing list and ranking is a personal view. Others may enumerate and rank the deterrents differently. The Canadian government at Ottawa, for example, would rank FIRA at the bottom of the list, since officials continually assert that it really has very little impact. The identification of applications that are never made is hardly a matter of record. The question here is one of perceptions, and I stand firmly on the views expressed. However, both the day-to-day administration of FIRA and policy formulation with respect to it appear to have undergone significant change in emphasis recently. With the passage of time, potential investors may become far less concerned about FIRA than they have been to date.

Future Opportunities

In the face of all these deterrents there are obvious attractive features of investment in Quebec. As the title of this chapter suggests, there are, in fact, investment opportunities in the province. They may not lead to the kind of future growth, such as high technology, that the new industrial policy of Quebec proposes to encourage. Instead, they more directly reflect the reasons why foreigners have historically invested in Quebec and will continue to do so:

1. a variety of natural resources in abundance;
2. cheap and plentiful electric power (on an inflation-resistant basis so that it has very strong long-term attractions);
3. adequate labor supply and skills;
4. a location adjacent to the largest population centers of North America, both in Canada and the United States;
5. easy shipping access to European markets; and
6. a well developed industrial and commercial infrastructure.

With economic recovery on both sides of the border, a renewed interest in these opportunities in Quebec among U.S. businessmen and investors is likely to produce a significantly increased investment flow. However, in the past such a listing would have also singled out Quebec's stable political situation relative to most other parts of the world. Hence the probability of major new investments is greatly diminished by the uncertainty that is likely to prevail at least until the next Quebec election, because of Premier Lévesque's declaration that separation will be the central issue when it is held.

4

Trade Union Relations

Jean Boivin

U.S.-Quebec trade union relations—an important bilateral domain of U.S.-Quebec relations—cannot be fruitfully examined independent of a broader Canadian context. The impacts of Quebec upon U.S.-Canadian union phenomena have been both unique and influential in more respects than might be assumed by Quebec's proportion of total Canadian union membership. These Quebec influences on the general Canadian union scene are linked with francophone Quebec linguistic, cultural, ideological, social, and related legal factors, which also bear directly on behavior of Quebec unions vis-à-vis U.S. involvements and interests in Quebec itself. This chapter will therefore deal first with the issue of autonomy for the Canadian labor movement and with specific Quebec influences over evolution in that domain. Second, it will assess the role of certain unique characteristics of the Quebec labor environment in explaining these influences and Quebec labor's role relative to U.S. economic relations with Quebec itself.

The Overriding Issue of Autonomy
for the Canadian Labor Movement

A particularly salient feature of Canadian industrial relations has been that a substantial proportion of Canadians are members of organizations with headquarters and an overwhelming majority of their membership in the United States rather than in Canada—the so-called international unions. This situation, moreover, has deep historical roots since it has existed from the establishment of national unions in the United States. In fact, as early as 1861 the Iron Moulders had established a local in Canada, and they were soon followed by Typographers, Cigarmakers, Railway Conductors, and Shoemakers.

Although some U.S. unions sent organizers into Canada, the initiatives for establishment of formal linkages came predominantly from Canadian trade unionists representing small, isolated local unions needing contacts and supports from their much larger and stronger emerging U.S. counterparts.[1] Furthermore, neither political factors nor considerations of U.S. labor self-interest seem to have played major roles on either side of the frontier in this development. According to one able analyst of the period, Roy J. Adams, "Americans, it appears, did not, in general, consciously calculate the peculiar benefits to them of having Canadians as members but, instead, simply thought of Canada as a natural extension of North American culture."[2]

Thus, the international boundary seemed irrelevant to the question of territorial jurisdictions as Canadians became dependent on U.S.-based unions in the late nineteenth and early twentieth centuries. However, U.S. labor leaders probably made wrong judgments about the Canadian workers' environment and temperament when they asserted that Canadian and U.S. workers were "one and the same in spirit, in fact, in union, with one common polity and policy, with identical principles, hopes and aspirations."[3] According to Robert H. Babcock, "a good many Canadians felt smothered by the AFL leader's verbal embrace."[4]

Although by 1902 approximately 95 percent of Canadian union members were in locals affiliated with a central union in the United States, the issue of the autonomy of the Canadian labor movement was raised from the beginning and it has never been abandoned since. Moreover, as will be noted shortly, specific factors originating from Quebec have played an important role in this question of autonomy.

Two criteria can be used to assess the degree of autonomy of the Canadian labor movement. First, an objective criterion is a look at respective shares of memberships held by U.S.-based international unions and Canadian national unions in Canada. Second, a more subjective approach is an evaluation of the degree of U.S. influence within both the major Canadian federation—the Canadian Labor Congress (CLC)—and the Canadian sections or locals of international unions.

Respective Shares of Memberships for
National and International Unions

Table 4.1 lists the percentages of Canadian union members who were affiliated with U.S.-based international unions between 1902 and 1980.

In the early years of this century an overwhelming majority of the Canadian union workers belonged to international unions, but starting in the mid-1960s, the percentage has declined until it reached a historic low of 46.3 percent in 1980. Among the many factors that help explain this situation, the rapid growth of public-sector unions that are independent of U.S. internationals—for example, the Canadian Union of

Table 4.1. Percentage of Canadian Union Members in International
Unions, 1902-1980 (selected years)

Year	Percent	Year	Percent
1902	95.0	1949	70.9
1911	89.7	1954	71.4
1921	72.8	1959	72.4
1929	72.1	1964	71.4
1934	57.4	1969	65.0
1939	60.4	1977	49.0
1944	64.6	1980	46.3

Source: Gary Chaison, "Unions: Growth, Structure, and Internal
Dynamics," in John Anderson and Morley Gunderson, eds., Union-
Management Relations in Canada (Don Mills, Ont.: Addison-Wesley,
1982), p. 157.

Public Employees, the Public Service Alliance of Canada, and the
Canadian Union of Postal Workers—is probably the most important.
However, some Canadian locals in the private sector have also severed
their relationships with international unions to become national unions.
Examples are the Paperworkers' Union, the Brewery Workers' Union,
the Chemical Workers' Union, the National Association of Broadcast
Employees and Technicians.

Even at the beginning of this century, when most Canadian union
members were affiliated with international unions, an important minority
preferred purely national unions. Most of this minority was found in
Quebec. Table 4.2 indicates that the tremendous growth from 1897 to

Table 4.2. Trade Union Locals of International Unions, 1897 and
1902, by Region

Region	End of 1897		End of 1902	
	Approx. Number of Locals	Percent of Total	Approx. Number of Locals	Percent of Total
British Columbia	27	8.4	137-140	13.2
Prairies	24	7.5	75- 77	7.2
Maritimes	30	9.3	94- 97	9.1
Québec	47	14.6	115-119	11.0
Ontario	192-194	60.0	612-627	59.0

Source: Robert H. Babcock, Gompers in Canada: A Study in American
Continentalism Before the First World War (Toronto: University of
Toronto Press, 1974), p. 52.

Table 4.3. Trade Union Locals in Quebec by Type of Affiliation, 1901-1921

Year	International	National	Catholic	Total
1901	74	62	--	136
1906	155	81	--	236
1911	190	--	--	190
1916	236	70	23	329
1921	334	38	120	492

Source: Jacques Rouillard, Les syndicats nationaux au Québec de 1900 à 1930 (Quebec: Presses de l'Université Laval, 1979), p. 119.

1902 of trade union locals affiliated with international unions was not nearly as impressive in Quebec as in other parts of Canada.

According to Babcock, "the relative decline in Quebec's position was at least partial testimony to the extraordinary obstacles faced by organizers in that province."[5] Some of these obstacles were: (1) the fact that the AFL's organizer in Quebec, John Flett, did not speak French; (2) the opposition manifested by the Catholic church toward international unions; and (3) the rivalry of some national unions. As can be seen from Table 4.3, the number of locals that did not affiliate with international unions remained important in Quebec during most of the time between 1901 and 1921.

It is not an exaggeration to affirm that the core of international unions' opposition in Canada has always originated in Quebec. For example, when the Knights of Labor and other "dual" organizations were expelled from the Trades and Labor Congress (TLC—ancestor of the current CLC) in 1902, sixteen of the twenty-three unions and 80 percent of the 10,185 members thereof who joined the new National Trades and Labor Congress set up two days thereafter were from Quebec. This new organization, which became the Canadian Federation of Labor (CFL) in 1907, defined itself as a truly authentic Canadian body the basic aim of which was to replace the TLC as the major federation in Canada.

Although some early successes doubled membership to some 20,000 by 1906, this Quebec-originated organization did not achieve its goal and by the end of World War I it had almost disappeared. Among the major causes for its final failure was its preponderance of members from Quebec, its perceived dominance by nationalist francophone leaders, and thus its identification with Quebec by many English-speaking unionists from elsewhere in Canada.[6] To remedy this image, CFL leaders decided in 1908 to hold their annual conventions regularly outside Quebec and make major efforts to involve non-Quebec leaders and members. However, as the CFL began to experience some organizational success in anglophone Canada, it lost popularity in Quebec. By 1915 only twelve of its sixty-three affiliates were from Quebec.[7] This drastic decline in Quebec was primarily due to the rise of "confessional" unions organized under Catholic church auspices starting in 1911, largely to counter organization by "secular" (termed "materialist" and "socialist") unions. The "confessional" unions came together in the Canadian Conference of Catholic Workers (CCCW) in 1921. Although the latter defined itself as an all-Canadian organization and for a time had a few affiliates among Catholics (largely francophones) in Ontario, its membership throughout most of its existence was almost exclusively in Quebec. There the CCCW built its grass roots organizations by working within locals whose Canadian unions were affiliated with the CFL. The combination of the domination by the church over most aspects of French-Canadian life during that period, the nationalist sentiment in Quebec (which earlier expressed itself in the Canada-wide CFL), and the generally isolated, inward-looking character of francophone Quebec society at that time permitted the CCCW gradually to replace the CFL as the major TLC opponent during the first two decades of this century.

Some argue that weakness of nationalist sentiments among Anglo-Canadians was a major cause of the CFL's lack of success,[8] which may well be the case. But Quebec's role was then all the more central in the establishment of the first authentically Canadian labor federation whose purpose was to challenge stronger continentalist organizations. And this role has never been abandoned since. The CCCW, which became the Confederation of National Trade Unions (CNTU) in 1960, kept increasing its membership over the years and now represents some 200,000 Quebec workers. It is the second largest federation in Quebec, behind the CLC's federation, the Quebec Federation of Labor (QFL), which claims approximately 320,000 members.

Degree of U.S. Influence on the CLC and on Canadian Locals of International Unions

By far the most important Canadian union federation, the CLC, represented in 1981 68 percent of all Canadian union members (see Table 4.4). The CLC resulted from the 1956 merger of the Trades and Labor Congress (TLC) and the Canadian Congress of Labor (CCL), a merger linked with that of the AFL and CIO the year before in the United States. Like the AFL, the TLC was organized in 1883 primarily among craft unions, whereas the CCL resulted from the merger of the All Canadian Confederation of Labor and industrial union locals expelled from the TLC in 1940, many of whose internationals became members

Table 4.4. Union Membership in Canada by Congress Affiliation, 1981

Congress Affiliation	Members	As Percent of Total
Canadian Labor Congress	2,369,775	68.0
Confederation of National Trade Unions	210,430	6.0
Central of Democratic Unions	44,463	1.2
Confederation of Canadian Unions	29,776	0.9
AFL–CIO only	2,958	0.1
Unaffiliated international unions	101,805	2.9
Unaffiliated national unions	641,430	18.4
Independent local organizations	87,018	2.5
Total	3,487,231	100.0

Source: Labor Canada, Directory of Labor Organizations in Canada (Ottawa: Minister of Supply and Services Canada, 1981), p. 18.

of the CIO established across the border, after they withdrew from the AFL.

The influence of U.S.-based unions on the major Canadian labor federation had always been felt heavily in the past, as the following examples illustrate. When the TLC and the AFL established regular contacts in the late 1890s, the AFL pressed the TLC to expel the Knights of Labor because they represented members in the same jursidictions as those of international unions. The TLC complied even though the Knights had been an active, important part of the Canadian labor movement, with Knights leaders holding the presidency of the TLC for several terms prior to their union's expulsion. Again in 1940, when the TLC leadership preferred to maintain within its membership the international industrial unions affiliated with the CIO which, under John L. Lewis, had withdrawn from the AFL across the border, intense AFL pressure forced their expulsion by the AFL's Canadian counterpart.

Immediately after World War II, the Communist-led Canadian Seamen's Union (CSU), which was then the most important Canadian affiliate of the TLC, was expelled after the Canadian officers of fourteen international unions, under pressures from their U.S. headquarters, informed the TLC executive council that they would withdraw their organizations from the TLC if it did not so act.[9] The rival union challenging the CSU's representation of Canadian seaman on the Great Lakes and eastern seaborad was the Seafarers' International Union (SIU), supported by the AFL. The SIU's Canadian director was the notorious Hal Banks, who had a criminal record in the United States. Under these circumstances, Banks and his organization, with the help of a number of "broad-shouldered boys" from the United States (as he described them), won a complete victory over the CSU by 1950, after a particularly ruthless and violent campaign.[10] A few years later, the CLC expelled Banks' SIU on charges of violence, illegality, and outright gangsterism used to suppress all internal opposition and to raid other unions. The CLC chartered a new organization, the Canadian Maritime Union, to take over jurisdiction of Canadian shipping from the SIU. However, the international executives of the SIU, the allied AFL-CIO Maritime Trades Department, and a majority of the AFL-CIO Executive Council supported Banks and his organization. The controversy precipitated the intervention of the Canadian government which, upon recommendation of a royal commission of inquiry, placed the SIU under trusteeship, pending the election of a new executive under democratic procedure.

Finally, when the merger between the TLC and the CCL was achieved in 1956, affiliation of the Quebec-based Canadian Confederation of Catholic Workers (CCCW) with the new Canadian Labor Congress (CLC) was seriously considered. However, the opposition of influential international craft unions made impossible the complete unification of Canadian trade unions by inclusion of the CCCW. The new CLC constitution provided that "where jurisdiction is affected, present affiliates to the Congress, which means mainly the international unions, can vote the affiliation of new bodies."[11] Subsequently the CCCW never joined the CLC for fear of its assimilation by international craft unions.

The relative decline in importance of international unions in Canada, which started in the mid-1960s (Table 4.1), was also felt within the CLC. The rate of membership growth of international unions between 1975 and 1981 was only 4.3 percent, but that of the national unions affiliated with the CLC was 40.8 percent (Table 4.5). Three of the five largest CLC affiliates are national unions, all of them representing public-sector employees.

With the increasing number of delegates from these new, more militant public-sector unions attending the CLC's biannual conventions, this federation has now developed into a less conservative, more nationalist organization than it ever was in the past. As a consequence, the CLC could more easily depart from traditional policies followed by U.S.-based labor organizations and continue its endorsement of the New Democratic Party; it could manifest publicly its opposition to U.S. military involvement in Vietnam, maintain its support for both the International Labor Organization and the International Confederation of Free Trade Unions, and express its discontent with the U.S. Burke-Hartke bill on foreign trade policy.

Two series of events that have considerably enhanced the position of the CLC as a more autonomous body vis-à-vis U.S. influence are worthy of mention. (Again, Quebec trade unionists were largely instru-

Table 4.5. Evolution of National and International Unions'
Membership Within the CLC, 1975 and 1981

	1975		1981		Growth	
	Number of Members	Percent of Total	Number of Members	Percent of Total	Number of Members	Percent of Total
International unions	1,392,994	68.4	1,453,029	61.3	60,035	4.3
National unions and directly chartered locals	630,993 19,497	31.6	905,322 11,000	38.7	265,832	40.8
Total CLC membership	2,043,484	100.0	2,369,361	100.0	325,867	13.7

Sources: Labor Canada, Labor Organizations in Canada, 1975 (Ottawa:
Labor Canada, 1975), p. XXI; Labor Canada, Directory of Labor Or-
ganizations in Canada (Ottawa: Ministry of Supply and Services
Canada, 1981), p. 18.

mental in the respective outcomes.) The first began at the 1970 CLC convention, which adopted three minimum standards of self-governance that were to be followed by the Canadian sections of international unions. These were (1) the election of Canadian officers by Canadians; (2) the determination of policies on national affairs by the elected Canadian officers and/or members; and (3) the authority of Canadian-elected representatives to speak for the union in Canada.

The issue of compliance with these standards was seriously raised by Quebec and other nationalist union leaders four years later at the 1974 CLC convention. These delegates also pressed for much more rigorous standards, but very few of their propositions were adopted. Nevertheless, two more standards were added: (1) that where an inter-national union is affiliated with an international trade secretariat, the Canadian section of that union should be affiliated separately to ensure a Canadian presence and voice at the international industry level; and (2) that international unions take whatever action is necessary to ensure that Canadian membership will not be prevented by constitutional requirements or policy decisions from participating in the social, cultural, economic, and political life of the Canadian community. At the same convention, three out of the four elections for the CLC's executive council were won by candidates supported by nationalist and radical delegates.

Although other nationalist propositions to impose very rigorous standards of autonomy were defeated (e.g., permitting Canadian locals of different internationals to merge even if the parent organizations were not merging themselves), the adoption of the new standards produced a near split within the CLC. Most of the construction unions withdrew their dues for months to several years, but a number of their locals either sent, or threatened to send, their dues directly to the CLC.[12]

In a second series of events a few years later, some of these construction unions would once again come to grips with CLC leaders. This second conflict, however, demonstrated the degree of autonomy achieved by the CLC and the important role played by Quebec trade unions in this regard.

The conflict started because the QFL accepted among its ranks local unions whose members were recruited among types of workers for whom some international unions, like the International Brotherhood of Electricians, had already established their jurisdictions. In fact, in the past, both the "dual" local unions and those affiliated with international unions were members in good standing of the QFL, until, one day, locals of some internationals threatened to disaffiliate unless the latter organization expelled the "dual" unions. Since these "dual" unions were among the most active and militant QFL affiliates in the construction industry, they had full support of the QFL leadership. The international unions involved thus pulled their locals out of the QFL and warned the CLC leadership that they would take similar measures against the national federation if the latter did not order the QFL to comply with its constitution, which forbade the affiliation of "dual" unions. Thus confronted with the issue, the CLC leadership could either revoke the QFL's charter, which would have meant setting up a new provincial organization in Quebec, or let the internationals disaffiliate from its ranks. For the first time in the history of the Canadian labor movement, the major Canadian federation decided in favor of its national constituency and backed up the QFL's position. (As a result, a number of trade unionists representing ten international craft unions left the CLC and established, in March 1982, a new federation, ironically with the same name as that of the first group that opposed domination from the United States, the Canadian Federation of Labor, or CFL.)

Thus, in recent years, Quebec unions affiliated with the CLC have found more allies than they ever had among other Canadian unions in their efforts to secure devolution of powers by U.S. headquarters of internationals to Canadian sections or locals. And this Quebec influence in the autonomy movement has had positive consequences. A study by Mark Thompson (1980), whose data were derived from intensive interviews with senior union officers in the United States and Canada and from analysis of documentary evidence from twenty-five international unions, indicated that the CLC minimum standards of self-governance were highly influential in the international unions' decision to implement changes. According to this study, eighteen out of the twenty-five unions in the sample changed the status of Canadians during the 1970s.[13]

Thompson's study identified three types of structural arrangements for Canadians in international unions; he calls them the "assimilationist" model, the "special status" model, and the "self-governing" model.[14]

The first model treats Canadians and U.S. union members no differently and makes few provisions for specifically Canadian issues. These unions have a Canadian vice president who is elected at large either by the full membership or by all convention delegates. In the "special status" model, Canada is designated as a separate region, with important rights and functions not found in U.S. regions. Among these rights are the election of a vice president by Canadians, the operation of a Canadian office, the organization of periodic Canadian policy conferences, and Canadian control over dues monies collected in Canada. Finally, in the "self governing" model, characteristics of the "special status" model are found but, in addition, there is a separate Canadian constitution, subject to interpretation by a Canadian president. Moreover, Canadian members determine their own dues structure and may have a separate strike fund. Power to approve strikes and supervise the union's activities is vested with Canadian officers. Canadians remain members of the international, are subject to its constitution, and are obliged to pay per capita taxes.

Relatively few unions have granted self-governing status to their Canadian affiliates. At least three have done so: the Brotherhood of Railway, Airline and Steamship Clerks (BRAC); the Office and Professional Employees International Union (OPEIU); and the Oil, Chemical and Atomic Workers (OCAW). The latter has gone as far as permitting the Canadian membership to establish a new national union—the Energy and Chemical Workers Union, which has merged with the Canadian Chemical Workers Union. Thus, in varying degrees there appears to be a definite trend toward greater self-governance on the part of Canadian sections of international unions. More unions are now in the "special status" category and fewer in the "assimilationist" category. In many instances, Canadian divisions or conferences have been created and led by Canadian officers. The members are playing a greater role in decisions about organizing, bargaining, and political activities.

Some Unique Underlying Aspects of Quebec Labor

The efforts over the years of Quebec labor to achieve greater autonomy for Canadian union organizations, and the behavior of Quebec labor in regard to U.S. investment and other relations directly with Quebec (to be discussed shortly), are reflections of more basic labor and related socioeconomic environments more or less unique to Quebec. Its francophone linguistic, cultural, and nationalist social and political developments are discussed in other chapters, but some of their implications for trade union behavior pertinent to the United States should be mentioned here.

Level of Unionization

Trade unionism is a more pronounced phenomenon in Quebec than in the United States generally, although in both cases an important decline has been noticed in the last decade. According to Thomas A. Kochan, the number of union members in the United States dropped from 27.3 percent of all nonagricultural employees in 1970 to 24.5 percent in 1976.[15] In Quebec, the respective figures were 37.9 percent and 33.5 percent for 1970 and 1976, and 32.5 percent for 1979.[16] The level of unionization in Quebec is slightly higher than in Ontario and slightly lower than in British Columbia. The figures for the year 1975 (the only ones available for comparative purposes) showed the following percentages: Quebec 33.8, Ontario 31.8, and British Columbia 36.5.[17]

The decline in the overall level of unionization does not, however, reflect the different realities of the private and public sectors. A study by the Quebec Employers' Council established at 21.2 percent the level of unionization in the private sector in 1976, as compared to the Canadian private-sector average of 20.8 percent. Ontario's and British Columbia's figures were 20.6 percent and 28.4 percent respectively.[18] On the other hand, the level of unionization in several areas of the public and quasipublic sectors in Quebec were 74.6 percent in education, 52.2 percent in health care services, and 49.9 percent in public administration.[19]

These phenomena, however, are not unique to Quebec and Canada. In the United States, the percentage of manufacturing and nonmanufacturing employees unionized declined from 51 percent to 45 percent and from 30 percent to 21 percent, respectively, between 1956 and 1976. However, the percentage of public employees in labor unions rose from 13 percent to 20 percent during the same period. Adding membership in bargaining associations to the government figure raises the latter figure to 39 percent.[20]

Thus, the pattern of unionization in Quebec follows the general characteristics that are also found in the rest of Canada and in the United States, namely, a sharp decline in the private sector and a great deal of stability or growth in the public sector. However, the overall magnitude of unionization is nonetheless higher in Quebec than in the United States by approximately 10 percent.

Table 4.6. Membership of Labor Organizations in Quebec for Selected
Years, 1957-1978 (thousands)

Year	CLC	QFL	CNTU	CEQ	CDU
1957	250	92	100	--	--
1960	250	99	94	30	--
1964	250	111	141	42	--
1966	325	141	204	54	--
1972	342	233	219	70	21
1978	420	300	178	85	42

Source: Fernand Harvey, ed., Le mouvement ouvrier au Québec (Montreal: Boréal Express, 1980), p. 287.

Trade Union Pluralism

An important and unique characteristic of the Quebec labor movement is trade union pluralism, which has prevailed since the expulsion of the Knights of Labor from the Trades and Labor Congress in 1902. Even if "confessional" unions never succeeded in gaining the adhesion of a majority of union members, they were nevertheless always the major source of opposition to international unions in Quebec. Those unions dropped their "confessional" status in 1960 and they are now the most important labor organizations in the public sector. In fact, 50 to 60 percent of the CNTU membership comes from the public and quasipublic sectors. This federation has also become a rather ideologically oriented organization and is committed to the goal of a socialist type of society. As a result of this radical ideological turnabout in the early 1970s, the CNTU lost a substantial portion of its membership, and some of the leaders who left the federation organized a rival federation, the Central of Democratic Unions, founded in June 1972.

Most teachers working at the pre-university levels belong to an independent teachers' federation, the Central of Education of Quebec. This organization has also started to recruit all types of people working in educational services like janitors, secretaries, and maintenance employees, but the bulk of its membership is still comprised of primary and secondary school teachers. The CEQ's ideology is quite similar to that of the CNTU.

Finally, the most important labor federation is the Quebec Federation of Labor, which represents, *on a voluntary basis*, all CLC affiliates in the Province of Quebec. As can be seen from Table 4.6, the QFL, which was formed immediately after the TLC-CCL merger in 1956, experienced some difficulties in convincing CLC's affiliates to participate in its activities in the early years of its existence. Nevertheless, according to some reliable sources, the QFL represented approximately 81 percent of CLC affiliates by 1982.[21]

This four-way competition explains why the QFL has pressed the CLC consistently to grant it greater authority than other provincial federations over such fields as union education, organizational services, appointment of local and regional officers (usually vested in the CLC), and information. Only after years of "hard lobbying" and maneuvering did the QFL obtain these powers at the 1974 CLC convention. Nevertheless, these powers are insufficient for the QFL to cope with potent competition from the other three Quebec federations. The QFL argues it also needs authority to retain local members who, dissatisfied with their national or international unions, have severed their relationships with them—unconstitutional under prevailing CLC statutes. The QFL notes that if it lets these members disaffiliate, they would be snapped up by one of its three rivals. Therefore the CLC has tolerated de facto some such retentions within the QFL, not without creating some turmoil, as has been noted.

Legal Aspects

Although Quebec's labor legislation borrows much from the U.S. Wagner Act, as do all other Canadian provinces, several pertinent Quebec laws are unique. Its 1934 *Collective Agreements Decrees Act*, inspired by French and Belgian laws but existent nowhere else on this continent, accords the minister of labor the power to extend terms of a collective agreement to all employees and employers in a given sector of the economy even though they might not themselves have been parties to it. Ministers have typically so decreed in industries characterized by a large number of small employers, to prevent unfair competition from nonunion shops by equalizing labor costs throughout the whole sector.

A second law unique in North America and of concern to U.S.-based unions and investors is the *Construction Industry Labor Relations Act* of 1968, related to the one above, but particularly designed to deal with the fierce rivalry between international unions affiliated with the QFL and Quebec associations affiliated with the CNTU, plus three different labor organizations in construction. This act applies compulsory industry-wide bargaining through agents designated by law. Because no labor organization possesses an absolute majority, coalitions are required to ensure that a collective agreement can be reached. Under this act, all types of crafts must bargain simultaneously. These institutional arrangements are of course in clear contradiction of traditional approaches of international craft unions.

Similarly, highly centralized bargaining contrary to the tradition of decentralized negotiations in much of the rest of North America prevails across the Quebec public and quasipublic sectors. International unions represent only a small minority of public-sector employees; thus, their leaders need to form a common front with the typically nationalist, frequently militant and ideological, Quebec-based and Canadian-based union leaders in order to bargain with the Quebec government and its state corporations.

Level of Strike Activity

An examination of person-days lost in strikes, as a percentage of potential person-days worked in the total nonagricultural economy, indicates a 0.34 percent loss for Quebec, contrasted with a 0.25 percent rate for the United States, during the 1965–1973 period. For the 1974–1978 period, the respective rates were 0.61 percent for Quebec and 0.20 percent for the United States. It should be noted that between 1976 and 1979 nearly 75 percent of the salaried persons involved in strikes in Quebec were either in the public or quasipublic sectors. However, these workers represent only 25 percent or so of total salaried employees in Quebec.

That the rate of person-days lost has increased over time in Quebec and diminished over time in the United States is due in part to the growth of trade unionism in the public sector in Quebec. It is also partly due to a slower realization of the competitive difficulties of the Quebec economy than has been the case in the United States. This attitude can also be demonstrated in the lack of cooperation between management and labor to cope with the competitive problems faced. Quebec trade unions in general are very reluctant to reopen collective agreements in order to postpone or even to drop wage increases and other benefits for which they had already bargained. Most of the unions are not interested in trading off these benefits against some institutional participation on companies' boards of directors.

This higher incidence of union militancy in Quebec as compared with that prevailing in the rest of Canada and in the United States could easily be attributed to the fact that Quebec trade unionists are more ideologically oriented than their other North American counterparts. But this interpretation should be carefully qualified. At least two labor organizations—the CNTU and the teachers' federation (CEQ)—have a radical ideology that could be called "marxist," although leaders of these organizations do not like this term applied to them. Several factors in relation to this situation reduce the explanatory power of the variable *ideology* for the high level of union militancy in Quebec.

First, it is well established that the vast majority of trade union members do not share the radical ideology of some of their leaders. Some organizations end up with a radical leadership for a combination of reasons. One is the general apathy of union members toward their organizations (which is common not only to Quebec). Another is the concentration of the membership in white-collar, public-sector or quasi-public-sector occupations where a higher level of education is found (the more educated and the more intellectual the union members are, the more radical their union tends to be). There is also the fact that the strong bargaining power of these unions vis-à-vis their employers, usually public agencies or the provincial government (which expends 50 percent of its budget on public-sector employees' wages and salaries), permits the unions to achieve substantial benefits for their members—and so long as the unions deliver the goods, the members do not mind the ideological rhetoric of the leaders. Moreover, there is always a way out; the existence of union pluralism, which favors the establishment of more homogeneous central labor organizations, allows dissident members to change their affiliation easily.

Second, except for the public and quasipublic sectors, the pattern of strike activity in Quebec does not differ substantially from that of the rest of Canada. There are, at times, some bitter conflicts the duration of which may be exceptionally long, but aside from the excessive language often used, these conflicts occur elsewhere. (The J.P. Stevens Company case is a good example of such bitter conflict in the United States.)

Third, one should not identify the higher level of militancy in Canada only with Quebec. In general, Canadian trade unionists, including anglophones as well as francophones, are more militant than their U.S. counterparts. Like Quebec trade unionists, they have been more reluctant to engage in "concession bargaining." The Chrysler Corporation case is a recent example that illustrates this point.

Quebec Labor and the Nationalist Movement

Integrally connected with linguistic and cultural differences is the strong francophone nationalist movement, reflected not only in supporters of the Parti Québécois (PQ) now in power, but also in varying forms and degrees among francophones associated with the Quebec Liberal Party (PLQ) and with the remnants of the National Union Party organized originally in the 1930s, but no longer represented at the National Assembly although it ruled over Quebec's destiny between 1944 and 1960.

Only minorities of 15–25 percent of Quebeckers have favored outright independence, with some 40 percent favoring sovereignty with economic association in a common market or customs union with a common currency. Larger minorities of the 82 percent of Québécois who are francophones have favored the latter course. However, majorities favor a dualist constitutional and political solution that would recognize Quebec as their linguistic and cultural homeland, clearly different from any other province—a francophone society in Canada that would have powers in respect to language, culture, communications, immigration, and related economic matters to protect and help develop their culture.

Francophone nationalism, manifested in different forms including agitation for independence, goes back two centuries to the forced cession of New France to Britain in 1763, and it will persist, undoubtedly, in militant form until at least a major compromise toward recognition of francophone jurisdictions is accepted by the federal government and the rest of Canada.

The Quebec trade union movement since at least the beginning of the Quiet Revolution that started in 1960 under Jean Lesage, former Pearson Liberal federal cabinet minister and Quebec Liberal Party premier from 1960 to 1966, has supported de facto the more nationalist, dualist, major party, at that time the PLQ. After René Lévesque's establishment of the sovereignty-association movement (later the Parti Québécois) in the late 1960s, most trade union militants and activists shifted their votes, their modest financial contributions, and in many cases their active support, at least as individuals, to the PQ.

Trade unions were a major factor in the PQ's victories in both the 1976 and the 1981 provincial elections, and in the PQ obtaining 40 percent of the votes in favor of negotiations toward sovereignty-association in the referendum of 1980. They provided much of the informal and organizational communications network, the volunteers to turn out the francophone labor vote and with it nearly a majority of the 47 percent of francophones who voted PQ in 1976, the 47 percent who voted "yes" in the 1980 referendum, and the 57 percent who voted PQ in 1981. However, only the QFL has officially endorsed the PQ in pre-election resolutions in 1976 and 1981, but this organization has no institutional relationships with the PQ. The commitment to support the PQ was made on an ad hoc basis, and it has always been asserted by the QFL leadership that such "moral support" could be removed at any time.

Although most CNTU and CEQ members are active PQ supporters, these organizations have refused to officially endorse the PQ in the last two elections. Moreover, the radical ideologues among CNTU and CEQ leadership view the Lévesque government and the party on which it is based as too "bourgeois," not sufficiently reflective of labor concerns, placing too much priority on the private sector and on attracting private foreign direct investment, and the like. Union leaders note that the Lévesque government is neither a labor nor a social democratic government, in which Lévesque has himself publicly concurred. Actually, these radical trade unionists have no place else to go on the political scene because the possibilities of a socialist or labor party in Quebec are rather remote[22] and the Quebec Liberal Party is widely regarded as increasingly pro-private enterprise.

Official endorsement by the QFL and active support by grass roots trade unionists have not only resulted in the PQ victories of 1976 and 1981, but they have also contributed to the election of trade unionists themselves. For example, a former vice president of the CEQ was elected in both the 1976 and 1981 elections, and a former vice president of the QFL was elected in 1981. In the latter case, the individual involved is a former UAW regional director for Quebec and vice president of the international union. He is also an anglophone. Overall some twenty persons with trade union backgrounds were elected to the National Assembly for the PQ in 1981. The total PQ delegation at the National Assembly includes two anglophones, Robert Dean and Stephen Payne.

It is thus rather surprising to realize that the only Quebec labor federation formally in support of the most nationalist provincial party represents international unions. However, one should not forget that the QFL also represents some very important national unions and that many union members affiliated with the CEQ, the CNTU, and the CDU are active PQ supporters despite the official neutrality of their organizations.

Conclusions

Quebec has been a major force in activating a slow but effective process of "Canadianization" of the labor movement. The Quebec context differs from that of the rest of Canada in respects that require international unions to behave differently from their habitual way of functioning in other provinces or in Canada as a whole. They must constantly modify and adjust their traditional modes to unique Quebec circumstances. The French language and the approaches to problems and ways of thought intimately related to it are of course an important consideration unique to Quebec. U.S. union leaders cannot ignore the linguistic difference, but like most Americans do not easily grasp the integrally associated cultural implications even as they impinge rather directly on relations with their Quebec affiliates. These linguistic and cultural differences also underlie, or affect, social and political considerations, such as the more ideological and militant character of Quebec labor unions compared with other, predominantly anglophone, U.S. and Canadian unions.

Despite these very specific characteristics of the Quebec labor and sociopolitical environments, foreign investors and policymakers should not look upon Quebec as a society that is hostile to their interests. All political parties are committed to the goals of a pluralistic and democratic society where the free enterprise system is encouraged to function efficiently. The presence of some radical union leaders may not be good for the overall labor outlook as viewed by U.S. investors, but it is heavily compensated by a trade union membership that is basically oriented toward "bread and butter" issues rather than ideologies. Radical union leaders also exist elsewhere in Canada, but because they do not control their own organizations like the CNTU and the CEQ, their voices are much less heard within a large organization like the CLC.

It is true that the level of Quebec strike activity is the highest in North America, but these statistics are heavily biased by strictly public- and quasipublic-sector phenomena. Quebec's pattern of private-sector strikes and level of unionization generally follows that of the rest of North America. Union membership is declining in the private sector as a whole and unions are virtually absent in the new high-technology sectors, as elsewhere on this continent.

Until recently, one of the major obstacles that some small and medium-sized firms faced was the pattern-setting conditions of employment established by some public-sector collective agreements, mostly in semi-urban or rural areas. However, the government has taken a very strong stance in its 1982–1983 negotiations with public-sector unions. It has unilaterally imposed substantial wage cuts (up to 20 percent in certain cases) and it has also increased employees' work loads in education, social affairs, and the civil service. The PQ government will probably have to pay a high electoral price by so alienating its traditional supporters, but it will certainly gain more credibility among business interests and prospective foreign investors.

Notes

1. Stuart Jamieson, *Industrial Relations in Canada,* 2nd ed. (Toronto: Macmillan, 1973), pp. 44–77; and John Crispo, *International Unionism* (Toronto: McGraw-Hill, 1967), pp. 11–23.

2. Roy J. Adams, "Canada-U.S. Link Under Stress," *Industrial Relations* 15 (1976), p. 296.

3. Samuel Gompers, *AFL Proceedings* (Washington, D.C.: American Federation of Labor, 1901), p. 21.

4. Robert H. Babcock, *Gompers in Canada: A Study in American Continentalism Before the First World War* (Toronto: University of Toronto Press, 1974), p. 54.

5. Ibid., p. 52.

6. Charles Lipton, *Histoire du syndicalisme au Canada et au Québec: 1827–1957* (Montreal: Editions Parti-Pris, 1976), p. 226.

7. Jacques Rouillard, *Les syndicats nationaux au Québec, 1900–1930* (Ottawa: Département d'histoire, Université d'Ottawa, 1976), unpublished Ph.D. dissertation, p. 152.

8. Lipton, *Histoire du syndicalisme*, and Rouillard, *Les syndicats nationaux*.

9. Robert W. Cox and Stuart M. Jamieson, "Canadian Labor in the Continental Perspective," in A. B. Fox, A. O. Hero, Jr., and J. S. Nye, Jr., eds., *Canada and the United States: Transnational and Transgovernmental Relations* (New York: Columbia University Press, 1976), p. 224.

10. Ibid., p. 224.

11. Charles Lipton, "Canadian Unions," in Gary Teeple, ed., *Capitalism and the National Question in Canada* (Toronto: University of Toronto Press, 1972), p. 102.

12. For details on the pertinent controversies at the 1974 CLC convention, see Robert Laxer, *Canada's Unions* (Toronto: James Lorimar & Company, 1976), pp. 136–145.

13. Mark Thompson, "The Evolving Role of Canadians in International Unions," in *Current and Future Perspectives in Canadian Industrial Relations* (Montreal: Canadian Industrial Relations Association, June 1980), p. 253.

14. Ibid, p. 250.

15. Thomas A. Kochan, *Collective Bargaining and Industrial Relations: From Theory to Policy and Practice* (Homewood, IL: Richard D. Irwin, 1980), p. 128.

16. For 1970, *Travail Québec* 13(2), March 1977 (Ministère du travail et de la main-d'oeuvre), p. 26; for 1976, *Le marché du travail* 1(1), May 1980 (Centre de recherche et de statistique sur le marché du travail, Bibliothèque nationale du Québec), p. 34; and for 1979, *Le marché du travail* 3(6), June 1982, p. 61.

17. Gary N. Chaison, "Unions: Growth, Structure and Internal Dynamics," in John Anderson and Morley Gunderson, eds., *Union-Management Relations in Canada* (Don Mills: Addison-Wesley, 1982), p. 150.

18. *Bulletin sur les relations du travail* 10(100), September 1979, p. 14 (Conseil du Patronat du Québec).

19. *Le marché du travail* 1(1), May 1980, p. 35.

20. Kochan, *Collective Bargaining and Industrial Relations*, p. 129.

21. Anne Parent, "La syndicalisation au Québec," in *Le marché du travail* 3(6), June 1982, p. 64.

22. A "Socialist Movement" was created in Quebec in early 1983. This group is led by two former trade union leaders, Marcel Pépin from the CNTU and Raymond Laliberté of the CEQ, who are now both university professors. This movement is dedicated to the idea of an independent and socialist Quebec. It has not yet decided to become an official political party, but if it chooses to do so, it should attract, in principle, the support of the radical minority among trade union members, mostly confined within the CEQ and the CNTU.

5

Population Exchanges Between Quebec and the United States over the Last Two Decades

Réjean Lachapelle

Although the United States, Canada, and Quebec have for many years considered themselves countries of immigration, they have not shared equally in the realization of this self-perception. The United States has had a net gain in immigration over emigration for more than a century, but Canada's departures have far exceeded its arrivals over the last four decades of the nineteenth century. For a large number of people, Canada has been but a stopover on the way to the United States. Canadians themselves have emigrated south. Nevertheless, Canada has been able to maintain a positive population balance during the last eighty years thanks to an immigration policy more expansive than that of the United States.

Quebec has almost always experienced losses in its population exchanges with other countries. Between 1840 and 1930, it saw the exodus of nearly 1 million people into the United States.[1] In spite of this drain, a rapid increase in population occurred, from 700,000 to 2.5 million in the course of this same ninety-year period. The fertility of the Québécoises more than made up for the migratory losses. After World War II, migration trends changed. Between 1951 and 1966, the balance became positive as important gains in the area of international migration more than made up for the slight losses that Quebec experienced by way of exchanges with the rest of Canada. Subsequently, international migration remained favorable to Quebec but less so than during the

I would like to express my appreciation to Minh Truong of the Quebec Ministry of Cultural Communities and Immigration for his invaluable assistance in this study, to Bernard Bonin and Alfred O Hero, Jr., for their comments and suggestions, and to Charlotte LeBlanc for this translation from French into English.

preceding fifteen years, and losses to other provinces became heavier. The balance of population exchanges once again became negative.[2]

During the last ten years, a change of focus has taken place in preoccupations concerning population exchanges between the United States, Canada, and Quebec. During the 1960s and early 1970s, interest lay principally in the study of the causes and effects of Canadian emigration to the United States.[3] Subsequently, attention was given to the study of U.S. draft dodgers and deserters in Canada,[4] to an examination of the causes of the progression of U.S. emigration,[5] to the analysis of the situation of immigrants from the United States in Canada,[6] and to measuring the fraction of Canadian immigrants who left the United States to return to Canada.[7] There is a striking parallel between the change in the themes of research and the evolution of migratory trends. If the rare statistics on the subject are to be believed, the Québécois as well as Canadians in general now emigrate to the United States at a much lower rate than formerly.

In Quebec, the sociocultural and particularly the linguistic consequences of immigration and the causes of the migratory losses to the rest of Canada have been the focus of attention since the early 1970s. These concerns will be examined first in this chapter. The population exchanges between the United States and Quebec during the last fifteen years will be examined next, within the framework of general trends in international immigration. Thereafter, the principal characteristics of U.S. immigrants to Quebec will be described. However, the characteristics of the Québécois who came to the United States are unavailable, because U.S. government official statistics do not distinguish constituent parts of a country but deal only with its whole. Canada, therefore, has its place in the nomenclature, but Quebec does not.

Quebec and Immigration

The British North America Act, by which Canada was created in 1867, ascribed shared jursidiction to the central government and to the provinces in matters of immigration. A provisional arrangement was concluded in 1868 that specified the responsibilities of the parties. Subsequently, the government of Quebec sent agents to Europe whose mission was to make Quebec known and to recruit either successful farmers who would serve as models to the Québécois, or investors and qualified workers who would strengthen industries related to agriculture. There was also a need in Quebec for farm hands and servants. However, immigrants, as was the case with nationals, had no desire to fill these jobs on a permanent basis. During the last four decades of the nineteenth century, departures from Quebec far exceeded arrivals. This was also the case throughout Canada. The ports served as gateways for immigrants wishing to migrate to the United States. The fraction of Quebec's population born outside the country diminished rapidly during the last half of the nineteenth century, going from slightly more than 10 percent in 1851 to 5 percent in 1901.

In 1875, Quebec, Ontario, and New Brunswick signed an agreement whereby their immigration agencies abroad were abolished. Each province was allowed to name a subagent who acted under the direction of Canada's general agent. Quebec seems to have found this arrangement somewhat advantageous financially. However, Quebec did express some reticence and reserved for itself the right to desist after one year.[8] Until the end of the nineteenth century, the government of Quebec's activities in Europe were sporadic. Attempts were made to increase French immigration, but the actions taken ran into numerous obstacles, and the results on the whole were rather mediocre. This is not surprising, given that the net number of Québécois emigrating to the United States continued to be more than 100,000 per decade from 1870 to 1930. To counteract this exodus, or at least diminish its impact, Quebec encouraged foreign investment and gave its support to the Catholic church and those societies created to colonize new territories. At various periods between 1870 and 1933, the government established repatriation programs aimed at inviting Franco-Americans to return.

In 1968, Quebec's Ministry of Immigration was created as a result of the government's renewed interest in immigration during the 1960s. Ongoing negotiations with the federal government led to the progressive increase of Quebec's power in the selection and recruitment of potential immigrants. In 1971 the Cloutier-Lang Agreement was signed with the federal government. Its provisions authorized the presence of immigration agents of Quebec in foreign countries to furnish information on Quebec society to individuals interested in meeting with them. The Bienvenue-Andras Agreement (1975) increased Quebec's powers in that the federal government was thereby obligated to take into consideration Quebec's opinion on any candidate contemplating emigrating there.

Subsequently, in 1978, the Couture-Cullen Agreement granted to Quebec important powers regarding the selection of foreign nationals wishing to settle there either temporarily or permanently.[9] The responsibilities of the Ministry of Information were further extended in 1981 and it became the Ministry of Cultural Communities and Immigration.

International immigration has often been invoked in the debate on the language question, a debate that has profoundly shaken Quebec's society for almost fifteen years. Its principal parameters begin in history. From 1850 to 1950, the French comprised about 80 percent of Quebec's population. The high fertility rate of the Québécois compensated for emigration to the United States, for an essentially British (or other than French) immigration, and for the assimilation of the latter into the anglophone community. From 1950 to 1970, however, the higher fertility of the francophones diminished radically and then disappeared altogether. During this same period, international immigration was rising and the number of immigrants sending their children to English schools and adopting English as their everyday language increased. The causes of this disturbing situation were well known: the socioeconomic inferiority of the French-Canadians and the mediocre status of the French language in certain areas of Quebec's collective life, particularly labor. This situation could not be redressed without profoundly altering the orientations of Québécois society. Such a step could not be achieved with a twist of the wrist.

During the first stage of dealing with the problem, from the end of the 1960s through the mid-1970s, numerous incentives were adopted by the government of Quebec. Much hope was placed in compensatory measures related to international immigration. However, facts had to be faced. International immigration could not resolve a problem the source of which lay at the heart of Québécois society. If immigrants learned and adopted English and were then integrated into the English community, it was because almost everything, especially in Montreal, fostered this course. Immigrants brought the disequilibrium to the surface, they did not create it. They could, however, amplify the imbalance and make setting it right more difficult. The Quebec government adopted the *Loi sur la langue officielle* (Law 22) in 1974, then the *Charte de la langue française* (Law 101) in 1977 which, as is stated in its preamble, intends to make "French the language of the State and of the law, as well as the normal language of work, teaching, communications, business, and commerce." As a general rule, children of immigrants must go to French schools. Immigration is no longer a phenomenon against which Quebec must defend itself, but a positive force.

After having dropped from 82.5 percent to 80.7 percent between 1951 and 1971, the proportion of francophones in Quebec's population rose to 82.4 percent in 1981. The percentage of anglophones dropped from 13.1 percent in 1971 to 11.0 percent in 1981. This decline is largely attributable to the heavy population losses incurred by Quebec in its exchanges with the rest of Canada since 1966. The anglophones figure prominently in these losses. However, there has been no observable fundamental modification in the structure of the population flow according to linguistic groups.[10] That structure predates the far-reaching language laws adopted in 1974 and 1977. To be sure, in the population exchanges between Quebec and the rest of Canada, losses in Quebec's population have increased in the five-year period 1976–1981, but this increase includes anglophones as well as francophones and other ethnic groups.

In short, international immigration is now seen in a favorable light. It reduces population losses that Quebec incurs in its exchanges with the rest of Canada, and it alleviates the decrease of Quebec's demographic weight in Canada as a whole. It is essential, however, that the immigrants who come to Quebec stay there. The current labor market is now the main barrier to an increase in international immigration. Investors, entrepreneurs, and highly qualified persons not easily recruited in Quebec are sought out. But these immigrants are proportionately few because of the stiff competition among countries to keep or attract competent professionals.

Population Exchanges with Other Countries

There is a mythology of immigration that fosters the idea that, with respect to its population, the United States receives a larger proportion of the masses who each year leave their homeland to seek a better life elsewhere. As with many ideas that are passed on, it has some basis in fact. But when the occasion arises, should not the validity of the idea be tested? For example, in proportion to their respective populations, does the United States admit more immigrants than does Quebec? The answer will show that the question is less trite than it would seem. Once the field of international immigration has been mapped out, it will be easier to describe and analyze the population exchanges between Quebec and the United States.

International Immigration

Since World War II, and through 1981, 12 million immigrants have entered the United States, while Quebec has welcomed about 925,000 during those same thirty-five years. Therefore, it would seem that immigration to the United States is twelve times greater than immigration to Quebec. In fact this index does not accurately express the incidence of immigration to the host country. A more accurate picture is obtained when immigration is considered in relation to the size of the population concerned. Toward the middle of the period in question, the U.S. population was 180 million, Quebec's 5.2 million. Based on these figures, the annual rate of immigration was 1.9 per 1,000 to the United States and 5.1 per 1,000 to Quebec. Considered proportionately, Quebec has admitted 2.5 times more immigrants than the United States in the last thirty-five years.[11]

However, in the course of that period the gap did begin to close. During the 1950s, the annual rate of immigration to Quebec reached

7 per 1,000 as opposed to 1.5 per 1,000 for the United States. In the following decade, the rate for Quebec was 5 per 1,000 and that of the United States 1.7 per 1,000. This convergence continued during the 1970s when Quebec's annual rate reached 3.7 per 1,000 and that of the United States exceeded 2 per 1,000. If these tendencies continue, the rates could be very close to each other during the next two decades.

In the United States, where the current population is about 230 million, a rate of 2 per 1,000 means 460,000 immigrants per year. At that rate, Quebec, with a population of 6.5 million, would have only 13,000. A rate of 3 per 1,000 equals 19,500 immigrants in Quebec and nearly 700,000 in the United States. Between 1979 and 1982, slightly more than 20,000 immigrants entered Quebec per year. Official U.S. statistics do not go beyond 1979. The Immigration and Naturalization Service's Statistical Yearbook for 1979 shows that since 1924, the number of immigrants accepted into the United States has never been as high as in the three years 1977–1979; during those years the United States accepted, on the average, 508,000 immigrants per year. The figure was probably much higher in 1980 and 1981.[12] It seems improbable, however, that the immigration rate to the United States will exceed that to Quebec in the coming years.[13]

In the United States as in Quebec, the character of immigration has changed in the course of the last decades. Between 1953 and 1965, immigrants born in Europe and Canada represented respectively 50 and 12 percent of immigrants to the United States.[14] These proportions have subsequently diminished due especially to the higher numbers of immigrants from Asia. In 1979, Europe accounted for only 13 percent of the immigration to the United States, and Canada only 3 percent. This same fundamental tendency spread to Quebec. Between the years 1962 and 1967, and 1979 and 1981, the proportion of European immigrants went from 73 to 28 percent, and that of American immigrants from 7 to 5 percent. International immigration is increasingly becoming Third World movements to other countries.

Population Exchanges Between Quebec and the United States

Table 5.1 shows the number of immigrants from the United States who declared Quebec to be their destination in Canada from 1956 to 1981. Between 1956 and 1964, this immigration to Quebec involved between 1,700 and 1,900 persons annually. The year 1965 saw a sudden increase (2,200 immigrants); a consistent growth in numbers continued until 1974 (3,600). After 1974 the numbers have decreased except for a one-year interruption in 1979. This pattern of ups and downs has been true of immigration in all of Canada, except for a slight increase from 1979 to 1981 (also Table 5.1).

Table 5.1. Number of Immigrants from the United States to Canada and to Quebec, 1956-1981

Year	To Canada	To Quebec	Percent of U.S. Immigrants to Canada who Declared Quebec Their Destination
1956-1960[a]	10,843	1,696	15.6
1961	11,516	1,819	15.8
1962	11,643	1,915	16.4
1963	11,736	1,902	16.2
1964	12,565	1,754	14.0
1965	15,143	2,225	14.7
1966	17,514	2,268	12.9
1967	19,038	2,301	12.1
1968	20,422	2,485	12.2
1969	22,785	2,671	11.7
1970	24,424	2,732	11.2
1971	24,366	2,739	11.2
1972	22,618	2,831	12.5
1973	25,242	3,531	14.0
1974	26,541	3,606	13.6
1975	20,155	2,474	12.3
1976	17,315	2,871	16.6
1977	12,888	1,618	12.5
1978	9,945	1,088	10.9
1979	9,617	1,165	12.1
1980	9,926	1,010	10.2
1981	10,559	944	8.9

[a]Annual average

Source: Commission on Employment and Immigration of Canada; Quebec Ministry of Cultural Communities and Immigration.

The increase in immigration from the United States from 1965 to 1974 can be attributed to several factors. Initially, this phenomenon was seen as being closely related to protests against United States involvement in Vietnam. But close examination of the data, notably the distributions according to sex and age of the immigrants, showed that draft dodgers and deserters accounted for only a part of the increase in immigration from the United States to Quebec and Canada.[15] The more general disenchantment of people in the states with regard to their society's capacity for change was also seen as a contributing factor. For example, a Gallup Poll showed a rise in the proportion of people wishing to leave the United States. In 1960, 6 percent wanted to live elsewhere; in 1971, 12 percent wanted to live elsewhere.[16] Canada's strong economic growth in the 1960s (including the development of multinational enterprises) and its expansive immigration policies were related to the increase in immigration.[17] As for the recent decline, it correlates with a reduction in economic growth since 1973–1974 and a consequent more selective choice of candidates for immigration by Canada and Quebec.

No close relation is evident between trends in immigration from the United States and those from other countries whose immigrants come to Quebec. From 1967 to 1972, total immigration figures for Quebec declined from 45,700 to 18,600, whereas immigration from the United States during the same period increased from 2,300 to 2,800. Moreover, it was in 1972 that immigration from the United States to Quebec reached a peak figure of 15 percent of the total immigration to Quebec. By 1981, the corresponding figure was less than 5 percent of the international flow to Quebec. It should be emphasized that the United States was the main source of immigrants to Quebec in 1971, 1972, and 1973; it followed France closely in 1970 and was exceeded only by Haiti in 1974 and 1976. This is proof of the importance of the United States to Quebec immigration in the early 1970s.[18]

It is interesting, by comparison, to study emigration from Quebec to the United States. Since U.S. statistics have nothing to say on the subject, one must turn to estimates and approximations. Table 5.2 shows estimates produced by Statistics Canada. These statistics are based on very weak hypotheses that even Statistics Canada calls into question.[19] The figures should be considered as indicating the maximum number of Québécois who may have emigrated to the United States in the given years.

Putting aside the overly arbitrary figures for the years 1961–1962 to 1966–1967—they are based on the premise that Quebec's proportion among Canadians emigrating to the United States corresponds to its place in the population of Canada—one notices a steady drop in the number of Québécois entering the United States from 1967–1968 (12,800) to 1975–1976 (2,300) followed by a sizable increase until 1977–1978 (7,300), and then by another drop in 1979–1980 (5,800). These trends are parallel to those occurring throughout Canada (Table 5.2). Essentially, they can be attributed to the changes in U.S. legislation on immigration.[20] A law passed in 1965, which went into effect on July 1, 1968, rendered immigration more difficult for nationals from countries in the Western hemisphere. Hence the drop in Quebec immigration to the United States. Beginning in 1976, the procedures in effect for the Eastern hemisphere were extended to the West, and an increase occurred in the number of Québécois coming into the United States. In 1978, the systems were combined. It is possible that this last modification of the legislation made immigration to the United States from Quebec more difficult.

Statistics Canada has recently developed another series of estimates of international emigration, notably emigration to the United States. This series deals with the years 1971 (more precisely April 1971 to

Table 5.2. Number of Emigrants from Canada and Quebec, 1961-1962 to 1979-1980

Year (June 1- May 31)	Total to all Countries		Total to the United States		
	From Canada	From Quebec	From Canada	From Quebec[a]	Proportion from Quebec (%)
1961-62	74,000	21,300	44,400	12,800	28.8
1962-63	79,500	23,000	50,000	14,500	28.9
1963-64	86,400	25,000	51,200	14,800	28.9
1964-65	95,800	27,700	50,000	14,500	29.0
1965-66	96,400	27,900	39,300	11,400	28.9
1966-67	104,200	32,700	33,800	10,600	31.4
1967-68	111,500	34,600	41,200	12,800	31.0
1968-69	91,700	25,500	30,200	8,400	27.8
1969-70	86,800	26,200	27,200	8,200	30.1
1970-71	78,200	25,200	22,900	7,400	32.3
1971-72	66,100	15,200	19,000	5,600	29.3
1972-73	62,300	14,300	15,100	4,500	29.7
1973-74	84,000	19,300	12,500	3,800	30.6
1974-75	79,400	18,200	11,200	2,900	25.9
1975-76	65,400	15,000	11,300	2,300	20.7
1976-77	69,600	14,700	14,000	3,000	21.1
1977-78[b]	78,500	24,300	23,700	7,300	31.0
1978-79[b]	75,200	21,700	20,800	6,000	28.9
1979-80[b]	74,200	21,400	20,200	5,800	28.8

[a]The figures shown are an approximation of the evolution of the Québécois emigration to the United States (U.S. immigration statistics do not list Canadian sources by provinces). Using data obtained from the U.S. Embassy in Canada on immigrant visas, Statistics Canada has been estimating by province since 1966-1967 the number of emigrants going to the United States. It is thus possible to calculate the Québécois emigration to the United States. It should be noted that the information obtained from the U.S. Embassy probably includes visas issued to nonresidents of Canada legalizing their status in consulates in Canada. It is safe to assume that this type of event occurs in Quebec more than in other provinces and that the numbers given correspond to maximum estimates of Québécois emigration to the United States.

[b]The figures shown are an approximation of annual emigration. There is reason to believe that emigration from Quebec has been overestimated for the last three years shown (K. G. Basavarajappa et al., A Comparison of Preliminary Census Counts and the Preliminary Post-Censal Estimates 1981: Canada, Provinces and Territories. Statistics Canada, Demography Division, working document, 1982).

Sources: Statistics Canada (1977, 1980, 1981).

April 1972) to 1978, and is based in part on unpublished information from the files on taxation of revenue. Because no detailed analysis of these figures has yet been made, they should be used prudently. They suggest, as do other data taken from the files on family allowances, that the number of Québécois leaving their province to settle in foreign countries, particularly in the United States, has been overestimated.

Is Quebec winner or loser in its population exchanges with the United States? An unequivocal answer is not provided by the facts and figures that have been put together. There is no available information on returns of immigrants to their country of origin, although undoubtedly these figures are not negligible.[21] In fact, according to a recent study of Canadian immigrants who arrived in the United States between July 1, 1970, and June 30, 1971, more than half had left the United States by January 1, 1979. This observation would indicate that immigration does not always have a high coefficient of permanence. Given this reservation, and taking into account legal migration only, it is probably true that Quebec has to admit to losses in its population exchanges with the United States. These losses were fewer in the second half of the 1960s and fewer still in the first half of the 1970s. It is even possible that Quebec experienced some gain between 1974 and 1976. Subsequently, however, the balance has been slightly negative.

Characteristics of Immigrants from the United States

Quebec as the ancestral home of many families in the United States has much to do with the later story of immigrants from the United States to Quebec. In this and other ways the comments that will be made about immigration will at times go beyond the theme of immigration in the strict sense. Some of the comments will also bear on the topics of foreign students and temporary workers.

To consider the cultural characteristics of immigration first, they are prefaced by the fact that Québécois emigrated to the United States in large numbers until the early 1930s.[22] As is always the case, this migratory trend brought forth a counter trend.[23] Its traces can be found in the Canadian census of 1971, which shows that French was the mother tongue of more than 70 percent of Quebec residents born in the United States who immigrated before 1946. However, the closer the period of immigration is to the census date, the less important the French language becomes (only 16 percent of the immigrants from the United States between 1966 and the census date, 1971, declared French to be their mother tongue). These data apply only to immigrants who stayed in

Table 5.3. Immigrants to Quebec from the United States According to Their Knowledge of the French and English Languages, 1968-1981

Knowledge of French and English	1968-1974	1975-1978	1979-1981
French only	746	545	144
(percentage)	(3.6)	(6.8)	(4.6)
French and English	4,310	2,124	959
(percentage)	(20.9)	(26.4)	(30.8)
English only	14,972	5,274	1,959
(percentage)	(72.7)	(65.5)	(62.8)
Neither French nor English	557	108	57
(percentage)	(2.7)	(1.3)	(1.8)
Total	20,585	8,051	3,119
(percentage)	(100.0)	(100.0)	(100.0)

Source: Quebec Ministry of Cultural Communities and Immigration.

Quebec,[24] not to the attributes of immigrants upon arrival. The gap can be filled, however, thanks to immigration statistics.

Since 1968, immigrants have been classified according to their knowledge of the French and English languages (Table 5.3). Nearly 25 percent of immigrants from the United States who arrived between 1968 and 1974 knew French. This proportion rose to 33 percent during the next four years[25] and reached 35 percent during the period 1979-1981. This fraction might seem quite small in relation to the large majority of the Quebec population whose mother tongue is French (more than 80 percent). But it is quite large in terms of the number of francophones in the United States (less than 1 percent).

Students play some part in the most recent data. More than 7,000 authorizations have been handed out to university students coming from the United States between 1978 and 1981. Nearly 85 percent of these students attended English universities (with 74 percent going to McGill), but 15 percent chose French universities (with 12 percent going to Laval). In 1981, the English institutions' share has dropped to 79 percent.

The socioprofessional qualities of immigrants coming from the United States is another interesting cultural statistic. One would expect that these qualities would be concentrated in management and in professions calling for scientific and technical training. The data confirm this prediction (Table 5.4). It is to be noted that the occupational nomenclature used before 1973 differs noticeably from that used since. There is also a breach in the series between 1972 and 1973; it is mostly artificial.

Table 5.4. Socioprofessional Qualities of Immigrants to Quebec from All Countries and from the United States, 1968–1981[a]

Year	From All Countries			From the United States		
	Total Immigrants in Labor Force	Percent of Entrepreneurs and Administrators	Percent in Professional and Technical Jobs	Total Immigrants in Labor Force	Percent of Entrepreneurs and Administrators	Percent in Professional and Technical Jobs
1968	19,128	1.8	29.8	1,266	5.3	61.9
1969	15,985	1.7	33.9	1,295	4.6	61.7
1970	13,384	2.1	35.5	1,388	4.9	62.7
1971	10,709	3.3	32.5	1,339	7.1	62.8
1972	10,059	4.5	33.0	1,268	10.0	58.3
1973	14,961	5.9	25.1	1,494	16.9	48.5
1974	18,118	5.7	23.5	1,521	14.5	45.6
1975	13,292	8.1	26.6	945	20.4	45.6
1976	13,304	9.9	24.7	1,089	18.9	43.1
1977	8,710	9.1	24.8	634	15.8	47.5
1978	6,027	7.7	22.2	467	15.6	43.5
1979	8,658	5.9	19.4	480	16.2	42.5
1980	9,889	4.7	18.4	436	12.2	43.3
1981	9,906	4.4	18.8	435	15.4	40.5

[a]From 1968 to 1972, the nomenclature used is that of the Dictionary of Occupational Titles (D.O.T.). From 1973 on, the Canadian Classification and Dictionary of Occupations (C.C.D.O.) is used.

Source: Quebec Ministry of Cultural Communities and Immigration.

Table 5.5. Temporary Work Permits Issued in Quebec (1978-1981[a])
According to Professional Groups and Country of Origination

Country and Year	Total Number of Work Permits	Entrepreneurs and Administrators		Professional and Technical Jobs	
		Number	Percent	Number	Percent
All countries					
1978	12,628	1,123	8.8	6,741	53.4
1979	14,832	1,111	7.5	7,476	50.4
1980	16,260	1,087	6.7	8,407	51.7
1981	16,519	1,148	6.9	8,519	51.5
United States					
1978	4,230	403	9.5	3,037	71.8
1979	5,159	395	7.7	3,669	71.1
1980	6,196	420	6.8	4,541	73.3
1981	5,954	406	6.8	4,343	72.9
Other countries					
1978	8,398	720	8.6	3,704	44.1
1979	9,673	716	7.4	3,807	39.4
1980	10,064	667	6.6	3,866	38.4
1981	10,565	742	7.0	4,176	39.5

[a]Certain cases on which important information was lacking have been excluded (24 in 1978, 38 in 1979, 27 in 1980, and 312 in 1981).

Source: Quebec Ministry of Cultural Communities and Immigration.

For the last three years reported, there has been a noticeable reduction in the proportion of immigrants in the labor force who hope to become administrators, managers, entrepreneurs, or who wish to have a professional or technical job. This observation, however, applies less to immigrants from the United States than to those from other countries, and it bears a definite relation to the increased numbers of refugees and humanitarian cases since 1979.

The distribution of temporary work permits according to the same professional groupings also reveals the concentration of individuals from the United States in professional and technical jobs (Table 5.5). It is to be noted that more than half of these professional groupings are made up of specialists in the arts, particularly musicians.

Probably a fair percentage of immigrants from the United States do not change employers when coming to Quebec. For them, this move is part of the evolution of their career in a large organization. Others are attracted by the alluring working conditions offered by Quebec companies. In a good number of cases, the persons attracted are highly qualified professionals in fields in which Quebec has shortages. But these same workers are generally equally in demand in the United States. Quebec should, therefore, not depend exclusively on immigration when looking to the development of its high-technology industries. To be sure, the extent of recruitment outside Quebec is limited. The government, however, gives its approval and support to those institutions and companies that cannot find the personnel they need in Quebec and that wish to call on foreign specialists.[26] Thanks to the broadening of the Quebec government's responsibilities in immigration matters, it can now simplify the formalities and, therefore, speed up the process.

Conclusions

Quebec suffered enormous losses in its population exchanges with the United States in the nineteenth century and during the first three decades of the twentieth century. The situation since World War II is clearly more balanced. Quebec's losses have diminished since the mid-1960s, and it is even possible that slight gains occurred in its exchanges with the United States between 1974 and 1976. However, the balance since then from the Québécois point of view has become slightly negative.

The last two decades have broken with an age-old past. Nowadays, travel between Quebec and the United States is increasingly by tourists, conventioneers, businessmen, and temporary workers and students, rather than by true immigrants. In 1980, at Quebec's border crossings, immigrants from the United States numbered about 1,000, but there were 3.2 million tourists and other visitors from the United States entering Quebec (and 5.6 million Canadians returning home). Immigration no longer has either the same meaning or the same scope it had in the nineteenth century. Increasingly, when it takes place between developed countries of the West, it is of a temporary nature for the individuals concerned.

Notes

1. Yolande Lavoie, *L'émigration des Canadiens aux États-Unis avant 1930: mesure du phénomène* (Montreal: Presses de l'Université de Montréal, 1972); "Les mouvements migratoires des Canadiens entre leur pays et les États-Unis au XIXᵉ et XXᵉ siècles: étude quantitative," in Hubert Charbonneau, ed., *La population du Québec: études rétrospectives* (Montreal: Editions du Boréal Express, 1973), pp. 73–88; and *L'émigration des Québécois aux États-Unis de 1840 à 1930*, 2nd ed., revised and updated (Quebec: Gouvernement du Québec, Conseil de la langue française, 1981).

2. *International and Interprovincial Migration in Canada*, (Ottawa: Statistics Canada, No. 91–208 in catalog, 1977, 1979, 1980, and 1981).

3. Yochanam Comay, "Determinants of Return Migration: Canadians' Professions in the United States," *Southern Economic Journal* 37 (1971), pp. 318–322;

78   *Réjean Lachapelle*

Claude Dionne, *L'émigration du Canada aux États-Unis de 1945 à 1968* (Montreal: Université de Montréal, 1971); K. V. Parkhurst, "Migration between Canada and the United States," *Annals of the American Academy of Political Science* 367, pp. 53–67; Louis Parai, *Immigration and Emigration of Professional and Skilled Manpower During the Post-War Period* (Ottawa: Queen's Printer, on behalf of the Canadian Economic Council, 1965); and T. J. Samuel, *The Migration of Canadian-Born Between Canada and the United States of America, 1955–1968* (Ottawa: Queens Printer, on behalf of the Department of Manpower and Immigration, 1969).

4. A. Luchaire, *Étude quantitative sur les réfractaires et déserteurs américains au Canada*, unpublished manuscript, 1972, and Roger N. Williams, *The New Exiles: American War Resisters in Canada* (New York: Liveright Publishers, 1971).

5. Ada W. Finifter, "American Emigration," *Society* 3 (1976), pp. 30–36.

6. Monica Boyd, "The American Emigrant in Canada: Trends and Consequences," *International Migration Review* 15(4), 1981, pp. 650–670.

7. Guillermina Jasso and Mark R. Rosenzweig, "Estimating the Emigration Rates of Legal Immigrants Using Administrative Survey Data: The 1971 Cohort of Immigrants to the United States," *Demography* 19(3), 1982, pp. 279–290.

8. The agreements concluded between the Government of Quebec and the Government of Canada in 1868 and in 1875 are presented and reproduced in Jean Hamelin, "Québec et le monde extérieur 1867–1967," *Annuaire de Québec 1968–1969* (Quebec: Gouvernement du Québec, 1968), pp. 2–36.

9. In most cases, the government of Quebec may accept whomever it wishes, as long as health and security requirements are met. The federal government retains all its powers in matters of admission and has some responsibilities regarding the settlement and adjustment of newcomers. French courses given in the *Centres d'orientation et de formation des immigrants* (COFI) are financed by the federal government. They are, however, managed by the Quebec Ministry of Cultural Communities and Immigration. Criteria for admission to the *Centres* are set by the federal government.

10. Réjean Lachapelle and Jacques Henripin, *The Demolinguistic Situation in Canada* (Montreal: The Institute for Research on Public Policy, 1982).

11. In the United States, persons born outside the country represented 4.7 percent and 6.2 percent of the total population in 1970 and 1980 respectively. In 1971, 7.8 percent of Quebec's population was born outside of Canada, and this proportion increased to 8.3 percent in 1981.

12. Select Commission on Immigration and Refugee Policy, *U.S. Immigration Policy and National Interest* (Washington, D.C.: U.S. Government Printing Office, 1981), p. 93.

13. This statement does not take into account the possibility that amnesty may be accorded on a large scale to illegal immigrants in the United States. Their number is evidently not well known; the most reliable estimates given are between 3.5 million and 6 million (David S. North, "Illegal Migrants in Northern America," *International Population Conference, Manila 1981* [Liege, Belgium: International Union for the Scientific Study of Population], pp. 473–489).

The number of illegal immigrants in Quebec is certainly no more than 10,000 and may be even less than 5,000 (Ministry of Cultural Communities and Immigration, *Les immigrants illégaux au Québec*, 1983).

14. Monica Boyd, "Immigration Policies and Trends: A Comparison of Canada and the United States," *Demography* 13(1), 1976, pp. 83–104.

15. Luchaire, *Étude quantitative sur les réfractaires et déserteurs américains au Canada*. The rise in immigration from the United States in 1973 and 1974 can be attributed in part to the Canadian government's special amnesty program established in 1973.

16. Finifter, "American Emigration," p. 33.

17. Boyd, "Immigration Policies and Trends," and "The American Emigrant in Canada."

18. During this period, 75 percent of the immigrants who declared the United States as their country of last permanent residence were native Americans.

19. K. G. Basavarajappa et al., *A Comparison of Preliminary Census Counts and the Preliminary Post-Censal Estimates 1981: Canada, Provinces and Territories*, Statistics Canada, Demography Division (working document), 1982.

20. Boyd, "Immigration Policies and Trends"; and Charles B. Keely and Patricia J. Elwell, "International Migration: Canada and the United States," in Mary M. Kritz, Charles B. Keely, and Silvano M. Tomasi, eds., *The Global Trends in Migration: Theory and Reserach on International Population Movements* (Staten Island, NY: Center for Migration Studies, 1981), pp. 181–207.

21. Jasso and Rosenzweig, "Estimating the Emigration Rates of Legal Immigrants."

22. Lavoie, "L'émigration des canadiens aux États-Unis."

23. Lavoie, "Les mouvements migratoires"; and Everett Lee, "A Theory of Migration," in J. A. Jackson, ed., *Migration* (Cambridge, U.K.: Cambridge University Press, 1969), pp. 282–297.

24. In 1971, 46 percent of Quebec's population lived in the Montreal region, including 87 percent of persons who had immigrated to Quebec. However, only 57 percent of immigrants born in the United States lived in that region. The proportion was much higher for those who had immigrated during the five years preceding the census (73 percent) than for those who had come to Quebec prior to 1946 (49 percent).

25. During the period from 1974 through 1977, two-thirds of the immigrants from the United Staes who knew French came from New England.

26. This was the reasoning behind the Quebec government's program of aid to research in biotechnology: *À l'heure des biotechnologies* (Quebec: Ministère du conseil exécutif, 1982), pp. 18–19.

6
Environmental Issues

John E. Carroll

Quebec shares a 500-mile border with the United States, a border that on its southern side touches four U.S. states: New York, Vermont, New Hampshire, and Maine. Quebec is downwind of significant portions of U.S industrial territory, is occasionally upwind of U.S. territory, and is downstream of the United States on the Great Lakes–St. Lawrence water system. Quebec also is geologically highly vulnerable to acidic precipitation from both the United States and Canada. These facts of geography ensure a transborder environmental relationship between Quebec and the United States, as well as some serious and some less serious transboundary environmental disputes or differences. It is the purpose of this chapter to describe Quebec's present and predicted bilateral environmental relationship with its southern neighbor.

What Are the Issues?

Transboundary environmental problems between the United States and Canada generally fall into the four broad categories of water quantity, water quality, air quality, and marine pollution. Only the last is not relevant to Quebec–U.S. relations. Issues such as international migratory waterfowl problems and differences of philosophy over the chemicals used in spraying—as in the control of spruce budworm in coniferous forests—will not be treated, although the latter can contribute to water pollution. The interpretation of the word "environment" used in this chapter refers to water pollution, air pollution, and marine pollution in all of their various forms. Although wildlife, waterfowl, or certain other topics might legitimately be included under this heading, these particular issues are not as relevant as are the various forms of pollution. In a less direct sense, internal environmental conditions and domestic controls in the United States or Quebec might also affect the relationship, as will be seen.

Water Quantity

In the quantitative sense, water differences between the United States and Quebec arise in two areas: the Great Lakes–St. Lawrence and Champlain-Richelieu systems.

Great Lakes–St. Lawrence System

Quebec is the farthest downstream of all the various Canadian and U.S. provinces and states that border, are dependent upon, or are affected by the Great Lakes. Human decisions made relative to the management or manipulation of that lake system, therefore, are of great consequence to Quebec; of the downstream U.S. states, only New York has a similar stake. Quebec's primary concerns relate to navigation and hydroelectric power generation.

Since the opening of the St. Lawrence Seaway, the port of Montreal has been in competition with numerous upstream Great Lakes ports for the opportunity to tranship grain and other products from the continental interior to overseas markets. To some extent, therefore, Great Lakes management decisions that favor those upstream ports can harm Montreal economically. High lake levels, mainly the result of natural cyclic causes but also caused by human manipulation, tend to favor general navigation in the system and thus favor those competing upstream ports. The development of all-season navigation through the provision of a winter navigation season (an effort advocated by the U.S. Army Corps of Engineers) could have a similar result. Natural low-level cycles, diversions out of lakes, and decisions to reject the expenditure of funds to promote navigation, especially all-season navigation, favor Montreal (and, therefore, Quebec Province) navigationally.

Hydroelectricity presents a somewhat different picture. High water in the lakes system favors hydropower generation, and Canada is more dependent on hydropower generated in the Great Lakes–St. Lawrence system than is the United States. Downstream Quebec shares in that dependency and in the benefits reaped from the works on the St. Lawrence Seaway. The greatest threat to those benefits, other than cyclically natural low lake levels, is diversion of the upper lakes through the Chicago Diversion Canal into the Mississippi River Basin. This diversion, essentially to carry Chicago municipal sewerage effluent south, has been a threat to all Great Lakes hydropower users, both U.S. and Canadian, for many years. Thus, Chicago's gain is Quebec's (and Canada's and New York's) loss. Recent proposals to divert portions of the Mississippi River and even Lake Superior westward to replenish high plains ground water for new coal slurry pipelines or to replace depleted aquifers may increase U.S. pressure to divert more lake water into the

Mississippi drainage. Such an eventuality would be costly to Quebec as well as to other downstream entities.

Champlain-Richelieu System[1]

The Champlain-Richelieu issue (see Maps 6.1a and b) is, from Quebec's perspective, a matter of too much water in the wrong place, i.e., flooding of downstream riparian farm and residential lands in the Richelieu Valley caused by naturally occurring cyclic high water levels in the Lake Champlain Basin of Vermont and New York. This problem is one of the most important as well as one of the most polarizing of all Quebec-U.S. transboundary environmental disputes of recent years, and deserves some attention for the potential damage it can do to transborder relations.

Professor Maxwell Cohen, who chaired the Canadian Section of the Canada-U.S. International Joint Commission (IJC) during much of the history of this dispute, has written, "The balance to be drawn between environmental protection through leaving nature alone, on the U.S. side, and flood control structures for protection on the Canadian side, has presented a mix of arithmetic and emotions unresolved to this day." Approaching the root of the problem, he continues, "There is very little common cause on this issue since the environmental values are measured so dearly on the U.S. side while the priority of feeling for flood control often has drowned out the modest environmental voice in Quebec."[2]

The Champlain-Richelieu issue to which he was referring involves a Canadian flood control structure that would alter water levels on U.S. territory. Champlain-Richelieu offers insight into polarized nationalist attitudes and demonstrates a case where basic thinking and perceptions differ greatly on both sides of the border. It is similar to the Skagit-High Ross Dam issue in the West in that it represents a failure of the IJC to come to grips with a transboundary flooding question. Also as with Skagit, it is an issue that may never be satisfactorily resolved, for both technical reasons and uncompromising attitudes, without recourse to forces external to the regions involved.

At Champlain-Richelieu, riparian flooding, a normal and formerly acceptable event to area farmers (given valuable silt deposition), became a hindrance with the development of waterfront housing. An international problem soon resulted.

Lake Champlain is a large and scenic lake of major recreational importance bordered by Vermont, New York, and a very small portion of Quebec. The lake drains northward into the Richelieu River, the entirety of which is in Quebec. The lake basin includes a large area of adjacent Vermont, much of which is a floodplain originally formed by the lake. Vermont's richest agricultural land (and most of the state's flatland), its largest city and university community (Burlington), its only

Map 6.1a. Richelieu River–Lake Champlain.

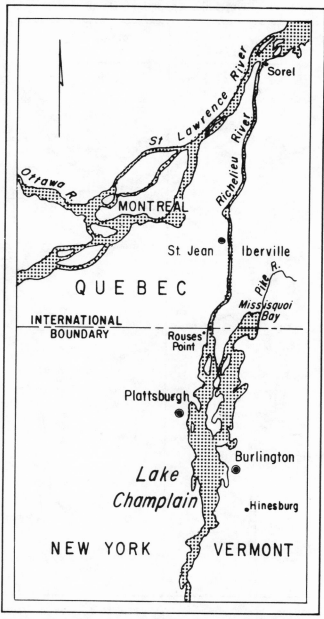

Source: International Richelieu Champlain Engineering Board, International Joint Commission, October 1974.

Map 6.1b.   Richelieu River–Lake Champlain, Detail.

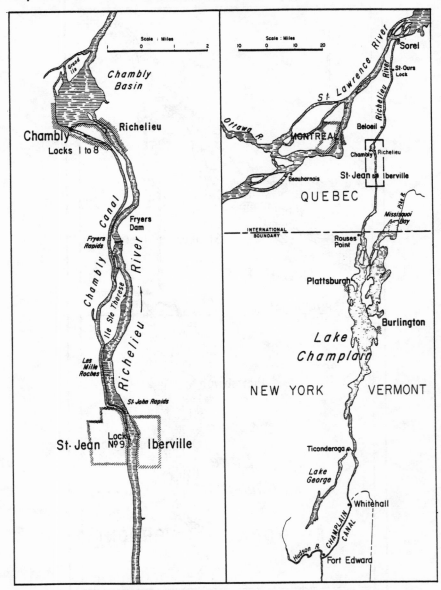

Source: International Joint Commission, *Regulation of the Richelieu River and Lake Champlain: An IJC Report to the Governments of Canada and the United States,* 1981.

shoreline, and islands and most of its wetlands are all on, dependent upon, or in some way associated with Lake Champlain, a fact that has had much to do with Vermont's strong role in this issue. New York has a small city and college community, Plattsburgh, on the lake, but for the most part this region of New York is sparsely populated and an economic and political backwater of that state. Quebec's portion of the lake is small and inconsequential to the province. The Richelieu River, entirely in Quebec, drains a very rich agricultural district, flowing past (and threatening in times of flood) a major regional urban center, St. Jean-d'Iberville. Recently, the riverfront has become host to small-lot waterfront housing subdivisions for second homeowners from Montreal. The United States has no stake in the river. These geographical facts set the stage for this issue.

The origin of bilateral involvement in the issue was the 1937 approval by the International Joint Commission for construction of water control works in the Richelieu River in Quebec to control flooding of lands adjacent to Lake Champlain and the river. This Canadian request for flood relief and the IJC acquiescence to the request was unopposed. The Fryer's Island Dam, constructed just downstream from St. Jean on the Richelieu River, resulted from this project, but the dredging and diking that would have made the project operative were not completed because of the outset of World War II. Thus, the purpose of this original project was never achieved.[3]

Many dry years ensued and serious problems did not develop until a period of high lake water occurred as part of Lake Champlain's normal fluctuation cycle in the early 1970s. Just prior to this high water period, extensive conversion of Richelieu Valley farmlands had begun, with new second-home housing subdivisions being carved out of riparian farmland in the immediate floodplain of the river. The high water cycles of Lake Champlain, and the Richelieu River flooding resulting from this only significant contributor to its water supply, is a natural phenomenon. The normal lake level range is five feet, although it can be greater depending on precipitation extremes. General high-water damages in the river include damages to permanent and seasonal residences and recreational facilities and some shoreline erosion and reduction of agricultural production by delays in spring planting. Low-water damages can also result, including reduced access to recreational facilities, effects on water supply intakes, the aesthetic problem of rotting vegetation, and low-flow-induced water quality problems.

The more housing development in the floodplain in years of low water, the more property damage that was bound to result when high waters returned. Real estate entrepreneurs, perhaps unsuspecting themselves, sold the land in dry years to unsuspecting buyers. These buyers began to feel the effects of high water in the early 1970s and called upon their provincial and federal governments to protect their interests. Hence, Ottawa asked Washington to join in a reference to the IJC. In March, 1973, the IJC received from the U.S. and Canadian governments a reference "to investigate and report upon the feasibility and desirability of regulation of the Richelieu River . . . for the purpose of alleviating extreme water conditions in the Richelieu River and in Lake Champlain."[4]

The IJC was specifically requested to make recommendations on the desirability of operating the 1937 Fryer's Island project or alternative works to alleviate the extreme water conditions, taking into consideration water supply and sanitation, recreation, navigation, environmental factors, including fish and wildlife, wetland reclamation, and other beneficial purposes. It was asked to recommend the most practicable and economically feasible system of regulatory works and methods to alleviate the extreme water conditions, and the costs, benefits, and impacts of each alternative. All this it was requested to do in one year. As the decade of the 1980s began some seven years later, the commission had still not completed its deliberations.

The IJC established its International Champlain-Richelieu Engineering Board in 1973. The board concluded its work in late 1974 and found that regulation of the lake for flood control on the river could be accomplished, but board members differed sharply on the environmental effects of such regulations. This board concluded that the environmental acceptability of the project could not be determined without further studies. After holding public hearings, the IJC recommended to the two governments that an intensive study be undertaken "to determine the environmental, physical and economic effects of regulations in both countries."[5] This was accepted and a second board, the International Champlain-Richelieu Board, was established and reported to the IJC in mid-1978.

In January 1976, after conclusion of the first set of IJC studies but prior to the beginning of the second board's work, the government of Canada, supported by Quebec, applied to the IJC for permission to dredge the river, thereby reducing peak water levels during flood, and to construct a fixed crest weir to maintain levels during low water.[6] The application noted that Canadian and Quebec government studies indicated that this weir and dredging arrangement "offer the best possibility of rendering a measure of flood control benefit at minimum cost and with minimum environmental disruption."[7] The IJC did not grant permission for this work, deferring to its new International Champlain-Richelieu Board and to its own ultimate decision on the whole issue.

The commission and its two boards have concluded that regulation of some sort is desirable. But before treating the findings of the second board, which the commission spent such effort deliberating over, consideration should be given to the roles of a variety of relevant actors who have succeeded in polarizing this issue.

Environmental Organizations. The local Quebec reactions to the IJC recommendations toward lake level regulation were positive, but the New York, and particularly the Vermont, reactions were quite the opposite. This polarization annoyed and even angered affected Quebec residents who viewed the U.S. reaction as selfish environmental elitism that valued birds and fish over property damage.

Given geographical realities, it is not surprising that Vermonters, with a much greater dependence upon Lake Champlain (over 80 percent of Vermont residents rely on the lake in one way or another), should react much more strongly than New Yorkers to the proposal to alter the lake's levels. Thus, the principal citizen environmentalist opposition formed in Vermont. The Lake Champlain Committee worked consistently through the 1970s. The committee has continually opposed any artificial change in lake levels, insisted upon full and detailed environmental impact statements prior to any actions affecting the levels, and opposed completion of the Fryer's Island Dam. It has insisted, as have other environmental groups and the state of Vermont, that strict floodplain zoning in Quebec's Richelieu Valley is the answer. Originally a regional environmental organization fighting water pollution in the lake, the committee with its intense lobbying has now moved into the forefront of this international issue.

Another group, the Champlain Coalition, has come together expressly to find an alternative to lake-level manipulation for flood control. This coalition is dedicated to floodplain land-use management in the basin and believes the IJC has given insufficient attention to floodplain zoning as an alternative.[8] New York environmentalists have generally supported these two Vermont-based organizations but have not seen fit to form a group of their own. Quebec environmentalist groups are not involved in the issue.

On the national and international level, the Canada-U.S. Environment Committee (CUSEC) has ascribed sufficient bilateral significance to this issue to find that dam construction will lead to even further floodplain development and harm wildlife habitats, and has therefore urged the IJC and the Canadian and Quebec governments to seek nonstructural alternatives, specifically including zoning and flood insurance, as the solution.[9] It should be noted that one Quebec organization (*Société pour vaincre la pollution*), fourteen other Canadian groups, and four U.S. groups endorsed this position.

Movement was made in the direction desired by environmentalists when the Quebec and Canadian governments signed a federal-provincial agreement designed to reduce future floodplain development. The agreement provided Can$ 5 million to identify and map flood risk areas, prohibited federal or provincial spending in these areas, and encouraged zoning where possible.[10] However, although it may well reduce or discourage future development on the Richelieu floodplain, it cannot affect in any way development that is already in place.

Vermont. Vermont has been in the forefront of adamant opposition to any structural controls on the Richelieu River that would in any way affect the levels of Lake Champlain, and has stated officially that it cannot abide by the findings of the IJC,[11] finding its documentation "misleading and inconclusive."[12] (Such a blanket refusal may be a precedent.) Vermont's principal concerns revolve around lake-level criteria needed to provide spawning habitats for northern pike, an important recreational fish. The state has a basic technical disagreement with the IJC on this matter. First, it disagrees with the commission's findings that the more rapid evolution of wet-meadow ecological succession will provide sufficient habitats for northern pike spawning requirements. Second, the state contends the total acreage loss itself is unknown because of an inadequate data base. Vermont's third technical concern is in the area of net benefits, wherein it questions the whole justification of this project. Put simply, it contends that the costs (U.S.$1.5 million average annual project cost) outweigh the annual damages (which it believes to be no greater than U.S.$1.39 million). The state also contends the benefit/cost analysis does not include lost revenue from the destruction of critical wetlands.[13]

The governor of Vermont, arguing that 22 percent of the state's wetlands would be lost, together with associated waterfowl, fish, and furbearers, has also expressed doubts about IJC findings and suggests that the commission might be undervaluing the basin's wetlands.[14] He complains of incomplete consideration of the true costs to Vermont, although he does not question the claimed benefits in Quebec. He advocates a detailed wetlands mapping and monitoring program, more research and a closer look at nonstructural alternatives in Quebec, including floodplain zoning. Finally, he wants consideration to be given to the purchase of development rights and the relocation and evacuation of existing development on the floodplain, and concludes:

> The extraordinary importance of Lake Champlain to the people of Vermont needs no special explanation to the Board. Our forefathers and their children have found that this lake speaks to them in a virtually sacred

fashion of the true meaning of Vermont. Whatever we can do to preserve that feeling is our debt and our duty to the future citizens of Vermont.[15]

Hence, Vermont's strong concerns focus on damage to wetlands habitats and associated recreation values and the state's general disagreement with the shoreline erosion, flooding of private property (particularly on Grand Isle and other Vermont islands in the lake), and possible navigation concerns in periods of low water. In all, Vermont's position has been clear, consistent, and absolutely uncompromising. The issue is well known and polarized statewide, and the political leadership has widespread support for its position, not only from such environmental groups as the Lake Champlain committee but also from the important University of Vermont community at Burlington and from the state's press as well. Compromise in Vermont appears unlikely and the U.S. State Department recognizes this and has generally supported the state's position and interests.

New York. Like Vermont, New York places a high value on the wetlands to be lost with lake-level regulation. New York echoes Vermont's concerns about IJC failure to consider the value of lost wetlands, noting that New York's loss would be 11,400 acres of wetlands, representing more than 22 percent of the total occurring under high-water conditions.[16] New York's own Freshwater Wetlands Law requires the state to place a high level of protection on these environments and to avoid altering them when their full values are unknown and when there are reasonable alternatives. Thus, New York cannot condone this Lake Champlain Basin wetland destruction and be consistent with its own statutes.

New York goes a step further than Vermont in questioning the negative effects of flooding across the border in Quebec, noting the type of flood damage sustained in Quebec is not the catastrophic life-threatening type associated with fast rivers and currents. For this reason and because most damages occur to grounds rather than structures, New York believes that property damage figures from flooding in Quebec are exaggerated, further reducing justification for a control structure (since by definition the protection benefits would be inflated as well). New York calls for additional and more refined information including the addition of replacement cost figures (acquisition and overhead) for wetlands lost through water-level regulation before it can take a final position on manipulation of lake levels.[17] New York joins Vermont and area environmentalists in advocating immediate implementation of nonstructural flood control measures in both countries and demands that the IJC withhold recommendation on any structural measures until a U.S.-type environmental impact statement, showing all resonable alternatives, is prepared.

Quebec. Quebec's position is tempered with the reality of existing flooding and property damage. Immediate political pressure within the province changes with the rise and fall of lake-level cycles. Quebec finds difficulty in understanding the vigor of U.S., and particularly Vermont, opposition. There is a tendency in Quebec to oversimplify and view the U.S. reaction as favoring fish and ducks over people, just as there is a tendency for oversimplification by U.S. environmentalists and state officials who advocate floodplain zoning as a solution to the problem. Neither position is helpful to the besieged property owners of the Richelieu Valley, who, by commonly held public values in both countries, deserve public protection and consideration of some sort. Hence, Quebec's position has been understandably to protect its people, and there is no reason why the province should be concerned about wetlands or wildlife habitats in the U.S. Lake Champlain Basin (although a small amount of Quebec's own shoreline would also be affected).

Another aspect of Quebec's position in this issue may lie in the nature of the people affected. Those who have purchased second homes on the Richelieu's floodplain are essentially middle-class, French-speaking Montrealers who, for the most part, are purchasing seasonal homes (or their own year-round homes) for the first time. It is inevitable that comparisons might be made between these people and those more affluent English-speaking Quebeckers who earlier built seasonal homes along the shores of Lake Memphremagog, a lake east of Richelieu, likewise on the Vermont border and likewise threatened by conditions (in this case, pollution) from the U.S. side. In the Lake Memphremagog case, the Canadian federal government moved quickly to protect the interests of those Quebec Canadians who were threatened from across the border. Will Ottawa move just as quickly and strongly to protect middle-class French interests as it did to protect more affluent English interests? Hence, the broader issues of French-English and Quebec-Ottawa relations may play a role here.

The Two Federal Positions. Washington must protect Vermont-New York interests from enforced lake-level alterations resulting from downstream regulation, and Ottawa must protect Quebec rights to implement river regulations. The basic federal response on both sides has been to put the issue in the hands of the IJC, where it has remained for most of the past decade. The federal role has been virtually nonexistent, and it remained so until the IJC disposed of the issue.

IJC Findings. The final recommendations of the last International Champlain-Richelieu Board, so vigorously opposed by Vermont and so vexing to the IJC for two years, include:[18]

1. refusal to recommend a nonstructural alternative by itself, believing only 20 percent of the damage could be eliminated in this way;

2. recommendations to implement a combined structural/nonstructural alternative to reduce flood damages while maintaining the seasonal rhythms of lake levels and protection of the lake and river ecosystem;

3. construction of a new gated structure near St. Jean and adoption of a regulatory scheme;

4. implementation of a flood forecasting and warning system and floodplain zoning regulations;

5. equal division between the United States and Canada of all capital construction and operational costs; and

6, additional environmental studies and monitoring during the first ten years of the gated structure's operation, with any overseeing or controlling board to contain representatives of area environmental control and management agencies in its membership.

The long two-year IJC deliberation, coupled with the fact that both governments turned the matter over to the commission nine years ago (1974), has not been lost upon the diplomats. Canadian diplomats have experienced particular problems with Quebec over the long delay, and some feel it would have been better for the IJC to admit it cannot handle the question and turn it back to government for action. As it is, with jurisdiction turned over to the IJC, the two federal governments have been able to do nothing, Richelieu Valley residents have remained threatened, and those concerned with the lake and its levels have remained burdened with uncertainty. Thus, regardless of the wisdom of its final findings, the IJC's image has been tarnished, in this case by what many perceive as inordinate delay and the costs in uncertainty that delay has caused.

In January 1981, after so many years of study and investigation, the IJC, operating with one vacancy and under the tangible threat of three or four more vacancies, submitted its final conclusions and recommendations on the last day of the Carter administration. The commission stated its difficulties in balancing the interactions between the environmental, physical, and economic aspects of this complex issue.[19] It concluded that the gated water-control structure at St. Jean was economically feasible, in that damage reduction outweighed the costs. However, it questioned whether the benefit-cost analysis used truly reflects the social gains and losses to be expected from regulation. Also questioned was the lack of attention given to intangible future options and social preservation values that the report concludes are worthy of separate attention. The commission sided with Vermont's strong arguments for wetlands and wildlife habitat protection and added a role for aesthetic values, noting that these resources were significant in the Champlain-Richelieu system and legal protection for them was consistent with U.S. policy. It also concluded that flow-management schemes under the gated-structure plan are capable of accommodating environmental criteria.

The IJC thus came close to concluding this thorny case, but wound up by handing it back to the two governments not only unresolved but as one of the two was about to undergo a change in administration. The final recommendation reads:

> Although the Commission has concluded that it is technically feasible to operate a gated structure at St. Jean that accommodates the proposed environmental criteria, the Commission was unable to determine the desirability of the gated structure and therefore is unable to make recommendations regarding the regulation of Lake Champlain and the Richelieu River.[20]

The International Joint Commission made a tangible contribution in overseeing a technical board's conduct of a study that helped both peoples, and particularly Vermonters and Quebeckers, to gain a greater understanding of the Lake Champlain–Richelieu system and of the complexities of solving this difficult problem. The commission's work also helped instill in Vermonters a greater love for "their" lake. However, by any reasonable standard, the commission failed in its basic task, and, unfortunately, further discredited itself by delaying its "nondecision" for an excessively long time, thus preventing diplomatic negotiators from tackling the issue. Such experiences as Champlain-Richelieu lend credence to the negative criticism that is sometimes directed at the IJC, namely, that too much of its work takes up excessive time and too many of its findings are indecisive and inconclusive.

The Difficulty of a Solution. Many have despaired of a solution, given Quebec's adamant desire to protect its flood-beleagered citizens and Vermont's unwillingness to alter its position on lake-level regulation. Maintenance of the status quo, through deadlock or for whatever reason, benefits Vermont and New York at the expense of Quebec, since this means no structural regulatory measures, no lake-level manipulation, and no flood protection in the high-water cycles. To achieve its goals, Quebec needs a break in the current long-standing impasse, but U.S. interests are protected, albeit weakly, by doing nothing.

An answer may lie in some type of U.S. payment to the afflicted Quebec property owners, however indirectly contrived, to enable them to vacate the floodplain so that Quebec can institute floodplain zoning, converting the land to some use that is not harmed by periodic flooding. It is not irrational to suggest that those benefiting most from this result, Vermont and New York lake users and shoreline business and recreational interests, should play a special role in raising the funds to enable this U.S. payment to be made. In any event, the major polarization that has developed in the region has reduced IJC effectiveness and may well negate diplomatic opportunities now that the matter is being returned by the IJC to the diplomats. As a result, it may be necessary to create another special body to adjudicate this specific issue.[21] Such a body would reduce surprise and dissipate much of the adversary atmosphere at present. Ultimately the new body might be converted into a planning and regulatory authority. Seasoned diplomats might well abhor the proliferation of such lower-level joint institutions on the scene of international relations. Yet where other lines of communication have failed and polarization has developed, is there an alternative to a more locally based institution? The alternatives may well be as limited as those available to Vermonters, New Yorkers, and Quebeckers adversely affected by the Champlain-Richelieu problem.

The experience of the Champlain-Richelieu transborder flooding issues illustrates that minor flooding issues affecting small geographical areas can easily become national causes célèbres and have impacts on the bilateral environmental relationship well out of proportion to their size— impacts that are long lasting and possibly unresolvable. The experience also teaches that the IJC does not always succeed, even in this, its most traditional area of transborder activity. The IJC deserves blame in Champlain-Richelieu for unwillingness or inability to face differences squarely and dispose of those differences in a timely manner. The lesson learned from these experiences are important, for similar flooding issues will continue to arise in the future. The tool is there to resolve them, but it must be used more effectively.

Dickey-Lincoln Dam

In view of the fact that northern Maine's once proposed Dickey-Lincoln hydro-dam has now been officially deauthorized by the U.S. government, it will be given limited attention here. However, mention must be made of the little known fact that Quebec and Canada once held the trump card to the completion of this project. As designed, completion of the dam required the flooding of 5,000 acres of Quebec woods. This is only a small percentage of the land that would have been inundated to form the giant reservoir behind the great Dickey-

Lincoln Dam, but nevertheless a critical percentage. Quebec and Canadian government approval would have been necessary to permit the flooding of this acreage and thus carrying out the project, and likely would have been given. But at what price? What kind of a trade-off between Ottawa and the United States, between Ottawa and Quebec City, and between Quebec City and the states would have been suggested? With deauthorization (purely on U.S. domestic grounds), we will never have the answer. However, Quebec clearly lost a bargaining chip.

Water Quality

Opportunity for transborder water pollution problems to arise between Quebec and the United States is limited and, in fact, the emergence of such disputes has been rare. Much of the Maine-Quebec and all of the New Hampshire-Quebec border is a drainage divide across which water cannot flow, and the Vermont-Quebec and New York-Quebec borders have relatively little water flowing across them. Only three instances of bilateral water pollution disputes involving Quebec can be identified.

Great Lakes Water Quality

The twenty-year debate over the bilateral consequences of Great Lakes water pollution normally depicts one province (Ontario) pitched against multiple states (stretching from New York west to Minnesota). Only rarely is Quebec acknowledged as a player with interests in this area. Contributing to overlooking Quebec in this regard is both its far-downstream position (on the St. Lawrence rather than the lakes themselves) and the fact that Quebec has been exceedingly slow to get its own house in order when it comes to the pollution of the province's own rivers and streams. Montreal's effluent contribution to the St. Lawrence has been quite notable, as has the contribution of Hull and other Quebec cities to the river and its tributaries, particularly the Ottawa River. Nevertheless, the Great Lakes contribute a deadly load of highly toxic substances to the St. Lawrence to be carried downstream to Quebec, and if Quebec is successful with present plans for sewerage control, the contributed load from upstream U.S. states (especially New York and its infamous Niagara River) and Ontario may present real problems. At present Quebec is represented in various bilateral Great Lakes water-quality negotiations, monitoring and research, albeit its role has been low in profile.

Lake Memphremagog

Quebec and Vermont share a particularly beautiful border lake, called Memphremagog, which generations of Anglo-Quebeckers have used as a recreational site for second-home development. The Vermont portion of the lake has seen more utilitarian usage, particularly by the economically depressed residents of the city of Newport. Newport was found to be polluting the lake to a greater than tolerable degree in the 1960s, leading to a transborder dispute and a relatively quick U.S. acknowledgment of the problem. Construction of the appropriate sewage treatment facilities by the city, largely with federal funding, followed soon thereafter. A few Quebec pollution sources have also now been controlled. Essentially the dispute is resolved but questions are occasionally raised, and the matter could flare again.

St. John River

The St. John River international water pollution problem is normally viewed as a Maine–New Brunswick matter, but the river's tributaries rise in Quebec and the river receives a small amount of its effluent loading from that province. Farther downstream the St. John forms the international frontier between Maine and New Brunswick, and thence flows across New Brunswick as that province's most important river. It receives effluent from municipalities, pulp and paper operations, potato and other farms, and food-processing operations. Bilateral environmental problems arose in the 1960s, due largely to pollution in the international section of the river. In response, a unique bilateral committee, the St. John Water Quality Committee, was formed to oversee clean-up of the river and resolution of the problem, as well as to conduct long-term monitoring. This committee subsequently became famous overseas when it was designated as the Canadian and U.S. model contribution to the North Atlantic Treaty Organization's multilateral environmental program carried out by NATO's Committee on the Challenges of Modern Society. Although most of the St. John committee's activity has focused on downstream Maine and New Brunswick, upstream Quebec has been represented and has participated from the beginning.

Air Quality

Other than the "megaissue" of acid rain, there have been no transboundary air pollution issues between the United States and Quebec of any significance to date. Undoubtedly, pollution from Montreal sources occasionally crosses the border into New York and Vermont, but thus far there has been no concern raised by the lightly populated portions of those two states that sometimes find themselves downwind. Acid rain, however, presents a different picture.

Map 6.2.   Regions Containing Lakes Sensitive to Acid Precipitation.

Source: John E. Carroll, *Acid Rain: An Issue in Canadian-American Relations* (Washington, D.C.: Canadian-American Committee, National Planning Association, 1982), p. 8. (Adapted from *United States–Canada, Memorandum of Intent on Transboundary Air Pollution,* Interim Report [February 1981], pp. 3–5.)

Acid Rain[22]

There is no Canadian province geologically more vulnerable to acidic deposition, and thus acidic precipitation, than Quebec (see Map 6.2). There may well be no province more economically vulnerable, given the vast commercially valuable forest resource of the province, the province's (and Canada's) great dependency on the processing and export of that resource, and given the grave suspicions thus far raised concerning linkage between acid deposition and growth retardation in the woods. Much research yet remains to be carried out in this area, but preliminary findings raise suspicions, suspicions that are exacerbated by the fear of ultimate irreversibility of ecological impacts, particularly if decisions are made too late to do any good. For a province (and a nation) as heavily dependent on the growth and export of wood products as is Quebec (and Canada), acid rain must of necessity be a major cause of concern.

Quebec is a vulnerable receptor of both acid rain and its precursors, sulfur dioxide (SO_2) and nitrous oxide (NO_x) gases, and also an emitter of such gaseous pollutants with their acidic effects. Quebec is immediately downwind of Ontario's Sudbury and other metal smelters and their sulfur dioxide emissions, as well as downwind of Ontario Hydro's coal-fired power plants. Somewhat more distantly, it is downwind of the heavy SO_2 emissions of the U.S. industrial heartland in the Ohio Valley and Great Lakes—emissions from large coal-fired power plants that lack controls on the stack gases. Quebec's vulnerability to these emissions has already been noted. Quebec's own SO_2 emissions are largely concentrated in the remote north from copper smelters at Rouyn-Noranda. Downwind of these emissions are the Maritime Provinces. The United States is not affected by Quebec's acidic emissions, with the possible exception of nitric oxide emissions from the Montreal metropolitan area.

The principal impact on Quebec of the bilateral acid rain debate stems from two conditions:

1. Quebec's previously mentioned high vulnerability to U.S. midwestern (as well as Canadian) emissions, coupled with its geographical location downwind of those emissions.
2. The possible impact of a rigorous international acid rain or air quality agreement on Quebec's own future SO_2 emissions and thus on the future economic viability of the province's metal-smelting industry. Indeed, Ottawa's determination to negotiate a hard line diplomatically with the United States is already placing great pressure on Quebec's smelting industry, if only to demonstrate a necessary Canadian determination to keep its own house in order.

The history of the acid rain issue in Quebec is shorter than it is in Ontario, at least partly due to the much lesser attention to the issue in the Quebec media, and especially francophone media, before 1981. Conversely, media coverage has been long and intense in Ontario through the English-language CBC and CP wire service networks, starting as early as 1975–1976. This coverage has included much in-depth analysis. The Toronto population has been particularly subject to very heavy media attention. Even places removed from the area of concern, like

Winnipeg, Calgary, and Regina, have been similarly exposed. The French-language media did not give such attention to acid rain until about 1980–1981, when the pressure of the issue overall, as well as Quebec's great vulnerability, ultimately prevailed. Not only is the issue now receiving French-language coverage more equivalent to that in anglophone Canada, but additionally, Quebec is taking a strategy leadership role in support of the strong Canadian federal diplomatic stance, as its population becomes increasingly aware of the seriousness of the problem for Quebec, for Canada, and for Canada-U.S. relations.

Analysis. The Quebec-United States environmental disputes or differences are not inherently different from those found elsewhere along the lengthy Canadian-U.S. border, with the exception of the dry prairies where water quantity takes on such a high degree of importance. Problems of flooding, water pollution, and air pollution can and do appear at almost any point along the border, the latter two often in direct proportion to industrialization. Transborder pollution problems are further exacerbated by border asymmetries where one nation's attempts to industrialize threaten the other nation's attempts to protect a prized environment such as a wilderness or a wild river. And acid rain is now more or less a universal problem from the Minnesota-Manitoba border region eastward to the Atlantic.

Because of Quebec's geographical location far downstream on the Great Lakes–St. Lawrence system, because it does not share a coastal border region with the United States, because its U.S. border is partly a drainage divide, and because it lies adjacent to very lightly populated U.S. terrain that is essentially a political backwater of its southern neighbor, Quebec experiences fewer transboundary environmental problems along the international frontier than does Ontario or British Columbia or even Saskatchewan or Manitoba. The case of Champlain-Richelieu stands as an exception, for there the resource at stake is vital to a U.S. population in Vermont that is by no means a backwater population and has thus made itself known, elevating the issue to a much higher level than could otherwise be expected. The case of acid rain also presents an exception of sorts, for it is Quebec's high vulnerability to long-distance transport of acid from points quite distant from the province that results in the province's being an increasingly important actor. There is, of course, potential for the development of future (now unforeseen) transboundary environmental problems in the narrow sense, but that potential is not as great as elsewhere due to the likely slow or no-growth prospects of northern New York, northernmost New England, and adjacent parts of Quebec. The development of small local issues, of course, continues to be likely.

If the Quebec-U.S. transboundary environmental problems are not substantively different from those elsewhere along the border, to what degree are they perceived or handled differently? On the U.S. side of the border, the states of Vermont and New York have strong environmental legislation and great environmental sympathy. This is especially true in Vermont, where much of the state's attention focuses north toward Canada. It is less true in New York, given that state's strong focus southward, as well as the economic depression and lack of political power of the far northern portion of the state. The positions of New Hampshire and Maine on environmental matters are not relevant, given the unpeopled nature of the border region and also the fact that these regions are not particularly prized as wilderness treasures. In Quebec, an historic focus on chronically high unemployment and depressed economic conditions (long predating the current recession), and a lack of intense interest in the mostly remote border region, have coupled to de-escalate potential problems. Language differences have also worked to create somewhat of a gap in the working relationships betweeen Quebeckers and citizens of the several states in the region (in comparison, for example, to working relationships between Minnesotans and Manitobans, or Michiganians and Ontarians), but perhaps not as much of a gap as some might expect.

Governments on both sides of the border have the now common array of air and water pollution control legislation in all aspects of the environment, though there is a difference in the legal approach between the Canadian (and Quebec) system of guidelines and recommendations and the U.S. system of inflexible statutory law. In day-to-day reality, however, differences in the region in question are not great, with Vermont having perhaps a higher level of enforcement complementing its greater political concerns, and Quebec perhaps choosing lesser enforcement given its more fundamental preoccupation with jobs and economic development.

As a general rule, Quebec is the principal actor and decision maker on the Canadian side of the border, with Ottawa's role secondary, while Washington is the dominant actor on the U.S. side, with the states secondary. However, in the current administration, Washington does not choose to utilize its powers. Thus, the province and the states at the present time are somewhat more equal in authority, though this will likely change in the future and the old imbalance between state and provincial authority will most certainly return.

In general, environmental issues are of lower priority and saliency among Quebeckers than among New Englanders and New Yorkers. Traditional Quebec concerns over economic underdevelopment and chronically high unemployment, for much of its modern history, contribute to this difference. One might therefore expect a high incidence of polarization over environmental differences between the two regions. However, such is not the case. New England environmental organizations are indeed highly organized, capable, and articulate, but they are Boston-based and with rare exceptions have never really focused on the border region. New York environmentalists seem to terminate their concerns geographically at the Adirondacks and do not look beyond. It is only Vermont groups such as the Lake Champlain Committee, with their intense but narrow interest in the lake and its basin, that have become strongly involved. Quebec environmentalists, low in numbers and weakly organized with little power by U.S. standards, have focused more on Montreal and other urban agglomerations, and on James Bay and other northern regions, and have played little or no role along the border.

Acid rain, however, presents a different situation. New England environmental groups (statewide and region-wide) are in the forefront of the national effort to alleviate the acid rain problem, albeit that most of their attention focuses on the domestic side of the issue (they have been slow to grasp the opportunity the foreign relations aspect represents). Quebec environmentalists, initially slow to respond, are now aligning with their Ontario counterparts behind the acid rain protests, and theirs is a concern that is highly cognizant of the international aspects. (The vulnerable receptor side is naturally more aware of transborder threats than the emitter, and Canadians are always more aware of Canada-U.S. relations and interdependencies than are most people in the states.) Thus, rather than being at odds, Quebec environmentalists and New England–New York environmentalists are very much aligned with one another against a common threat. Both reside in acid-vulnerable environments, and neither has a great stake in protecting the rights of emitters (with the exception of northern Quebec's few copper smelters). A further common interest is the northeastern U.S. dependency on Quebec newsprint, pulp, and paper from forests that could be threatened by acid rain. It would be interesting to know what the economic impact will be for the United States should Quebec forests become less profitable due to acid rain. The power of this common environmental (and perhaps economic) interest to *align* the two regions is infinitely greater than is the power of any transborder environmental dispute to pull them apart, and that power extends well beyond the level of citizens' environmental groups to the highest levels of state and provincial governments, the media, and other influential sectors of both societies.

As Quebeckers become increasingly concerned over acid rain and increasingly aware of its bilateral aspects and its potential for alliance-building, they will undoubtedly seek to capitalize on the situation. Necessity demands that they support Ottawa's hard negotiating stance with Washington, if only to protect them from U.S. midwestern emissions and give them an entrée to negotiation with Washington. Hence, Quebec saw fit to join with Ontario, with Canadian federal acquiescence, as an intervenor in U.S. Environmental Protection Agency rule-making proceedings. Necessity also dictates that they must further develop that natural alliance regarding acid rain with northeastern U.S. states, both as a way to utilize domestic U.S. political clout against the midwestern emitters and as a way to maintain better U.S. linkages for Quebec trade, energy export, and perhaps ultimately, political support.

This developing Quebec-northeastern U.S. alliance is off to a slow but nevertheless tangible start with the recent signing of two accords with New York and Vermont on acid rain research, monitoring, and information exchange. Quebec has also joined New York to establish an "Acid Rain Institute" to facilitate exchange of information between these two governments and disseminate information on acid rain to the public. These Quebec–New York and Quebec-Vermont initiatives are agreements to cooperate in the sharing of data. They are not agreements to abide by any findings of data and do not imply cross-border recognition of the validity of each side's data, which is the case with the IJC. These steps are positive and are not politically risky, nor are they financially demanding. They will also likely result in greater human linkages among scientists and officials of the three governments.

Quebec has additionally used its participation in New England Governors/Eastern Canadian Premiers conferences and its participation in Governor Carey's New York acid rain meetings further to secure this alliance.

There are other issues in Quebec-U.S. relations that, while not indicative of transborder environmental problems *per se* are matters of consequence that are affected by environmental decisions. Energy is undoubtedly predominant in this area, and many examples can be cited:

1. The political climate in New England and New York now is such that no new nuclear power plants can readily secure construction licenses. Regional environmentalist groups made a contribution to that change in climate, assisted by economic conditions working against the nuclear alternative, creating greater opportunity for Quebec to export hydro-generated electricity into the New York–New England region. This increases the likelihood that the Quebec Government will further develop hydropower potential in the northern and eastern wilderness regions of the province, with consequently greater impact on the northern ecosystems and on the Cree Indian peoples who reside there.

2. Major air quality and acid rain concerns of New Englanders and New Yorkers are gravitating against the burning of high-sulfur fuels (oil and coal) in the region, making imported hydropower more economically competitive.

3. In spite of the fact that the environmental costs of hydropower generation at the site of the impoundment are well known, hydropower is renewable and is widely viewed today as "clean" even among environmentalists, making the U.S. climate more conducive to the acceptance of Canadian imports.

4. New Englanders and New Yorkers are working toward U.S. sulfur emission control legislation that will make high-sulfur midwestern coal-fired electricity more expensive and increasingly less competitive with hydro sources, further aiding Quebec export plans.

5. Quebec's electricity exports must be transported to and through U.S. territory. Although no one seriously envisions problems at the border where the high-voltage transmission lines must cross, nevertheless there are issues of aesthetics about those high-voltage transmission lines in New England. New Englanders, unlike Canadians, are not accustomed to the very large size and the great height of these lines; they are accustomed to much smaller lines. And most New Englanders do not realize that some of these lines coming into New England will be of this larger size, unless technology develops rapidly to reduce that size and consequent aesthetic impact. Health effects of high-voltage transmission are little known, signifying a very soft area scientifically, but research is ongoing in New York and Minnesota into the impacts of such transmission both on livestock and on human health. Little of consequence can be said at this time. In five or ten years much more will be known, perhaps enough to show that there is no need for concern. But a potential threat looms in the background of this issue today.

In another area, increasing U.S. health and environmental concerns over the use of asbestos could well gravitate against this extremely important Quebec export. U.S. market potentials will be reduced if this particular environmental and health concern continues.

Given the great interest in the impacts of Québécois independence sentiment and perhaps Quebec's ultimate disassociation from Canada, the question naturally arises as to the potential influences of such an event on Quebec-U.S. environmental relations. A corollary concern is Quebec's relationship with international bodies such as the International Joint Commission, and its possible dealings with nongovernmental environmentalist organizations.

If Quebec should leave the Canadian federation, obviously it would lose the Boundary Waters Treaty and its vehicle the IJC, and would probably have to renegotiate them or replace them with something else. On the acid rain issue, the big one, it could be argued that as long as Quebec remains part of Canada, it needs Ottawa for one basic reason; namely, that Washington (i.e., the U.S. federal government) will not deal directly with the government of Quebec on this or any other issue. Canada is the more vulnerable nation, the more afflicted nation. Quebec is particularly afflicted within Canada, and it needs to have its interests effectively represented in Washington by professional diplomats who can deal with U.S. diplomats on a peer basis. In this respect, Quebec City needs Ottawa at present, simply because of Washington reactions and response. If Quebec were not so vulnerable, Quebec City could probably ignore this debate. But it cannot.

The Quebec-IJC relationship has historically been a cooperative one. There invariably has always been, on the Canadian side of the commission, a respected Quebecker in the membership, so that Quebec has been represented by one-third of the Canadian membership. (There are three Canadian and three U.S. commissioners.) Some could argue that Quebec has been overrepresented on the IJC. And Ottawa has been very careful to maintain one of those three positions for a Quebecker. The province has never had to deal very much with the IJC, the Champlain-Richelieu issue being probably its biggest involvement with the commission. In that instance the commission did fail, but it failed for both countries.

In the area of Quebec contact with U.S. environmentalist organizations, it must be said that this contact is certainly no greater than and probably much less than the contact developed between Ontario or Ottawa and U.S. environmentalists. Language differences inhibit such contact and, in any event, U.S. environmentalists would likely shy away from any significant direct contact with the Quebec or any other foreign government, certainly if there were any suggestion from the U.S. State Department that such was inappropriate.

The overall prospect for Quebec–northeastern United States environmental relations is for a positive future. Champlain-Richelieu will continue to remain a thorn in the side of the bilateral environmental relationship, especially in cyclic years of high water levels, and there is no clear resolution in sight. However, acid rain and "clean energy" export will both serve as positive forces. As noted, acid rain may drive the two nations farther apart, but it will drive Quebec and the northeastern U.S. closer together in the sharing of a common community of interest. Likewise, the growing New York–New England support for Quebec hydropower import, even among environmentalists who perceive it to be a desirable alternative to nuclear and coal sources, holds promise for solidifying the relationship.

The foundation is laid for an increasingly profitable relationship of great mutual value. It is now up to the people of New England, New York, and Quebec to capitalize on this foundation and build a structure to ensure that the profits are accrued to the people of this international region.

Notes

1. The section on Champlain-Richelieu is derived from the author's recent work *Environmental Diplomacy: An Examination and Prospective of Canadian-U.S. Environmental Relations* (Ann Arbor: University of Michigan Press, 1983).

2. Maxwell Cohen, "Transboundary Environmental Attitudes and Policy—Some Canadian Perspectives," unpublished paper prepared for the Harvard Center for International Affairs, Cambridge, MA, October 21, 1980, p. 37.

3. International Champlain-Richelieu Board, *Regulation of Lake Champlain and the Upper Richelieu River, Report to the International Joint Commission by the International Champlain-Richelieu Board* (Ottawa and Washington, D.C.: IJC, 1978), p. 1.

4. Ibid., p. 75.

5. Ibid., p. 1.

6. International Joint Commission, news release, Ottawa and Washington, D.C., January 22, 1976.

7. Ibid. By mandate of the Boundary Waters Treaty of 1909, such application must be made to the IJC. Article IV states that neither country "will . . . permit the construction . . . of any remedial or protective works or any dam or other obstruction in waters flowing from boundary waters or in waters at a lower level than the boundary in rivers flowing across the boundary the effect of which is to raise the natural level of waters on the side of the boundary unless the construction or maintenance thereof is approved" by the IJC.

8. The Champlain Coalition, information sheet, Burlington, VT, undated. The coalition is comprised of a group of existing organizations, including the Sierra Club.

9. Canada-U.S. Environment Committee, list of resolutions, Third Meeting. Ottawa, March 16–17, 1977, p. 4.

10. Fredrick W. Statson, "Vermont Environmentalists Welcome Reduced Flood Plain Development," *Burlington Free Press*, Burlington, VT, October 10, 1976.

11. Brendan Whittaker, secretary of environmental conservation, state of Vermont, personal interview, Montpelier, VT, June 25, 1980.

12. Vermont Agency of Environmental Conservation, "A Case Against the Regulation of Lake Champlain," Montpelier, VT, June 10, 1980, p. 1.

13. Ibid., p. 4.

14. Richard Snelling, governor of Vermont, transcript of remarks to the International Joint Commission hearing, September 26, 1978, pp. 5–6.

15. Ibid, p. 13.

16. Peter A. A. Berle, commissioner of environmental conservation, state of New York, statement of New York State to the International Joint Commission public hearing at Plattsburgh, New York, June 7, 1978, p. 3.

17. Ibid., p. 5.

18. International Champlain-Richelieu Board, *Regulation of Lake Champlain and the Upper Richelieu River*, pp. 3–4.

19. International Joint Commission, *Regulation of the Richelieu River and Lake Champlain: An IJC Report to the Governments of Canada and the United States*, 1981, p. 11.

20. Ibid., p. 24.

21. Justin Brande and Mark Lapping, "Exchanging Information Across Boundaries: The Richelieu-Champlain Experience," *Canadian Water Resources Journal* 4(4), Fall 1979, p. 49. Brande and Lapping have written, "We must strive to develop . . . a recognized, continuing institution as will allow us at the outset at least to discuss our interests, ideas and plans on a regular basis. This could be done by treaty, compact and/or simple agreement."

22. For a detailed analysis of acid rain and its influence on the bilateral role, including Quebec's role, see John E. Carroll, *Acid Rain: An Issue in Canadian-American Relations* (Washington, D.C.: Canadian-American Committee, National Planning Association, 1982). See also John E. Carroll, "Acid Rain Diplomacy: The Need for Bilateral Resolution," *Alternatives* 11(1), Winter 1983; and Kenneth M. Curtis and John E. Carroll, *Canadian-American Relations: The Promise and the Challenge* (Lexington, MA: Lexington Books, D. C. Heath & Company, 1983).

7
American Cultural Influence
in Quebec: A One-Way Mirror

Yvan Lamonde

Henry David Thoreau, who crossed "the invisible frontier between the United States and Canada" in 1850, said that the only thing he retained from his journey to Quebec was a cold.[1] This may have been true for the philosopher of the forests but it certainly does not adequately describe the cultural relations between Quebec and the United States over the past two hundred years!

Little questioning of the climate takes place unless there is a crisis— or a head cold—and this holds equally true for culture, in particular for the pervasiveness of U.S. influence on the culture of Quebec. Chroniclers of this influence reflect the model of a cultural consciousness that is disturbed and awakened at moments of crisis or when events occur that mark the crossing of a threshold, a change of scale. A definitive historical analysis of American cultural influence in Quebec has yet to be made; opinions and surveys there are, certainly, but no real synthesis exists setting forth in decisive fashion the cultural and intellectual history of both Quebec and the United States.[2]

It seems symptomatic that studies on the U.S. or "American" cultural presence have been spasmodic in Canada and Quebec since the 1930s: now about radio, now arts and letters, now publications, then radio and the arts once again, as if cultural research were amnesiac and incapable of establishing any sort of continuity that might provide a proper measure of what was actually happening. This pattern is still true of Quebec, where research into the American cultural presence is limited to random studies of this or that sector.

The relative absence of research on this cultural influence stems largely from the cultural and linguistic attraction of France for Quebec's intellectuals and their consequent alienation from the mass popular culture of Quebec, which is fundamentally North American. Another part of the problem is the slowness with which anticapitalistic, leftist ideology, not very empirically inclined until recently, has become aware of U.S. cultural influence in particluar.

These research shortcomings can be explained, but they are more difficult to understand in light of the fact that, after trade and investment, culture forms the strongest bond between Quebec and the United States. The gap between the omnipresent mass U.S. culture (in media and advertising) and the limited understanding of this reality is not the least of paradoxes, for the cultural and political consequences seem decisive at a time when communication technologies, such as cable, satellite, pay TV, and computers, are reinforcing U.S. influence in Quebec and the rest of the world and will continue to do so.

Tracing the historical network of the cultural influence of the United States upon Quebec appears to be a task of the utmost urgency and one that must be systematically followed up. By dealing with the various evolutionary phases of these influences I will try to trace their roots back to the American Revolution, show the change of scale that occurred in both the infrastructure and in cultural awareness after World War I, and demonstrate the intensification of change after World War II with the development of the media.

Ideas and Entertainment

In the eighteenth century and up to the time of the Civil War at least, republican ideas and the image of the "Great Republic" gripped the imagination of the democrats of Quebec. Historians agree that the *L'appel du Congrès aux Canadiens* of October 26, 1774, did have a certain appeal, and in particular that scarcely fifteen years after their conquest by Britain the French-Canadians' "benevolent neutrality" toward the American troops was an indication of something to come.[3] A certain ambivalence developed that was to lead to a three-dimensional cultural time and space: the distant space of "eternal" France, the ever-present Laurentian space of Britain's North American colonies, and the Laurentian-American space of a possible future.

Half a century later, during the uprisings of 1837 and 1838, under Louis-Joseph Papineau, Quebec's "Sons of Liberty" were to find inspiration in the principles and statements of rights of the American Declaration of Independence, before benefiting, in exile, from the "benevolent" hospitality of the citizens of Vermont, Maine, and the state of New York.[4]

After the abolition of protectionism and the Corn Laws by England in 1846, the 1849 movement toward annexation by the United States once again revealed the continuing, spontaneous attraction of the United States for the people of Quebec, even within a "logic of despair" in which disappearance by annexation seemed preferable to disappearance through the recent union of the two Canadas.[5] In a series of lectures, the great intellectual and democrat Louis-Antoine Dessaulles once again expressed this fascination for the "colossal republic of the New World" and condemned "any political principle which is not synonymous with the sovereignty of the people, any organization which is not a republic."[6] Citing the example of French Louisiana and religious freedom in the United States to strengthen the nationalism of his compatriots, Dessaulles nevertheless opted for democracy. In doing so he clearly formulated one of the classic dilemmas of Quebec's intellectual and political tradition: nationalism and/or democracy, nationalism and/or socialism.

But at the time of Canadian confederation, the admirable republic had already spiked the cultural guns of a Quebec that dreamed of a French America. The clear-minded bookseller, poet, and exile Octave Crémazie wrote nostalgically:

Canada could have won its place in the literary circles of the old world had it found amongst its children, before Fenimore Cooper, a writer capable of introducing Europe to the splendour of our forests, the legendary exploits of our trappers and "voyageurs." Even if today a talent equal to that of the author of *The Last of the Mohicans* should appear among us, his works would produce no sensation in Europe, for he would make the irreparable mistake of coming second, that is to say, too late.[7]

Between the American Revolution and World War I, the United States' cultural influence on Quebec was not limited to republican ideas. A *continental culture* was in the process of creation in all its varied forms. Over and above the symbolic experiment of a Fleury Mesplets, who came with his press from Philadelphia, historians of the printed word in Quebec have noted not only the significant number of printers from the United States in Quebec City and Montreal but have also shown that the production and distribution of printed matter was carried on until at least the mid-nineteenth century in the U.S. style—successive roles for the printer, publisher, and bookseller—rather than in the French manner where the bookseller assumed all three roles.[8] Moreover, very early on, imports from the United States of printed matter, printing materials, and art objects were revealed, for certain products, to be greater than those from Great Britain and France combined.[9] In the realm of printed matter, the establishment of the telegraph in 1846 and of the telegraphic line from the U.S. Atlantic coast via Albany, for example, was already changing journalistic practices. As early as 1868, the American Press Association was providing Quebec newspapers with information; these papers were to become, after 1880, newspapers in the U.S. style—*La Presse* dates from 1884.[10]

This continental culture was just as dependent, if not more so, on a nonliterary, oral, and visual culture constituted by the world of the theatre: touring theatrical troupes that came from Paris via New Orleans to play in French in Montreal,[11] circuses and entertainments of all kinds,[12] including burlesques, essentially American,[13] that were seen in Montreal between 1880 and 1930. The prime examples of this trend were the "moving" pictures, which could be seen in Montreal from the summer of 1896 on, and whose popularity in the years before World War I marked a new high in the cultural impact of the United States in Quebec.

Between 1775 and 1920, the North American cultural influence formed part of the British colonial political framework, and the attraction of Quebec's republican neighbor to the south clearly demonstrated a north-south political culture that has tended to persist. This nineteenth century continental culture often followed the lines of the economy, the continental dimensions of which are best exemplified by the annexation movement and the Treaty of Reciprocity. But most important, toward the end of the nineteenth century a social cleavage became apparent in cultural practices, and this division continues today. A section of the middle class has since been "on the Paris wavelength," although the mass of the people have been avid adherents of the essentially visual, spectacular entertainment world of the United States. A clear cultural awareness of this new situation was expressed in no uncertain terms in the 1920s.

Go North! Americanization, the New "Conquest" (1920–1945)

The ideological and cultural shock produced by the U.S. investments made in Quebec between the end of World War I and the crash of 1929 has been amply demonstrated.[14] People in Quebec quickly adapted their language to what was happening, and more and more frequently one heard the new word, *Americanization*, a vague enough term but one that covered a widespread phenomenon indicative of the new feeling in the air.

The cinema was without a doubt the most important medium of this new, visual culture imported from the United States. During the period of silent films after World War I, there was a tremendous rise in the number of movie houses in Montreal, from forty-six in 1915 to seventy-three in 1921. With the advent of the "talkies" in Quebec in 1930, 148 commerical houses sprang up, fifty-one of them in Montreal. Of the films imported into Canada between 1919 and 1930, an average of 96 percent came from the United States.[15] This virtual U.S. film monopoly applied to cinemas in Montreal and throughout Quebec province as well. The 1914–1918 war interrupted the production and export of French films, opened up the market to the United States, and instilled in Quebeckers a taste for U.S.-produced films[16] that lasted for over fifteen years, until the coming of French talkies after 1930.

Moreover, the periodicals associated with the U.S. film industry presented a "continental" view of the cinema in Quebec and Canada, as statements like the following indicate: "the Dominion of Canada is regarded by members of the American film industry as part of its domestic market."[17] The U.S. presence was equally powerful in the commercial operation of movie houses. Famous Players (Paramount), which in 1923 bought the largest Canadian chain, in 1925 controlled eight of the fifty-one movie houses in Montreal including the *Capitol* and three other first-run houses.[18]

The press also felt the effects of Americanization. Quite apart from the explicitly "yellow" press, the sensationalism, the photography, and the comics, the Sunday press saw the addition of the U.S.-type tabloid (1919) and expansion of that tradition with the establishment of *Le Petit Journal* (1925) and *La Patrie du Dimanche* (1935).[19]

The number of cars in Quebec, 400 in 1908, multiplied by ten between the war and the depression, rising from 14,159 in 1916 to 140,802 in 1930.[20] The burgeoning culture of the automobile was the advance guard of the consumer culture that was taking root, already identified at that time as "the American way of life." It was this new material culture that was to make the region north of the forty-fifth parallel the mirror of that to the south. The rise of private radio stations and the increase in advertising after 1936 were yet another indication of the attraction of the American way of life.[21] As for the invasion of professional sport, it resulted in a certain questioning of the traditional Catholic way in which the human body was perceived in the cinema and the cabaret.[22]

Americanization literally pervaded the cultural spirit of the time. It poured forth in the novel[23] and became one of the warhorses of the new cultural awareness personified by the groups responsible for *L'action française*, a review that first appeared in 1917.[24] For these men of the predepression period, Americanization was "the greatest misfortune in our history, much worse that the English conquest," for the latter "was imposed on us but did not succeed in breaking our French spirit, while today this spirit is going under, swamped by foreign influence."[25] One even spoke of "a soul already changed," "a hybrid spirit" (a spirit *métissé*).[26]

These cultural influences, which accompanied the movement of financial investments, were intensified at a time when urbanization was on the rise in Quebec and the population of Montreal was rapidly increasing.[27]

It is certainly possible to imagine an urbanization and industrialization process per se in such a way as to single out what is specifically of North American derivation. But the situation between 1911 and 1921, when Quebec was becoming predominantly urban, was quite different. From that time on, capital invested in Quebec was no longer British but primarily U.S. capital; business firms became continental in scope. In the cities, architecture and urban planning were distinctly U.S.-influenced in character, like entertainment and material culture. It is in this sense that urbanization was not only synonymous with modernity, but also with Americanization, with American-ness. The highest praise was "Just like the States!"

This simultaneous urbanization and Americanization was a manifest shock to the intellectual elite of the time, the conservative middle class, as well as the clergy. The rural ideal, the family, marriage, language, and the faith were beset by new practices and new values, and in the minds of these "well-bred persons" the words "the people" and "the masses" took on a definite class meaning bordering on the pejorative.[28] The social cleavage in Quebec's cultural life became increasingly marked as the lines were drawn between the elitist, Atlantic, "French" world and the American continental mass culture.

The intensification of the U.S. impact on Quebec life obliged the nationalists and the intellectuals of the period to seek their identity in a new diversity, compounded of an enhancement of French culture, a clear awareness of the distance separating them from English Canada, and an increasingly significant continental mentality. This rejection of Americanization, begun in the 1930s, gathered speed with the increase in U.S. investments in Quebec and the unrest created by the depression. The period between 1930 and 1936, which saw the end of the Liberal regime and the beginnings of the *Alliance libérale nationale* and the party of Maurice Duplessis, was a time of youthful revolt against U.S. holdings, often the target of criticism by newspapers such as *La nation* and *L'indépendance*, which advocated national independence as a solution. But such efforts had no effect whatsoever on the grip of the U.S. "cultural industry" represented by the media and the world of entertainment. In short, the thesis of U.S. cultural imperialism had not yet been written.

This new awareness of the Americanization of all sectors proved to be a turning point for French-Canadians in search of their identity. The dream of a French America within the greater North American domain had to make way for a new dream, the dream of a Laurentia which from that time on would have to face squarely the challenge of the continental mentality.

"Bringing It All to Montreal" (1945–   )

The United States may not have expected the immense cultural impact of the mass media in Quebec; nevertheless, after World War II this cultural impact in Quebec made a great leap with the introduction (1952) and rapid spread of television. The powerful effect of this medium was to strengthen the trend toward liberalization after 1960, when traditional values began to crumble: the drying up of sources of recruits for the priesthood and the religious orders and the taking over of responsibility for health and education by the state were to mark the end of a religion; the dramatic drop in the birthrate and the move upwards in the divorce rate were to radically change marriage and the family. The "difference" was to dwindle, being reduced, for some, to a matter of a language consecrated by legislation, and turning an increasing number of Quebeckers into French-speaking Americans.

Television, that cultural canning industry of sound and image, made it possible for a private anglophone television station in Montreal to give itself the credit, daily, for "bringing it all to Montreal"—"all" referring primarily to the United States.[29] This identification of U.S. culture with the media, restrictive as it was, has in a way been encouraged by recent works on U.S. cultural imperialism that are aimed essentially at the media.[30]

Despite the lack of research, there are sufficient data available to add up to a sort of robot portrait of the U.S. cultural presence in Quebec at this moment.

The dominance of the automobile in the American way of life, with its car services and car washes, became a firm part of the way of life in Quebec after 1950; the number of cars increased from 287,657 in 1950 to 1,485,757 in 1969.[31] Private radio with its commercials, its "Hit Parade," and its promotion of the "soaps" as well as records controlled 25 percent of all transmission power in Canada in 1936, but 70 percent by 1956.[32] Between 1950 and 1959, U.S. periodicals and magazines whose circulation was controlled by ABC captured 60 to 65 percent of the Canadian magazine market.[33] What does Benjamin News distribute in Quebec compared with the French distribution agency Periodica?

Internationally, Americanization of industry and the cinema has been going on since immediately after World War I. Between 1946 and 1966, Canada ranked third, after Ireland and Italy, as importer of U.S.-produced full-length films (Table 7.1). Over a longer period, from 1946 to 1976, on average Canada imported from the United States more than

Table 7.1. Percentage of Feature Films, by Country, Imported from the United States, 1946–1967

Country	'46	'47	'48	'49	'50	'51	'52	'53	'54	'55	'56	'57	'58	'59	'60	'61	'62	'63	'64	'65	'66	'67	Average
Ireland[a]	70	64	76	75	73	87	83	79	65	75	69	69	67	65	50	55	54	52	60	59	58	--	65
Italy						67	62	62	68	66	63	65	64	54	41	47	51	56	52	52	58	--	61
Denmark[a]	44	55	77	75	71	69	66	65	53	40	17	44	58	58	52	51	45	49	50	46	49	--	54
Canada	80	76	72	71	68	75	60	44	58	60	56	52	47	41	43	37	37	33	33	42	36	34	54
United Kingdom				69	69	72	64	62	57	61	59	57	56	50	40	38	36	37	38	35	40	--	52
Finland	60	58	58	65	69	69	65	61	53	49	48	54	53	48	40	34	29	32	41	42	36	43	50
Norway	48	57	49	55	61	59	62	55	50	48	51	48	49	40	41	38	44	47	48	45	37	--	49
Sweden				63	63	61	59	53	49	53	48	48	50	43	39	40	38	39	38	40	40	35	48
Netherlands	40	59	66	69	67	64	59	56	48	52	50	45	47	43	35	29	28	31	32	30	32	--	47
West Germany						49	57	49	43	46	41	41	41	37	33	33	29	32	29	31	29	--	38
Spain	58	49	48	41	35	37	40	40	47	41	21	17	18	32	32	26	27	25	31	26	24	--	34
France	40				40	40	40	39	36	33	32	33	32	32	30	28	29	27	27	27	25	--	32

[a]Feature films subject to censorship.

Sources: Thomas H. Guback, The International Film Industry (Bloomington: Indiana University Press, 1969), passim; Yvan Lamonde and Pierre-François Hébert, Le cinéma au Québec (Quebec: Institut québécois de recherche sur la culture, 1981), Tables 126 and 129.

Table 7.2. Feature Films Passed by Quebec's Bureau de surveillance
du cinéma (BSCQ), by Place of Origin, May 1971–December 1981

| | Films Passed | |
Place of Origin	Number	Percent
Quebec	287	2.76
Canada (other than Quebec)	555	5.33
France	1,548	14.86
French-language countries (other than France)	90	0.86
United States	3,638	34.92
Great Britain and other English-language countries	876	8.41
Foreign-language countries	3,423	32.96
Total	10,417	100

Source: Rapports mensuels of the BSCQ, May 1971 to December 1981
inclusive. Compilation by Jeal-Paul Baillargeon, Annuaire de
statistiques culturelles du Québec (yet to appear), Institut
québécois de recherche sur la culture.

half the feature films shown in movie houses in Canada, the peak period
being reached just before the advent of television in 1952.[34] There are
no data available for Quebec for the period before 1958, but it seems
likely that the average was slightly less given the particularly active
import market for feature films from France after 1930. Between 1971
and 1981, 34 percent (Table 7.2) of the full-length films viewed by the
Bureau de surveillance du cinéma du Québec (Quebec film supervisory
board) came from the United States, two and a half times the proportion
from France.[35] And between 1958 and 1978, full-length films given a
first showing in Montreal were 37.3 percent from the United States,
19.3 percent from France, and 4.2 percent from Canada.[36]

With regard to the commercial operation of movie houses, U.S.
ownership was constantly on the rise. In 1950, four companies owned
50.5 percent of Montreal's cinemas and controlled 62 percent of available
seats. United Amusements, which was to be taken over by Famous
Players Canadian Corporation, a U.S. subsidiary, in 1966 and from then
on known as *Les Cinémas Unis*, owned 25.3 percent of the houses in
Montreal and 29.3 percent of the seats in 1950, the golden age of the
cinema. Famous Players then controlled 6 percent of the movie houses
in Montreal and 13.9 percent of the seats (because two of its three
houses had 2,000 seats or more). Nearly 30 years later, the concentration
was intensified. In Quebec City, three companies controlled one-third
(34.2 percent) of the cinemas: U.S.-controlled *Les Cinémas Unis* (Famous
Players), 16.7 percent; Odeon (Canadian-owned), 8.7 percent; and France
Film (Quebec-owned), 8.6 percent. But in Montreal, these same companies had control of two-thirds (66.8 percent) of the houses: *Les Cinémas*

Unis held 37.8 percent, Odeon, 21.3 percent, and France Film, 7.7 percent.[37]

Without attempting a systematic analysis of the U.S.-produced programing shown by television stations that were "bringing it all to Montreal" since the inception of the Canadian content policy of the Canadian Radio-television and Telecommunications Commission (CRTC) in 1961, it has nonetheless been possible to make a general assessment of the U.S. hold over Quebec television. Analysis of the ten most popular programs broadcast by the French networks between 1973 and 1982 shows an ever-increasing proportion of U.S. content. In 1979, three U.S. programs took sixth, seventh, and tenth places in the ratings. In 1982, three U.S. programs broadcast by TVA, the main commercial chain in French, over ten different stations and attracting between 2 and 3 million viewers according to the ratings, were ranked in the first, second, and fifth places. These sixty-minute programs were obviously broadcast at prime times (Tables 7.3–7.6). To the top ten can be added a whole string of other U.S. programs, including feature films. In 1980, close to half the full-length films presented by the two main francophone networks, CBC (45.9 percent) and TVA (44.4 percent), came from the United States. This proportion reached 57.3 percent for the CBC English network in Montreal and 67.9 percent in Quebec City. On private station CTV, "bringing it all to Montreal" counted among the feature films it presented 71.4 percent from the United States (Table 7.7).

Audience data correspond to these figures. Two identical inquiries, the first made in 1971 and the second in 1979, indicated that the francophone audience had increased its viewing of U.S. programming by 8 percent, compared to 20 percent for anglophone viewers. Quebec's francophones, who accounted for 81 percent of the population in 1971, made up 72 percent of the viewing audience for U.S. television programs in Quebec and 75 percent of the viewing audience of English-language television. This bias toward entertainment rather than information is, among francophones, positively correlated with income level, schooling, Montreal as opposed to other parts of Quebec, and above all age (youth) and the degree of bilingualism.[38] The young, as in most other places in the world, seem particularly receptive to this anglophone U.S. culture, which is becoming increasingly accessible and with the increase in sophisticated electrotechnology will become more so. An inquiry[39] conducted among students of 15 to 17 years of age has clearly demonstrated the broad impacts of English contents through the spoken media (Table 7.8).

It is clear that in a daily cultural situation where the media occupy first place,[40] "Made in the U.S.A." labels—television, radio, magazines, records—are the most sought-after cultural products in Quebec. At

Table 7.3. The Ten Most Popular Programs Broadcast by the French Networks of TVA and CBC, March 5-18, 1973

Rank	Program	Audience (thousands)	Network	Origin	Day and Time	Length (min.)	Type	No. of Stations Broadcasting
1	Les Berger	2,836	TVA	QC	Mon. 7:30 p.m.	30	serial	9
2	Rue des Pignons	2,515	RC	QC	Tues. 9:00 p.m.	30	serial	17
3	Symphorien	2,371	TVA	QC	Tues. 8:30 p.m.	30	serial	9
4	Quelle famille	2,156	RC	QC	Sun. 7:00 p.m.	30	serial	17
5	Mont Joye	1,943	RC	QC	Mon. 8:30 p.m.	30	serial	17
6	La p'tite semaine	1,797	RC	QC	Mon. 9:00 p.m.	30	serial	17
7	Cinéma Kraft	1,775	TVA	(various)	Thurs. 7:30 p.m.	90	feature film	8
8	Les forges de St. Maurice	1,749	RC	QC	Mon. 8:00 p.m.	30	serial	17
9	Hawaii 5-0	1,632	TVA	U.S.	Tues. 7:30 p.m.	60	serial	8
10	La soirée du hockey	1,563	RC	QC	Sat. 8:00 p.m.	158	sport	15

Source: Bureau of Broadcasting Management (BBM), Television Network Program Report, March 5-March 18, 1973, two-week average, Toronto, 1973, 215 pages. Compilation by Christine Eddie, Annuaire de statistiques culturelles du Québec (yet to appear), Institut québécois de recherche sur la culture.

Table 7.4. The Ten Most Popular Programs Broadcast by the French Networks of TVA and CBC, February 23-March 14, 1976

Rank	Program	Audience (thousands)	Network	Origin	Day and Time	Length (min.)	Type	No. of Stations Broadcasting
1	Rue des Pignons	2,538	RC	QC	Tues. 9:00 p.m.	30	serial	18
2	Les Berger	2,508	TVA	QC	Mon. 7:30 p.m.	30	serial	6
3	Y'a pas de problème	2,294	RC	QC	Mon. 8:00 p.m.	30	serial	18
4	Symphorien	2,073	TVA	QC	Tues. 8:30 p.m.	30	serial	4
5	Avec le temps	1,984	RC	QC	Mon. 8:30 p.m.	30	serial	18
6	La p'tite semaine	1,805	RC	QC	Tues. 8:00 p.m.	30	serial	18
7	La petite patrie	1,784	RC	QC	Sun. 7:00 p.m.	30	serial	18
8	Télé-sélection	1,689	RC	(various)	Mon. 9:00 p.m.	90	feature film	18
9	Le monde de Disney	1,393	RC	U.S.	Tues. 7:00 p.m.	60	program for the young	15
10	Le 60	1,385	RC	QC	Tues. 9:30 p.m.	60	information	18

Source: BBM, Télévision Réseaux, Spring 1976, Toronto, 1976, 139 pages. Compilation by Christine Eddie, Annuaire de statistiques culturelles du Québec (yet to appear), Institut québécois de recherche sur la culture.

Table 7.5. The Ten Most Popular Programs Broadcast by the French Networks of TVA and CBC, February 26–March 4, 1979

Rank	Program	Audience (thousands)	Network	Origin	Day and Time		Length (min.)	Type	No. of Stations Broadcasting
1	Grand Papa	2,646	RC	QC	Tues.	8:00 p.m.	30	serial	20
2	Jamais deux sans toi	2,401	RC	QC	Tues.	8:30 p.m.	30	serial	20
3	Dominique	2,258	TVA	QC	Mon.	7:00 p.m.	30	serial	8
4	Terre humaine	2,086	RC	QC	Mon.	8:00 p.m.	30	serial	20
5	Le clan Beaulieu	2,006	TVA	QC	Mon.	7:30 p.m.	30	serial	8
6	La petite maison dans la prairie	1,903	TVA	U.S.	Wed.	7:30 p.m.	60	serial	8
7	La femme bionique	1,795	RC	U.S.	Sat.	7:00 p.m.	60	serial	14
8	Les grands films	1,793	RC	(various)	Thurs.	8:30 p.m.	120	feature film	19
9	Du tac au tac	1,657	RC	QC	Thurs.	7:30 p.m.	30	serial	20
10	Le monde de Disney	1,609	RC	U.S.	Tues.	7:00 p.m.	60	program for the young	19

Source: BBM, Télévision Réseaux, February 26–March 4, 1979, Toronto, 1979, 96 pages. Compilation by Christine Eddie, Annuaire de statistiques culturelles du Québec (yet to appear), Institut québécois de recherche sur la culture.

Table 7.6. The Ten Most Popular Programs Broadcast by the French Networks of TVA and CBC, March 1-7, 1982

Rank	Program	Audience (thousands)	Network	Origin	Day and Time		Length (min.)	Type	No. of Stations Broadcasting
1	La petite maison dans la prairie	2,347	TVA	U.S.	Mon.	6:30 p.m.	60	serial	10
2	Chips	2,167	TVA	U.S.	Tues.	6:30 p.m.	60	serial	10
3	Terre humaine	1,873	RC	QC	Mon.	8:00 p.m.	30	serial	20
4	Marisol	1,870	TVA	QC	Mon.	7:30 p.m.	30	serial	10
5	Drôles de dames	1,782	TVA	U.S.	Thurs.	6:30 p.m.	60	serial	10
6	Chez Denise	1,668	RC	QC	Sun.	7:00 p.m.	30	serial	20
7	Le temps d'une paix	1,538	RC	QC	Wed.	8:00 p.m.	30	serial	20
8	Les grandes films	1,512	RC	(various)	Thurs.	8:00 p.m.	120	feature film	20
9	Boogie Woogie '48	1,421	RC	QC	Thurs.	7:30 p.m.	30	serial	20
10	Les beaux dimanches (part I)	1,353	RC	QC	Sun.	7:30 p.m.	75	varied	20

Source: BBM, Télévision Réseaux, March 1-7, 1982, Toronto, 116 pages. Compilation by Christine Eddie, Annuaire de statistiques culturelles du Québec (yet to appear), Institut québécois de recherche sur la culture.

Table 7.7. Percentage of Feature Films Broadcast in Quebec, by Station and Country of Origin, January–December 1980

Stations	Canada	United States	Other Anglophone Countries[a]	France	Other Francophone Countries[b]	Italy	Other Countries	Not Known	Total	Total
RQ										
CIVM-Montréal[c]	10.3	13.2	6.6	37.5	1.5	15.5	14.7	0.7	100.0	136
RC										
CBFT-Montréal[d]	3.9	34.9	10.2	33.4	3.3	6.4	6.6	1.3	100.0	699
CHAU-Carleton	3.9	36.2	10.4	31.9	3.7	5.6	6.9	1.4	100.0	629
CKSH-Sherbrooke	2.2	57.7	7.9	16.2	1.4	7.3	5.8	1.5	100.0	1035
CKRS-Jonquière	2.5	48.2	8.2	23.8	1.6	6.0	7.6	2.1	100.0	939
CKTM-Trois-Rivières	2.2	52.6	10.5	19.5	1.5	6.7	5.9	1.1	100.0	1028
TVA										
CFTM-Montréal[e]	0.4	40.7	12.1	22.1	0.1	16.1	8.4	0.1	100.0	751
CJPM-Chicoutimi	0.4	46.5	12.5	20.1	0.1	12.9	7.4	0.1	100.0	690
CHLT-Sherbrooke	0.6	42.6	12.0	22.0	0.1	14.2	8.2	0.3	100.0	718
CHEM-Trois-Rivières	0.5	40.8	11.0	22.2	0.1	15.8	8.7	0.1	100.0	798
CFCM-Québec	0.4	51.7	11.1	18.7	---	11.8	6.2	0.1	100.0	828
CBC										
CKMI-Québec	5.9	67.9	18.2	1.1	---	5.3	1.1	0.5	100.0	187
CBMT-Montréal	9.6	57.3	25.0	2.2	---	2.2	2.2	0.5	100.0	136
CTV										
CFCF-Montréal	5.8	71.4	15.3	1.8	---	2.4	1.8	1.5	100.0	615

[a] Includes Great Britain, Australia, and New Zealand.

[b] Includes Switzerland, Belgium, and Luxembourg.

[c] Valid also for CIVQ-Québec, CIVO-Hull, CIVN-Rouyn-Noranda, and CIVA-Val d'Or.

[d] Valid also for CJBR-Rimouski, CBGAT-Matane, CBVT-Québec, CKRT-Rivière-du-Loup, CBOFT-Ottawa, and CKRN-Rouyn-Noranda.

[e] Valid also for CFER-Rimouski, CIMT-Rivière-du-Loup, CHOT-Hull, and CFEM-Rouyn-Noranda.

Source: Compilations by Christine Eddie, based on TV-Hebdo 20(52), Dec. 29, 1979–January 4, 1980 to 21(52), Dec. 27, 1980–January 2, 1981 (pages "Cinéma-tv cette semaine"); to appear in Annuaire de statistiques culturelles du Québec, Institut québécois de recherche sur la culture.

Table 7.8. Percentage of Audience Use of Some English-Language
Media by Students Aged 15-17, 1978

Census Area	Radio	Television	Shows (singers)	Cinema	Records or Cassettes
Quebec, Francophone	16	22	35	--	45
Jonquière, Francophone	13	21	26	1	41
Montréal, Francophone	32	29	32	39	46
Montréal, Anglophone	51	44	45	17	57
Montréal, Allophone	41	37	40	6	60
Hull, Francophone	56	49	45	29	66

Source: Edith Bédard and Daniel Monnier, Conscience linguistique
des jeunes québécois. Influence de l'environnement linguistique
chez les elévès francophones de niveau secondaire IV et V, Québec,
Éditeur officiel - Conseil de la langue francaise, 1981, vol. I,
pp. 51-52.

present, this consumption of U.S. culture seems to be disturbing more
because of its effects on the language of Quebeckers, particularly the
young, than the fact that it increases the movement toward integration
into, first, a continental culture, and ultimately an international one.
On the political level, Quebec legislation is more concerned with the
language of work and of signs than with impacts of the media. The
reason for this is simple: the media fall under federal jurisdiction, one
of the major bones of contention between Quebec and Ottawa.

In one sense, the continental integration of Quebec's culture is not
only an established fact, but is enhanced, personalized, and made
Quebec's own as much by the American theme in poetry as by the
popular songs of a Robert Charlebois or a Sylvain Lelièvre, or the
novels of a Roger Lemelin.[41] Quebeckers' awareness of cultural depen-
dencies and imperialisms (I use the plural form deliberately) has become
much stronger since their experience with French-owned Hachette's effort
to purchase Garneau, a major Quebec-owned bookstore chain, and the
crushing failure of the negotiations with France with regard to the
dubbing, in Quebec rather than France, of U.S. films for the international
French-language market, including France. Such imperialisms can come,
in two languages, from both sides of the Atlantic.

Tracing the historical background and identifying the periodic fluc-
tuations of American cultural influence in Quebec have very clearly
indicated where the shortcomings lie and what the specific research
needs are. The research possibilities are many; it is in any case essential
to avoid certain well-beaten paths, which to date have been too confined

to the official statements of a conservative bourgeoisie of liberal professions, a class that has been resisting Americanization since the beginning of the century. It would be much more informative to study the culture of the majority, forgetting the written word for the moment. One promising path of research concerns the development, at the turn of the century, of a material culture, both domestic and technological, that brought "the American way of life" into Quebec's cities. A differential analysis of the daily environment would give a better picture of the continental scope of the habitat, clothing, and in short of the consumption *patterns* of average Quebeckers.

A systematic analysis of the history of the media and their content would provide a more exact measure of the domination of the American way in Quebec. Study of the financial and cultural structure of television, cable and, more recently, pay TV, as well as of the sociocultural evolution of television programming since 1952, would reveal profound changes in the *pattern* of values generally and, unquestionably, in that of the family. Greater attention to the cultural infrastructure, to cultural industries (records, audiocassettes), would also help pinpoint one of the major problems of Quebec culture today, the market.

Conclusions

It is revealing that the U.S. cultural influence in Quebec has come largely by way of the media, particularly the cinema in one period and television in another. The fundamental importance of the market in the establishment of the cultural industries of entertainment and communications should be remembered. Since the end of World War II it has become clear that culture is synonymous with the media and the market. The United States occupies an overwhelming place in this market, as well as in the worldwide infiltration of its culture.

The basic conceptual ambiguity of the cultural situation in Canada and Quebec will only be resolved when a valid answer is found to the following question: How, in a context of mass culture, which means the culture of the market, can countries with small, inadequate markets cope with cultural domination of the media by larger countries?

This question of mass culture is most certainly one that confronts Quebec today; the exercise is not as banal as it first seems, for traditionally culture referred to the culture of the elite. It is above all important to understand that for over 200 years the question of Quebec culture has been considered only in relation to nationalism. This culture-nationalism binomial seems irreducible. Since the 1960s the culture of Quebec has been closely linked with the concept of a people or a nation, more specifically with a state that has assumed cultural responsibility through its departments (cultural affairs, education, communications, and tourism). But the failure of the Parti Québécois referendum has raised a new question: does Quebec's cultural identity necessarily mean cultural sovereignty and consequently political sovereignty? This seems to be the message of the majority regarding culture.

The state has nonetheless designed a cultural policy and invested in the cultural sector; it has intervened in what is representative of Quebec, its heritage, and in *certain* sectors such as publishing, dance, and the theatre. But here one finds a paradox: the state intervenes where it can, but not in the most crucial area, that of mass popular culture or the culture of the market. This market, this culture of the majority, of the average Quebecker, is U.S.-dominated.

The thorny but basic question of the market seems to lie at the heart of the matter. How can the state, as promoter of a "national" culture, and by necessity interventionist, be reconciled with a majority that says "no," that consumes and appreciates mass culture? In the end, the interventionist state will be logically obliged to demonstrate its liberalism by not acting, on the cultural plane, wherever culture is synonymous with the market—the American cultural market.

Curiously, these paradoxes seem to reveal what is most American in the culture of Quebec—an implied liberalism, taken for granted by the average Quebecker, inevitable for the government or even for the state. It is precisely this that the word "quiet" in Quiet Revolution means.

It is clear that the challenge of American culture is more or less the same for both Quebec and Canada.[42] Has the cultural strife between Quebec and Ottawa over communications diverted attention from the real issue of coming to grips with the pervasiveness of the U.S. influence?

The same question could also be asked with regard to relations between Quebec and France. But changes have occurred, and one has to acknowledge that the recent activities of the Quebec Ministry of Intergovernmental Affairs in and with respect to the United States are an indication of a new policy of adjustment to continental realities, both cultural and political.

My conclusions can be summed up by one question: If the management of Quebec's most popular television network were to assume direction of the cultural affairs department, how would this affect Quebec's cultural policy? Would the American nature of Quebec's culture manifest itself in other ways, or would it only become more accentuated?

Notes

1. Henry David Thoreau, *A Yankee in Canada* (Montreal: Harvest House, 1961), pp. 13 and 19.

124   Yvan Lamonde

2. For overviews and some bibliographies dealing specifically with American cultural influences in Quebec, excluding the more comprehensive question of cultural exchanges, see Edmond de Nevers, *L'avenir du peuple canadien-français* (Paris: Jouve, 1896; Montreal, 1964); Jean Ethier-Blais, "L'influence culturelle américaine," in Raymond Morell (ed.), *La dualité canadienne à l'heure des États-Unis* (Quebec: Presses de l'Université Laval, 1965), pp. 65–72; Pierre Savard, *Jules-Paul Tardivel, la France et les États-Unis (1857–1905)* (Quebec: Presses de l'Université Laval, 1967); Richard Pouliot, *Influences culturelles des États-Unis sur le Québec: état sommaire des travaux* (Quebec: Université Laval, Centre québécois de relations internationales, 1972); Guildo Rousseau, *L'image des États-Unis dans la littérature québécois (1775–1930)* (Sherbrooke, Quebec: Editions Naaman, 1981); Jacques Cotnam, "Americans Viewed through the Eyes of French Canadians," *Journal of Popular Culture* 10 (1976–1977), pp. 784–796.

3. Gustave Lanctôt, *Canada and the American Revolution 1774–1783*, translated by Margaret M. Cameron (Cambridge, MA, and Toronto: Harvard University Press, and Clarke and Irwin, 1967); Jean-Pierre Wallot, "La pensée révolutionnaire et réformiste dans le Bas-Canada (1773–1815)," in *Un Québec qui bougeait: trame socio-politique au tournant du XIXe siècle* (Montreal: Editions du Boréal Express, 1973), pp. 255–260.

4. Ivanhoe Caron, "Influence de l'indépendance américaine et de la Déclaration des Droits de l'Homme sur la Rébellion canadienne de 1837 et 1838," *Proceedings of the Royal Society of Canada* 25 (1931), pp. 5–26; and Jean Bruchési, "Influences américaines sur la politique du Bas-Canada, 1820–1867," in Gustave Lanctôt, *Les Canadiens français et leurs voisins du Sud* (Montreal: Editions Bernard Valiquette for the Carnegie Foundation, 1941), pp. 185–236.

5. Jean-Paul Bernard, *Les Rouges: libéralisme, nationalisme et anticléricalisme au milieu du XIXe siècle* (Montreal: Presses de l'Université du Québec, 1971), p. 73; and Jacques Monet, *The Last Cannon Shot: A Study of French Canadian Nationalism (1837–1850)* (Toronto: University of Toronto Press, 1969), pp. 334–353, 375–392.

6. *Six lectures sur l'annexion du Canada aux États-Unis* (Montreal: P. Gendron, 1851).

7. Letter to Henri-Raymond Casgrain, January 29, 1867, quoted in Rousseau, *L'image des États-Unis*, p. 114.

8. John Hare and Jean-Pierre Wallot, "Les imprimés au Québec (1760–1820)," and Claude Galarneau, "Livre et société à Québec (1760–1859): état des recherches," to appear in Yvan Lamonde, ed., *Aspects de l'histoire de l'imprimé au Québec (18e–20e siècles)* (Quebec: Institut québécois de recherche sur la culture, 1983).

9. Yvan Lamonde and M. Ambrosio, "Les importations culturelles au Bas-Canada (1850–1867)," unpublished.

10. Gustave Lanctôt, "Le Québec et les États-Unis, 1867–1937," in G. Lanctôt, *Les Canadiens française et leurs voisins du Sud*, p. 299.

11. Baudoin Burger, *L'activité théâtrale au Québec (1765–1825)* (Montreal: Parti Pris, 1974), pp. 146–150; and John Hare, "Panorama des spectacles au Québec: de la conquête au XXe siècle," in Paul Wyczynski (ed.), *Le théâtre canadien français* (Montreal: Fides, 1976), pp. 59–108.

12. Groupe de recherche en art populaire (Raymond Montpetit, ed.), *Travaux et conférences 1975–1979* (Montreal: Université du Québec, Département d'Histoire de l'Art, 1979).

13. Chantal Hébert, *Le burlesque au Québec* (Montreal: Hurtubise HMH, 1981), pp. 18–44; and Rousseau, *L'image des États-Unis*, p. 116.

14. Yves Roby, *Les québécois et les investissements américains (1918–1929)* (Quebec: Presses de l'Université Laval, 1976).

15. Yvan Lamonde and Pierre-François Hébert, *Le cinéma au Québec: essai de statistique historique (1896 à nos jours)* (Quebec: Institut québécois de recherche sur la culture, 1981), p. 27 and Table 8; and Michel Brûlé, "Les impacts du cinéma américain sur le cinéma et la société québécoise," *Sociologie et sociétés* 8(1), April 1976, pp. 25–41.

16. Alban Janin, "Notre américanisation par le cinéma," special issue of *Revue dominicaine* (February 1936), pp. 69–88.

17. *Film Yearbook* (New York and Hollywood: Wid's Films and Film Folks, 1928), p. 831.

18. Lamonde and Hébert, *Le cinéma au Québec*, p. 25 and Tables 6 and 7.

19. Georges Pelletier, "Notre américanisation par le journal," *Revue dominicaine* (May 1936), pp. 273–282; Jean Bruchési, "Notre américanisation par le magazine," *Revue dominicaine* (July–August 1936), pp. 5–21; and "Nos importations littéraires," *Almanach de la langue française* (1922), pp. 113 and 116.

20. Lamonde and Hébert, *Le cinéma au Québec*, p. 81 and Table 79.

21. Elzéar Lavoie, "L'évolution de la radio au Canada français avant 1940," *Recherches sociographiques* 12(1), 1971, pp. 17–50; Gilbert Maistre, "L'influence de la radio et de la télévision américaines au Canada," *Recherches sociographiques*, pp. 51–76; and L. Desbiens, "L'infiltration américaine par la radio," *Revue dominicaine* (March 1936), pp. 134–149.

22. C.-M. Forest, "L'américanisation par le sport," *Revue dominicaine* (June 1936), pp. 348–363.

23. Rousseau, *L'image des États-Unis*, Chapter III.

24. Susan Mann Trofimenkoff, *L'action française: French Canadian Nationalism in the Twenties* (Toronto: University of Toronto Press, 1975).

25. Adélard Dugré, *La campagne canadienne* (1925), quoted in Rousseau, *L'image des États-Unis*, p. 109.

26. Hermas Bastien, *Le bilinguisme au Canada* (1938), quoted in Rousseau, *L'image des États-Unis*, p. 118.

27. Yvan Lamonde, Lucia Ferretti, and Daniel LeBlanc, *La culture ouvrière á Montréal (1880–1920): bilan historiographique* (Quebec: Institut québécois de recherche sur la culture, 1982), pp. 25–26, 31.

28. For example, A. Janin, "Notre américanisation par le cinéma," pp. 69–70.

29. Y. Lamonde, "A History of Mass Culture and the Media," *Cultures* (UNESCO) 8(1), 1981, pp. 9–16.

30. Pioneer works by Canadians H. A. Innis and Dallas W. Smythe; W. H. Melody, L. Salter, and P. Heyer, *Culture, Communication, and Dependency:*

126   Yvan Lamonde

the Tradition of H. A. Innis (Norwood, NJ: Ablex, 1980); D. W. Smythe, *Dependency Road: Communications, Capitalism, Consciousness and Canada* (Norwood, NJ: Ablex, 1981); and the work of Herbert Schiller, Armand Mattelart, and Jeremy Tunstall.

. Lamonde and Hébert, *Le cinéma au Québec*, p. 81 and Table 79.

. Maistre, "L'influence de la radio et de la télévision américaines au Canada," p. 66; Roger de la Garde, "L'information internationale dans les médias québécois et anglo-canadiens: la fenêtre américaine," *Communication et Information* 4(1), 1981, pp. 7–31; and Gertrude Joch Robinson, *News Agencies and World News in Canada, the United States and Yugoslavia: Methods and Data* (Fribourg, Switzerland: University Press of Fribourg, 1981), particularly pp. 149–187.

. *Royal Commission on Publications* (Ottawa: Queen's Printer, 1961), p. 228; André Patry, "La dualité canadienne et les relations canado-américaines," *La dualité canadienne*, pp. 16–17; and *Rapport sur la distribution des périodiques et du livre de poche au Québec* (Quebec: Éditeur officiel du Québec, 1976). For partial summaries on American aid for Quebec research (Carnegie, Rockefeller, Guggenheim, etc.), *Report of the Royal Commission on National Development in the Arts, Letters and Sciences,* Special Studies (Ottawa: Queen's Printer, 1951), pp. 436–439, 441–442, 497–500.

. Lamonde and Hébert, *Le cinéma au Québec*, pp. 103–104 and Tables 125 and 126.

. Ibid., pp. 105–107 and Table 127.

. Ibid., pp. 106–107 and Table 129.

. Ibid., pp. 74–77 and Tables 72-74.

. Daniel Monnier, "Les québécois, la langue et les médias," in *Conférences sur la situation de la langue française au Québec* (Quebec: Conseil de la langue française, Notes et documents 13, 1981), pp. 75–92; and Louise Gendron, "Incertitude québécoise. Télévision: Good morning America," *Le monde diplomatique* 321 (December 1980), p. 37.

. Edith Bédard and Daniel Monnier, *Conscience linguistique des jeunes québécois: influence de l'environnement linguistique chez les élèves francophones de niveau secondaire IV et V* (Quebec: Éditeur officiel—Conseil de la langue française, Études et recherches 9[1], 1981), 164 pp.

. Carol Kirsh, Brian Dixon, Michael Bond, *A Leisure Study: Canada 1972* (Ottawa: Secretary of State, 1973); and Rolf E. Schliewen, *A Leisure Study: Canada 1975* (Ottawa: Secretary of State, 1977).

. Jonathan M. Weiss, "Les Plouffe et l'américanisme au Québec," *Canadian Review of Studies in Nationalism* 3 (1975–1976), pp. 226–230.

. Susan Crean and Marcel Rioux, *Deux pays pour vivre: un plaidoyer* (Montreal: Editions coopératives Albert-St. Martin, 1980).

8

A Return to Roots?
Quebec in Louisiana

Gerald L. Gold

Background

In Quebec over the last fifty years there has been a recurring interest in establishing a relationship with Louisiana, and in particular with French-speaking Louisiana. The first series of exchanges, from 1930 to 1937, were organized by Omer Héroux of *Le Devoir* in Montreal, and Dudley LeBlanc, an entrepreneur-politician from Abbeville, Louisiana.[1] Though these visits, or "pilgrimages," did not involve the participation of the government of Quebec, the participants included prominent priests, politicians, judges, and representatives from both Laval University and the University of Montreal. The Quebec involvement was strongly linked to an ideology of French "survival" in North America and its rhetoric evoked a messianic myth of Acadian survival. The rhetoric of the Louisiana initiative alluded to reunification of the two Acadias. Its thrust depended on the political guile of a single man, LeBlanc. The thousands of Louisianians who welcomed the "Acadian" visitors from Quebec and New Brunswick neither shared a national ethnic ideology nor supported an ethnic institutional infrastructure such as a national church, a national association, or French-language schools.

The details of *Le Devoir's* extensive front-page attention to the rediscovery of French Louisiana are well documented elsewhere. But it is important to consider the rationale behind this intensive interelite exchange—now forgotten by Québécois, Acadians, and Louisiana French—because it can be viewed as a prelude to the sudden establishment of formal Quebec-Louisiana ties in 1969 and the emergence of a Quebec policy for dealing with the Louisiana French. It is equally important to identify a continuity in Quebec influence on ethnic nationalism in Louisiana and, specifically, the role of Quebec in the rise of a movement within Louisiana for the revival of French language and culture. The objectives of this discussion are first to bring out those cultural and social factors that have influenced the definition of a "Louisiana dossier" by representatives of the Quebec government and by those who shape public opinion in Quebec. A second objective is to identify the perception of Quebec within French Louisiana and some of the impact that Quebec policies have had on what some French-speaking Louisianians refer to as *Le mouvement*.[2]

These objectives are not easily met because Louisiana has always been a peripheral part of Quebec's involvement in the French-speaking world, even though the Lafayette delegation was one of the first that the Quebec government opened in the United States.[3] Official documentation on Quebec's presence is sparse, and there has been a considerable turnover of personnel responsible for the Louisiana dossier over the thirteen-year period of formal Quebec-Louisiana ties (1969–1982). This official relationship spans three different political regimes in Quebec and four successive Quebec delegates in Lafayette, Louisiana.

My data for this period comes from interviews with three of the four official delegates, from discussions with officials of the Ministry of Intergovernmental Affairs (*Ministére des affaires intergouvernmentales*), from Quebec French teachers in Louisiana, and from extensive participant observation between 1975 and 1980. The perspective of this inquiry is an integral part of the research by *Projet Louisiane*,[4] an interuniversity project that has completed three regional studies and six related subregional studies that seek to unravel the complex relationship between the changing social and cultural adaptations of dispersed French-speaking Louisianians and regional support for ethnic revival.

An important finding of this research is that there are a number of contradictions between the regional manifestations of French revival and the changing objectives of CODOFIL, the Council on Development of French in Louisiana (*Le conseil pour le développement du français en Louisiane*), which is the most visible promoter of an organized revival of French language and culture in Louisiana. Because the CODOFIL program involves the placement of Quebec (and French and Belgian) teachers within regional school systems, the Quebec presence has exerted an important influence from the inception of a Louisiana French movement in the 1960s. The Quebec government was instrumental in the original design of the CODOFIL school program and successive Quebec delegates influenced the Louisiana "French movement" with direct and indirect actions.

On an individual level, when Québécois university graduates from Lac St. Jean, Gaspé, or Montreal become visible temporary newcomers within insular French-speaking communities such as Ville Platte or Rayne, Louisiana, regional ethnic identities come into contact with the transnational program to preserve Louisiana French. For the successive Quebec delegates and for their counterparts in Quebec City, the actions of individual teachers are part of an unfolding Quebec understanding of French Louisiana society and its significance to Quebec government objectives. In terms of actual programs, this assessment brought about a major redefinition of Quebec objectives in Louisiana. But in terms of the underlying Quebec ideology of involvement in French Louisiana, there has been little if any change from the first renewal of Quebec contacts in 1968.

The most significant development is the increasing importance of Quebec as a model for supporters of the Louisiana French movement. This change is also tied with an attempt to organize ethnic associations that represent all Franco-Americans. The prospect of an organized Franco-American collectivity, rather than a return to providential myths of an earlier era, is an astute political move to concentrate efforts at getting more resources from Washington for the teaching of French language and culture. Quebec has shown a particular interest in such ethnic alliances, at least during its pre-referendum period, because the American francophone minorities provide an alternate constituency to the Canadian French minorities in supporting and legitimating the Québécois claim to be a francophone nation in North America.

Change in South Louisiana and the Decline of Elite Contacts with Quebec

Creoles and Quebec

Contacts between the Louisiana French and French-Canadians were not always channeled through the Acadian elites of Southwestern Louisiana. In the nineteenth century, white Creole elites in New Orleans established a range of institutions ranging from schools to theaters and publishing houses. Their contacts were predominantly with France and French civilization in Louisiana. Liaison was renewed regularly in transatlantic links that followed nineteenth-century arrival of planters from the French West Indies and European French who migrated to Louisiana after the two Napoleonic wars and throughout the nineteenth and early twentieth centuries. Though the white Creoles and the French immigrants were a relatively small population compared to the more heterogeneous, rural, French-speaking population, they were primarily, though not exclusively, an urban group and initially they shared little interest in the Acadian and Canadian origins of Cajun farmers and fishermen whom they did not consider to be cultural kindred.

This European orientation of the white Creoles was hardly effective in countering the Americanization of Louisiana and a decline in economic and political power of planter elites after the Civil War. Few of the Creole leaders saw the unification of the linguistically and culturally heterogeneous francophone population of the state as a means of maintaining their class position. The institutional response of the old elite and the creation of cultural groups such as *l'Athènée Louisianaise* in 1876 were inner-directed actions that would not delay the Americanization of their milieu.[5] Cultural contacts between New Orleans Creoles and Cajuns (Acadians and other non-Creole French-speakers in Southwestern Louisiana) had always been discouraged because of the class differentials between the two groups. It follows that links with France were of a higher priority than ties to Quebec. Even in 1977, interviews revealed that many white Creole respondents placed a higher value on contacts with France than with a lower-status Quebec.

Another reason for the absence of linguistically-defined ethnic unity is that, until the late nineteenth century, language and class also crossed the color line; Louisiana had a large number of communities of "people of color" (*gens de couleur*) who participated in many of the French-language institutions of the state. However, with the Jim Crow laws that followed Reconstruction, ambiguities in the color line were relegated to regionally-recognized distinctions and were of no wider political importance. In the late nineteenth century the meaning of the term Creole gradually shifted to also include black French-speakers.[6] The superimposition of sharper racial divisions on the French/"américain" division (where the "américains" were the English-speaking outsiders) would later lead to the situation in which blacks abstained from participating in the French revival movement.

This fission of the francophone population troubled many visitors from Quebec throughout the fifty years of recent contacts. The French-Canadian historian and ideologist Lionel Groulx capsulizes the reaction of many Québécois to the tension between French-speaking "Acadian" whites and French-speaking blacks by resolutely assigning the Louisianians their martyred Acadian status: "This goes on in the land of this little exiled people who have suffered so much and who should be able to understand the misery of others! Oh the misery of Protestantism that permits human brotherhood to be forgotten!"[7]

It may be the very "cultured" status of the white Creoles and their distance from the Acadian myth that earned them little sympathy from French-Canadians. Nonetheless, Creole cultural leaders began to turn toward Quebec at the time when their institutions were facing catastrophe. At the turn of the century, the more cosmopolitan white Creole leaders were already known to the Quebec elites. This tenuous link was maintained by leaders such as historian Alcée Fortier, president of *l'Athènée Louisianaise*, who traveled to Montreal in 1912 to report on the tragedy of the dismantling of French institutions in Louisiana.[8] Quebec and Acadian reactions to the significance of this appeal are aptly captured by historian Antoine Bernard: "Let us say it frankly. The French elite of New Orleans, refined to the point of 'preciosity,' demonstrate a clear indifference toward the 'Acadian' speech of the Bayous that prejudices the overall cause of the French language in the state."[9]

Quebeckers' Perceptions Versus Acadian Realities

Though the first Quebec links with the Acadian elites were closer and more enduring, after the first few enthusiastic inter-elite exchanges, the continuation of the relationship was relegated to a few individuals who were committed to the survival of a wider *Acadie*. The Quebec Catholic church received the Louisiana visitors of 1930 with unrestrained enthusiasm, but the number of Quebec priests sent to Louisiana did not increase, and within Louisiana the Catholic church was at best lukewarm toward the idea of encouraging the establishment of national parishes[10] or of promoting cultural and linguistic ties with Quebec.

Quebec elites continued to regard Louisiana Cajuns and Creoles as Acadians and the Louisianians tended to support such an image by visitors from Quebec until the 1970s. The northern visitors were primarily concerned about the survival of a large Catholic French-speaking community. Few of the published reports, however, show that the visitors had more than a rudimentary knowledge of where the Louisiana French worked, and more importantly, to what extent French identities influenced state politics.

The major Louisiana supporters of an expanded relationship with Quebec were drawn from the Acadian elites of St. Martin and Lafayette parishes where there is a concentration of Acadian settlers, as well as descendants of Creole planters who have in many cases redefined themselves as Acadian by emphasizing their Acadian ancestors. The region also has a large black minority, which is also French speaking and culturally heterogeneous. Though the black population of Breaux Bridge, as well as some of the white population of the same region, speaks Creole French, this community served as the model Acadian town for visiting francophone dignitaries ranging from Lionel Groulx in 1931 to René Lévesque in 1979.

Acadian identity in Louisiana was nurtured by a small fraction of the region's population. Moreover, though the Acadian elite of the region has succeeded in attracting a national and international network, there was never any concerted attempt to mobilize popular ethnic sentiment among the French-speaking farmers, fishermen, and petroleum workers.

The elite identity, infused with the metaphor of Longfellow's *Evangeline*, remained a symbol of a transplanted legitimacy, unstained by the tar brush of the racial pluralism of antebellum Louisiana.

Except for the small group of known contacts in Breaux Bridge and Lafayette, the Louisiana French were considered to be beyond the sphere of influence of French Canada. After the second Conference on the French Language, held in Montreal in 1937, Quebec contacts with Louisiana were left to Louisianians and Québécois who worked with the Committee for the Survival of French (*Comité de la survivance française*) of the newly established Council on French Life in America (*Conseil de la vie française en Amérique* or CVFA) in Quebec City. The CVFA sent an Acadian historian, Brother Antoine Bernard, to Louisiana in 1941 and again in 1949, with the objective of keeping its contacts in Acadian southwestern Louisiana. But Bernard's Louisiana network atrophied as his prewar elite contacts lost their prominence in the socioeconomic changes that followed the war.

Another visible Québécois in Louisiana elite circles was politician-genealogist Bona Arsenault, who made repeated trips to Louisiana in the postwar years. Arsenault, Dudley LeBlanc, and the CVFA again attempted to renew the vigorous exchanges of the 1930s on the occasion of the bicentennial of the Acadian expulsion in 1955 when a delegation of 132 Québécois traveled to southwestern Louisiana. But by then there was no widespread interest in the minority French within Quebec. In Louisiana, assimilative pressures in Cajun and Creole communities increased dramatically in the postwar years and few were optimistic about the future of the French language. Despite this pessimism, channels of communication that were left open between Louisiana "Acadian" and French-Canadian elites facilitated the renewal of contact in the 1960s.

Before World War II, French was spoken by all generations in a thirteen-parish (county) triangle of southwestern Louisiana. Even in 1970, 572,162 Louisianians were reported by the U.S. census to be of French mother tongue, a figure that exceeds similar census statistics for every Canadian province except Quebec and Ontario. But the decline of the French language in Louisiana had already begun after the Civil War. The decline was gradual due to the concentration of French-speakers in rural primary resource industries and the relatively late extension of effective universal education in the state of Louisiana.

Post-1945 Developments

After the war, French use receded most sharply among those who were born after 1952 and in urban areas. It is important to emphasize that French remained the language of work in small towns, in farming communities, in fishing, and in the blue-collar domains of the petro-chemical industry that have became economically important in the last thirty years.[11] Within the towns, where much of the population has been recently displaced from manual farming of cotton and sugar and from wild resource-capture industries, there was a revival of traditional music and dance as the former inhabitants of isolated rural hamlets reconstructed their social life in the towns.[12] Most of this popular revival, expressed in radio programs, recordings, and French-language control of local politics,[13] was invisible to the non-French population of Louisiana and, until the 1970s, even more transparent to Québécois and other francophones.[14]

Most French-speaking Louisianians were sufficiently removed from the French culture of the cities that they are still predominantly unaware of the removal of French language rights by the state legislature during the nineteenth century, which was a period when many rural Cajuns were antagonistic toward compulsory education.[15] In this light, the creation of a legally bilingual Louisiana in 1968 did not have the same impact as a similar action in a Canada where language has been a political issue.

Within individual families, the decision not to raise children to speak French appears to be correlated with the shame and stigma felt by many French-speaking Louisianians after their first contacts with film, exclusively English-language schools, middle-class consumer culture, and the difficulties of coping with an English-speaking U.S. Army or Navy during World War II.

By far the most important economic factor contributing to the decline of French was the breakup of the domestic unit of production in farming, fishing, and trapping. Oilfield work and wage labor led to the separation of male and female work worlds and to the emergence of linguistic-dimensioned sex roles. Rural and small-town women expressly prepared their children for an English-speaking middle-class United States, al-though their husbands, often speaking French in their work, projected a very different image within the local community.[16] In many families the major force keeping French alive was (and is) an insistence by functionally unilingual grandparents on speaking French with their children and older grandchildren.

Quebec's second involvement in this complex socioeconomic milieu was not a result of any of these regional changes. But since Quebec was to send teachers into the changing rural areas and interact extensively with French-speaking leaders, and because there are some similarities to the minority situation of French-Canadians in Canada, Quebec representatives have developed a more thorough understanding of the minority situation in Louisiana than have their French or Belgian counterparts.[17]

When Quebec Premier Jean Lesage quietly made an official trip to Louisiana in 1963, after consulting the financiers and policymakers in New York and in Washington,[18] the notion of *l'Amérique française* or of a French "race" in North America was of low priority to the new Quebec nationalism of the Quiet Revolution, and thereby to the Liberal Lesage government. In another respect the French-speaking minorities in the United States provided Quebec with an opportunity to extend its political influence with a powerful neighbor. However, within the United States, the Lesage initiative toward an "international vocation for Quebec" had little immediate impact—perhaps as one source claims, on account of anti-American indiscretions by Eric Kierans, then Quebec Minister of Revenue.

Another elite pilgrimage to Louisiana would have sparked enough interest to make the social pages rather then the headlines of *Le Devoir*. In the minds of some nationalists, the image of a French Louisiana had became a negative symbol of the future of Quebec. In the words of a past president of the *Société Saint-Jean-Baptiste* who maintained channels of communication with Louisiana: "It was when I was in Louisiana that I decided to become an indépendentiste in Quebec. I could see clearly an image of a future Quebec where French would be reduced to insignificance . . . I am indebted to them for the making of my political commitment."[19]

The Lesage cabinet kept its options open. In 1965, Minister Pierre Laporte traveled to Louisiana for the events connected with Léonard Forêt's work for the National Film Office to commemorate the 210th anniversary of the Acadian deportation. Historian Guy Frégault, representing the Quebec Ministry of Intergovernmental Affairs, followed Laporte in June 1965, in a trip that permitted Bona Arsenault to introduce Frégault to his network within the Louisiana "Acadian" elite (Wade O. Martin, then secretary of state for Louisiana, and Roy Thériot, who was considered a pivotal figure in the statewide contacts between Acadians). Frégault held unprecedented discussions with Louisiana's superintendent of education and strongly urged his colleagues to consider a cultural agreement between Quebec and Louisiana.[20] The stage was set for a shift in Quebec's policy. Between 1965 and 1968 a number of events both in Quebec and in Louisiana served to push both sides toward a formal partnership.

Within Quebec several factors favored a Quebec presence in Louisiana:

1. The Gaullist emphasis on *francophonie* was strongly supported within the Union Nationale government of Daniel Johnson (1966–1968) and by his successor Jean-Jacques Bertrand

(1968–1970). During this period Quebec was opening a number of delegations and seeking to define its own role within a North American *francophonie* with which Québécois had built up strong networks of contact over the previous decades. The contacts with the United States were, however, somewhat more delicate in that Quebec City did not wish to do anything to disturb Washington following the De Gaulle affair in Montreal. This notion of a special role for Quebec vis-à-vis Franco-American minorities emerges more clearly with the Parti Québécois "Louisiana policy," but it was an integral part of the rationale that led Quebec to a relationship with Louisiana.

2. But as Frégault explains in his memoirs, his exploratory trip to Louisiana was "part of small competition with Canada." He enjoyed the parallel between his aloofness toward English Canada and the manner in which many Cajuns would situationally refer to English speakers as "Américains."[21]

3. Frégault's policy in intergovernmental affairs was not to reject the value of conservative traditional minority leaders—the elites of the traditional resistance—partially because it is this leadership that controls the only associations that could give Quebec access to the minorities. The private social networks of these leaders were otherwise closed to outsiders.[22]

4. A fourth factor is more subtle and "primordial" in terms of Quebec culture. It ties in to a revival of Quebec folk music in the late 1960s and a new appreciation for Acadian folklore. Many Québécois had been captivated by the Cajun music they heard at Montreal's Expo 67 and elsewhere. Once in Louisiana, they felt, they could strongly identify with traditional Cajun culture as something distantly related to them. In the same way as Quebec's mission in Louisiana would become more explicit, the inflow of Louisiana musicians and of Cajun music would have an important effect on Quebec popular culture.

    It is difficult to assess the emotional power of Louisiana oral culture on the first official Quebec delegations, though the first delegate, Léo Leblanc, spent several weeks at the beginning of his six-year posting becoming familiar with the musical style of the Cajuns and the philosophical meanings and double entendres within Cajun music.

There is reliable indirect evidence that Quebec's actions in Louisiana were strongly encouraged in Paris, particularly by Philippe Rossillon, Rapporteur of the *Haut Comité de la Langue française*, who was expelled from Canada in 1968 for allegedly encouraging radicalism among fran- cophone minorities. Rossillon came to Louisiana in 1969, shortly after

Quebec signed a cooperation agreement, and through his committee role continued to monitor closely the activities of CODOFIL and of the Louisiana French movement. It would be an error, however, to link Quebec's Louisiana policy too closely with French foreign policy. The Quebec delegates have enjoyed considerable freedom of action in Louisiana and the Louisianians are difficult to manipulate. Finally, many Québécois who have been sent to Louisiana have been uneasy about the French presence or about the attitudes of superiority of some of the French.[23]

The Louisiana disposition toward Quebec is far more complex principally on account of the decentralization of the political process. In Louisiana, power and decisions often emanate through the influence and charisma of a leader, and conflict over objectives within government is more apparent than is the case in Quebec. The situation is appropriately capsulized in Huey Long's (borrowed) electoral slogan "Every man a king but no one wears a crown."[24] In Cajun communities, politicians can carry the rhetoric of equality to extremes. As one candidate for parish policy jury said of his opponent (in French): "I'm not against the 'big dogs' . . . but I certainly like you as much as I like them."[25] It follows that there is no single Louisiana policy toward Quebec, and the attitude of politicians toward Quebec participation in CODOFIL varies greatly from parish to parish.

In the late 1960s, white ethnic movements flourished throughout the United States, following the earlier rise of the civil rights and black power movements. In southwestern Louisiana there was widespread feeling that something should be done to save French language and culture. Moreover, in keeping with regional political style, there were several claimants to the throne, or in the words of one astute observer, "kings in waiting."

James Domengeaux, member of the House of Representatives before World War II and prominent Lafayette lawyer and politician, had been raised in Lafayette and Breaux Bridge, with an Acadian mother and a Creole father (who also had been a politician). Early in his political career, Domengeaux was a political opponent of Dudley LeBlanc and was unlikely to have supported LeBlanc (a claimant to the throne) at the helm of an association to preserve French in Louisiana. A brief summary of the events leading to the founding of CODOFIL is necessary to bring out how Guy Frégault was brought back into the Louisiana negotiations and why Louisiana moved so quickly toward an agreement with Quebec.

According to Domengeaux and others who worked to found CODOFIL, it took three outsiders, Raymond Rodgers, an entrepreneurial British political scientist, and two traveling Quebec students, to contact him in 1967 and persuade him that he was the person who could lead a new organization. For the balance of the year, Rodgers researched the juridical basis of a bill to establish CODOFIL and worked on a first draft of an agreement between Quebec and Louisiana. Rodgers also began negotiating an agreement with the Director of Cooperation (*Directeur de la coopération*) of Quebec's Ministry of Cultural Affairs (*ministére des affaires culturelles*), billing himself as an "aide-de-camp of Governor McKeithen."

As a result of the various representations by Rodgers, on September 7, 1967, the governor received a draft agreement from Quebec with a proposal for a summit meeting or an exchange of official letters. However, Quebec's Jean-Paul L'Allier, a minister in the Union Nationale government, considered the letters to be an inadequate base for an agreement and insisted, in February 1968, that Governor McKeithen and Premier Johnson meet before the signing of any agreement. Rodgers took the next step by arranging the official twinning of Lafayette and Longeuil (where Mayor Robidas initially thought that the proposal was for a twinning with New Orleans).

Quebec was still silent when the Louisiana legislature unanimously passed the CODOFIL legislation and several bills that restored symbolic official bilingualism to Louisiana, facilitated the training of second-language specialists, and supported the development of French-language educational television. There was no mention of extensive transnational assistance, and there was also no appropriation for the new bills. Domengeaux, a supporter of Governor McKeithen, arranged that there be no opposition.

When the new bills arrived in Quebec City and the Quebec memorandum of September 1967 was still unanswered, a puzzled Gaston Cholette of the Ministry of Intergovernmental Affairs advised Baton Rouge that an agreement was premature. He was then contacted by Wade O. Martin, Jr., secretary of state of Louisiana and prominent Acadian from St. Martin parish who had traveled to Quebec with his father in 1937 for the Second Congress of the French Language (*Deuxième Congrès de la Langue française*). Martin suggested an official Quebec mission to finalize preparations for a final agreement. Gaston Cholette departed for Louisiana in October 1968, with the personal objective of justifying a Quebec role in the linguistic and cultural revival of French in Louisiana.[26]

The Cholette Report

Cholette's brief visit led to a position paper that became an influential document in the framing of a Quebec policy toward Louisiana. Significantly, he did not attach much importance to his contacts with the old Acadian network or to Martin's warnings that Louisiana was reluctant to exacerbate tensions between France and Canada. Cholette did attach a great deal of importance to a meeting in St. Martinville of a thousand people, including the governor, fifty legislators from Baton Rouge, and the French consul general, at which a CODOFIL chapter was founded in St. Martin parish. He notes sardonically that Canada's roving ambassador, Lionel Chevrier, refused an invitation to the same meeting even though he was in Lafayette, ten miles away, to donate books to the University of Southwestern Louisiana library. In a drama that could not have been more appropriately arranged in Quebec City or in the law offices of Mr. Domengeaux, Quebec became the Louisiana ally for the nascent French movement.

In a few days of observation, Cholette demonstrated his understanding of Louisiana minority French populations and his belief in international francophone cooperation as the solution to their problems:

1. Cholette concurred with Frégault that the identity of the Louisiana French was reduced to a private ethnicity that called for a situational use of French. Delegates from Quebec would need to make the effort to penetrate the intimateness of those groups who seemed to be ashamed of speaking their language poorly and who used it only within their own circles.
2. With a Québécois emphasis on education, Cholette realized that the schools had "depersonalized" the "Acadians," though education had given them access to positions of command. He then seriously misinterpreted the CODOFIL legislation with the conclusion that "French would be required at all levels" and that the schools would be "one of the pillars of the French revival."
3. Québécois and French participation would ensure that Louisianians could discover that it "is normal to live in French." In assuring the salvage of French in Louisiana, Quebec would be demonstrating "its special role in a North American *francophonie* . . . without having to limit its ambitions to being a province like the others [Canadian] within the framework of confederation."
4. Cholette recommended massive exchanges that could lead to a "visible Frenchness" in Louisiana (a proposal that included a Richelieu Club in Lafayette).

The Quebec Presence in Louisiana

The Delegate and His Role

Léo Leblanc was appointed by Quebec Prime Minister Jean-Jacques Bertrand as the first Quebec delegate to Louisiana in 1969. Leblanc began a series of actions with CODOFIL that were of great importance to the Quebec presence and to the Louisiana French movement in the years that followed.

Léo Leblanc was a strategic choice as Quebec's first delegate. His background and training made him acceptable to several constituencies. As a bilingual Acadian he was acceptable to the Louisianians and understood their minority status. His family name was one of the most common among Louisiana Acadians. Leblanc was married to an American, a graduate of Laval University and a former journalist. All of these characteristics proved to be important assets when Domengeaux turned to the new Quebec delegate to assist him in the organization of CODOFIL.

The first challenge faced by Leblanc was to convince his own government of the urgency of signing a formal agreement with Louisiana. In practice, this plan involved convincing the lanky Louisiana governor and a contingent of supporters, including a tin-starred sheriff and Cajun musicians, to travel to Quebec City in 1969. In its implementation the plan did not have the diplomatic luster appropriate to Quebec City but the strategy did work. After convincing Quebec that Lafayette was a plausible location for the Quebec delegation, rather than Baton Rouge or New Orleans, a Quebec delegation headed by Minister Marcel Masse signed a cooperation agreement in Natchitoches, Louisiana, in November 1969. The Quebec-Louisiana Permanent Committee, which emerged from the Natchitoches agreement, continues to meet annually to renegotiate the terms of the exchange. This series of circumstantial events, combined with official cultural policies, led the Quebec government to negotiate an official presence among the Louisiana French.

Leblanc arrived in Lafayette with the objective of pursuing "an international objective for Quebec . . . an opening to the world (*rayonnement*)." Initially, he found it difficult to define precisely a unique role for Louisiana in Quebec. His task was complicated by the absence of a mass participation in CODOFIL and by the concentration of authority by Domengeaux. Meanwhile, the Quebec delegate wrote numerous CODOFIL press releases, the CODOFIL parish manual, and assisted in the preparation of a much-quoted speech by Congressman F. Edward Hébert, which defended the need for international participation in the French movement and the value to the United States of making Louisiana a "window on the French-speaking world."[27] With these actions, Quebec was, in effect, cooperatively creating an institutional French presence in Louisiana.

Quebec and CODOFIL

A constant concern of the Québécois was that the CODOFIL program be legitimated by the public and by government. Thus when several surveys were carried out in 1969–1972 to verify the number of French-speaking Louisianians, Leblanc recognized the action as a political maneuver and Quebec cooperated. Likewise, when Bill 714 (1975) was passed in the Louisiana legislature to permit parents to petition for French elementary instruction, and when the CODOFIL appropriation eventually did become an issue, the Québécois (with French and other francophones) were present in the state capitol to see if all went well. Some of the information on Quebec's intentions and on CODOFIL's (Domengeaux's) intentions reached the delegates or Domengeaux through managed leaks in either the Quebec or the CODOFIL office, where it was known that certain staff members had a tendency to keep the other side informed.

At the same time, Quebec agreed to the CODOFIL strategy of presenting the French language program as a second language that would be taught to an international standard. Quebec also agreed with Domengeaux's strategy of insisting that the CODOFIL policy would not be a nationalistic course of action and that in no way would the program envisage "the supplanting of English."[28] Foreign French teachers were to be sent to both English-speaking and French-speaking parishes with the emphasis to be placed on the international value of a second standard language. Though Quebec, and to some degree CODOFIL, would later retreat from this position, these were the objectives presented to the French teachers who arrived from Quebec in 1972.

In one respect the opening of Louisiana to the world francophone community was an immediately successful step. A constant stream of international francophone visitors turned up in Lafayette: journalists, politicians, muscians, artists, and businessmen. For many the decision to visit Lafayette was motivated by curiosity and the feeling that something exciting might be happening to the French language in South Louisiana. By 1972 Louisiana had already carved a place for itself in the new *francophonie*, and Domengeaux traveled to France and opted to use the familiar *tu* to charm President Pompidou into sending a large contingent of *coopérants militaires*, conscripts who were carrying out alternate military service, as French teachers in Louisiana schools. A substantial level of international aid followed to assure that the metropolitan French teachers would bring an acceptable international French to Louisiana.

As the Quebec delegate became more involved with CODOFIL, he also, like CODOFIL itself, was isolated from the regional roots of Cajun culture. Quebec's visible contribution between 1969 and 1972 was the provision of specialists to work with the Louisiana State Department of Education on the design of a second-language French program for Louisiana elementary schools. A second initiative, with the greatest long-term benefits for Quebec, was the opening of a summer study program for Louisiana students, first at the CEGEP (approximately equivalent to a U.S. junior college) in Jonquière, Quebec, and then later in Rivière-du-Loup. As a consequence of over twelve years of operation thousands of Louisianians have become familar with "living in French" in Quebec, and some of these summer students later took an active role in the French movement.[29]

The Quebec participation in the CODOFIL school program drew Leblanc and his succesors into the politics of education in Louisiana. Domengeaux's political network became critical to CODOFIL in that two successive superintendents of education (Michot and Nix) and the director of foreign language programs (which is where official bilingualism enters the State Department of Education) depended on Domengeaux's influence with the superintendent of education. It did not take long for Leblanc to enter the network of communication that is managed through daily telephone calls to the State Department of Education in Baton Rouge.

When the first contingent of Quebec teachers was recruited in 1972, most were CEGEP graduates and many were unsuitable for teaching in conservative rural schools. Even after teacher qualifications were raised, Quebec was unable to contribute trained teachers. An additional problem arose when a jurisdictional dispute broke out between the Lafayette representative of the Cooperation Office of the Quebec Ministry of Education and Leblanc, representing the Ministry of Intergovernmental Affairs. Leblanc rejected an application of the "French cooperation model" to Louisiana. The problem, as he explained it to me in 1975, is that "everything is unstructured in Louisiana, a point that the people in Quebec do not always understand."

The Québécois in CODOFIL

> We are North Americans who speak French. . . . The history of the Acadian deportation moves us deeply—it's visceral—and we are not here to find out whether it's going to work with our Acadian brothers. It is an act of faith to the challenge that they have brought forward. [A Quebec French teacher on arrival in Louisiana in 1975.]

Quebec hired an average of forty French teachers a year from 1972 through 1982 to assist with both the CODOFIL program and the U.S. Title VII bilingual education programs. In general, Québécois teachers adapted well to the everyday activities of French-speaking communities and many managed to make friends with Cajun musicians and with young Cajuns who were seeking cultural or grass roots revival of the oral culture of their grandparents. In many other instances teachers from Quebec would not hesitate to break what they considered to be archaic or racist social conventions (e.g., dating across the racial line).

Louisiana French teachers and local elites were not always accommodating to Québécois syntax and pronunciations. In Lafayette, several of the delegates noted that the elite were biased toward according greater respect to the European or "real" French teachers. Other administrators reacted strongly to the Quebec nationalism expressed by some of the teachers. School administrators could not rely on European supervisors (the *conseillers pédagogiques*) to control Quebec teachers in that they would not respond to the threat of demerit that would affect their future job opportunities. In a number of cases in which Quebec teachers were unhappy they went home for Christmas and did not return.

But these problems were not exclusive to the Québécois. The delegates did manage to solve most of the difficulties. Few foreign teachers, with the exception of the Belgians, were trained in teaching and fewer still were knowledgeable second-language teachers. Also, until recently, the orientation session was very minimal and incoming teachers knew little about the society in which they would be working (for up to three years). Finally, teachers received an often hopelessly contradictory set of instructions from homeroom teachers, principals, superintendents, CODOFIL supervisors, *conseillers pédagogiques* of their respective nations (Quebec has sent as many as two, France has had as many as five), and so-called "bilingual specialists" working with the Louisiana State Department of Education.

The Quebec solution became to focus on social and cultural *animation*, something that Louisianians generally felt was best done by Québécois. Quebec teachers and the delegation staff took a relatively important role in community activities organized by CODOFIL. The Québécois also did a great deal to better adapt the European-developed CODOFIL teaching techniques (the Frère Jacques method) to Louisiana. Finally, the Quebec teachers were regrouped so that most worked in the vicinity of Lafayette where there was always a small Québécois support network and a compatible and nonauthoritarian *counseiller pédagogique*.

Almost all the Quebec French teachers interviewed in 1977 were troubled by the loss of Cajun French and cultural identity. Frequently, in the metaphor of Gilles Vigneault's *Quand nous partirons pour la Louisiana* ("When we all leave for Louisiana"), the loss of identity was seen as something that could well happen to themselves as Québécois. However, despite statements by CODOFIL leaders that the Québécois teachers were linguistic missionaries, most of our respondents were cautious about the question of Quebec's responsibility to Louisiana. They did not wish to be paternalistic or to be present if they were unwanted.

Some were disturbed because formerly stigmatized aspects of regional culture—music, folklore, and Cajun or Creole French—were still given a very low profile in the classroom. The closest that most CODOFIL students could get to those who still speak French as a dominant language was with the maintenance men, the cooks, or their own grandparents.

The Quebec teachers and the delegate himself were for the most part anxious to encourage cultural revival in French Louisiana and at the same time inculcate an awareness of Quebec as a source of serious assistance for that revival. There was a general malaise before 1979 that Quebec was participating in a program that was neither of its own making nor compatible with Québécois objectives. The French infused five times the number of teachers and three times the overall budget, and it was their ideology of cooperation that prevailed. In the words of the first delegate in a letter to his first permanent *conseiller péda-gogique*:

> It is shameful that Quebec must use overseas methods for the teaching of her mother tongue at home and on her own continent. Teachers arriving for their training period in Baton Rouge must immediately cope with French methods that were largely "dumped" on the Gulf Coast without charge. It is a standard practice in these French teaching methods not to discuss Quebec. This situation profoundly shocks newly arrived Quebec teachers. When the Québécois will be a proud people they will create their own teaching methods for themselves and for the continent that they founded.[30]

Broader changes came after Leblanc was replaced by a new delegate. A transnational appraisal team strongly criticized the lack of objectives and consistency in the CODOFIL program and its failure to establish effective linkages with French Louisiana culture.[31] But by 1977 the Quebec officials were aware that Quebec could not reform the problems in Louisiana's school system, and though Quebec continued to send teachers and cultural resource persons, the greatest impact of Quebec over the four years ending in 1982 has been, in my assessment, on the direction taken by the French movement.

The Parti Québécois in Louisiana

Québec is discovering Louisiana.
But Louisiane is also discovering Québec.

                                Jules Poisson, Quebec delegate in Lafayette, July 1977

De nouveau, l'Acadie est en exil,
Volontairement pour une fois, pour une
   raison.

A Québec, à Moncton, à Paris.
Richard, Broussard, Guidry,
Jeunes Cadiens s'attachent à
  des nourrices
Pour de préparer pour une
rennaissance, Cette fois
vraie, née d'un mariage légitime
La musique ayant enfin épousé la langue
. . . . *31*

[Once again, Acadia is in exile
This time voluntarily, and for a
  reason.
In Quebec, Moncton, and Paris.
Richard, Broussard, Guidry,
Young Cajuns cling to
  wet nurses
To prepare for a
revival, this time
authentic, born from a legitimate marriage
Music has finally been wed with the language
. . . .]

There was no dramatic shift in Quebec's relations with Louisiana after 1976. It is more accurate to state that the political consequences of the French movement began to emerge during this period and that these events were indirectly assisted by the presence of Quebec. For the first time since the relationship was renewed, many Cajuns had come to accept the Québécois invitation of looking to Quebec as a North American place of French origin, or in Quebec government terminology, the Cajun could look at his travel to Quebec as a "return to roots" (*retour aux sources*). If this ideological link was implicit in the earlier relationships, it is explicit in the Parti Québécois policy with regard to the Louisiana French. Cajuns would never have suffered this relationship to be forced upon them. Few if any of the leaders are alienated from their country, and most are not anxious to get involved in Canadian political quarrels. The major change comes from the leaders of the French movement, particularly the network of young Cajuns.

If this category seems somewhat vague to the reader, it was equally elusive to the Quebec delegates who heard about the younger leaders of the French movement from Quebec French teachers who had been in Louisiana. It is easier to situate this group sociodemographically. With several exceptions,[32] all of these leaders are white Cajuns. The oldest was in her or his early thirties in 1983. Rather than constituting a group in the strict sense of being a corporate entity, the young Cajuns in the French movement make up an identifiable social network, whose members more or less know each other. One subset of the network is centered around the University of Southwestern Louisiana (USL) graduates in Lafayette, most of whom speak Cajun French and come from small towns in strongly French-speaking parishes. Many can read and write in French because they have taken French as a foreign language at their university. There is no single leader, but several persons are important in our discussion of the relationship with Quebec.

A subsidiary network that began in Baton Rouge and extends into New Orleans includes students who have studied linguistics, anthropology, and French at Louisiana State University (LSU) in Baton Rouge. In 1977, this latter part of the network formed the LSU Cajun Club, a short-lived and more militant group under the leadership of Randall Whatley and Debbie Clifton, which at first disapproved of all foreign francophones in Louisiana and blamed CODOFIL for the rejection of Louisiana French language and culture. Since Quebec worked closely with CODOFIL, Quebec became politically suspect to some of the new leaders. This antipathy toward Quebec representatives was a challenge recognized by the second Quebec delegate.

The Young Cajuns and the Quebec Delegate

Jules Poisson came to Louisiana as the second Quebec delegate with a very different background than his predecessor. In his Quebec government posts he had never before had to speak English on a daily basis and his insertion into Louisiana life made him reconsider the meaning of a minority status. But identity interested him as a practical concern, and as a graduate in economics and business he pondered whether he was best equipped to handle a cultural problem, and culture was the only justification that Poisson or his successor could offer for a Quebec presence in Lafayette.

But Poisson's management of culture was very effective. He reasoned that the Quebec presence in Lafayette called for "a cultural team—commandos—possibly directed by a delegation located elsewhere." He saw Lafayette as an *antenne culturelle* for Quebec, but the reality of the isolation in Lafayette comes back to what Leblanc discovered: the delegate determines Quebec policy in Louisiana.

The first major initiative by the new delegate followed several months after the visit of PQ Minister of Intergovernmental Affairs Claude Morin to Southwest Louisiana, an occasion that Morin used to reconfirm the Quebec commitment to the Louisiana French movement. I am told that Morin or others in his ministry approved of a modest proposal by

Poisson to assist younger Cajuns in organizing and participating in a national association. Similar approbation was received from Domengeaux who remained aloof from the organizing that followed, although he has had a number of active disagreements with some of the persons on the Quebec delegation's list. Poisson's dual mandate was limited to facilitating the creation of a new association by constructing documented lists of names with the appropriate contact information and then drawing on the assistance of Cajuns whom he had already met and his own staff of the Quebec delegation.

The new organization—*L'Association des francophones de la Louisiane*—did not endure. Initially, the use of the name "francophone" triggered a bitter war of words between the LSU Cajun Club group and the USL group in Lafayette. It was almost like seeing a replay of some of the rivalries between musicians and radio announcers. However, the Baton Rouge group was very wary of any cooperation with CODOFIL, and to them *if Quebec was involved, then CODOFIL must be involved.* But their protest was a false alarm in the sense that most of the leaders of the LSU group were also scheduled to some form of voluntary exile in Quebec.

The new association did create action patterns of those who applied their energies to specific projects such as the creation of a bilingual newsletter, *Louisiane française* (now in its fifty-first issue), a theater group, and a publishing venture. Some members worked to reinvigorate the annual Cajun Music Festival in Lafayette. Though the festival was originally associated with CODOFIL, that linkage has been partially a matter of convenience in that the actual organization was carried out by Barry Ancelet and others outside of CODOFIL. The very emergence of these organizations is timely and most of the leaders look to Quebec as a major cultural resource.

Despite this cultural activism, the network of participants is very small in relationship to the number of youth in small towns and in other regions who do not benefit from these activities. One might ask, as did a visiting Canadian Acadian advisor, who was sent by his federal government, whether all these activities do not end in the creation of a new cultural elite? If that is so, then do summer festivals in Quebec not fall into the same category?

The second major initiative of the Parti Québécois period was a direct invitation to young minority Franco-Americans and Cajuns to participate in Quebec culture and use the occasion for mutual benefit. *Le Retour aux Sources* was first held in Quebec City in July 1978 and restaged in subsequent years in a somewhat different format. This festival did more than demonstrate Quebec to be a living showcase for the survival of the French language. It offered vocal leaders of all francophone minorities, on a continental basis, an opportunity to discuss seriously their common problems in workshops. *Le Retour*, organized in Louisiana by the staff of the Quebec delegation who invited a planeload of Louisianians, was considered by Québécois and Cajun alike as the first real meeting of the renewed French movement and the new Quebec.

Timed to coincide with the referendum, *Le Retour aux Sources* conveyed a role for Quebec that went beyond its traditional relationship with French-Canadian minorities. But the message was for the minorities, and not English Canada. The Canadian French minorities were not an issue in Quebec during the referendum, but rather outside of Quebec where specific minorities used the occasion as a bargaining point.[33]

One of the Louisianians attending the sequel to *Le Retour*, the *Rencontre des francophones* in 1979, spoke out against being used by Quebec to support its political plans. René Lévesque replied specifically to the attack in his banquet address; "The Cajuns are Americans and wish to stay that way. We do not want support or a crutch. All we want is understanding." He added that the "political changes in Quebec can only rebound on the francophone world and on the immediate neighborhood." Two well known Louisiana leaders immediately supported Lévesque in a press statement. They insisted that Quebec does not interfere in their affairs and noted that *Rencontre* does show that they are not standing alone in this world.[34]

Quebec seems intent on continuing the new relationship and demonstrated its disposition in the appointment, in 1980, of Marc Boucher as Quebec delegate. As a McGill and University of Maine product, Boucher appears to have the personal flexibility and knowledge of French minorities that characterized the first Quebec delegate. His appointment follows a period in which Quebec is moving away from seeking to turn the Lafayette operation into a business office and back toward some of the attitudes that prevailed during the Johnson regime. The difference is that the Ministry of Intergovernmental Affairs seems to be most concerned in aiding the next generation of leaders.

Conclusions

This brief discussion presents Quebec's relationship with Louisiana as a kind of dialectic. In Quebec popular culture, Louisiana has symbolized the death of a French nation and the rebirth of its folklife. This rebirth is expressed in the metaphor of a bidirectional "return to roots." As Québécois discovered the metaphors of their roots in the living oral traditions of the bayou country, French Louisianians have turned to Quebec in an exile that would give them the instruments to rebuild their own society. That at least is the insider's view, a logic that is not entirely plausible when one is on the outside looking in.

Viewed from a wider perspective, the contacts of the 1930s repeated, at a rather late date, the manner in which French Quebec replicated its institutions throughout French America. In this instance, contact was made and then broken because the French-Canadian delegations could find no structured, overarching institutions, including the Catholic church, that would permit French Canada to deal with their rediscovered Acadians.

The renewal of contact is difficult to understand from the purely instrumental terms of a balance sheet of profit or loss to Quebec or to Louisiana. It is also unacceptable to conclude that Quebec was duped into an agreement in 1967–1969. Furthermore, though it is never mentioned by Quebec government officials, there is some continuity from the ideology and organization of Quebec's earlier contacts. Cholette's report provides insights into the bureaucratic recycling of the providential ideology that made the first page of *Le Devoir* in another era.

What the new Quebec is looking for is the birth of a political consciousness among the minorities, an ideological change that can only work to sustain an independent or autonomous Quebec that will then be somewhat less than an isolate in English-speaking countries. Cholette, Masse, Vaugeois, Claude Morin, and Lévesque all received reasonable evidence that French-speaking Louisianians were looking for an acceptable political solution to cultural stagnation. This was a more positive response than much of what they might have experienced in nearby New England, or even in some Canadian provinces.

Notes

1. For a more detailed discussion of the 1930–1937 exchanges between Louisiana, Quebec, and New Brunswick, see Gerald L. Gold, *The Role of France, Quebec and Belguim in the Revival of French in Louisiana Schools* (Quebec: Centre International de recherche sur le bilinguisme, Université Laval, Publication B 91, 1980); Gerald L. Gold, "The Mission of Quebec in Louisiana," in G. L. Gold, ed., *Ethnicity and the Mother Country* (St. John's, Newfoundland: Institute of Social and Economic Research, Memorial University, forthcoming 1983).

2. For further details on the Louisiana French movement see Gerald L. Gold, *The Role of France, Quebec and Belgium*; and Eric Waddell, "French Louisiana: An Outpost of Amérique française, or Another Country and Another Culture," Working Paper 4 (1980), Quebec, Département de géographie, Université Laval. A critique of the Louisiana French movement appears in Gerald L. Gold, "The Cajun French Debate in Louisiana," in Albert Valdman, B.

Hartford, and C. Foster, eds., *Issues in International Bilingual Education* (New York: Plenum, 1982).

3. A chronology of recent Quebec involvement in the United States and a discussion of a shift in Quebec's U.S. policy in the 1960s is found in Jean Louis Roy, "Les relations du Québec et les États Unis (1945–1970)," in P. Paichaud, ed., *Le Canada et le Québec sur la scène internationale* (Quebec: Les Presses de l'Université Laval, 1977), pp. 503–509.

None of the people whom I interviewed in 1975–1980 could recall the 1963 trip by Jean Lesage.

4. *Projet Louisiane* was directed by Gerald L. Gold (York University) and by Louis-Jacques Dorais and Eric Waddell (Université Laval). Dean Louder (Université Laval) joined the project in 1977 and carried out some of the interviews upon which this chapter is based. This portion of the research was financed by a grant from the Ford Foundation and leave time fellowship from the Social Sciences and Humanities Research Council of Canada.

5. See John-Smith Thibodeaux (pseudonym), *Les francophones de la Louisiane* (Paris: Editions entente, 1977), pp. 36–40.

6. For an account of the semantics of this shift see V. R. Dominguez, "Social Classification in Creole Louisiana," *American Ethnologist* 4(4), pp. 589–602.

7. Lionel Groulx, *Mes mémoires, cinquième volume 1926–1931* (Montreal: Fides, 1952), p. 160. Author's translation.

8. The decline of the juro-political protection for the linguistic status of white Creole elites is well documented. See Heinz Kloss, *Les droits linguistiques des Franco-Américains aux États-Unis* (Quebec: Les Presses de l'Université Laval, 1970).

9. Antoine Bernard, *Histoire de la Louisiane de ses origines à nos jours* (Montreal: Conseil de la vie française en Amérique, 1944), p. 383. Author's translation.

10. In practice, Bishop Jeanmard of the diocese of Lafayette discouraged the creation of French ethnic parishes. He also wished to limit the number of Quebec priests in South Louisiana (Glenn Conrad, Center for Louisiana Studies, University of Southwestern Louisiana, personal communication).

11. For a discussion of French as a language of work in Cajun communities see Gerald L. Gold, "Language and Ethnic Identity in South Louisiana: Implications of Data from Mamou Prairie," in R. Breton and P. Savard, eds., *The Quebec and Acadian Diaspora in North America* (Toronto: Multicultural History Society of Ontario, 1982).

12. A discussion of the effects of urbanization and the end of the manual cultivation of cotton appears in Gerald L. Gold, "The French Frontier of Settlement in Louisiana: Some Observations on Cultural Change in Mamou Prairie," *Cahiers de Géographie du Québec* 23(2), 1979, pp. 263–280; and Gold, "Language and Ethnic Identity in South Louisiana."

13. Gold analyzes a local election campaign that was fought in French, in the 1977 democratic primary. See Gerald L. Gold, "*Cousin* and the *gros chiens*, the Limits of Cajun Political Rhetoric," in Robert Paine, ed., *Politically Speaking: Cross Cultural Studies of Rhetoric* (Philadelphia: Institute for the Study of Human Issues, 1981).

14. Few francophone journalists or commentators on southwestern Louisiana have reported on patterns in the regional use of French.

15. Brasseaux finds historical continuity in popular Cajun opposition to universal education. See Carl Brasseaux, "Acadian Education: from Cultural Isolation to Mainstream America," in G. R. Conrad, ed., *The Cajuns: Essays on their History and Culture* (Lafayette: USL History Series No. 11, Center for Louisiana Studies, University of Southwestern Louisiana, 1978).

16. See Gold, "Language and Ethnic Identity in South Louisiana," pp. 49–60, for a discussion of sex differences in French language use and patterns of retention. These differences are particularly strong in maritime regions such as the southern part of Lafourche parish where the fishery is a male, French-language activity. See Alain Larouche, *Ethnicité, pêche et pétrole: les Cadjins du Bayou Lafourche en Louisiane francophone* (Quebec: Monografie no. 1, Projet Louisiane, Département de géographie, Université Laval, 1981), pp. 185–187.

17. For a trinational comparison of foreign French teachers in Louisiana, see Gold, *The Role of France, Quebec and Belgium in the Revival of French in Louisiana Schools.*

18. Jean-Louis Roy, "Le Canada et le Québec sur la scène internationale," pp. 503–509. None of my Louisiana interviewees in 1975–1980 could recall this visit by Premier Lesage.

19. Author's translation.

20. Guy Frégault, *Chronique des années perdues* (Montreal: Léméac, 1965), pp. 193–194.

21. Ibid., p. 196.

22. Ibid., pp. 198–200.

23. This point emerges frequently in interviews.

24. T. Harry Williams, *Huey Long* (New York: Bantam Books, 1970), p. 276.

25. Gold, "*Cousin* and the *gros chiens*," p. 153.

26. Much of the account that follows is summarized from Cholette's unpublished report.

27. F. Edward Hébert, "The New Louisiana Story," *Congressional Record*, Proceedings and Debates of the 93rd Congress, 2nd session, March 5, 1974.

28. Gold, *The Role of France, Quebec and Belgium in the Revival of French in Louisiana Schools*, p. 5.

29. Francis Debyser et al., *Evaluation of Louisiana State-wide CODOFIL French Program* (Baton Rouge: Louisiana State Department of Education, 1978).

30. Author's translation.

31. Jean Arceneaux (pseudonym), "Exil II," in J. Arceneaux, ed., *Cris sur le Bayou: naissance d'une poésie acadienne en Louisiane* (Montreal: Les Editions Intermède, 1980), p. 37. Author's translation.

32. The two major types of exceptions are black Creoles who became involved in the French movement at LSU and at USL, where they interacted primarily with white Cajun networks.

33. Gold, "*Cousin* and the *gros chiens*."

34. "Rencontre des peuples francophones," *Le Soleil*, July 11, 1979.

9
Franco-Americans and Quebec: Linkages and Potential in the Northeast

Armand B. Chartier

Quebec is nearly always mentioned in studies of Franco-Americans, yet there exists no serious survey of Quebec's influence on Franco-Americans through the years, no scholarly inventory of the linkages between the mother country and the emigrants or their descendants.[1] This state of affairs is particularly surprising because the subject is so obvious, vast, and varied, lending itself to serious research in so many disciplines, because linkages have existed in all major spheres of activity from athletics to theology. Systematic study of this symbiosis would require the expertise of historians specialized in diverse domains, genealogists, demographers, specialists in literature and linguistics, anthropologists, sociologists, psychologists, economists, and political scientists.

Pending such empirical studies by diverse talents, the following analysis is necessarily based upon incomplete evidence combined with the author's impressions derived from varied experience and considerable speculation. The objectives are to provide a historical framework and summary survey of the nature and extent of early and later linkages, to indicate knowledge gaps and potentially fruitful areas for future inquiry, and to suggest promising endeavors in which Quebec's collaboration would be particularly helpful.

Quebec migration to what is now the United States began with the initial French settlements along the Mississippi River Valley to its mouth and on the shore of the Great Lakes during the first half of the eighteenth century. Many last names of Normandy and Brittany origin that are widespread in today's Quebec are also frequent in St. Louis and particularly along the Mississippi in Louisiana. Approximately a million Québécois, typically from large, poor families, left poor farms and villages for comparatively attractive employment in textile mills, shoe factories, and other plants in the industrializing northeast and the Great Lakes states as far as Minnesota beginning in the 1840s, expanding considerably after the Civil War, and continuing until the Great Depression. Although a significant fraction of the pre-1870 migrants went to the states on the Great Lakes, a majority of those thereafter went to nearby New England and upstate New York. Post-1945 migration has also been large—some estimate as many as half a million—half of them illegal—in Florida; a quarter of a million in California and the southwest; and more than a hundred thousand more dispersed elsewhere across the United States.[2]

This chapter will focus on those in the northeast, especially in New England, who are geographically within a day's drive from the land of their ancestry and are able, with but modest effort and expense, to establish contacts and communications with it. There, Franco-Americans are also sufficiently numerous to foster effective institutions to preserve and develop their heritage in ready collaboration with Quebec. They are also the Franco-Americans with whom the author is particularly familiar and of whose society he is himself a part and an active participant.

Linkages Throughout a Shared History

The Immigrant Generation and Their Children

Variously referred to as an exodus, an *hémorragie démographique* (demographic hemorrhage), and the departure of *la canaille* (riff-raff, rabble), the mass migration from Quebec extending over nearly a century since 1840 has not proven to be *le cimetière de la race* (the cemetery of the race), as Curé Labelle and other Quebec leaders had feared—at least not yet. By 1850, the first Franco-American parish in New England—St. Joseph's in Burlington, Vermont—was established with a Quebecker, the Rev. Joseph Quevillon, as pastor. Over a hundred fifty more Franco-American parishes would eventually be created, as the immigrants brought with them a heritage founded on the French language and the Catholic religion.

Contemporaneous with the establishment of parishes and the building of churches was the creation of parochial schools. Just as many founding pastors were born in Quebec, so too the nuns who taught in these schools came from French-Canadian orders: by 1880, the Sisters of Jesus-Mary had come to Fall River, Massachusetts; the Grey Nuns to Lewiston, Maine; the *Dames de la Congrégation* to St. Johnsbury, Vermont. More would come later. Their histories as yet unpublished, one can only speculate on the impact of several thousand sisters, during the course of a century, on the minds of many thousand youngsters and on adults as well. One hopes that social historians will some day describe and evaluate these vast, intricate networks made up of diverse religious communities and Church-related agencies. Although they were dispersed in their work in dozens of localities in New England, these communities remained juridically dependent upon and in regular communication with their headquarters in Quebec. This system facilitated not only the free flow of ideas and information in the areas of pedagogy and religion, but also continuing rapport of individuals and institutions and reinforcement of cultural values associated with Quebec and the French language.

Throughout the latter half of the nineteenth and the early twentieth centuries, lay persons also created linkages across the border. Immigrants like Ferdinand Gagnon, born in Quebec and active on the New England scene, themselves remained living links with the mother country. Moved by dreams of some day seeing a New (French-speaking) Canada in New England, these men and women devoted lifetimes to the development and preservation of linkages, to such an extreme that *L'Etendard National,* one of Ferdinand Gagnon's newspapers, became the U.S. edition of the Montreal-based *L'Opinion Publique* in an attempt to achieve constant communication. In addition, both *La Presse* and *La Patrie* in Quebec ran regular columns on French-Canadians in the United States. By the 1890s, both represented serious competition in New England for Franco-American newspapers.

Simultaneously, fraternal societies were established to provide life insurance services to the immigrants, and *caisses populaires* (credit unions) were founded to encourage thrift. From the outset, these societies combined business with ethnic interests, as many of them became avowedly "patriotic," advocating loyalty to the immigrants' adopted country along with faithful remembrance of the ancestral homeland. These local and regional groups would merge to form the *Association Canado-Américaine* (ACA) in 1896, based in Manchester, New Hampshire, and *Union Saint-Jean-Baptiste* in 1900, headquartered in Woonsocket, Rhode Island. Today, one-third of ACA's more than 20,000 members are Quebeckers.

With Franco-American churches, schools, newspapers, and societies emerging everywhere in New England and looking to Quebec for inspiration and role models, their myriad links were virtually "organic." One could hardly conceive ties closer than those existing during these years of immigration, for these ties involved close family, religion, and education. They were an integral part of the immigrants' daily lives, part of an existential reality, quite the opposite of a fad, a hobby, or a fond memory, which today's ethnicity increasingly threatens to become.

Present in the day-to-day existence even of its humblest offspring, Quebec took on added meaning on certain special occasions. For example, some 18,000 Franco-Americans led by Ferdinand Gagnon attended the mammoth *Congrès* organized by *Société Saint-Jean-Baptiste de Montréal* (St. John the Baptist Society of Montreal) in 1874. New links were formed and old ones reinforced during a similar gathering in Quebec City in 1880 and at the Franco-Americans' general convention held in Cohoes, New York, in 1882. Several hundred Quebeckers attended this latter assembly, including the outspoken conservative Bishop of Trois-Rivières, Louis-François Laflèche, and eminent political leaders such as Laurent-Olivier David and Honoré Mercier. At the general convention held in Nashua, New Hampshire, in 1888, L.-O. David was present again, along with Faucher de Saint-Maurice. Both were official representatives of Honoré Mercier, by then prime minister of Quebec. Indeed, with Mercier, Franco-American relations with Quebec reached a peak not attained since, and by 1892, even after his fall from power, Mercier remained an idol of French-Canadians on both sides of the border.

The Louis Riel controversy proved to be another occasion for renewed linkages between Franco-Americans and the homeland. Riel himself spent several days in Worcester, Massachusetts, in 1874, speaking publicly about the *Métis* and the "troubles" in Manitoba in 1869–1870. He visited New England as least twice more and was well received. Hence his execution in 1885 caused outrage among French-Canadians everywhere. Franco-Americans from eleven states assembled in a general convention in Rutland, Vermont, in 1886, unanimously denounced his hanging as a *meurtre judiciaire* (judicial murder) perpetrated by the Canadian government.

Notable occasions through the 1920s emanating from longstanding leadership linkages included Franco-American attendance at the Eucharistic Congress in Montreal (1910) and at the First Congress of the French Language in Quebec (1912). Other elite-level linkages were made possible after the establishment of the *Société Historique Franco-Américaine* (the Franco-American Historical Society) founded in Boston in 1899, which over the years attracted many prominent guest lecturers from Quebec and often published the texts of their lectures.

Linkages across the forty-fifth parallel also found expression in various forms of support and encouragement by prominent Quebec leaders to Franco-American cultural preservation efforts. Quebec newspapers published articles inveighing against assimilationist U.S. bishops; modest financial assistance was occasionally extended, and guest speakers from Quebec traveled the Franco-American lecture circuit. At the same time—

and through the 1950s—several thousand Franco-American youth studied in Quebec colleges, seminaries, and convents. In time, some members of this new elite would become living links with Quebec as well as dynamic leaders in Franco-American organizations.

During the half-century from the Civil War to World War I, literature of common interest also provided a significant link between French-Canadians in Canada and those in the United States. For instance, Honoré Beaugrand, an immigrant journalist, published his immigration novel, *Jeanne la fileuse*, in serial form in his newspaper *La République* (Boston and Fall River, Massachusetts) in 1875, and in *La Patrie* (Montreal) in 1880, and again as a book in 1878 in Fall River and in 1888 in Montreal. Thus its earliest readership spanned the border, suggesting its common appeal. Even a full century later, *Jeanne la fileuse* is variously regarded as a Franco-American novel or as a Québécois novel, just as its author is considered a Franco-American by some and a Quebecker by others.

In the 1920s, a stormy ethno-religious conflict buffeted the Franco-American world. At issue was the right of the Bishop of Providence, Rhode Island, to levy taxes for the development of diocesan high schools and to impose his will, generally, on Franco-American parishes. In public speeches and in their newspaper *La Sentinelle*, sentinellists defended the Quebec-inspired conception of the parish as a sacred entity to be zealously protected against the encroachments of assimilationist bishops. This heated controversy probably never would have occurred had it not been for certain well established linakges between sentinellist leaders in New England and clergymen in Quebec.

Even through the depression, organizations continued to formalize exchanges and linkages. The *Société Saint-Jean-Baptiste de Montréal*, for example, developed a continuing liaison program with the *Association Canado-Américaine* whereby the latter would have air time on a francophone Montreal radio station for a series of programs on different aspects of Franco-American life. In this same spirit of solidarity, the *Société* organized several Franco-American tours for some of its directors and donated prizes for the ACA-sponsored French contests in Fall River. These New England activities of the Montreal society were not, however, favorably regarded by the Woonsocket, Rhode Island-based *Union Saint-Jean-Baptiste*, which denounced these programs, though without much effect, as an intrusion. The denunciation was symptomatic. By the 1930s, *Union Saint-Jean-Baptiste* had adopted a policy of developing preferential relations with France, while ACA was doing the same with Quebec. Such divergences persist to this day.

Finally, the Second Congress of the French Language in Quebec City in 1937 was attended by over 4,000 Franco-Americans and was surrounded by considerable publicity in both New England and Quebec. As an outgrowth of the Congress, the *Conseil de la Vie française en Amérique* (Council on French Life in America) was founded in 1937 and today (1983) still provides liaison among North American francophone elites through publications and meetings. In 1947, the council helped create an independent New England counterpart, the *Comité de Vie franco-américaine* (Committee on Franco-American Life), an elite group that organized eleven large-scale conventions to discuss Franco-American sociocultural problems with a view toward practical solutions. The committee has maintained both formal and informal communication with the council since its founding. Even as late as 1952, the Third Congress of the French Language (organized by the *Conseil de la Vie française en Amérique*) was also attended by a large number of Franco-Americans. It was destined, however, to be the last such major gathering.

Widening of the Gap

The 1940s are a watershed in the history of Franco-American–Quebec relations. Few Franco-Americans, for instance, empathized with Quebec's opposition to conscription and participation in World War II. Viewed against the background of an identity formerly shared, this lack of empathy dramatizes the growing rift between Franco-Americans and Quebeckers. The war also hastened the assimilation of Franco-Americans; many had their first prolonged contacts with non–Franco-Americans in military service and even married outside their ethnic group during and after the war. Also during the 1940s and 1950s, many religious communities achieved autonomy from their headquarters in Quebec, which meant fewer contacts between Quebec and *la Franco-Américanie*, fewer Québécois teachers in Franco-American schools, and a generally lessened Québécois presence in New England. That this presence should be diminishing at the same time as the *sense* of belonging to a North American French tradition and the perceived *need* to belong to that tradition were also diminishing amounts to an unfortunate combination of circumstances. This growing gap between Franco-Americans and their French-Canadian homeland and traditions constitutes a major characteristic of Franco-American life today.

But assimilation was forestalled by that vast network of linkages, and the French-Canadian cultural heritage thus was preserved. For a surprisingly long time, *survivance* obtained, thrived, and prevailed.

Contemporary Linkages

Although many linkages have weakened or disappeared, particularly since World War II, a number still persist to some degree. Some new linkages have also been established, especially with the modernization of Quebec society accelerated by the Quiet Revolution that began in the early 1960s. The older New England–based groups have tended to remain relatively traditional, not only in continuing their activities in French rather than in English, but also in their staunchly Catholic spirit and inspiration. With some exceptions, their active memberships are understandably upper middle-aged and older. Newer groups, notably those established since 1970, are religiously neutral or pluralistic, and they increasingly use English, or at least English with French, because many of their members are younger and few are bilingual.

More Traditional Groups

Some of the traditional groups are more active, effective, and promising than others, especially in terms of possible collaborative efforts either with the public or the private sectors in Quebec. Many traditional groups show no visible interest in self-rejuvenation and it would be difficult, at the present time, to justify any hope of enlisting their support in projected joint ventures with Quebec. Such groups are distrustful of modern-day Quebec and often condemn the rapid rise of religious indifference in what was once a monolithic, practicing Catholic province. Thus, their loyalty to Catholicism alienates them from Quebec, even as loyalty to the French language separates them from younger generations of Franco-Americans. But two traditional groups do show considerable promise.

The ACA, with some 20,000 members, 7,000 of whom are Quebeckers, constitutes a fully functional network of linkages through its system of local lodges scattered throughout both New England and Quebec. A new leadership has proven to be dynamic, flexible, innovative, and eager to increase an already high level of sociocultural activities on both sides of the border.

Another active and effective traditional group is the *Fédération Féminine Franco-Américaine* (Federation of Franco-American Women), founded in Lewiston, Maine, in 1951. The federation sponsors carefully planned conventions, French-language contests, concerts, youth festivals, colloquia, scholarship funds, and cultural trips. Many of these activities have had Quebec dimensions, an analytical history and evaluation of which could provide lessons and prototypes for implementation by others. The federation also continues to publish a *Bulletin* that reflects its intellectual and social life. It is anticipated that once the group moves beyond its "French only" policy and allows the use of English in some of its deliberations, it will appeal to younger women and will thereby gain added strength.

Pluralistic Present- and Future-Oriented Agencies

Even an overview focusing solely on Franco-American organizations created during the past fifteen years lies beyond the scope of the present chapter; their number is large. In the selection of groups for discussion here, the following criteria have prevailed: a demonstrated openness to new ideas, the ability to work creatively with other groups, and receptivity to the possibility of collaborations with Quebec institutions, public or private.

At the national level, the Association of Franco-Americans (AFA), founded in Lafayette, Louisiana, in 1980 for the express purpose of creating links among Franco-Americans, Acadians, and other franco-phones and francophiles in the United States, also seeks to create new links with Quebec and francophone groups abroad. The association is represented on the Advisory Committee of the *Corporation des rencontres francophones de Québec* (Corporation of Quebec Francophone Meetings) and its annual national meetings have proven increasingly successful. If, as seems likely, the association continues to broaden its support base nationally, it could become the U.S. equivalent of the *Fédération des francophones hors Québec* (Federation of Francophones Outside Quebec), with a strong potential for fruitful linkages between the two.

At the regional level, the most promising of the newer groups is Action for Franco-Americans in the Northeast (ActFANE [sic]), a small secretariat and clearinghouse in Manchester, New Hampshire. Established in July 1981 with technical and financial assistance from the Quebec government, this central office implements policy decisions made by a board of directors representing New York and each New England state. The organization's main purposes are to stimulate exchanges of infor-mation and ideas among the northeast region's Franco-Americans, to help coordinate and initiate cultural activities and to facilitate Franco-American cooperation with various public or private agencies in Quebec. Considering its modest size—it is staffed by a full-time coordinating secretary and a growing number of volunteers—and limited financial resources, ActFANE has been pursuing its goals with increasing success, particularly through the multitude of meetings it sponsors and through a highly informative newsletter. In a short span of time, ActFANE has proven itself, and its potential is impressive.

In most New England states, there has existed since the late 1960s an agency similar in spirit to the American and Canadian French Cultural Exchange Commission created by the Massachusetts legislature in July 1968. The purposes of these statewide commissions are to develop cultural ties between Franco-Americans and French-Canadians and to foster interest in the historical backgrounds of both groups. The fortunes of these commissions have in fact varied from state to state depending on qualities of leadership, priorities accorded them by governors and legislatures, and the limited budgets provided them. Some observers regard their accomplishments as modest, but they have, to varying degrees, raised public awareness about Quebec. Further, they do constitute an officially recognized mechanism for cultural exchange with French Canada and as such they should not be overlooked in program and policy development.

At the grass roots level, thousands of Franco-Americans have been drawn to genealogy during the past decade, with the result that several small to medium-sized (1,500 plus) genealogical societies have been established to facilitate members' research and information exchange. As yet there has been no discernible effort to federate these societies, although a federation would assuredly facilitate the creation of a communications network capable of covering New England and New York. Existing genealogical societies have, however, held meetings in Quebec and provided technical advice to members wishing to do research in Quebec. It is therefore not unrealistic to think that genealogy may well lead to an interest in the history of the towns and regions from whence one's ancestors emigrated; to genealogical/cultural tourism; to the development of ongoing relations between certain U.S. and Quebec towns in which today's residents—Franco-Americans or Quebeckers—share a common ancestry.

In the academic area, the major event in recent years has been the founding of the French Institute at Assumption College in Worcester, Massachusetts, in 1979. The development of the institute, largely the work of its director, Professor Claire Quintal, ably supported by various members of the college faculty, has stimulated new linkages among intellectuals, academics, and other thoughtful, interested, and often influential Franco-Americans and Quebeckers. The institute searches out talent, salient data, and ideas pertinent to Franco-American phenomena, and elicits systematic studies and papers by Quebec and U.S. scholars for discussion at annual colloquia, four of which have taken place since 1980. Topics have included Quebec immigrants since 1850, Quebec's economic evolution, postmigration linkages, high culture, and popular culture in nineteenth-century Quebec.[3] The institute's growing collection of Franco-American newspapers and other materials also provides data for serious analyses by researchers from both sides of the border. If it can alleviate its financial strictures, as it is now in the process of doing, the institute could become an increasingly influential center for documentation, serious research, and its dissemination.

Assumption College, along with others including Anna Maria College, Clark University, Johnson State College, the University of Vermont,

Central Connecticut State College, Bridgewater State College, and all Quebec universities have, for the past year, participated in the Quebec/ New England Student Exchange Program. Although the program is not directed exclusively at Franco-American students, one might expect the latter as well as other students to explore its possibilities. However, no exploration on a broad scale is occurring, attributable in part to a general unawareness of the program's existence. A publicity effort involving the Franco-American media and departments of French in the area's high schools and colleges is needed to stimulate interest in this long-overdue program.

Media

Franco-American media are also clearly in need of empirical study. Such study would reveal substantial losses of communications vehicles over the past generation. For example, of the numerous daily and weekly French-language newspapers that survived into the 1960s, only one, Wilfrid Beaulieu's *Le Travailleur* of Worcester, Massachusetts, founded in 1931, lasted into the 1970s. But it, too, closed in 1978.

A Franco-American periodical of opinion is published eight times yearly by the Franco-American Resource Opportunity Group (F.A.R.O.G.) at the University of Maine, Orono. Founded in 1973, *Le F.A.R.O.G. Forum* is youthful, brash, iconoclastic, and reminds some readers of *Le Canard enchaîné* rather than of any Québécois model. Still, the *Forum* publishes articles on Quebec with some regularity and with considerable variations in degrees of perceptiveness. The *Forum* is moreover the only paper in recent memory to have argued the importance to Quebec of developing more effective communications with Franco-Americans. Regardless of likes, dislikes, enthusiasm, or skepticism, however, the *Forum* appears to have a secure role and constitutes a significant element in the dynamics of modern Franco-American life.

Two other newspapers, *Le Journal de Lowell* (founded 1974) and *L'Unité* (founded in Lewiston, Maine, in 1977), have reflected mostly local Franco-American life in these cities with large Franco-American populations. These two monthlies reveal a number of contacts with Quebec, particularly visits to these cities by Quebec officials and visits to Quebec by local people.

In the audio-visual media, numerous losses have been only partly offset by some gains. The disappearance of many French-language radio programs since the 1950s has drastically reduced the amount of Québécois music and discussion heard in New England. Cable television, however, has been gaining steadily, with the result that over 250,000 homes in some 160 towns throughout the three northern New England states and some Massachusetts communities now have access to Radio Canada television programming in French. But there have been no impact studies or surveys to determine frequency of viewing or programs preferred, or to learn how useful, usable, beneficial, or desirable this programming really is. Nor is there any mechanism for ongoing dialogue between the Quebec stations whence these television programs come and the Franco-American communities they serve. Satellite transmissions from Quebec could broaden the availability of its television to minority audiences as this vehicle becomes more widespread.

Public television in the United States could also serve as a link between Quebec and Franco-Americans, especially in regions where they are numerous, as evinced by a 1982 New Hampshire public television series on the heritages and customs of various regions in Quebec, which included interviews with writers and artists. But here again, no audience surveys are available.

Recent Roles of the Quebec Government

The Quebec government began to institutionalize its relations with Franco-Americans and other North American francophone groups during the initial years of the Quiet Revolution, with the creation of the *Service du Canada français d'outre frontière* (French-Canadian Service for Outside Quebec) in 1961. Through this agency, cultural materials were disseminated and support was given to groups and some individuals.

Another major step was taken with the establishment of the Quebec Government Bureau in Boston in 1969, which later became the Quebec Government Delegation in New England. From the start, Franco-Americans were welcome to use this bureau, which many of them perceived as a major means of providing better contact with Quebec. The bureau, and later the delegation, has actively encouraged Franco-American efforts to preserve and develop their heritage, has provided modest financial assistance and more effective links with appropriate governmental agencies, private institutions, and individuals in Quebec, and has helped staff a diversity of programs across the region, both in French and in English. Members of the delegation have also attended these programs. The Boston-based delegation was, for example, crucial in the successful campaign mounted by Mr. Paul Blanchette of Lowell, Massachusetts, to bring Radio Canada television programming in French via microwave to northern New England and several Massachusetts cable systems.

The delegation also played a critical role in bringing about negotiations leading to the establishment of ActFANE, the previously described secretariat-clearinghouse. During those negotiations, extensive discussions took place involving three Franco-American community leaders, senior civil servants, and appropriate cabinet ministers of the Quebec government. The substance of those discussions, which took place in 1980–1981, might still serve as the basis for a master plan of Quebec–Franco-American collaboration.

Priority areas identified during those talks include youth and media. Youth then became the theme and focus of the 1982 *Rencontre francophone de Québec* (Quebec Francophone Meeting) organized by the Quebec government, and plans have been formulated to create an association of francophone youth, with representation from all parts of Canada and the United States. As for media, efforts deemed especially worth pursuing were those designed to develop contacts between cable television firms in the northeast and relevant personnel in the Quebec television industry. It was also agreed that the feasibility of bringing Quebec satellite television to the northeast would be explored during the next several years as the industry itself continues to evolve. Likely collaborations in the areas of cultural affairs, education, and recreation were also outlined.

The Quebec government has developed two programs of special interest to Franco-Americans. The first is a series of annual *Rencontres francophones de Québec* (Quebec Francophone Meetings), medium-sized gatherings, held since 1978, of French-speaking North Americans committed to the preservation of the cultural heritage. Representatives from different regions on the continent exchange information and ideas, compare experiences, and discuss strategies. Each meeting has a different theme and those invited to participate are usually dynamic and dedicated leaders in their home regions.

Another ongoing program complements the work of these annual meetings. It is implemented by the *Secrétariat permanent des peuples francophones* (Permanent Secretariat of Francophone Peoples) and consists in staffing a cultural center located in Quebec City. The center is available year-round to Franco-Americans and others who wish to make known to Quebeckers some aspect of their heritage. The center has hosted a number of exhibits and meetings of special relevance to different regions. Such activities, it should be noted, transcend mere symbolism in that they provide frequent opportunities for repeated linkages with Quebec.

Conclusions and Recommendations

Most Franco-Americans today are uninvolved in the preservation of their ethnic heritage. Those who are active in development efforts to maintain their heritage are often locally rather than regionally organized. It is this author's contention that such a situation is not irreversible and that there are indeed energies to be tapped, however latent they may seem. It could also be argued that efforts to preserve Franco-American culture have not fully or systematically exploited Quebec's geographical proximity or its advances in technology, particularly in the area of communications.

Moreover, for the past half-century, Franco-American leaders have often debated the question of what the precise nature of Quebec's role in Franco-American life should be, without ever reaching unanimity on the subject. It seems clear, however, that without injections of even modest human, technical, or financial resources by the public and/or private sectors in Quebec, virtually total assimilation will take place within a generation or so. This would mean that awareness of as well as interest in the Franco-Americans' ethnic heritage would be lost beyond possibility of recovery, with the exception of a very few indomitable souls.

In considering ways of delaying assimilation while maintaining or even increasing the United States' cultural diversity, the very highest priority should be given to media, for only through the various media can one hope to reach mass levels as well as elites, and all age groups including the crucially important youth. Making Quebec and/or Canadian French-language television programming available to all of New England and New York state either by extending the cable system connected via microwave, or by any other means, would be a critical first step. Effectiveness could moreover be maximized by the use of English subtitles when feasible and by utilizing television for teaching French in attractive formats at the beginning and intermediate levels. Importation of Quebec-produced video and audio-cassettes, films, radio programs, records, and printed media should also be intensified in Franco-American centers while at the same time the Franco-American population should be kept informed about the development of Quebec satellite television.

To begin working toward this goal of augmenting the presence of Quebec media in the northeast, a permanent committee, to include broad representation of all the parties concerned, is essential. Action for Franco-Americans in the Northeast (ActFANE) could serve as that committee's facilitator and coordinator, especially if small annual subsidies were given to or channeled through ActFANE to hire part-time media consultants. From the outset, representation and the active ongoing participation of Franco-American business persons as well as of southern New England Franco-American centers not now receiving cable television programming from Quebec would be especially critical in such an undertaking. Obviously, this effort requires a dynamic and committed group willing to meet frequently until the goal is reached, and willing also to act as "lobbyists" for the idea in their home communities in order to gain popular support. Working through existing Franco-American networks such as the *Association Canado-Américaine*, the Federation of Franco-American Women, the various genealogical societies, and, on a local level, private clubs similar to *Le Foyer* in Pawtucket, Rhode Island, would hasten progress toward the desired goal.

As diverse Quebec media become increasingly available in the northeast, their potential as educational tools for use by secondary schools and colleges throughout the region should be emphasized to social science and French departments. In this way, the general student population could benefit from the use of these tools, as could Franco-American youth. If encouraged by the Franco-American population at large, the presence of Quebec media in the schools and colleges might well inspire Franco-American young people to become involved in the preservation and development of their cultural heritage.

Other techniques and approaches must be found in order to stimulate youth involvement. Youth exchanges allowing Quebec and Franco-American youth to spend one or two weeks during the summer visiting one another's families in their respective milieus could be arranged with minimal effort and substantial gain. Concert tours throughout New England by young Quebec performing artists and in Quebec by Franco-American performers could very likely be organized by the Franco-American Resource Opportunity Group at the University of Maine (Orono) working with the Federation of Franco-American Women and the *Association Canado-Américaine*, if a small operating budget were provided.

The development of media, youth exchanges, and concert tours would also facilitate breaking the language barrier that has grown between Franco-Americans and Quebec as well as between older and younger Franco-Americans. Motivation for unilingual anglophone Franco-Americans to learn French is far more likely to be generated by such activities than from any purely academic or filiopietistic approach. In the United States, historical interpreters such as Reid Lewis of Chicago and John Rivard of St. Cloud, Minnesota, and performing artists such as the Beaudoin family of Burlington, Vermont, and the Lil Labbé/Don Hinckley duo of Orono, Maine, can also serve as motivators for Franco-Americans to regain interest in their heritage, including the French language. These individuals and groups deserve encouragement on both sides of the border.

It is regrettable, of course, that more Franco-Americans do not speak French. Several facets of this language issue command attention. To begin with, a more conciliatory attitude is needed on the part of French-speaking Franco-Americans toward those who do not speak French. Only meager results (if any) have been produced by their scorn for or condemnation of unilingual Franco-Americans who wish to retain their heritage but were deprived by circumstances of the opportunity of growing up in a predominantly French-speaking environment. French-speaking Franco-Americans tend to minimize unilingual Franco-Americans' claims to an ethnic heritage, refusing to believe in ethnicity without language. But staunch loyalty to the French language at the cost of alienating young people completely will only continue to foster indifference or animosities. A more positive approach is both crucial and feasible.

It is not difficult, for example, to envision collaborations involving the Quebec government and Franco-American groups that share its deep commitment to the French language, for the purposes of implanting Quebec media in schools and of developing attractive, innovative French-language instruction programs for unilingual Franco-American adults. A cultural component on Quebec's past, its present, and its special relevance for Franco-Americans would be critical to the success of such programs. Some of the larger Franco-American organizations that are either potentially or in actuality bilingual—the *Association Canado-Américaine* and the Federation of Franco-American Women, inter alia—have within their present membership the talent, competencies, and energies required to help carry out such programs, especially if encouraged to do so through loans of audio-visual materials by the Quebec government's Departments of Education, Communications, Cultural Affairs, Tourism, and Recreation. These Franco-American organizations could also help underwrite the costs of sending Franco-American young people to Quebec for total immersion programs in French.

The resources of these same governmental departments could also be used to reach unilingual Franco-Americans in order to help them develop awareness of their heritage. For although the phenomenon of "ethnicity without language" may leave some observers skeptical, it is not an insignificant reality but rather a fact that, if judiciously dealt with, could benefit both Quebec and the Franco-American community. Like other Americans, and regardless of language, Franco-Americans have a felt need to develop awareness of their roots, to know that they belong somewhere on a definite historical continuum, in order to secure an effective palliative against the depersonalization of the modern age. Few experiences can provide or deepen a sense of roots as completely as do visits to Quebec, especially to towns from which one's ancestors emigrated. Hence a promotional campaign aimed at fifteen to twenty northeastern cities with large Franco-American populations could measurably increase the number of Franco-American tourists going to Quebec, thereby increasing as well the chances of forming new linkages and of making possible cultural discoveries which could be profitable to everyone concerned. These same Franco-Americans also form a sizable potential market for Quebec television programming and films produced in English or kept in their original French but with English subtitles.

In education, further linkages are both desirable and feasible to enhance Quebec's visibility and increase understanding of its uniqueness. The use of Quebec textbooks in schools, especially schools located in Franco-American communities, and the introduction of Quebec and Franco-American content in social studies and French courses are viable means of reaching younger generations. Proximity to Quebec makes it possible to "twin" classes across the border, with exchanges of correspondence, visits, and locally-produced audio and video cassettes frequently during the school year and summer. Effective publicity about opportunities for summer study in Quebec, Junior Year in Quebec programs, and scholarship aid available to Franco-American students wishing to study in Quebec would be likely to attract growing numbers of young Franco-Americans. Supplementing these programs of study with genealogical/cultural excursions will increase the likelihood of formation of lasting ties with Quebec, ties the students may well want to renew through frequent future visits. Teacher exchanges and joint meetings of professional associations are also facilitated by geography and are worth pursuing.

There are many needs as well as opportunities in the areas of research and publication. The most pressing need is for greater recognition, by the public and the private sectors in Quebec and by the Franco-American community, that Franco-American history is an aspect of Quebec history. Recognition of the massive emigration to the United States as a central fact of Quebec history is occurring slowly and the process needs to be hastened before parts of Quebec's history disappear irretrievably. There already exists a small core of historians and social scientists in Quebec and in the United States with specialized knowledge of the Franco-American reality, but that core must be expanded considerably before basic research needs are met. Encouraging doctoral candidates to write dissertations on Franco-Americans would bring new talent into this neglected area. Additional talent and assistance may also be available at Quebec's *Institut national de la recherche scientifique* (National Institute of Scientific Research), and at the *Institut québécois de la recherche sur la culture* (Quebec Cultural Research Institute), as well as in Quebec's university community generally. Joint ventures involving individuals or teams from those institutions working in collaboration with Assumption College's French Institute are likely to yield optimal results.

The most urgently needed scholarly publications for which talent teams or pools could be assembled include: works in the field of cultural history in which scholars would analyze and evaluate Quebec's contributions to Franco-American religious life and education, both at the conceptual and at the practical levels; systematic, in-depth analyses of Franco-American newspapers (in which a quite considerable portion of Quebec/Franco-American history and literature remains buried); comparative surveys of Franco-American and Québécois popular culture in the nineteenth and early twentieth centuries; works on Franco-American folklore; studies of Quebec influences on the arts in Franco-American life, particularly in the neglected field of religious art (*e.g.,* church architecture) to be preceded by inventories of Franco-American art and artists. The overall need for empirical studies of Quebec/Franco-American linkages has already been noted at the beginning of this chapter.

Of the many desirable nonscholarly publications, a directory of francophone and Franco-American resources is probably the most critically needed; expanding the *Répertoire de la vie française en Amérique*[4] is one possible approach. A quarterly magazine similar to *Forces* in scope and format, published as a joint venture by Franco-Americans, Quebeckers, and others, if interested, could do much to develop a positive image of the participants and a sense of community between north and south. Lastly, a *revue de presse* (newspaper clipping and photocopying service) or newsletter dealing with Franco-Americans and North American francophone groups generally would also foster a sense of belonging and create new linkages.

In sum, the potential for creating new linkages exists and should be tapped. Some specific ways for achieving that goal have been discussed, and others may be uncovered as the dialogue between Franco-Americans and Quebec develops. However, permanent and fruitful linkages not involving the media, youth, Franco-American business persons, and other elites, as well as large numbers of unilingual anglophone Franco-Americans, are difficult to imagine.

Notes

1. This author is not aware of any study focusing solely on Quebec–Franco-American linkages. The subject does recur, however, in the classics of Franco-American history and in other sources consulted in the writing of this chapter. It is therefore a pleasure to acknowledge my indebtedness to Alexandre Belisle, *Histoire de la presse franco-américaine et des Canadiens-français aux États-Unis* (Worcester, MA: L'Opinion Publique, 1911); Félix Gatineau, *Historique des Conventions générales des Canadiens-français aux États-Unis, 1865–1901* (Woonsocket, RI: Union Saint-Jean-Baptiste d'Amérique, 1927); Josaphat Benoit, *L'Ame franco-américaine* (Montreal: Editions Albert Lévesque, 1935); Association Canado-Américaine, *Les Franco-Américains peints par eux-mêmes* (Montreal: Editions Albert Lévesque, 1936); Robert Rumilly, *Historie des Franco-Américains* (Woonsocket, RI: Union Saint-Jean-Baptiste d'Amérique, 1958); Renaud Albert

et al., ed., *A Franco-American Overview* (Cambridge, MA: National Assessment and Dissemination Center, 1979–1981) 8 volumes. Several histories of Quebec have also been utilized.

2. Alfred O. Hero, Jr., "The American Side of the Cultural Relationship," unpublished manuscript, December 1982, pp. 36–37.

3. Proceedings published to date are Claire Quintal and André Vachon, eds., *Situation de la recherche sur la Franco-Américanie* (Quebec: Conseil de la Vie française en Amérique, 1980); Claire Quintal, ed., *L'émigrant québécois vers les États-Unis: 1850–1920* (Quebec: Conseil de la Vie française en Amérique, 1982); and Claire Quintal, ed., "The Little Canadas of New England" (Worcester, MA: French Institute/Assumption College, 1983).

4. *Le répertoire de la vie française en Amérique* (Quebec: Conseil de la Vie française en Amérique, 1981).

10

How America Sees Quebec

Stephen Banker

Virtually everything the United States hears about French Canada comes from English-Canadians. In U.S. newspapers and magazines and on radio and television, Quebec news (on those rare occasions that it travels across the border) is gathered, edited, and presented by Anglo-Canadians. The lack of Québécois voices might be expected because the linguistic barrier is fundamental to the Canadian struggle. But that U.S. news services have opted to let Canadians report the news for them instead of seeing for themselves is remarkable.[1]

Such reporting has led to an unbalanced perspective in the United States, which is further distorted by scholarly studies that fail to take the real world into account, by the peculiar habits of wire service and broadcast news gathering, and by the clumsy efforts of the Quebec government to rectify the situation. The result is that the prevailing U.S. attitude favors "a united Canada," a phrase that has been used by several Washington administrations.

The Just-Like-Us-ification of Quebec

In mid-1981, Henry Giniger, then Ottawa correspondent of *The New York Times*, told a Quebec City audience that the Parti Québécois had aroused hostility among such important U.S. institutions as the government, the business community, and the military. "Yes," said a member of his audience, "but what do the workers think?" Giniger replied the U.S. workers don't think about Quebec at all. "Quebec is the furthest thing from their minds," he explained. "They don't read about it in whatever papers they read. And they certainly don't get much on television, which is where they get most of their information." This, Giniger remembers, "shocked the hell out of the audience."

Perhaps the surprise was because Quebeckers are conscious of their special cultural position in North America. Yet, as I hope to show here, coverage of French Canada in the U.S. media is hit with a double whammy: not only does one disputant present both sides of the argument, but overall attention suffers from the "just like us" fallacy, which only slightly more justifiably diminishes consideration of the rest of Canada.

General Tone of Coverage

The press in the United States covers dramatic events in Quebec—mainly calamities and confrontational politics. The border areas of New England, for reasons of consanguinity as well as geographical proximity, are relatively sensitive to French-Canadian issues. And in many parts of the United States, there is an attempt by local newspapers to cover economic news, such as billion-dollar sales of hydroelectricity or subway cars when those regions are directly affected.

Occasional efforts are made to do scenesetters or backgrounders, usually as spinoffs to other ongoing stories. For example, during the Falklands War, Giniger was able to write about St. Pierre and Miquelon, two small islands in the North Atlantic, trading on the thesis that they might someday be central to a similar tug-of-war between France and Canada. But such opportunities occur only sporadically. "It is true," says John Anderson, editorial writer of *The Washington Post*, "that some events—the sharp, hard ones—are much more susceptible to reporting. We can report the referendum in Quebec, but to give American readers a week by week, month by month, account is a much more difficult thing to do."

The task is difficult for a number of reasons, not least of which is apathy on the part of the U.S. public. Canadian nationalism has also worked against the flow of news southward from Quebec. The Ottawa policy that resulted in the demise of *Time Canada* in the mid-1970s also resulted in the abandonment of *Time's* major office in Montreal. So the United States' most popular newsweekly no longer has the antennae in Quebec that it previously had.

When news of Quebec appears in *Time, Newsweek,* or *US News & World Report*, it is frequently in the business section. Economics, after all, is the principal issue to most U.S. readers with respect to Canada. This conforms with the "service revolution" that has swept the news business in recent years. The idea is to make news more useful to its consumers. Thus the refrain of many editors is, "How is this going to affect the reader (or the viewer)?" That question is easiest to answer in the business section.

When magazines of opinion treat Quebec, they do so, predictably enough, when they find grist for their mills. *The National Review*, a conservative voice in U.S. politics, featured a June 25, 1982, article by

Lubor J. Zink on "The Unpenetrated Problem of Pierre Trudeau." Zink, a Canadian, sees Trudeau as a leftwing threat to North American society, and he details the paradox of Trudeau's relationship with his home province: how Quebec has provided him with both heavy support and burdensome problems.

Rolling Stone, a voice of the new left, published Jane Alpert's article, "I Bombed the Federal Building," on July 23, 1981, in which the writer describes assisting members of the radical Quebec group, Le Front de Libération du Québec (FLQ), to hijack an airplane to Cuba in 1969.

In book publishing, there has been one significant event in the past few years. That was the appearance in 1981 of *The Question of Separatism*, a thoughtful, discursive approach to the Quebec situation by Jane Jacobs, a Pennsylvania-born woman who is now resident in Toronto. The publisher, Random House, expended money and effort promoting the book and it received good reviews, well played, around the United States. Quebec's premier, René Lévesque, even told the American publication *Barron's* (June 7, 1982) that he found the book persuasive. Nonetheless, it sold only 7,500 copies in both hard and soft cover.

If there is one area of U.S. press coverage in which Quebec has been favorably presented, it is the travel sections of newspapers and magazines. Many stories still express naive delight and wonderment that French is spoken in the province. Typical is the lead concocted by a *Newsday* (Long Island) writer for the May 2, 1982, paper: "You'd like to take the children to a foreign land, to expose them to a foreign culture, another history. But the price, inflated by the cost of air travel, is prohibitive. What to do?"

In a more serious vein, but equally up-tempo, are such articles as Margaret Atwood's piece in the June 1982 *Vogue*, "Canada Coming on Strong," which makes a special bow to *les artistes* of Quebec.

The gentle treatment on the travel page is the other side of the undercoverage coin, for if more were to be made of Quebec's turbulent politics and innovative economics, the travel editors would quickly be disenchanted.

The proliferation of newsletters has resulted in increased dissemination of specialized news about Quebec. Audiences tend to be well-to-do people of industry, heavily engaged in their work. Government officials, academics, union officials, and the general press also read these publications. Two such newsletters that frequently refer to Quebec are *Pulp & Paper* and *Energy Daily*.

Canada Today/d'Aujord'hui is put out monthly by the Canadian Embassy in Washington. In the decade ending in 1982, it has devoted half a dozen issues to Quebec, and there have been numerous mentions in other issues. There is a discernible federalist point of view in the publication, but it is uncommonly well written (by Tom Kelly, a U.S. national) and goes down easily. The propagandistic tone is limited to emphasis and selection—it is very careful with facts. *Canada Today/ d'Aujord'hui* has a circulation of almost 100,000 U.S. residents. They include federal, state, and local government officials; business, professional, and cultural affairs people; members of the press; teachers and students; and U.S. residents who like to vacation in Canada. The publication receives more than a thousand postal communications per month, which, if nothing more, means that it has a very active relationship with its readers.

Less successful is *Quebec Update*, a four-page newsletter published forty-six times a year by the Quebec government through its offices in Atlanta, Boston, Chicago, Los Angeles, Lafayette (Louisiana), and New York. It goes to businessmen, journalists, academics, Quebeckers resident in the United States, and anybody else who wants it. The distribution from Quebec House in New York (probably the largest list) is just over 2,000. The tone of the letter varies under different editors, but by and large it is determined to squeeze in every positive-sounding economic development, no matter how far-fetched, and to omit everything else, no matter how important.

Newspapers

There are about a dozen staff reporters for U.S. publications stationed in Canada. Of these, only Alan Freeman of *Dow-Jones/Wall Street Journal* and Leo Ryan of *The Journal of Commerce* are based in Quebec. Both are in Montreal. Both men are bilingual Quebeckers from basically Anglo backgrounds (though Ryan's mother was French-Canadian). Both normally write skeptically about the Parti Québécois and its agenda. Ryan explains that he reflects "the point of view of the majority of the business community in Montreal."

Many news organizations have "stringers" (freelancers, sometimes on retainers) in Quebec. Because of the informal nature of these arrangements, the personnel change rapidly. The stringers for U.S. outlets are often full-time employees of Canadian news organizations; virtually all of them are Anglo-Canadians.

Naturally enough, English-language publications choose their correspondents from among those whose first language is English—but there is something more subtle at work here. News in Quebec is channeled to the United States through unilingual U.S. reporters or through bilingual Canadians whose loyalties are distinctly Anglo-Canadian. No matter how bilingual those Canadians may be, their involvement in the great national upheaval of Canada forms their opinions and perceptions. To reach a U.S. audience, the reality of French Canada must overcome numerous obstacles—linguistic, cultural, national.

Despite all this, Henry Giniger of *The New York Times* received high marks from all sides for his explications of French-Canadian life and his "fairness." An American, he felt at home in the French language and took a special interest in reporting Quebec life. In the days leading up to the May 1980 referendum, Giniger focused on a Quebec family who described themselves as nationalists, but who lined up three to one against the sovereignty-association proposal of the Parti Québécois. This was a journalistic coup, if not a scoop, and later some of his colleagues called him "prescient."

But Giniger, who in 1982 was transferred to New York, believes his coverage suffered from his being based in the federal capital. He says, "You can't cover Quebec sitting in Ottawa. It's an entirely different world, a different point of view. In Ottawa, you were constantly pounded by federal propaganda against the Parti Québécois. The Liberals, after all, were in power in Ottawa, and for them the main enemy was René Lévesque and the PQ."

As for his role as an American, Giniger says: "I have fewer hangups as a foreigner than if I were part of the struggle. I didn't start off with deep prejudices that the Canadian-English community is apt to have. I could move from one world to the other. I can understand both— but I'm not involved in the damn thing. If Quebec wants to be independent, it's okay with me."

That "okay with me"—the mildness, the willingness to let the *Québec-libre* philosophy sink or swim as it deserves—is not an attitude found among many Canadians.

When There Is Attention . . .

Although U.S. reporters in Canada regularly make get-acquainted tours through Quebec, and most Quebec government officials speak English, the opportunity to communicate with the man on the street (or the farm) is denied them, except through interpreters. But despite the lack of direct coverage, U.S. newspapers and magazines are comfortable expressing freewheeling opinions about Quebec. *The Arkansas Gazette* wrote on April 20, 1982, "Premier René Lévesque of Quebec calls the Constitution a 'betrayal' of French Canada and his followers will likely continue their agitation for separation." *The Baltimore Sun*, however, opined a week later that, "With the Constitution finally 'patriated,' there is a distinct impression that the most perilous of secessionist times is over." The editorial did not state for whom the peril existed.

Just as Giniger was an exception to generalizations about covering Quebec from Ottawa, some editorialists write perceptive copy from their armchairs many miles away. *The Houston Post* seems to have an unusual sensitivity to Quebec issues. After describing the components of the constitutional question on April 17, 1982, the paper continued:

> Puzzlingly, all this was done without the consent of Quebec and against the vociferous opposition of Quebec's Premier René Lévesque. The provincial governments have always been strong. They think more in terms of a confederation of provinces than a federal union. Each is more aware of its assets and selfish interests than most American states. Western Canada is intent on making the most of its oil wealth. Quebec is determined to be a French nation within the federation.

Hot Off the Press?

U.S. reporters in Canada often feel frustrated by the way their home offices handle their copy. It is cut, played badly, and frequently shelved despite its timeliness until a suitable space appears. Says Giniger: "Much of what I did, [the *Times*] sat on for days in New York."

An example of this pattern can be seen in the coverage of what came to be known as *l'affaire Charron*. The story involved the young majority leader of the Quebec legislature, Claude Charron, who resigned his post early in 1982 after being caught stealing a jacket from Eaton's department store in Montreal. The story was further spiced by allegations of Charron's unorthodox life-style and by accounts of his capture by a store detective, also an Olympic sprinting hopeful, who tackled him in a snowbank.

Despite the clear-cut nature of the crime, the political atmosphere was such that the incident became another point of contention between French and English factions in the province. Many of Charron's partisans claimed that Eaton's prosecuted their leader only because of his political beliefs. The most astonishing element may have been Eaton's subsequent acknowledgment that it indeed would not have taken Charron to court if he, as a first offender, had given back the coat and apologized, rather than running out the door when apprehended.

All this is by way of noting that *l'affaire Charron* amounted to an excellent news story: an eccentric celebrity involved with crime and politics. For the tabloids, there was even a chase. And for any reader, the story provided a sharp focus of French-English bitterness in Quebec. Yet when reporter Susan Brown of the Knight News Service wrote an article about it, her dispatch was carried in the *Detroit Free Press* on March 22, 1982, and in *The Buffalo (NY) News* on May 16, 1982. Same story, two months apart.

Scholarly Contributions

In a study of U.S. newspaper coverage of the 1980 referendum, Vernone M. Sparkes, James P. Winter, and Pirouz Shoar Ghaffari of Syracuse University said their "most surprising finding" was that *The Wall Street Journal* ran only five stories on the subject during May, the month of the voting, but seventy-four nonreferendum stories about Canada. Frozen by their academic stance, the scholars ingenuously wondered if the newspaper had "purposefully downplayed the referendum."

In 1981, Sparkes and Ghaffari concluded after another study that "The American press . . . has somewhat improved its coverage of Canada." This time, they based their finding on various quantifiables, such as column inches. But such measurements are frequently misleading, according to John Anderson of *The Washington Post*, who says, "There are a lot of people who tend to equate column inches with moral standing. That is a calculus we are not prepared to deal with."

In their study of the 1980 referendum, Professor Sparkes and his university colleagues made the elementary mistake of confusing what a newspaper's outside contributor wrote with the position of the newspaper itself. As they put it, "*The Washington Post* suggested [that the referendum] 'may be as ominous as was South Carolina's decision in 1860 to withdraw from the United States.' " And again, they assert:

> *The Washington Post* proposed that civil war in Canada was a serious possibility, a prospect that Canadians and the Canadian press would regard as ludicrous. The *Post* said:
>
> > If the referendum does fail, then, there is a serious possibility that violence will break out in Montreal and perhaps other cities, and that Trudeau would again send in troops. In that case, the specter of civil war would hang over Canada.

In fact, *The Washington Post* did not say any of that. Those words came from an individual named Don Nuechterlein. Unlike anonymous editorials that reflect the thinking of the newspaper, his signed article was buried on page 4 of the financial section, where people of various political and economic positions—sometimes extreme—are invited to set forth their views. If the *Post* is to be criticized at all, it is for wasting a part of the limited space it would devote to the Quebec referendum on such an outlandish view.

But it was not *The Washington Post* that anticipated a revolution in Canada over Quebec rights. It was an outside contributor who has never had any connection with the newspaper. Professor Sparkes and his academic colleagues should be asked: Who said, "We have met the enemy and they is us!"? Was it *The Washington Post*? Or was it Pogo?

It is worthwhile to pause over this misinterpretation because it fits so neatly into the preconceived notions of many observers of the U.S. press, especially in regard to coverage of Quebec. Charlotte Gray, writing in the May 1982 issue of the Canadian magazine, *Saturday Night*, gullibly picked up the accusation against *The Washington Post*, failed to check it, but seized the opportunity to heap scorn on the U.S. press through this secondhand and unsubstantiatable allegation.

The *Post's* actual position on the referendum, as expressed on the editorial page of the news section, was quite moderate: "[G]rowth and stability now depend on those political leaders who urged Quebec to vote 'non.' On their response . . . depends whether the issue of separatism has now finally been put to rest."

But as in the news business, there is no catching up with a mistake. *The Washington Post's* "ludicrous" statements will pass into history as such on the basis of publication by those academic "researchers" from Syracuse University.

Business Publications

If one is looking for clear hostility to the separatist movement in the U.S. press, the best places to search are business publications. It has already been noted here that the only U.S. publications with full-time employees in Quebec are *The Journal of Commerce* and *Dow-Jones/ Wall Street Journal*. The Montreal bureau of *Dow-Jones* often gathers information that is not even intended for publication. In an article that appeared on January 6, 1982, reporter Leo Ryan of *The Journal of Commerce* returned to the subject of Quebec's operational deficit and concluded, "Premier René Lévesque is skating on thin ice."

Similarly, *Barron's*, in the issue of November 9, 1981, comments editorially:

> Americans often assume that the Quebec Anglophones are paying for past sins. This is naive. The Anglophones largely built Quebec, their rule was mild by world standards and the Francophones' prolonged failure to participate fully in the commercial system was mainly the fault of their own rural predilections and rapacious politicians.

The editorial also calls attention to the budget deficit, and charges that Quebec's finance minister, Jacques Parizeau, "talked of extorting $150 million a year" from Hydro-Quebec in order to bring more money into the provincial coffers.

So when, in July 1982, *Standard & Poor's* and *Moody's Investor Service*, both New York firms, lowered their credit ratings for Quebec, the news got heavy play in financial chronicles.

The harshness among business publications, if that is what it is, should be seen in the light of their responsibilities to their readership. They are providing information that is designed to be useful for investments. It is the wish of every investor to eliminate variables. Political unrest is a very large variable. The financial community is uncomfortable with it, and its publications reflect that discomfort.

The uncertainty is not just a question of independence. The problem to business writers is the overall social and political outlook of the Parti Québécois, which considers itself social democratic, i.e., left of center. Early on, the PQ expressed ideas about foreign investment and Quebec control of its natural resources that it modified after achieving power. But for the U.S. capitalist world, those statements had an ominous ring whose resonance continued to be heard.

Unpredictability

The United States government does not control what reporters write, but it briefs reporters on request before they visit Canada and, through its embassy and consulates, while they are there. To a traveling reporter who has too many stories to cover in too short a time, the briefings are crucial to his orientation. And those briefings express the U.S. tilt in favor of "a united Canada." Presidents have used that phrase and so have State Department officials. Such an attitude comes naturally in a situation in which the United States has better relations with Canada than with any other country, and Canada's crises appear manageable compared to difficulties that confront the United States in other parts of the world. An independent Quebec would be an unknown, a counterweight to predictability.

When the PQ talked about taking Quebec out of NATO and NORAD, this disturbed the Pentagon, which also gives journalistic briefings. When the PQ reversed itself on the military pacts, the U.S. Departments of State and Defense wondered if the new position was not opportunistic, something that might be re-reversed when the right moment presented itself.

This background may help to explain why Lévesque has sometimes been defiled in the U.S. press with epithets ranging from "another Castro" to "fascist." The first is tied to the nationalization of a few industries. The second is a product of "the language police" and the flight of Quebec Jews, both of which received more coverage than they might have without those frightening phrases.

News Agencies Set Tone

Many newspapers and radio and television stations in the United States depend on The Associated Press (AP) and United Press International (UPI) for their foreign news, including news of Canada and Quebec. Even those publications with their own correspondents in Canada (there are no broadcasters) sometimes print wire service stories because their reporters are otherwise occupied.

Wire service copy is much more widely distributed than anything that is staff-written for a newspaper. Wire copy is also the most important basis for local and network radio and television news. Frequently, the copy is read on the air word for word as it appeared on the wires.

Yet neither wire service has a single person stationed in Quebec. The AP, which has one correspondent in Toronto, depends on Canadian Press (CP) for its Quebec coverage, and UPI has a contractual relationship with its offshoot, United Press Canada (UPC).

This is important because what the people of the United States are seeing and hearing is an Anglo-Canadian version of events in Quebec. As of mid-1982, all four UPC reporters in Quebec were Anglo-Canadians. CP, with a much larger staff, had three French-Canadians among the twenty-two filing on the English wire from Quebec. Moreover, all CP and UPC copy goes through the agencies' Toronto clearinghouses before it is passed on to New York for U.S. distribution, and those who run the desks in Toronto were, without exception, Anglo-Canadians.

There is no charge of conspiracy here, nor even a suspicion that the editors in Toronto are supressing certain stories or details. The problem is more complex, having to do with differing world views. It is exacerbated by the ill feeling that exists between the two societies.

A personal example may illustrate that difficulty. I was told by a Quebec government official about what he considered the proclivity of the Anglo press to "exaggerate" violence in Quebec. This official referred to a June 25, 1981, story put out by UPC that in his opinion unnecessarily lumped the previous day's celebration of St. Jean Baptiste Day, a "national holiday," with some "mafia" killings. "Such murders," he told me, "sometimes take place in New York or Chicago, but when they happen in Montreal, UPC makes them look as though the separatists are doing them."

I asked a New York Quebec House spokesperson to get me a copy of the story. She called UPC's senior news editor for Canada, Bob McConachie, in Toronto, who told her, "I won't release the story because I know what use you people will make of it." I then called McConachie, explaining that I did not represent the Quebec government, that I was a U.S. journalist looking into the ways Quebec news travels to the United

States. "I don't see where we fit in," he said, When I reminded him that he was the conduit through which all Quebec news flows from UPC to UPI, he moderated his tone and told me, "We've had a running battle with the Quebec government, which is why I was so touchy."

But still he refused to release the story. I told him I thought it was absurd to hold back a news story that had been sent all over the world a year earlier. He did not change his position, but he agreed to discuss the circumstances of the controversy with me. He said:

> Previously, we were a division of UPI. Since 1979, we have been a separate corporation—80-percent owned by Sun Publishing, which puts out newspapers in Toronto, Edmonton, and Calgary—but we remain an affiliate of UPI. Most of the criticism we receive from the Quebec government has to do with how American newspapers rehandle Canadian copy. When we were a division of UPI, we wrote our copy for American consumption, but now we write for Canadian newspapers. There is more than a subtle difference. When you write for the Americans, particularly on a subject like the Canadian Constitution, you oversimplify. If Allan Singer is mentioned, you have to explain that he is a Montreal businessman who took the Quebec government to court because he refused to change his [stationery store] sign to French, and so disobeyed the law. Then you have to explain what the law is. The story builds up and up. Now we just write for Canadian newspapers and give a drop to our New York office. It's picked up there and rewritten with the American perspective. There is an attempt to simplify and that obviously is very touchy, so this is where you run into difficulties.
>
> We are happy with the job we are doing in representing Quebec to the United States. But the Quebec government misunderstands the relationship between UPI and UPC. They think that any criticism amounts to "misinterpretation by the English press," which then becomes "the American press." You cannot persuade them the UPC is not an American organization in Canada.

In Washington, a UPI executive adds, "There are not a lot of Canadian stories that make the U.S. wire. Two stories a day would be a lot—unless they have violence, death, and destruction."

The St. Jean Baptiste Day story had those elements, though not to the extent that some stories of mayhem do. The story, as it appeared in *The Toronto Sun*, is reproduced in Figure 10.1.

After having gone the extra mile to find the story, I was surprised at its innocuousness. I disagree with the Quebec official who said that the juxtaposition of the murders and the celebration was unwarranted. I do not see how it would have been possible to tell that story without mentioning what the crowd was doing.

Figure 10.1.   The St. Jean Baptiste Day Story—Objective or Biased?

3 DIE AT QUEBEC FESTIVAL

Gunman blasts crowd

MONTREAL (UPC-Special) — A gunman who hit six people when he sprayed bullets into a crowd of 200 St. Jean Baptiste Day merrymakers early yesterday continues to elude police.

Three people were killed and three others were injured when the lone gunman opened fire in an apartment house courtyard at about 1 a.m.

Police said two men slain, Serge Desmarais, 20, and Bruno Michaud, 23, had criminal records and theorized the shootings may have been motivated by a drug-related "settling of accounts."

But a young girl also killed, Manon Laprise, 19, appears to have been an innocent victim of the violence which marred observance of Quebec's national holiday, police said.

Confusion swept the crowd as the gunfire rattled against the noise of the festivities.

"People didn't know what was happening until people started falling," police spokesman Charles Poxon said. The gunman escaped through the crowds.

"We don't have a heck of a lot to go on."

Source: *The Toronto Sun*, June 25, 1981.

And on Television—the Same Story

The U.S. television networks have no staffers anywhere in Canada. When there is a Canadian story of substance in Quebec or elsewhere, it is frequently reported to the enormous U.S. TV audience by Peter Jennings or Barrie Dunsmore of ABC, by Morley Safer of CBS or Robert MacNeil of PBS—all of whom are Anglo-Canadian in origin, though the networks never identify them as such.

Computer checks using the cues "Quebec" and "French Canada" of the ABC and CBS evening news programs between April 1980 (the month before the referendum) and July 1982 reveal that CBS had thirteen stories on the air during that time. Five were about violent crimes or calamities. Two were about the air controller strike. Two were about patriation of the constitution. And four were about the referendum. There was less coverage on ABC, where only eight stories were presented in the same period. One of them bears repetition here in full. Anchorman Peter Jennings reported from New York on April 15, 1980, as follows:

> Political news from north of the border today. The residents of Quebec have learned they will vote on May 20th for or against partial independence from the rest of Canada. It's a vote on political independence for the largely French-speaking province while retaining economic and monetary links. The rest of Canada thinks it won't or shouldn't work.

Surely that final sentence would have had a different ring to it if the audience had known that the speaker was a product of the opposing force.

When the networks are confronted by a fast-breaking story in Canada, they have no hesitation about using reporters from CBC or CTV. Again, the Anglo-Canadian perception is the one transmitted, even though the stories are sometimes especially done for the U.S. networks. Canada is the only country in the world in which the U.S. networks frame reports by foreigners as if they had been done by U.S. network staffers. Even from England, BBC reports, when they are used, are identified as such. The reason must be that the Anglo-Canadian accent falls so easily on south-of-the border ears. If so, that disadvantages Quebec, since Anglo-Canadians are the only ones who are permitted to tell the United States the Anglo-Canadian news *and* the Franco-Canadian news. This discrimination amounts to a tilt on the part of the U.S. networks in favor of the Canadian confederation.

In the Quebec context, television's need for interesting pictures means that the issue of independence is reduced to personalism. The TV eye in the United States sees Pierre Trudeau as a hero. Always the most casually dressed at any summit conference, he is a statesman who has been humanized by the ordeal his wife put him through. He is a smiling, athletic nation-builder.

If Trudeau is a builder, Réne Lévesque is a termite. He is a crybaby, a nuisance. He appears infrequently on U.S. television, but every appearance is to complain. He does not like the constitution, which would snap the apron strings to Mother England. He ungraciously objects to the visit of a perfectly pleasant Queen Elizabeth. His legislature even votes to withhold congratulations on the birth of Prince Charles' son—as if saying something courteous would introduce disturbing sunshine into a nice, gloomy day.

These caricatures exist because of television's preference for confrontation, preferably of a violent nature. But the quick glimpses have resulted in a distortion. Trudeau, given time on television, comes across as aloof, academic, and close to humorless, while Lévesque, a professional TV performer in the past, is an amusing, persuasive, sometimes brilliant speaker. His television appearances in Quebec have been, according to Giniger, "masterpieces." But the U.S. television audience has not seen any such thing.

There is a competition for time on television that is much more intense than the battle for space in newspapers. Stories usually have to justify themselves in terms of visual interest as well as importance. That is why many people in the industry hope that the evening news on U.S. networks will be lengthened to a full hour. In arguing that case before the Radio and Television News Directors convention in Hollywood, Florida, in December 1980, CBS News anchorman Dan Rather said:

> The evening news ought to be an hour. . . . We need that time to tell the American public the important things that are going on in the world.

I see things that are happening that are interesting but that simply don't get told because we don't have the time. . . . Most days, Central America winds up on the [editing room] floor. . . . The Quebec separatist movement— what an extraordinary story—on the floor. . . . I'll tell you, it gets pretty crowded on that floor.[2]

Since Rather made that speech, there has been significant expansion of network television news in the morning and late at night. It will be interesting to take stock after a few years to see whether or not the additional time has been used to fulfill Rather's agenda.

Quebec Fights Back

Despite formidable obstacles to fair and thorough treatment in the U.S. press, Quebec keeps trying. Lise Bissonnette, editor of *Le Devoir*, in *The American Review of Canadian Studies* (Spring 1981), describes "*Operation-Amérique*," devised in 1978. Its purpose was, in part, to establish a communications program aimed at opinion leaders in the U.S. media. She writes, "Budgets increased, energetic public relations operations had the effect of improving American press coverage following the disastrous distortions of 1976–'77."

According to a Canadian reporter, Quebec officials "worry about American opinion, they think about it, they're oriented to it." But their actions sometimes belie that concern. Lévesque has said that he prefers the United States to English Canada. He is proud to have worn a U.S. uniform during World War II, and he still spends some of his vacations in New England. He was, inconveniently, on vacation in Maine in July 1982 when *The New York Times'* managing editor, Seymour Topping, wanted to interview him as part of a series of conversations with provincial premiers. Topping, the son-in-law of the well known Canadian diplomat, Chester Ronning, has a particular interest in Canada and has been a force in favor of more Canadian coverage in the *Times*. With him on the swing through the provinces was Michael Kaufman, who was soon to replace Henry Giniger in the Ottawa bureau.

There were those in Quebec's Department of Intergovernment Affairs who felt that the opportunity to sit down with a high-level executive of the most prestigious and influential newspaper in the United States, along with the individual who was going to be covering Quebec for that paper for the next few years, would have been worth a day's interruption of the premier's vacation.

It is true that Lévesque had met with those people before and would again, but that special moment would not reappear. It was an occasion in which the *Times* was not pursuing a particular story, it was asking the premier to survey present circumstances in reflective terms. The *Times* was printing verbatim interviews with the premiers, not stories in which the subject's words and thoughts were rearranged. Finally, it was an opportunity to give Kaufman a firsthand version of the Parti Québécois' point of view before he began his regular duties as the paper's chief Canadian correspondent. The fact that this opportunity was allowed to glide by hints that the Quebec government—at the top, at least—was not fully commmitted to its own priorities.

Earlier the same month, Lévesque visited Washington at the invitation of Republican senators, who meet on a regular basis with foreign officials. Before the visit, Quebec spokespersons sent out numerous, conflicting messages to reporters in Washington and New York. First, the prime minister would hold a news conference in Washington. Then, the prime minister would not hold a news conference but would be available to those who "staked out" (hung around) the Senate Foreign Relations Committee room. Then, the prime minister would not be available to reporters because this was a private visit. And so on. After this carousel had gone around a few times, one Washington reporter told the Quebec official who had been telephoning him, "Thank you very much. Please tell the prime minister that if he wants to see me, I will be in my office."

The uncertain signals, the lack of coordination, unnecessarily created a negative feeling about Lévesque himself and the plausibility of working with the Quebec government. In a two-paragraph item, *The New York Times* noted that Lévesque had "slipped into Washington" and that the Canadian embassy was not involved with the arrangements. All in all, it was a maladroit performance that did nothing to modify the U.S. image of René Lévesque as a nay-sayer.

Conclusion

Barring dramatic news events of global consequence, U.S. press coverage of Quebec can be expected to remain at about the present level, with television the most likely area of enhancement. There will undoubtedly be a surge in coverage when national and provincial elections are held, but there is nothing on the horizon to suggest a fundamental change in the present system of news gathering and dissemination—a system that has led to the inequities, distortions, and omissions described in this chapter.

Notes

1. See also Alan K. Henrickson, "Le Canada français dans la press américaine," in Albert Legault and Alfred O. Hero, Jr., eds., *Le nationalisme québécois à la croisée des chemins* (Quebec: Centre Québécois des Relations Internationales, *Choix* 7, 1975), pp. 261–277.

2. Marvin Barrett, ed., *Broadcast Journalism* (New York: Everest House, 1982), p. 145.

11
Quebec Nonfrancophones and the United States

Martin Lubin

This chapter explores images of Quebec projected by its nonfrancophone inhabitants to the United States and, to a lesser degree, impacts of the United States on the thoughts and actions of these Quebeckers relative to developments in their province. Emphasis will be placed on the period since the election of the first Parti Québécois (PQ) government on November 15, 1976.

The discussion will focus first on the relevant background, composition, and structure of the many diverse minorities that comprise the nonfrancophone minority. Second, it will turn to their perceptions of and reactions to developments in Quebec since Law 22 of the Liberal Bourassa government in 1974 made French the official Quebec language, limited access to English schools to children already fluent in that language, and urged opening of attractive private-sector careers to francophones otherwise qualified but not necessarily fluent in English. Third, the linkages of these Quebec minorities with the United States and their impacts on American perceptions will be examined. And fourth, a few brief observations will be made concerning U.S. influences on nonfrancophones' behavior toward the demands of the francophone majority and the PQ government. The chapter will conclude with a brief review and some suggestions for priority research on these hardly explored transborder impacts.

A substantial body of diverse empirical research exists about the nature of nonfrancophone communities: who they are; *where* they are geographically, socially, and economically; and their attitudes and actions toward developments in Quebec and Canada since the beginning of the Quiet Revolution in 1960.[1] Here only a brief summary of these findings is possible, insofar as they are essential to American understanding of who these groups are and their likely impacts on the United States.

Very little thought, attention, or discussion and virtually no systematic research have focused on linkages of these Quebec minorities south of the border. Even less reliable information is known about influences of these Quebeckers on U.S. images and actions regarding Quebec, or the impacts of the United States and its people on the perceptions and behavior of these nonfrancophones toward the issues facing them in their province, and between it and the rest of Canada. This chapter is an initial attempt to piece together the very limited existing evidence using the author's personal experience as a Montreal native living for some years in the United States, varied experiences brought to his attention by others, and his interviews on linkages of U.S.-based ethnic organizations with counterpart Quebec groups. Thus, the following discussion of reciprocal impacts will necessarily be speculative, hypothetical, preliminary, and piecemeal, pending more systematic and exhaustive empirical analyses.

Who and Where Are the Nonfrancophones?

Quebeckers whose native language is not French comprise two general categories, anglophones and allophones.[2] The former are inhabitants of the province, irrespective of ancestry, who learned English as children at home prior to any other language, and for whom English is the language they use predominantly, at home and usually at work. Allophones are immigrants, and children of immigrants, whose native tongue learned as youngsters at home was neither French nor English, whose language in their families remains very often the same, and who may or may not work regularly in that language.

Allophones

Allophones particularly are a very diverse category, not only as to ethnic background, but also as to degree and spheres of integration or assimilation into an increasingly francophone society. Quebec contains some thirty ethnic groups, few of which spoke either of Canada's official languages in their country of origin. They may work in a retail establishment or other enterprise where most or all the others are of the same ethnic origin, in a neighborhood where most or many are likewise, and where they use their native language predominantly or regularly. Others may deal predominantly with anglophones as employers, colleagues, and/or clienteles; fewer deal with francophones, but some deal with both anglophones and francophones, speaking both languages in addition to their own. Moreover, some allophones have married outside their ethnic group, so that their family language may be different from their native tongue. More often than not the family language is English, but it is French among a growing minority of allophones. The second generation has attended or is attending predominantly English schools, especially children of post–World War II immigrants, and as adults this generation works more often in English-speaking rather than French-speaking business communities.

Anglophones

The anglophone category is also quite diverse, though less so than allophones. Catholic Irish began arriving in Quebec in significant numbers during the potato famine of the late 1840s and continued to do so for over a century. Their native language on arrival, other than Gaelic, was English, and they have been reported in census and most other data in the general "British" category of origin. But before the arrival of the Irish, the English-speaking Quebeckers were mainly descendants of Protestant British Loyalists who left the thirteen colonies during and shortly after the American Revolution, joined by other Protestants from Scotland, England, Wales, and Ireland. In the 1871 census, and for decades thereafter, the descendants of these combined "British" immigrants, now including the Irish, comprised overwhelming majorities of nonfrancophones. However, they were joined beginning in the last quarter of the nineteenth century by increasing numbers of Jews—the third largest group after francophones and the anglophones of British backgrounds, until Italians overtook the Jews in numbers in the 1950s.[3] Except for a minority of Sephardics, most of whom came from North Africa beginning in the 1950s, Jews overwhelmingly integrated into anglophone rather than francophone society. Italians who arrived before World War II—most came thereafter—were more inclined than any other ethnic group of nonfrancophone immigrants to send their children to French Catholic schools rather than to Irish-controlled English Catholic schools; the Italian language resembled French more than English.[4]

However, until language legislation of 1974 and especially 1977 inhibited them from doing so, the vast majority of immigrants whose native language was not French sent their offspring to English schools, and the offspring thereafter joined anglophone society. By the 1980s probably more than a third of anglophones were of other than Irish or United Kingdom extraction.

Thus, popular definitions and identities attached to anglophones and allophones vary, as do some of those used in empirical studies of their attitudes and behavior. Nevertheless the relevant trends and distribution of attitudes on basic issues facing Quebec are clear.

Table 11.1.   Quebec Population by Native Tongue

	1976 (Census)	1981 (Census)	1976 to 1981		
			Net Natural Growth	Net Migration	Net Population Change
French- speaking Population					
Number	4,989,245	5,307,010	290,371	27,394	+317,765
Percent	80.7	82.4			+6.4
English- speaking Population					
Number	800,680	706,115	46,606	−141,171	−94,565
Percent	12.9	10.9			−11.6
Other Population					
Number	444,520	425,275	25,875	−45,120	−19,245
Percent	7.1	6.7			−4.3
Total Population	6,234,445	6,438,400	362,842	−158,897	+203,955

Source: La Presse, July 24, 1982, p. A-11, Table 1.

The Declining Nonfrancophone Population

During the initial five-year mandate of the PQ government of René Lévesque, the total number of francophones grew by 6.4 percent, from 80.7 percent of the total Quebec population to 82.4 percent; the number of native-language anglophones declined by 11.6 percent, from 12.9 percent to 10.9 percent of the population; and the number of others (of neither of these two languages) declined considerably less, by 4.3 percent, from 7.1 percent to 6.7 percent of all Quebeckers (Table 11.1). But the several sources of these changes in absolute and relative numbers were of differing importance among the three linguistic groups.

From one of the highest birthrates in the industrialized world and the highest in Canada among religious, linguistic, and ethnic groups as late as 1951, francophones (almost all of Catholic upbringing) had lower natural replacement rates over these five years than native anglophones and allophones, including many Irish and other Catholics. Francophones were no longer replacing themselves, while the other two groups were barely doing so (but losing by emigration). No longer would "revenge of the cradle" make up for francophones' formerly massive departures for better jobs outside Quebec, or the very few francophone immigrants since the British conquest of over two centuries before, or the migration of peoples of many other nationalities to Quebec and the assimilation of the vast majority of their offspring into anglophone Montreal or its suburbs rather than into francophone Quebec as a whole.

This decline in francophone birthrates, combined with major post-World War II immigration of nonfrancophones (until Canadian policies sharply restricted it in the early 1970s), and even alleviated by continued emigration of native anglophones, resulted in decline of the francophone proportion of Quebec's population from 82.5 percent to 80.7 percent between 1951 and 1976 (Table 11.1 and 1951 census statistics). Yet except for the integration of most immigrants and their progeny into Anglo-Montreal, the anglophones too would have declined in both absolute and relative numbers between World War II and 1976. In other words, only allophones would have increased in their proportion of the population.

By 1976 Quebec francophones had become sharply less inclined to leave their French-speaking society than either anglophones or allophones (Table 11.1). Economic recession notwithstanding, francophones were very much less apt to depart than some 1.5 million of their ancestors who left for the northeastern United States and the shores of the Great Lakes of both the United States and Ontario (and other Canadian points west) during the century ending with World War II. Indeed, more francophones *came* to Quebec than departed after 1976 (Table 11.1). Some came from abroad, but most of the francophone immigrants were of Québécois ancestry, living across Canada and even in the United States (see Chapter 5). Anglophones were by far the most inclined to leave—particularly younger, better educated ones with talents to offer elsewhere in North America. Ninety percent of net emigration in the five years from 1976 to 1981 was of anglophones; very few anglophones migrated to Quebec, for reasons probably associated with the shift of the economy away from Montreal, initially to Toronto and more industrialized Ontario, then increasingly to the energy- and resource-rich Canadian prairies and west.

Immigration from abroad to Quebec sharply declined as well, due in the first instance to much less permissive Canadian immigration policies since the early 1970s. However, the flow of immigrants was further reduced by a combination of more dynamic economic opportunities to the west of Quebec, the new language laws (Law 22 in 1974 under the Bourassa Liberal government and the more stringent Law 101 in 1977 under the Lévesque government, requiring immigrants' children to attend French rather than English public schools, and making French the only official language and language of work), and finally the agreement in 1978 between the Lévesque and Trudeau governments authorizing Quebec to determine which immigrants, refugees, temporary workers, students, and others from abroad could come to that province.

The accelerated emigration of anglophones and to a lesser extent of allophones is due only in part to the advent of the PQ government, to perceived state interference in and mismanagement of the economy, to threat of independence with or without economic association, and to Laws 22 and especially 101. Moreover, this accelerated emigration may be relatively short-term, depending on future developments.

The shift of the Canadian economy westward from Quebec resulted in growing anglophone emigration well before Law 22 and election of the PQ government two years thereafter. Furthermore, immigrants, although directly affected by schooling provisions of Laws 22 and 101, have remained considerably less inclined than anglophones to leave Quebec. The reasons are probably multiple: their lower average education, skills, and talents saleable for better career opportunities elsewhere; their lesser connections with relatives, university colleagues, friends, and acquaintances in managerial, professional, and other roles outside Quebec apt to provide them with attractive jobs; their lesser capital and self-confidence in English and in its associated North American culture; their lesser sense of loss of previous status, influence, and privilege; and their generally greater willingness to accommodate to the francophone majority.

Moreover, among both nonfrancophone groups, the lowest net emigration occurred just prior to and after the first election of the PQ government. The peak took place in the year from June 1, 1977, to May 31, 1978, during which the PQ proposed, discussed, and passed Law 101. Thereafter, through 1981, net emigration steadily declined, although at the end of this period it was still well above the rate for the months just before and after the November 15, 1976, election.[5] Most nonfrancophones who preferred to move to careers elsewhere, where English is spoken, rather than to learn French, compete in French with ambitious, younger, well-educated francophones, and participate in a society and economy requiring fluency in that language, may largely have done so by the early 1980s. Those who still remain, particularly younger people in growing numbers, have often learned French in immersion schools, some in French schools, and more in French courses in English schools. They are probably disproportionately among those willing to accommodate (see below).

Furthermore, the more extreme unemployment and general recession in Quebec relative to Ontario, prairie and western Canada, and most of the United States have particularly encouraged those whose native language is English to leave for jobs elsewhere, thus expanding the difference in rates of departure between them and allophones and, especially, francophones. A related phenomenon took place during earlier post-1945 recessions as well.[6]

However, even if net emigration of anglophones decreases considerably henceforth, their proportion of the Quebec population seems destined to decline further in relation to francophones. Law 22 and especially Law 101 have already reversed the long-persisting pattern whereby anglicized children of immigrants replaced departing anglophones. The former law required children to pass English fluency tests to enter English rather than French public primary and secondary schools. The latter law requires children of immigrants who had no siblings in English schools after 1977 to attend French schools. French is the primary working language in medium-sized and larger firms, except in roles requiring regular business, professional, research, or other contacts in anglophone Canada, the United States, and elsewhere outside Quebec. The law requires examinations in French to practice law, medicine, and other professions and prohibits most commercial establishments from displaying signs in English outdoors. Thus, the historic replacement of departing anglophones with English-schooled children of immigrants will decline. Furthermore, the number of nonfrancophone immigrants, and of those unwilling to learn French and work in that language, will decline as well.

Anglophone Assimilation of Allophones

The motivations for immigrants to aspire to anglophone rather than francophone society until the two language laws were passed were powerful indeed. Many would have preferred to have come to the United States, but post–World War II Canadian immigration policies were much less restrictive. Many came hoping that Montreal—until the 1960s Canada's metropolis and banking, trade, business, and cultural center where many nongovernmental decisions were made for the rest of the country—would be a stepping stone to the United States. Montreal was moreover where their ships docked until the opening of the Saint Lawrence Seaway in 1954 permitted them to continue into the Great Lakes, and until transocean air travel became cheaper than ship passage. The inhabitants of the continent and country to which they thought they were moving spoke English. Indeed, many arrived in Montreal without being particularly aware, or at least considering important, that most of the inhabitants of the province in which it is situated speak French.

Montreal decision makers, managers, and the jobs and careers they controlled were English-speaking. Economic, social, and geographic mobility and prestige in North America, and in Canada itself, would be achieved in English. Francophones isolated themselves from immigrants, as they did from virtually everybody else. They had no welcoming programs or institutions, their elites lived to themselves and offered no jobs in their usually small, locally-oriented, family-owned enterprises.

Until the mid-1960s, there were few jobs requiring French in the small provincial government. Provincially controlled corporations such as Hydro-Quebec, with careers to offer to francophones, were either in their beginnings or did not yet exist.

The ultramontane clergy who controlled French schools preferred to exclude not only Protestant, Jewish, and other non-Catholic children who might erode the faith of their francophone pupils, but even Irish and other Catholic children who they feared would erode their homogeneous, defensive, agrarian thinking and conservative and inward-looking society and culture. Irish and other Catholics were actively encouraged to establish their own, separate, English-speaking schools, where nonreligious instruction was subsidized by the province, as it was in French Catholic schools. With the exception of an Italian minority before 1939, immigrants were thus actively discouraged by francophone institutions and individuals from integrating into the francophone society.

The francophones whom immigrants were most apt to meet, blue-collar workers in Anglo-controlled enterprises—many of them migrants from poorer farm and village families—were generally hostile to immigrants competing for such jobs. Neither political nor trade union authorities—mainly francophones—acted to mitigate such conflicts. At virtually no levels were there relatively harmonious, give-and-take relations between immigrants and their francophone peers.[7]

Thus, as successive waves of immigrants came into Quebec, francophones foisted them, with their religions and cultural pluralism, onto the anglophone minority. Although "charter-group" Protestants were not eager to welcome them, their Protestant school boards—financed primarily by local property taxes—accepted, at times reluctantly, Eastern Orthodox, Jewish,[8] Hindu, Moslem, and other non-Catholic religious groups of widely divergent languages, cultures, and national origins. Formerly Protestant schools became neutral in terms of religion. Previously predominantly Irish Catholic schools took in children of Italians, Portuguese, Dutch, German, Polish, Hungarian, and other Catholic families. Thereafter, children of immigrants got jobs, intermarried, and lived with English as their sole or primary language far more frequently than with French.

Anglophone Ascendancy

Protestant Anglo-Saxon settlers of the eighteenth and nineteenth centuries had been concentrated in Montreal, Quebec City, the Eastern Townships between the upper St. Lawrence and the U.S. border, and the southern Gaspé coast. However, by the 1970s most of their descendants had migrated to greater Montreal. After arriving in Montreal, very few immigrants or their descendants migrated elsewhere in Quebec. At the time of the 1971 census, over four-fifths of all Quebec anglophones, whatever their ancestry, lived there,[9] as did 99.1 percent of Jews and Greeks, 94.4 percent of Italians, 92.4 percent of the Hispanics, 91.3 percent of Chinese, and more than 85 percent of most other ethnic groups. By contrast, only 49 percent of Quebec's francophones were in greater Montreal. Conversely, in rural areas and the smaller towns that served these rural areas, francophones typically exceeded 95 percent of the population, and only small minorities learned much English.[10]

Thus it was primarily in Montreal that anglophones and the larger immigrant groups built networks of educational, social, health, and service institutions separate from the francophone ones. Until the 1960s these institutions were church-operated. The most prestigious and well financed were funded, run, and until relatively recently staffed at professional levels by descendants of the Protestant "charter group." Examples of these institutions are McGill University, Royal Victoria Hospital, Anglican and Presbyterian churches, museums, theaters, the Montreal Symphony Orchestra, the YMCA, downtown and country clubs, the Montreal *Gazette* and *Star*, and so on. In their self-contained society in western Montreal the anglophones had a network of bookstores, cinemas, retail establishments, and the like to live out their existence without learning French or knowing much about the francophone majority in Quebec. Contacts with francophones were typically perfunctory, superior-to-subordinate, and in English.

Moreover, from western Montreal the descendants of this Protestant "charter group" of anglophones controlled and managed most of the Canadian economy until Toronto challenged their dominance after World War II and surpassed Montreal in the 1960s. Until the last decade or so, Protestant Anglo-Saxons largely excluded most university-educated descendants of non-British immigrants from the most attractive careers in the enterprises they controlled. Irish Catholics, many of them in Montreal for generations, were the first to be so admitted, but until the 1960s they too were few at influential levels of major banks, investment firms, law firms, and anglophone-controlled manufacturing firms and services. Although Jews valued education, sent their children through university degrees, and ascended relatively quickly the economic scale in their own individual and family businesses and the professions, they were effectively excluded from professional and managerial careers in Anglo-Canadian firms—especially banks and investment houses, but also others. Jewish firms, like francophone ones, remain mostly small and medium-sized, labor-intensive, and locally rather than export-oriented. The few larger Jewish enterprises, like the lesser ones, are in wholesaling, or in retailing chains such as food, clothing, and hardware, or in other consumer-oriented production and distribution businesses such as soft and alcoholic beverages (see also Chapter 2). Private enterprises operated by other ethnic groups that were almost wholly excluded until recently from many careers in Anglo-Canadian firms generally fit descriptions somewhat like those of the Jewish-owned enterprises.

As the non–Anglo-Saxon anglophones prospered, educated their children as anglophone Canadians, and became influential in their own ethnic groups, a few successful children and grandchildren of immigrants were gradually drawn into governing boards and professional staffs of community-wide anglophone service, educational, philanthropic, and cultural institutions. Their participation became necessary to fundraising among their particular ethnic groups, as well as to improve the credibility and broaden the outreaches of the organizations they joined. But even today Jews and members of a number of other ethnic groups are infrequent or nonexistent in some clubs and other prestigious and influential private institutions. Jews have therefore developed an institutional network of their own, the most extensive of the ethnic groups— for example, the YMHA, schools, clubs, and the Baron de Hirsch Institute (which after 1971 became the publicly funded Jewish Family Social Services Center, but continued to service mainly Jewish ethnic needs).

Though less so than heretofore, these heterogeneous nonfrancophones continue to comprise a vertically ordered pyramid with Anglo-Saxon Protestants concentrated disproportionately at the top in respect to their influence (in both Quebec and North America as a whole), income, and prestige. At the bottom of the pyramid are Haitians and Orientals.[11] Anglo-Saxon Protestants still largely control and staff the upper levels of the larger, more productive, export-competitive firms with important international business in the United States and elsewhere, and occupy most decision-making roles in Canadian subsidiaries of U.S. and other foreign-controlled corporations as well. Some Irish and other second- and later-generation ethnic groups have in recent years also gained access to such roles. Jews as a group are relatively affluent and well educated, but their economic, political, and other influence beyond their group and its institutions is still quite limited. Significant numbers of even the relatively prosperous Anglo-Saxon and Jewish groups are still in the working class below the poverty line and are of little influence beyond their immediate families, friends, and jobs.[12] Conversely, a few members of less privileged groups are professionals, managers, and relatively well off.

Lower-class and lower middle-class nonfrancophones, virtually regardless of ethnic background, tend to accept and project the highly selective views of contemporary Quebec life advanced by media, organizations, and other communications controlled by their elites, still predominantly Anglo-Saxon Protestants. Coalitions between these diverse groups designed to oppose majority francophone demands and objectives are far more prevalent than any based on common economic, social, or other interests vis-à-vis similar francophone strata. Yet there have recently been sufficient differences both across these ethnic groups and within them (between elites and others) to make a continuation unlikely of the pre-1960 patterns of accommodation between nonfrancophone and francophone elites who have been able to "bring along" their former flocks on conflicts regarded as threatening to linguistic minorities.

Even by the mid-1970s, relatively few native francophones had ascended into the predominantly anglophone elite that controlled or managed larger, internationally competitive Canadian or foreign-subsidiary firms.[13] Anglophone decision makers argued until the last decade or so that francophones, even the relatively few who had university educations, did not have the fluency in English, the background, the work ethic or other values, or the correct training for professional and managerial jobs. Even the relatively few francophones with university degrees were educated primarily in the humanities—literature, philosophy, and theology—rather than in business, engineering, the sciences, and other specialties needed by a modern industrial economy. It was only after francophone education, including its universities, became secularized and shifted its emphases toward these practical fields in the 1960s that there began to be a pool of appropriate talent, but mainly at young, entry levels. Before Law 101 was passed, francophones could be excluded due to their faulty command of English, but forceful pressures from francophone university graduates to open such careers to them without requiring that they work primarily or exclusively in English resulted in the legislation to achieve that end.

As late as 1983, francophones in managerial and professional positions were still concentrated primarily in provincial public and parapublic institutions. Francophone-controlled commercial firms, like Jewish and other ethnic ones, were mostly relatively modest to small in size, local in their markets, and low in capital and technology. Bombardier and the National Bank were major exceptions, but even the exceptions normally were successful expansions of smaller francophone-controlled firms rather than a result of francophone decision makers in Anglo-Canadian or foreign-controlled firms. Younger francophones by the 1980s were growing in number in leadership-oriented careers at the lower and middle levels in a number of firms controlled by U.S., European, and Anglo-Canadian interests, but few of these francophones had yet reached senior executive offices and boards of directors.

Nonfrancophone Images of Quebec

The nonfrancophone minorities' perceptions of and reactions to most of the objectives, policies, and actions of the Lévesque government have been predominantly negative. So have the reactions of most nonfrancophones across Canada, but those of nonfrancophones in Quebec have been even more negative than in other provinces.[14] The latter is not surprising in light of Quebeckers' much more direct involvement and sense of threat to their basic interests and ways of life.

Among Quebec minorities, anglophones have been more opposed to most of the nationalist objectives of the francophone majority since at least the early 1970s than have allophones of more recent immigration. Although Law 22 and Law 101 restrictions against entry into English schools have applied primarily to immigrants' children, old-stock anglophones felt overall greater shock and status deprivation because they had for generations enjoyed prestige, privileges, and economic and social standing in such apparent security that few had ever learned any language other than English. Furthermore, the allophones, being of lower average income and more in need of social welfare, transfers of wealth, and other state action, have not been so opposed to the PQ government's progressive and interventionist economic policies.

Nevertheless, many immigrants and especially their anglicized children and grandchildren read the same English-language papers, frequent many of the same economic, educational, and other institutions, and often perceive their interests as being as much challenged as do older-stock anglophones. Politically, both anglophones and allophones overwhelmingly vote Liberal in provincial elections, oppose the PQ and independence with or without economic association, and subscribe to prevailing anglophone attitudes toward francophone demands. The immigrants, none of whose children were in English schools by 1977, were especially angry at being forced to send their children to French schools unless they could afford private English ones.

Allophone as well as anglophone elites, media, and intermediary opinion leaders have continuously attacked the basic tenets and the concrete programs of Québécois nationalism. Opinion surveys document that their arguments represent the views of most of their ranks-and-files.[15] The arguments comprise three general recurrent, overlapping, and mutually reinforcing themes.

General Opposition to Francisation

First, the nonfrancophones object to critical features of francisation in such areas as education, professional eligibility, labeling of products, and billboard advertising. Nonfrancophone spokesmen often express support for, or at least acquiescence in, general goals such as the desirability of more widespread use of French in large corporations. Nevertheless, they denounce as illiberal and unjust the means that francophone majorities feel to be essential to accomplish such ends. Widespread apprehension is expressed about future prospects for survival of the social insititutions that constitute the core of minority linguistic communities. Nonfrancophones disavow the concept that francophone majority collective rights should take precedence over inalienable individual rights, despite their often-asserted acknowledgment that the general objectives of francisation are acceptable. Nonfrancophones also view their linguistic minority-group institutional prerogatives as rights acquired over generations; francophones, on the other hand, see these prerogatives as unjust privileges resulting from over two centuries of monopoly over economic power. Nonfrancophones assert that their collective minority rights should be a central part of a new social contract binding upon the francophone majority and guaranteed, in law, by the federal as well as the Quebec government.

Notwithstanding francophone assurances to the contrary, nonfrancophones fear that francophone ethnic mores and Catholic origins as well as fluency in French will be de facto prerequisites for equitable treatment in the job market—particularly at upper levels in francophone-controlled institutions—and for minimal acceptance and integration into the Québécois majority community. They note the very few individuals who are not native francophones in provincial governmental agencies and corporations,[16] the absence of any anglophones or allophones in the PQ cabinet, the negligible number of nonfrancophones in private enterprises controlled by francophones, and the clannish traditions and closed ethnocentric and xenophobic attitudes that they allege still pervade most of francophone society, whether secularized or still based on religious practice. They further complain that the burden of bilingualism has suddenly been shifted to them from the francophones in a vengeful, unjust, and economically counterproductive way. Some suggest that as they become more bilingual and francophones more unilingual, the traditional economic hegemony favoring nonfrancophones in more dynamic sectors involving business in English outside Quebec may well be reinforced. At the same time the awareness of anglophones that better career opportunities exist elsewhere in North America has been heightened by their concerns about their futures in Quebec.

Nonfrancophone opposition to francisation by the Quebec government has not been limited to the current PQ government. Italians' demonstrations against their children's choice being limited to French schools in St. Leonard in the late 1960s were directed against a conservative, relatively laissez-faire National Union government. Although the vast majority of nonfrancophones voted for Liberal candidates in the 1973 election, they vehemently opposed the Liberal government's version of francisation, Law 22, the next year. In part because of Law 22, sufficient numbers of nonfrancophones dissaffected temporarily in 1976 to vote for National Union candidates against Liberal and PQ candidates and help put the PQ into office through plurality votes in a number of constituencies around greater Montreal.[17]

PQ Government Blamed for Economic Malaise

A second claim of nonfrancophones is that the negative state of the Quebec economy has been exacerbated by the priorities, policies, and practices of the Lévesque government. Disparaging comparisons are cited particularly with regard to Ontario, but also with the rest of North America. Nonfrancophones take their cues from anglophone corporate elites and media that reflect and support their views. In the economic domain, English-language media feed upon and amplify the fears of the less educated, less well off, and often poorly informed rank-and-file nonfrancophones. The latter are predisposed to believe the worst about the economic policies and intentions of the generally disliked government. More affluent native anglophones feel that the vigor, speed, and means with which the PQ government is pursuing francisation of the economy threatens both the economy itself and their own deserved status within it, achieved by individual effort.

While the majority agree that Quebec's economic difficulties of the early 1980s are part of a North American and worldwide malaise, nonfrancophone elites note that unemployment, stagnation, and other negative aspects in Quebec are about the worst on the continent. They point to the only provincial succession taxes in Canada, the most progressive personal income taxes and the highest ones on the continent on the types of technical, professional, and managerial talent that Quebec most needs, counterproductive policies to make French the language of work in larger businesses interdependent with the rest of Canada and the United States, and a government and party led by impractical intellectuals, artists, academics, and "progressives" with no experience in business and virtually no rapport with, sympathy for, or support by businessmen. The government's policies are alleged to have discouraged both Canadian and foreign-owned enterprises already in Quebec from modernizing and further investing there, have deterred new companies from coming in, and have motivated those companies based in Quebec to move elsewhere.

Anglophones and allophones have portrayed government efforts to open jobs to francophones and limit assimilation of immigrants' children into anglophone society as having little plausible justification, as designed to deny nonfrancophones their democratic rights, to make their presence virtually invisible, and to encourage them to leave Quebec. They feel Quebec cannot work its way out of its profound economic difficulties and prosper without their talents and that such linguistic requirements will drive out needed younger talent and render virtually impossible attracting this talent from outside. The problems of recruiting promising young people in other provinces even for jobs outside Quebec when those jobs are with a firm with Montreal headquarters are cited as growing, because the potential applicants fear a successful career would bring them to Montreal, where they would have to learn French at mid-career and put their children in French schools.[18]

Anglophone arguments selectively downplay, criticize, or ignore both the objectives and achievements of PQ economic and related linguistic actions, as well as their historical contexts. For example, although the anglophones concede the efficient management and notable achievements of Hydro-Quebec (the creation of which in 1962 they vociferously opposed), they criticize the lack of profitability and other shortcomings of state corporations such as SIDBEC (steel), SNA (asbestos), and SOQUIP (oil and gas). They also fail to note the profitable and generally successful operations of SOQUEM (mining), REXFOR (forest products), and the *Caisse de dépôt et de placement* (which manages pension and savings funds of public and semipublic Quebec agencies). The latter is widely portrayed as using its investments to gain control of important private Canadian corporations and to shore up economically less prom-ising Quebec enterprises for political, "socialistic," and other controversial purposes of the PQ, rather than to achieve optimal investments for its clientele of public workers. Virtually no favorable note is taken of such state corporation objectives as rationalization of markets, facilitation of investments desirable to Quebec's future economy but regarded as too risky by private investors, and joint ventures with foreign and domestic private enterprises for these purposes.[19]

Moreover, the fact that most of these state enterprises and other forms of provincial intervention were initiated not by the PQ government but by the Liberal Lesage government during the early 1960s is seldom noted. Lesage and his successors had to intervene to modernize an inherently anachronistic society: to convert a minimal, laissez-faire government to successful dealings with industrialized and urbanized Quebec's economic and social problems; to catch up economically, socially, and culturally with the rest of North America; to educate and motivate the long-stagnant francophone majority to participate actively in the modern world; and to open up careers so they could do so. There were no ministries of education, public health, culture, communications, or economic development, and there was virtually no francophone participation in the modern economy above blue-collar and clerical levels. Succeeding National Union, Liberal, and PQ governments continued and further developed these basic policies and instruments to achieve the ends widely supported by the francophone majority.

Negative Effects of Separatist Nationalism

The third nonfrancophone criticism focuses on the PQ's *raison d'etre* of "separatism," that is, ill-defined sovereignty or independence from the Canadian federation and, even if attainable, an unstable economic association (with a common currency) and customs union with Canada. This objective is widely described as a "leap into the unknown," a new arrangement with provisions that are unclear and with consequences, particularly but not only economic, at least harmful and probably horrendous.

Nonfrancophones predict unequal, prejudicial treatment of their minority interests and rights, notwithstanding any written guarantees negotiated with Ottawa and included in some new Quebec constitution. In this regard the PQ and the Lévesque government are considered embodiments of evil. Even francophones who are conditional federalist nationalists, active as articulate supporters of the Quebec Liberal Party or the National Union—Claude Ryan, for example—are criticized as "closet separatists" for their criticisms of Prime Minister Trudeau's policies pertinent to Quebec, their refusal to support the 1982 patriation of the constitution without veto powers for Quebec over amendments (or rights to opt out with full compensation from amendments of which the Quebec government and people disapproved), and so on.

Growing Polarization

Few anglophones, and not many more allophones, have voted for the PQ, voted "yes" in the 1980 referendum, favored linguistic or like legislation, or held positive images of many policies of the Lévesque government.[20] Whereas most francophones identify more with Quebec than with Canada, Quebec nonfrancophones are more likely to emphasize their Canadian over the provincial identity and to favor more rather than fewer centralized federal powers.[21] Francophones of virtually all political persuasions and party preferences have increasingly perceived themselves as "Québécois," whose culture, society, and geographical home base is Quebec, rather than as merely French-Canadians or Canadians living mainly in Quebec, but also elsewhere in Canada, who happen to speak French.[22]

However, although "Québécois" is the literal French translation of "Quebecker," it now has such francophone nationalist connotations that relatively few nonfrancophones, even those whose ancestors have been in Quebec since the late 1700s, tend to apply the term to themselves. If they do, they often thereafter differentiate their political stance from the nationalist tones that "Québécois" has acquired among much of the francophone majority.

This polarization and marginalization from majority francophone Quebec life have been partly self-imposed, partly reinforced by legitimate francophone objectives and by French Quebec social and especially political institutions. Anglophone marginalization particularly has been intimately linked with the tendency of anglophones to overlook changes in outlook and aspirations of the francophone majority, and to act as though privileges accruing to a dominant economic minority can be defended as eternal prerogatives under the guise of civil liberties, acquired rights, and freedom of linguistic choice. When rapid changes do occur, as they have in French Quebec society since 1960, formerly privileged minorities tend to develop siege mentalities, which further distance them from major currents of thought and action permeating the majority.

The images described above are those that anglophone Quebeckers transmit either directly or through their relationships with other Anglo-Canadians in Toronto, Ottawa, and elsewhere, insofar as anglophone Quebeckers have any influence in the United States.

The nonfrancophones who merit exception to these generalizations are an apparently slow-growing minority. They are mostly young, functionally bilingual, and university educated. They usually have close francophone friends, and some have married francophones. Some have voted for PQ candidates, and a few even voted "yes" in the referendum. Proportionally more allophones than anglophones have voted PQ, and more did so in the 1981 than in any previous provincial election. Some social democratic nonfrancophones who would vote NDP elsewhere in Canada have voted PQ, but many have not done so because of the francophone nationalist and independentist objectives. However, even though nonfrancophones may vote Liberal and prefer that Quebec remain in the federation, growing numbers particularly of the younger non-francophones have decided to remain and to accommodate to the Québécois, at least until their roles in increasingly francophone Quebec and Quebec's future with respect to the rest of Canada become clearer. How many would remain if Quebec left the federation is difficult to estimate.

Impacts on the United States

Neither anglophones nor allophones have made any intentional, concerted efforts to transmit their perceptions of Quebec to people in the United States, although many of them have made concerted efforts to convince their Canadian anglophone compatriots and the federal government of their perceptions. Whatever impacts they may have on people in the United States are generally inadvertent and unorganized, by informal conversations between individuals, business and professional colleagues, family members, acquaintances, and strangers of chance encounter, or by the exposure of people in the United States to English-language U.S. media coverage derived directly or indirectly from Quebec nonfrancophones. Nonfrancophone images may reach some Americans in more or less their original form, but probably more often they are attenuated, second or third hand, via Toronto, Ottawa, elsewhere in Ontario, and the rest of Canada. Therefore, degrees and qualitites of influence on perceptions in the United States probably vary considerably depending on frequency and types of exposure, alternative sources of information, and the groups involved both in Quebec and in the United States.

American Proclivities Preponderantly on the Anglophone Side

Linguistic and cultural affinities between native Quebec anglophones and Americans, and related anglophone access to both formal and informal transborder communications networks, markedly privilege anglophone views that reach unilingual Americans over other views prevailing among the majority who are not fluent in English. The nonfrancophone side of the "two solitudes" is part of the network of both formal and informal interpersonal communications in the *lingua franca* of North Americans, but the nationalist francophone majority side is not. U.S. contacts with unconditional independentists and supporters of sovereignty-association are especially few, and those contacts even with qualified federalist nationalists who favor decentralization are also quite infrequent.

The interpretations of Quebec developments drawn from anglophone Canadian sources in U.S. printed and electronic media (documented in Chapter 10) are much reinforced among U.S. individuals who read Canadian media. U.S. readers of Quebec media are limited to the relatively few with significant interests in developments there; the Montreal *Gazette* and anglophone business newsletters and other periodicals comprise most of that exposure. The views advanced in such publications are generally reflective of those summarized above, and certainly very different from those in *Le Devoir, La Presse*, and weekly, monthly, and other periodicals in French. By definition those who read the latter are among the very small minority of interested U.S. individuals fluent in that language.

A rather different U.S. audience has been exposed to anglophone Canadian novels, plays, and other literature bearing on the Quebec conflict in more personal terms, like the novels of Montrealer Mordecai Richler.[23] Such works by Quebec nonfrancophones, like those of Canadian anglophone writers elsewhere, virtually never exhibit much comprehension of or empathy with the emerging purposes and identities of post-1960 francophones. The points of view and emotional tones are very different from the nationalist ones of such francophone counterparts as Hubert Aquin, Michel Tremblay, Marie-Claire Blais, Roch Carrier, Jean Barbeau, Michel Beaulieu, Michel Garneau, Jacques Godbout, or Gaston Miron—with whom only a handful of U.S. individuals, largely French teachers at the university level, are at all familiar.

U.S. readers of *The Globe and Mail*, published in Toronto, or of the *Financial Post* or other Canada-wide English-language periodicals are much more numerous than the readers of Quebec media. Although Toronto-published and other non-Quebec media devote much less attention to Quebec and are usually more moderate in their interpretations than Quebec-based English publications, their Quebec sources, like those of U.S. media, are primarily anglophones or more or less unqualified federalist, bilingual francophones.

U.S. private-sector elites and their staffs with Canadian business interests are among the most influential groups who follow Canadian media and, in some cases, read Quebec English-language publications as well. Federal, state, and other public officials charged with economic relations with Canada—in Washington in the Treasury, Commerce, and Energy Departments, in the Bureau of Economic and Business Affairs in the State Department, and in several agencies—read similar Canadian material in English. Officials concerned with Canada at the Defense Department have likewise read primarily or exclusively Anglo-Canadian sources, including some from Quebec. Few if any of these individuals read the francophone counterparts of these Canadian English publications. Even among academics, intellectuals, and other research people in the United States interested in Canada, most do not read French, and few other than those with Quebec interests read francophone material that is reflective of a cross section of francophone views on Quebec.

American Business and Professional Elites

The Quebec anglophone corporate and related professional community speaks the same language as their U.S. counterparts and is of very similar culture. Much more than their francophone counterparts, they are apt to have attended elite universities in the United States as undergraduates. If not, they often went to business, law, or other professional or graduate schools in such institutions. They have often continued "old boy" networks with classmates and other acquaintances who have attained comparable or more influential roles in the United States. And as earlier noted, they predominate on corporate boards of U.S. subsidiaries, their U.S. parent companies, and larger Canadian firms with extensive trade, investment, and other business relationships in the United States. They are on telephones daily and on airplanes frequently back and forth, to and from the United States. They deal regularly with U.S. clients, customers, consultants, lawyers, and other influential persons. They participate much more than do francophones in U.S. business and professional organizations, and in Canadian anglophone ones with close links to the U.S. organizations.

Although there are fewer Canadian and U.S. subsidiary headquarters in Montreal than formerly, executives who came from Montreal, maintain family and other ties there, and reflect the views prevailing there, frequently hold responsible positions in corporate headquarters in Toronto and elsewhere outside Quebec. Colleagues are affected by the "first hand" views of these executives, and by those of their Montreal regional headquarters staffs. Thereby Montreal anglophone views are transmitted directly to other parts of Canada and indirectly to U.S. private-sector elites.

At least the more sophisticated and prudent of U.S. business contacts of Anglo-Canadians weigh the views received from their Montreal or Toronto informants with what they read in *The Wall Street Journal, Business Week, The Journal of Commerce, The New York Times,* or other publications (see Chapter 10)—in some cases anglophone Canadian publications. In major U.S. firms with important Canadian interests the senior executives or their staffs have inputs from other observers, including U.S. observers in Canada. Some executives have dealt directly with ministers and senior civil servants—virtually all francophones— in the Lévesque government. In some sectors the executives have negotiated with English-speaking francophone officials of Hydro-Quebec, REXFOR, or another provincial public corporation. As Chapter 3 observes, impressions of top U.S. executives in corporations operating in or dealing with a number of other countries are usually more detached, nuanced, and balanced than the views advanced by Montreal anglophone elites. Nevertheless, only an atypical handful of such executives have been exposed much to countervailing interpretations they could hear from more nationalist francophone elites, including more conditional federalists than the few francophone corporate elite members whom they know.

The above observations seem to apply with some modifications to business-related professionals who deal with, but are not employees of, U.S. banks, other services, manufacturers, and other corporations—

examples are corporate lawyers, consultants, engineers, commercial and industrial architects, and accountants. Though some of their professional and technical staffs received part of their training in the United States, usually at graduate levels, the major engineering and other consulting firms populated primarily by francophones tend to be specialized in hydropower and other sectors particularly important in Quebec—their foreign business has been relatively little with the United States. Larger U.S. consulting firms, such as Arthur D. Little, have Canadian subsidiaries run by anglophones and, more recently, based in Toronto and other centers outside Quebec. U.S. consultants, with few exceptions, likewise deal primarily with anglophone elites in Quebec.

Francophones, since the Quiet Revolution, have been brought into and thereafter gained partner status in top law firms, architectural firms, accounting firms, and other professional services formerly staffed exclusively or nearly so by anglophones mainly of British extraction. In some cases the francophones deal with counterparts in the United States, usually in similarly cosmopolitan firms, often on legal, accounting, or other problems of multinational and other transborder corporate business. But insofar as Boston firms are valid examples, interfirm contacts with Quebec lawyers are still only exceptionally with francophones, and moreover include not many more Jews, Italians, or members of other ethnic groups apart from Anglo-Saxons and Irish. U.S. lawyers involved with lawyers in Montreal tend to be from elite law schools and leading firms, as do their Montreal contacts, and to be internationally sophisticated, to have professional contacts in other countries, and to weigh interpretations with those from other sources, as do their U.S. corporate equivalents in other businesses.

Religious and Ethnic Groups

U.S. Protestant and Jewish religious leaders—influential lay persons and the clergy and religious institutions in which they are involved—have virtually no francophone counterparts to counter the interpretations they receive from Quebec and other Canadian anglophone clergy and lay persons of their respective religious denominations. Even the U.S. Catholic hierarchy, clergy, and members of religious orders of both sexes have much more contact and rapport with their anglophone, often Irish, Montreal and other Canadian counterparts than with francophone archbishops, bishops, clergy, and religious orders representing nearly half of Canadian Catholics. The two cultural-linguistic dualities apply to the Catholic church as they do to most of Canadian society. The Jesuits are a typical example of orders organized in two provinces (or other jurisdictions) along linguistic rather than geographical or other lines; the anglophone Jesuits have close contacts with U.S. Jesuits, but the francophone Jesuits have very few. Anglophone Jesuits, Dominicans, Sacred Heart sisters, etc., often attended U.S. graduate schools or seminaries, see U.S. counterparts at meetings, sometimes work on projects together, and are part of multiple anglophone North American networks. Whereas members of francophone missionary orders tend to serve in francophone Africa and other French-speaking societies, anglophone missionaries are more apt to meet U.S. colleagues in English-speaking societies.

Francophone Catholic clergy, members of orders, and active church people are considerably less apt to be independentists and to vote PQ than less involved and less practicing Catholics,[24] but their views on Quebec diverge considerably from those prevalent among their anglophone counterparts.

Anglophone, largely Ashkenazic rabbis of East European ancestry in Montreal, and ex-Montreal rabbis in the United States and elsewhere in Canada, have often received their rabbinical training in the United States. Many of them maintain extensive contacts with U.S. rabbis and lay people. But contacts between U.S. Jewish clergy and laity and francophone Sephardic rabbis and lay people are almost nil.

The author's pilot study in 1982 of linkages of U.S. ethnic organizations headquartered in New York with comparable Quebec organizations and individuals of their ethnic background revealed significant differences, but on the whole few contacts and still fewer, if any, impacts beyond the headquarters staffs and governing boards of these agencies.

Some of these organizations had limited links with ethnic institutional counterparts in Canada that are still headquartered in Montreal, or that have Quebec-based agencies. Most did not have members in Quebec and heard relatively little directly from individuals or groups there. Even among those with significant contacts, whatever perceptions reached them from their ethnic colleagues in Quebec were considerably more moderate than those described in the preceding section of this chapter. In none of the U.S. organizational headquarters where interviews were conducted was Quebec perceived as being among the important problem spots around the world.

For instance, the Italian-American Anti-Defamation Alliance has chapters and members in Toronto, but not in Quebec. No organizational channels linked it with any Italo-Quebec organization despite the numbers of Italian immigrants and their descendants in Quebec. The appropriate senior official of this organization in the United States noted he knew little about Quebec, that he had never heard complaints from his chapters or members in Canada, or from individual Italians in Quebec, about prejudiced treatment of Italians there, and that the organization he represented was neither for nor against language developments in Quebec.

On the other hand, the Historical Branch of the American Italian Congress has many members in Quebec, receives considerable correspondence from ethnic confreres there, and sponsors visits back and forth. However, a senior official there had received no complaints from Quebec Italians relative to their treatment by and relations with the francophone majority. His concern was mainly that Quebec Italians are forgetting their heritage as they assimilate into predominantly anglophone, but more recently francophone, society. With respect to Quebec itself he had only positive reactions.

Greek-American organizations in the United States had virtually no communications with their Quebec counterparts. For example, the ethnic periodical most widely read in English in the U.S. Greek-American community, *The Greek Daily National Herald*, had no reporters or contacts in Quebec, not even "stringers" or other sources, had never received material for publication from there, and thus contained no content on Greeks in Montreal.

The Quebec Jewish community had the most extensive ethnic organizational links with the United States. However, contacts varied widely from one Jewish organization to another. In no case did their U.S. counterparts regard the problems of Quebec Jewry as deserving special concern or attention.

The Canadian Jewish Congress (CJC), like the American Jewish Congress (AJC), is affiliated with the World Jewish Congress (WJC). Both of the latter are headquartered in New York, as are the major U.S. organizations of most other ethnic groups aside from those of Latin American backgrounds. The WJC receives regular reports from both the Canadian and American Jewish congresses. The president of the CJC at that time was a prominent McGill University law professor, and the CJC headquarters was in Montreal. The president of the WJC was a prominent ex-Montrealer living in New York, Edgar Bronfman, chief executive officer of Seagram's U.S. operations.

The director of organizations of the WJC, the executive responsible for links with member national Jewish congresses, regarded the reports from the CJC concerning Quebec developments as balanced. He noted anxieties among the Montreal leadership about departures from the city and province particularly of younger, university-educated, ambitious people with professional and entrepreneurial talents. The rising costs of social welfare, health, and other needs of the increasingly aged Jewish population would have to be defrayed by the Quebec government as the number of prosperous younger contributors to Jewish agencies declined. Moreover, adaptation to francisation by older Jews who had not felt the need to learn French under the prevailing conditions of their youth was becoming a difficult problem.

Nonetheless, the responsible WJC executive could recall no complaints from Montreal Jewry about anti-Semitism, discrimination against them for jobs, or other maltreatment by the Quebec majority. He was aware of the substantial francophone Sephardic minority in Montreal and the 80-percent provincial subsidies to private Jewish schools for teaching secular subjects. However, he had heard little more since the 1980 referendum from or about the Montreal Jewish community. He argued that developments relative to Jews in other parts of the world had overshadowed any "Quebec question," if indeed either PQ governmental policies or relations with the francophone majority in general really posed any significant problems at all to Jewish well-being.

Thus these nuanced, sophisticated appraisals coming out of Quebec have not been such as to be translated into programs, publications, or other communications by one of the WJC's affiliates, the AJC, for its membership. Quebec developments are reported no further down than the few interested staff and board members at the national level. Quebec had not been a significant matter on the AJC agenda or the subject for any statements or other vehicles of associated agencies in the memory of an appropriate official of AJC's international affairs section. A colleague in this section had recently visited Montreal for two weeks as a tourist, during which he had contacted professionals with major Jewish social welfare agencies. They had reported concern about where Quebec society was headed and what roles such agencies would play, but made no references to anti-Semitism, unfair treatment, discrimination, or the like.

The Anti-Defamation League (ADL) of the B'nai B'rith is the Jewish agency specifically charged with such concerns, in respect to which it has worldwide contacts. However, its U.S. headquarters' reactions were quite like those of the WJC and AJC. Quebec was not regarded by pertinent ADL staff as one of the numerous problem environments for Jews.

The New York section of the National Council of Jewish Women, by far its most populous section in the United States, is composed primarily of elderly "people from another era." Its members and its leadership have few international interests other than Israel, and focus primarily on local matters. Its executive director had no concept or view of Quebec or its Jewish community, either positive or negative. She was unaware of such articles as those in *Commentary*, the *Jerusalem Post*, and other periodicals noting anxieties among Quebec Jews, unequal treatment by francophone institutions or individuals, or fears about the future.

This preliminary survey leads to several working hypotheses about the flow of images of Quebec from its ethnic minorities and their institutions, either directly or via their Canada-wide organizations to

U.S. ethnic organizations. As in the case of religious and most other groups, whatever is communicated comes almost exclusively from anglophone and allophone sources even when some ethnic members, such as North African Jews and some descendants of Italians who arrived before World War II, have integrated into the francophone majority. The more formal the organizational links, the more regular the flow of perceptions from Quebec. The more regularized the links and communications, the more multidimensional and detailed the impressions of leaderships of U.S. counterparts. But absence of such communications, and of perceptions that might result from them, and indifference about Quebec were more typical than exceptions. Furthermore, even when organizational elites had impressions from such communications, seldom did their impressions conform to alarmist tones prevailing in any of these groups in Montreal; thus, U.S. ethnic representatives did not consider Quebec a special problem for their ethnic groups. Moreover, any communications and resulting impressions that may have affected the national leadership were unlikely to be transmitted beyond the U.S. organizational headquarters of the ethnic groups involved.

Whatever impressions of Quebec do reach U.S. ethnic groups from their Montreal counterparts are apt to be transmitted informally, between individuals, rather than via ethnic organizations or publications. Montreal Jews, Italians, and other ethnic groups, particularly those of first- and second-generation descendants of immigrants, frequently continue contacts with relatives, friends, or acquaintances who have come to the United States. Some visit from time to time back and forth across the border, as they do with kinsmen and friends in Toronto, Ottawa, Edmonton, and other parts of Canada (who, in turn, have similar contacts in New York, Los Angeles, Dallas, Boston, or elsewhere in the United States). Jews, for instance, may meet U.S. Jews at ethnic and religious gatherings or on visits to New York, southern Florida, Israel, or wherever.

Counterpart francophone transborder ethnic relationships, with Franco-Americans of the U.S. northeast and Acadians and Creoles in Louisiana, are examined in Chapters 8 and 9 in this volume. Those authors note not only sharp declines in those still able to exchange ideas with Quebec francophones in French, but also relatively little interest in Quebec's post–Quiet Revolution francophone–nonfrancophone controversies, and little sympathy for independence, sovereignty association, Law 101, or the allegedly left-of-center "progressive" or "socialistic" economic and social policies and high taxes of the Lévesque government. Those in Louisiana as well as the U.S. northeast who still can converse in French, mostly late middle-aged or elderly, identify often with a traditional Quebec that no longer exists. Younger Americans of Quebec ancestry are frequently concerned that Quebec's unilingual policies will reduce communication with the majority of Americans of Quebec and Acadian ancestry in the northeast and Louisiana who no longer speak French.

Furthermore, the influence of francophone Americans of Quebec descent beyond their own ethnic group, and particularly beyond their geographic areas, on perceptions of their compatriots is minimal. Their minor impacts are no match for those of the diversity of contacts of the combination of Montreal anglophones and the diverse ethnic groups who speak English.

Other Networks

The communications channels mentioned to this point are far from all the varied routes by which predominantly negative allophone and, particularly, anglophone perceptions reach diverse individuals and groups in the United States. A number of anglophones over the years have migrated to the United States where they tend to occupy more influential, higher status roles as businessmen, doctors, lawyers, consultants, engineers, and the like, unlike the declining number of francophone migrants (see Chapter 5). The more recent departees have often left partly because of their opposition to the objectives and policies of Quebec nationalism, and those who left earlier maintain ties with family and friends who "keep them abreast" of anglophone views on these issues.

Individuals from the United States temporarily in Montreal with U.S. subsidiaries or in other roles derive their views primarily from local anglophones before they return to the United States. Increasing numbers of francophones of most strata visit the United States for business or pleasure, but they are more likely than their nonfrancophone colleagues to congregate together in southern Florida, the northeast U.S. Atlantic coast, or wherever. The contacts and rapport of anglophones with U.S. residents are apt to be both more diverse and more communicative. U.S. visitors to Quebec, again largely because of their English language, seldom leave their business sessions with other anglophones, or their tourist network, to compare perceptions with francophones. These generalizations apply across most leadership and otherwise more sophisticated exchanges, and to miscellaneous, largely chance contacts, overwhelmingly with nonfrancophones.

One of the more direct impacts on U.S. perceptions derived primarily from the nonfrancophone side of the Quebec conflict has been on majority-group anxieties about bilingual and associated ethnic heritage programs in the United States. Those concerns have been centered on Hispanic groups in their regions of concentration, particularly in states along the Mexican border such as California and Texas, and also in southern Florida, where people of Hispanic origins constitute large minorities, and in some political districts, majorities.[25]

The contexts and real issues involved are of course very different from Quebec's to anyone more than very superficially familiar with both, but very few on either side of the Hispanic bilingual controversy know much about Quebec. Vague images and clichés derived from the anglophone side of the Quebec conflict are used to articulate opponents' arguments. Some suggest that states like California (bordering on Mexico) and Maine (adjacent to Canada), each containing significant nonanglophone minorities, will become another Quebec (or Canada). Concessions to bilingual arguments will confer unjustified privileges on a minority group that "hasn't worked for these privileges," which will violate the principle of individual advancement based on objective criteria of merit. The result will be minority fractiousness, divisiveness, inwardness, and negation of the American melting-pot ideal of give-and-take (in English). Some critics even raise the spectre of growing illegal Hispanic migration leading to long-term "separatism" to "rejoin" Mother Mexico, from which the states concerned were separated a century and a half ago.

Few Mexican-American proponents of bilingualism are particularly informed about Quebec, but biased allusions by their antagonists to linguistic conflict there have encouraged both interest in and sympathies for francophone Québécois aspirations. As this U.S.-Hispanic conflict continues, Mexican-American leaders may further sympathize with the Québécois, despite the policy of official unilingualism in Quebec.

Until relatively recently, especially since initial election of the PQ government, U.S. academics, intellectuals, and other analysts of Canadian affairs concentrated their attention on anglophone Canada. Possibilities of election of a PQ government and thereby of departure of Quebec from the federation were seldom taken seriously. Anglophones not only constituted the Canadian majority, they made the federal governmental, private business, and most of the other decisions affecting U.S. interests. Only a few analysts could read French readily; very few could participate in meetings or informal discussions in French. For most, outside a few French teachers, Canadian literature meant Anglo-Canadian literature; U.S. economic relations were with anglophone Canada and were analyzed by anglophone economists; Canadian history was written by Anglo-Canadian historians; and Canadian politics as they interested U.S. observers were those reported by anglophone political scientists.

Since 1976 the number of U.S. residents reading materials in French and interacting directly with representative francophones has increased substantially. Nevertheless, the above preponderance of anglophone sources of interpretations of Quebec has so far only been partially attenuated.

The Lévesque government, particularly since its reelection in 1981, has applied itself increasingly to redressing these imbalances. Cabinet ministers have met with influential persons from the United States. Financial aid for universities, cultural institutions, and individuals to develop interests in Quebec—and efforts of Quebec delegations in the United States to develop wider U.S. understanding of Quebec—have grown considerably. However, particularly in light of the much longer-enduring, more all-embracing affinities and communications earlier noted, plus the much greater visibility, resources, and entrée of Canadian federal officials, their embassy, and consular offices, the competition remains very unequal.

The U.S. Department of State's Office of Canadian Affairs, its Ottawa embassy, and its consulates general in Montreal and especially Quebec City have broadened considerably both the quantity and quality of their sources of information and interpretation across francophone Quebec elites. The proportion of professionals relatively fluent in French, and particularly those able at a minimum to follow the media in that language on at least the diplomatic side of U.S. relationships, has grown significantly. Conversations reveal a range of inputs and level of knowledge with respect to the spectrum of influential francophone opinion seldom apparent among even most journalists and academics with supposedly serious interests in Canadian affairs.

American Impacts on Nonfrancophone Attitudes

As Yvan Lamonde's analysis in Chapter 7 documents, U.S. impacts on the culture, behavior, and thinking of nonfrancophone Quebeckers, as on English-speaking Canadians in general, are significantly greater than those on francophones. Nevertheless, the impacts on francophones have also become increasingly massive. Influences from south to north are of course much more pervasive than those from north to south. Not only the native-born Quebec anglophone minority, but large majorities of almost all newer nonfrancophone ethnic groups, identify with the North American English-speaking majority, in many cases almost as much as, or even more than, with the particularly Canadian one.

Although the majority of immigrants who would have preferred to come to the United States have within a few years reconciled themselves to the reality that they will probably remain Canadians, "America" (the United States) still provides for them the dream and goals for which they strive. They are among the most pro–United States of Canadians.

For anglophones as well as allophones the obvious model is the dynamic, powerful, and varied country of 230,000,000 anglophones only an hour's drive away. The United States is omnipresent across their media, their economy, their life-styles, their daily lives, and their aspirations. They visit New England, New York, Miami, and elsewhere for amusement, shopping, business, and for both products and ideas they may bring back to Montreal. Nearby "America" provides a sense of security and a prototype for their resistance to francophone nationalism's demands, which 18,000,000 other Canadians alone could not supply.

Even relatively recent immigrants, like native anglophones, manifest pervasive U.S. middle-class aspirations, which they feel are frustrated by the pressures, requirements, and objectives of francophone nationalism and its majority government. They want "American" opportunities for upward economic and social mobility for themselves and their children, based on individual abilities, initiatives, and hard work. They too emphasize economic progress through private entrepreneurship and the ultimate responsibility of individuals for their own success, the priority of individuals over collective majority rights and objectives, and freedom of choice (as opposed to governmental restriction) in regard to the education of their children to compete on this continent. For them the U.S. constitution's Bill of Rights, defending individuals against such incursions, should set the example for application of the Canadian constitutional Charter of Rights in their defense in Quebec.

Nonfrancophones admire assumed U.S. superiority in scientific, technological, managerial, and other fields, want more of it in Canada, and attribute it to the spirit of individual initiative and liberties and to English as *lingua franca* in the North American economy. Replacement by French in education, in employment, and in Quebec life generally they fear will unnecessarily inhibit their achieving these successful ends in their own milieus, and will, moreover, cut them and other Quebeckers off from essential communication on this continent and with the English-speaking world in general. As the language of a small, noncompetitive continental minority, French will inhibit Quebec as a society and the immigrants and their offspring as individuals from ever "catching up" with the rest of North America and will isolate them from the media, the contacts, the ideas, and the many other advantages to which they would be open in English.

Proximity contributes to the heightened sense of relative deprivation among nonfrancophones. They compare their own lots unfavorably with those of Americans, particularly with relatives, maybe their own children, friends, acquaintances, and others they know who have gone south to practice their professions, invest their capital, make names for themselves in the arts, sciences, or whatever. "America" represents for them freedom not only from restrictive language legislation, but also from "confiscatory" taxes and the tensions and impending economic "chaos" due to "separatism." The United States contrasts vividly with perceived statist regimentation by the PQ government, in which they have no influence, although it impacts particularly unjustly on nonfrancophone minorities.

Nonfrancophone Quebeckers tend to exaggerate the degree of Americans' interest in and sympathy for their plight and agreement with their views. Particularly those with frequent contacts with U.S. residents draw a feeling of broad support for their "American" points of view in resisting the Lévesque government's policies and actions. Even chance encounters in restaurants, in public transportation, or in business dealings reveal virtually no one from the United States agreeing with "the other side" in these controversies, and this erratic sampling is often interpreted as solidarity of opinion in accord with the Quebec nonfrancophones' own.

Conclusions and Recommendations

Nonfrancophone resistance to nationalist objectives and policies in Quebec draws far more vitality from the many mutually reinforcing, frequently subtle and subconscious, forces associated with geographic proximity to the United States than these minorities are willing to admit. This virtually all-encompassing "North Americanness" nourishes in anglophone and allophone Quebeckers alike visions of what Quebec could and should be like. This stands in glaring contrast to developments there under a PQ government, which has not received much electoral support from either anglophone or allophone minorities. Many may even see the United States as the penultimate restorer of the status quo ante 1976, or even ante Law 22 of 1974, when U.S. political and economic elites finally perceive the threats to vital U.S. interests that "separatism" poses (if and when that possibility again becomes credible).

These minorities' direct influences on even those relatively few individuals in the United States with whom they have contacts are probably on the whole quite limited. As Chapter 3 implies, few influential banking, investment, or other corporate decision makers take typical views out of western Montreal at face value; their own impressions are much less one-sided, more balanced. The same generalization probably applies to U.S. Jewish organizational elites, similar elites in U.S. Catholic institutions, among those dealing with Canada in the U.S. government and state governments, and in academic life.

Thus, decisions by utilities leaders and state governments and their representatives in New York and New England relative to importing Quebec hydro-power, and of the New York Metropolitan Transit Authority relative to purchasing Bombardier's subway cars, and of Louisiana relative to accepting and helping to finance Quebec teachers and communications specialists in its bilingual programs, have been little or not at all affected by minority reports from Quebec. Nor are decisions by Reynolds Metals, General Motors, Pratt and Whitney, Celanese, IBM, Gillette, and other U.S. multinational corporations widely experienced with foreign operations much affected by such reports. Several large U.S. paper and pulp companies have decided to work jointly with REXFOR, partly at the Quebec government's expense, in modernizing production to render it more competitive with the newer plants in the U.S. southeast, undoubtedly without according much attention to these reports. U.S.-controlled enterprises in Quebec are widely considered to adapt themselves more readily to the requirements of Law 101 than do Anglo-Canadian firms. Moody's, Standard and Poor's, and other bond rating systems derive information from much more objective considerations, as do banks, investment houses, and other internationally knowledgeable lenders.

Yet, however sophisticated they may be, Americans in most walks of life feel naturally greater rapport and identity with Quebec anglophones than with most francophones. Their personal contacts with anglophone Quebeckers are reinforced by others with Anglo-Canadians elsewhere and by North American media coverage of Quebec. With very few exceptions, even relatively knowledgeable and influential Americans are more comfortable with Canadian anglophones, in their common language and similar culture, clubs, restaurants, and mores, than with their francophone equivalents. Decisions contrary to Quebec majority interests may be influenced to one degree or another by nonfrancophone Quebec inputs, direct or indirect. For instance, the departure of anglophone scientific, technical, and managerial talent and the hesitations of their counterparts to move to Quebec from elsewhere in Canada (or other English-speaking societies including the United States) due to Law 101 probably weighed in the 1982 decision of Ayerst Laboratories to concentrate its research and development in New Jersey rather than Montreal. Such considerations probably also compound other inhibiting factors surrounding the Lévesque government's efforts to attract more high-technology investment, including talent-intensive research, in competition with the existing critical mass in Ontario's "silicon valley," as well as its counterparts in the United States.

Research to trace these complex networks of linkages and their impacts in both directions would require the expertise of a number of disciplines and individuals, their application over a decade or more, and major funding. Neither the required money nor the interested talent is apt to be forthcoming.

More realistic, more feasible, and nearly as significant would be careful studies of U.S. elites, "gatekeepers" and "influentials" in roles that influence decisions and actions pertinent to Quebec in trade, direct and indirect investment, tourism, communications, and public policy not only in the relevant federal departments and agencies but also in state governments, especially those in the U.S. northeast and north central regions that are especially important economically, culturally, and politically to Quebec. Such studies, involving frank interviews with carefully selected samples, would need to delve into the spectrum of nuanced perceptions pertinent to developments in Quebec and its relations with the rest of Canada, from whence those perceptions are derived, and how these perceptions influence important decisions and recommendations of these elites. Within that broad context several probing questions could be posed about influences in the thinking and actions of individuals, groups, media specialists, and so forth by Quebec itself. U.S. researchers are apt to gain access to and establish the rapport required with the Quebec government more readily than anglophone Canadians.

The much more potent impacts of the United States on both anglophones and allophones in Quebec, and how these impacts differ from those on English-speaking Canadians elsewhere on the one hand, and on the francophone Quebec majority on the other, in the context of implications for nonfrancophone perceptions and actions toward critical issues facing Quebec, should be of sufficient priority to attract requisite research talents in Quebec. Moreover, such research should be more manageable, less complicated, and much less expensive and more readily fundable than that suggested for the United States. Both the relevant phenomena and the social scientists, Ph.D. and master's thesis candidates, thoughtful journalists, and other appropriate researchers are predominantly in one city, greater Montreal.

Notes

1. For example, John R. Mallea, ed., *Quebec's Language Policies: Background and Response* (Quebec: Les Presses de l'Université Laval, 1977); Marcel Rioux, *Quebec in Question* (Toronto: James Lorimer, 1978); Gary Caldwell, *Anglophone Quebec Outside of the Montreal Area in the Seventies: Socio-Demographic Evolution* (Quebec: Conseil de la langue française, 1980); and Jean Meynaud and Guy Bouthillier, *Le Choc des langues au Québec 1760–1970* (Quebec: Les Presses de l'Université Laval, 1972). For a more exhaustive documentation of most of the generalizations under the initial two subheadings following, see Alfred O. Hero, Jr., and Louis Balthazar, *The United States, Quebec, and Canada* (tentative title—forthcoming volume), particularly Chapters 3, 5, and 6.

2. Allophones are sometimes termed *néo-Québécois* in French, or *New Quebeckers* in English. However, in light of the francophone nationalist connotations the term *Québécois* has acquired, most immigrant groups resent the label *allophone* less. In their eyes, both *Québécois* and *allophone* imply second-class treatment of immigrants to a greater or lesser extent.

3. In the 1971 census Italians numbered 169,655, or 2.8 percent of the Quebec population. Jews were 115,990, or 1.9 percent, including both English-speaking, largely East Eurpoean Ashkenazic Jews (the vast majority) and the much smaller number of francophone Jews, mostly Sephardic from North Africa. See Sheila M. Arnopoulos and Dominique Clift, *The English Fact in Quebec* (Montreal: McGill-Queen's University Press, 1980), p. 229.

4. Jeremy Boissevain, *The Italians of Montreal: Social Adjustment in a Plural Society* (Ottawa: Studies of the Royal Commission on Bilingualism and Biculturalism, 1970), Chapter 5.

5. In the 1971 census, nonfrancophone Quebeckers of British origins numbered 640,000, of other backgrounds 628,000. Although 13.1 percent of Quebeckers in that census learned English as their primary language—typically at home as well as at school—only 8.3 percent of Quebeckers claimed English, Scottish, or Irish origins (Arnopoulos and Clift, *The English Fact*, pp. 228–229, Tables 1 and 2). In light of significantly higher emigration rates and much lower immigration rates of anglophones than allophones since 1971, the proportion of anglophones of non-British origin is now probably considerably higher.

6. *La Presse*, July 24, 1982, p. A-11, Table 2. This phenomenon of greater increases in emigration of mother tongue anglophones than francophones during recessions has applied to New Brunswick and Nova Scotia as well, whose francophones are predominantly Acadians. (*Le Devoir*, July 12, 1982.) The 445,000 Canadians who failed to indicate their native language in the 1981 census, probably 25 to 30 percent of them in Quebec and most of them likely to have learned languages other than the two Canadian official ones, undoubtedly contributed to an underestimate of the proportion not only of allophones but also of anglophones vis-à-vis francophones in Quebec (*Le Devoir*, July 22, 1982).

7. See, for example, Paul Cappon, *Conflit entre les néo-Canadiens et les francophones de Montréal* (Quebec: Les Presses de l'Université Laval, 1974).

8. As late as the 1920s, some Protestant school boards discriminated against Jewish students. They encouraged their parents to establish private Jewish schools (whose nonreligious instruction would likewise be provincially subsidized after 1965). By 1930 the movement to establish a separate Jewish School Commission proved to be abortive. See David Rome, *On the Jewish School Question in Montreal, 1905–1931* (Montreal: Canadian Jewish Congress, 1975).

9. Ninety percent of anglophones in 1971 lived in urban, largely industrialized areas, and of these, nine out of ten were in greater Montreal.

10. Ministère des communautés culturelles et de l'immigration, *Quebecers Each and Every One: The Government of Quebec's Plan of Action for Cultural Communities* (Quebec: Gouvernement de Quebec, 1981), p. 18.

11. This review of the hierarchy of ethnic groups and their differential gradations of power and status is extrapolated from the classic work on Canadian society by John Porter, *The Vertical Mosaic: An Analysis of Social Class and Power in Canada* (Toronto: University of Toronto Press, 1968).

12. About 20 percent of the Montreal Jewish community live below the poverty line, partly because the proportion of members of this community 65 years of age and older is increasing much faster than that of other anglophones

and francophones. See Martin Lubin, *The Politics of Social Policy in Quebec: The Case of Bill 65 (1971)* (New Haven: Proceedings of the 2nd Annual Colloquium of the Northeast Council for Quebec Studies at Yale University, 1981), forthcoming.

13. The statistical validity of this assertion is confirmed in Arnaud Sales, *La bourgeoisie industrielle au Québec* (Montreal: Les Presses de l'Université de Montréal, 1979), especially Chapter 5.

14. See, for example, John H. Pammett et al., "Political Support and Voting Behavior in the Quebec Referendum," unpublished paper for Duke University Conference on Political Support, November 21–22, 1980; CBC survey of March 1979; and Harold D. Clarke et al., *Political Choice in Canada* (Toronto: McGraw-Hill Ryerson, Ltd., 1979), p. 74.

15. For supporting survey findings, see Hero and Balthazar, *The United States, Quebec, and Canada* (forthcoming), Chapters 3 and 4.

16. In 1979 only 2.6 percent of over 300,000 Quebec civil servants and public employees were of nonfrancophone origins.

17. Richard Hamilton and Maurice Pinard, "The Parti Québécois Comes to Power: An Analysis of the 1976 Quebec Election," *Canadian Journal of Political Science* 11(4), December 1978, pp. 739–775; also by the same authors, "The Independence Issue and the Polarization of the Electorate: the 1973 Election," *Canadian Journal of Political Science*, 10(2), June 1977, pp. 215–259; and John Saywell, *The Rise of the Parti Québécois 1967–1976* (Toronto: University of Toronto Press, 1977).

18. If the Canadian Supreme Court supports the lower court decision of 1982 that English schools must be available to Canadian children who previously attended an English school anywhere in Canada, this concern relative to families of Canadians moving to Montreal will be much reduced. In practice, U.S. citizens and other anglophone foreigners "temporarily working in Quebec" are permitted to send their children to English schools for three years, with the likelihood of extension for an additional three years.

19. The argument that public enterprises pose no threat to the existing dominant private firms in Quebec is articulated in Pierre Fournier, *The Quebec Establishment: The Ruling Class and the State* (Montreal: Black Rose Books, 1978). Arguably, the PQ government has not fundamentally altered the mandates of these essentially state capitalist institutions. See also Gouvernement du Quebec, *Bâtir le Québec* (Quebec: Éditeur Officiel du Québec, 1979).

20. For survey and other empirical documentation, see Hero and Balthazar, *The United States, Quebec, and Canada*, Chapter 3. However, the minority of allophones who voted PQ in 1981 increased over 1976 and over the "yes" votes in the referendum. Two nonfrancophones were elected PQ deputies to the National Assembly in ridings with significant allophone populations, and a francophone was elected in the Mercier riding in Montreal with the essential votes of a significant minority of Greeks and other allophones.

21. Clarke et al., *Political Choice in Canada*, p. 74, and Joel Smith and David K. Jackson, "Restructuring the Canadian State: Prospects for Three Political Scenarios," unpublished paper, Duke University, 1980.

22. See, for example, Léon Dion, *Quebec: The Unfinished Revolution* (Montreal: McGill-Queens University Press, 1976), p. 31; Marcel Rioux, "Bill 101: A Positive Anglophone Point of View," *Canadian Review of Sociology and Anthropology* 15(2), 1978, p. 143; Kenneth McRoberts and Dale Posgate, *Quebec: Social Change and Political Crisis* (Toronto: McClelland and Stewart, 1980), p. 96; and Andre Bernard, *What Does Quebec Want?* (Toronto: James Lorimer, 1978). A 1979 survey discovered that among all Quebeckers, including nonfrancophones, 47.5 percent between 18 and 24 years of age designated themselves as *Québécois* rather than *Canadien* (Canadian) or *Canadien Français* (French-Canadian); 41.6 percent between 25 and 34 years of age, and only 24.0 percent among older age groups designated themselves as *Québécois*. Percentages were significantly higher among francophones alone, and a majority among younger ones. (Edward Cloutier et le Centre de recherches sur l'opinion publique, "Sondage sur la perception des problemes constitutionels Québec-Canada par la population du Québec." September 1979, p. 26.)

23. Richler's *St. Urban's Horsemen, The Apprenticeship of Duddy Kravitz,* and *Joshua Then and Now,* urban North America Jewish novels set in Quebec, provide a valid interpretation of the bittersweet immigrant encounter with the Montreal version of "America" but little understanding or sympathy for the francophone majority just beyond immigrant neighborhoods. To the contrary, Richler has been an outspoken opponent of Quebec nationalist ends and policies. For example, he referred to Quebec government "tongue troopers" in the Sunday, July 12, 1982, sports section of *The New York Times*, just prior to the annual All Star major league baseball game, which was about to take place for the first time in Montreal. As usual, there was no appropriate rebuttal in this influential paper from majority Quebec francophone perspectives.

24. Francois-Pierre Gingras and Neil Nevitte, "Religion, Values and Politics in Contemporary Quebec," paper for the American Political Science Association Annual Meeting, New York, New York, September 3–6, 1981.

25. Bilingual French programs with active Quebec official participation in Louisiana and to a lesser degree in New England have seldom generated such concerns. Indeed, many people in Anglo-Saxon Protestant northern Louisiana have in some respects demonstrated more enthusiasm for their children participating in the bilingual programs than a considerable number of southern Louisianians of French ancestry. However, the numbers involved in Louisiana are much smaller and the programs to reinforce dwindling French among youth of such backgrounds very different from the situation prevailing among people of Hispanic origins, many of whom are relatively recent, both legal and illegal entrants, speak little English, and are feared to become a growing threat in both numbers and culture to U.S. mores, values, and political control in areas where the Hispanic peoples are concentrated.

12

Quebec's Policies
Toward the United States

Louis Balthazar

There are no political relations in the normal meaning of that term between Quebec and the United States. The government in Washington, D.C., does not accept communications from any Canadian provincial government. For the Departments of State, Commerce, or Energy, the Office of the President, or other executive agencies, the only legitimate spokesman for Quebec and its inhabitants is the government in Ottawa. For Washington officials, Quebec is but one of ten Canadian provinces with the same status as all the others. None have any international status, in that they are not sovereign states.

Washington has always scrupulously respected this Canada–United States orthodoxy. U.S. executive officials are particularly careful to avoid any contacts that could possibly concern their Canadian federal counterparts. Thus when Quebec Minister of External Trade Bernard Landry evoked the possibility of closer economic ties between Quebec and the United States as part of a Canada–United States liberalized trade arrangement, the State Department promptly issued a rebuttal on February 2, 1983:

> It would not be appropriate for the United States Government to enter into special trading relationships with provincial governments as distinct from Canada as a whole. . . .
> . . . We do not intend to involve ourselves in internal Canadian issues.[1]

However, the U.S., like the Canadian, political system is very complex; ideas, influences, and actions bearing political implications affecting Quebec's interests are not limited to those of the U.S. federal government. Moreover, although formal initiatives and management of diplomatic relations and foreign policy are lodged in the federal executive branch, the Senate and in some spheres the House of Representatives play important roles in foreign affairs in general and, especially in economic matters, in problems of serious concern to Quebec. State governments and, to a lesser extent, certain local governments are of as great or even greater significance to Quebec's interests. And with all of these, other than the federal executive branch, Quebec has or can establish varying degrees of contact and communication.

Particularly in Quebec-U.S. relations, as in Canadian-U.S. relations generally, complex networks of economic, technical, environmental, and other transnational and transgovernmental linkages of overriding significance exist. They are, moreover, intimately related to, and often perceived as part of, domestic affairs, over which the Congress, lower levels of government, and private actors together often have more influence than the federal executive and particularly more than its formal foreign-policy apparatus. In these respects Quebec's relations with the United States are more extensive and consequential than the relations between most sovereign states, and more so than Quebec's relations with any other foreign country, including France.

Thus Quebec governmental officials travel frequently across the U.S. border, maintain as close and in some cases closer relations with certain state governments than with most other Canadian provincial ones, and meet with members of Congress and their staffs, officials of city governments, even some federal civil servants in less politically or diplomatically sensitive positions, and various politicians in and out of office. They negotiate and sign agreements and carry out coordinated or interrelated programs. U.S. governors, their staffs, congressmen, and politicians also meet with Quebec officials in Quebec.

The State Department's consulates general in Montreal and, particularly, Quebec City have extensive, albeit "correct" (meaning relatively apolitical), contacts with Quebec officials.

Nevertheless, as real as these diverse relations may be, they lack autonomous status. They moreover take place within the limiting context of policies of the two federal governments with respect to each other, the actions and precedents established by other provincial governments with respect to the United States, and Quebec's ventures elsewhere abroad. This chapter will examine, first, this setting, second, long-term Quebec interests and corresponding policies, and, third, some contingencies that might henceforth affect those policies.

The Setting

The Quebec-Ottawa-Washington Triangle

Whatever interests, policies, and actions Quebec may pursue in the United States in its pretenses to conducting foreign policy, the Canadian government alone can pursue real diplomacy and sign binding agreements with the United States government. Moreover, Ottawa can display impressive assets in asserting its claims of representing the interests of Quebeckers, as it does for those of citizens of other provinces.

First, Canada's representatives provide Quebec's only access to federal officials whose decisions affect its interests. Second, Ottawa's material and human resources in relevant federal ministries and in its large Washington diplomatic establishment and fifteen consulates general or consulates in important cities (where Quebec has no agents) far exceed Quebec's resources for dealing with its U.S. interests. Canadian officials have contacts and entrées throughout the United States, aside from those with the U.S. federal authorities, which Quebec's much more humble and less well provided U.S. delegations cannot hope to duplicate.

Perhaps the Canadian government's most important advantage is the very favorable biases the vast majority of Americans manifest toward Canada and its government. This contrasts with their anxieties and suspicions about the political objectives in the United States of a PQ Quebec government; their general leanings are toward the Canadian side of Ottawa-Quebec political and constitutional conflicts.

In spite of the many controversial issues between the two federal governments, bitter resentments by certain U.S. economic interest groups against Canadian economic "nationalism," complaints about the National Energy Policy of 1980, opposition to ratification of the fisheries treaty, reactions against the Canadian Foreign Investments Review Act (FIRA), and so on, Canada is generally considered by U.S. elites and masses alike as a privileged partner, a friendly country par excellence, and the United States' best friend.[2] To many people in the states anglophone Canada is a country and society very like their own. Moreover, at least since the time of Abraham Lincoln, not only most northerners, but most Americans generally, have come to celebrate the ideal of national unity as a great benefit. They also feel in common that maintenance and reinforcement of the Canadian unit is an important U.S. interest. Indeed, many consider Canada as much more unified than it actually is.

Hence it is virtually a foregone conclusion that Quebec, and particularly U.S. relations with the predominantly French-speaking province, will be perceived and acknowledged in an essentially anglophone Canadian framework. Inasmuch as Quebec-Ottawa antagonisms are reflected in the United States, Ottawa's point of view will normally prevail as the more reasonable and realistic.

Nonetheless, there is a widespread feeling among Quebec francophone elites that Quebec's interests, particularly insofar as they may differ from those of Canada as a whole, are not well represented in the United States by the Canadian government. Prime Minister Trudeau is himself a Quebec francophone, as are a number of other cabinet members. However, his views and those of his government on the role of Quebec in the United States diverge significantly, not only from those pressed by the Lévesque government since its reelection in 1981, but also from those of the several previous Quebec governments since Trudeau came to power.

While Quebec-Canadian federal differences have applied especially in cultural domains, Quebec businessmen complain about the degree and character of federal assistance accorded them in private commercial relations as well, the primary focus of Quebec's interests and policies in the United States. Moreover, French-speaking Quebeckers have been few in Canadian diplomacy with the United States, at the U.S. Bureau in the Department of External Affairs, in Washington, and in American cities.[3] Conferences, symposia, and other meetings and papers take place in both countries, sponsored or financed in part by the Canadian government, with virtually no participation, or only token participation, by Quebec francophones.

Some Quebec economic interests are, however, effectively served through Canadian agencies, as in the case of the successful conclusion in 1982 of Bombardier's contract to sell a billion dollars of subway equipment to the New York Metropolitan Transit Authority. But in other cases Quebec businessmen have complained about inadequate assistance by Canadian consular officers when their products may have competed with those of Ontario or other provinces already selling in the U.S. market. The Quebec Minister of Intergovernmental Affairs, reporting such cases, drew a bitter conclusion in May 1982 before a U.S. audience: "Here is the federal apparatus playing against the laws of competition. The Quebec product could be of better quality, cheaper, that is not important. That is an attitude we cannot accept."[4]

Controversies about representation by Canadian federal agents are much more persuasive in culture-related spheres. The Trudeau administration rejects the cultural duality conception of Canada, accepted by a majority of Quebec's francophone population, by the report of the federally appointed Task Force on Canadian Unity (Pépin-Robarts report) of 1979, by other authoritative studies before and after, and by all Quebec governments since World War II.[5] This principle views the French language and culture as integrally related and comprising a distinctive North American society whose only potentially secure home is Quebec. Canadian officials in the United States and in their relations with Americans in Ottawa and elsewhere project the contrary image of a single "Canadian culture," expressed in two offical languages, and of Quebec as a province in Canada similar to the others except that the majority of its population speak a different tongue.

The Liberal Lesage government that opened the Quiet Revolution beginning in 1960 transformed the modest Quebec office of narrowly commercial functions in New York, established in 1940, into a *délégation générale* (general delegation) with much broader purviews. The more conservative but staunchly Quebec-nationalist Bertrand National Union regime opened two delegations in the late 1960s in Chicago and Lafayette (Louisiana). Its less nationalist Liberal successor under Premier Robert Bourassa created two more at Boston and Los Angeles in 1970. Premier Bourassa and his ministers stressed economic relations with the United States. He moreover joined the former New England Governors' and Atlantic Provinces Premiers' Conference in 1974, thus transforming it into a more dynamic New England Governors' and Eastern Canadian Premiers' Conference wherein Quebec–New England relations became increasingly more important relative to those of the Atlantic Provinces with New England.

The Lévesque government elected in 1976 further expanded these linkages. It opened two more Quebec delegations, in Atlanta and Dallas (the latter closed in 1981), broadened both the economic and cultural outreaches of its delegations, and sent its senior ministers repeatedly across the United States explaining the PQ government's objectives, including sovereignty-association.

Since the reelection in 1981 and particularly since Jacques-Yvan Morin, Deputy Prime Minister, replaced Claude Morin (no close relative) as Minister of Intergovernmental Affairs in early 1982, the PQ government has markedly raised the priority of particularly its economic relations with the United States. It has accorded particular importance to economic relations with the U.S. northeast. Delegates general to New York City and Boston appointed in 1982 to replace predecessors of cultural and educational expertise were from business and engineering consulting backgrounds. Budgets and personnel in the ministry headquarters and its U.S. delegations for economic functions expanded both in absolute terms and in relation to those for cultural purposes.[6] A new Ministry of External Trade, with broad responsibilities across international economic domains, was also established in late 1982 under a dynamic minister close to Premier Lévesque, Bernard Landry. Although responsible for overseas trade as well as that with the United States, his emphasis has been on the latter for reasons noted in Chapter 2.

After his election in 1981 as a PQ member of the National Assembly, Rodrigue Biron, former leader of the pro-private enterprise, but francophone nationalist, National Union Party, became Minister of Industry, Commerce, and Tourism. The only successful former businessman in the cabinet, he has actively urged and aided the Quebec tourist industry, and small and medium-sized businesses wherein francophone entrepreneurs are concentrated (see below), to develop their business especially with the United States.

The meeting of Messrs. Lévesque and Morin with Republican senators, public criticisms of FIRA's restrictions on foreign investment, Minister Landry's proposal for North American free trade, and the agreement with the New York state government to share developmental data referred to in Chapters 2 and 6 and in this chapter were part of this post-1981 election emphasis on economic relations. With fanfare, Premier Lévesque and Minister of Energy and Resources Yves Duhaime also signed in New York and Boston agreements for expansion of electricity exports over the 1980s, accompanied by optimistic public statements of considerably more to be negotiated. The government moreover offered particularly low electricity rates and other inducements to U.S. resource companies and other energy-intensive industries and suggested it was seriously considering reducing provincial personal income taxes affecting especially higher paid managers, professionals, and technicians to levels competitive with other parts of North America.

While the government's hard-line stance with public-sector trade unions in 1982–1983 was due primarily to its own budgetary problems, broader implications were not lost on potential U.S. investors. The PQ government's image in the United States shifted perceptibly from its former social-democratic, state interventionist, pro-public corporation, pro-union image of the 1970s to one that accorded priority to private initiative, including foreign direct investment.

Also to improve its image in the United States, the Lévesque government changed by the end of the second year of its first mandate its pre-election semipacifist, neo-neutralist stances on international strategic and political issues toward congruence with U.S. policies. From stating or implying that if it succeeded in leaving the federation and gaining control of its foreign policy it would reduce its armed forces to primarily domestic police functions reminiscent of Costa Rica and withdraw from NATO, NORAD, and other expensive bilateral and multilateral commitments (unless the United States defrayed the expense), since 1978 the government has repeatedly announced it would continue these and other international commitments of the Canadian government. It would act to maintain an efficient, cost-productive St. Lawrence Seaway, would press no irredentist claims on its neighbors such as in respect to primarily francophone border regions in New Brunswick and Ontario, and would submit any territorial claims regarding Labrador to decision or arbitration by the International Court of Justice or other appropriate neutral international body. The government has moreover been careful to avoid either the substance or the rumor that it is attempting to draw United

States citizens, including those of francophone Canadian ancestry, into its arguments with Ottawa.

In these growing contacts, Quebec representatives have not resisted temptations of letting U.S. audiences know about their feelings of being poorly served, even frustrated, by Canadian diplomacy and representation in the United States, and of differentiating their view of Quebec and Canada from that advanced by federal authorities. Thus rivalries and quarrels between Ottawa and Quebec City have often been projected on U.S. ground. Particularly since the PQ gained power (in 1976) until the referendum of May 1980, most Quebec officials traveling in the United States have tried, over and over again, to demonstrate to their U.S. audiences that the federal regime had been deleterious to Quebec and that the processes whereby the French-speaking province hoped to acquire its political sovereignty would be peaceful, democratic, normal, and without any prejudice to U.S. interests.

However, even under the Lévesque government, Quebec's emphases and continuing policies in the United States have not been to project quarrels with Ottawa or defend sovereignty-association, but to promote Quebec's cultural and economic interests. While the PQ government gradually brought some new people into relations with the United States as others departed, most Bourassa appointees remained in office and continued their duties pretty much as they had under the Liberals. Though most were francophone nationalists of one or another stripe, many preferred a truly reformed, more devolved, federal system to sovereignty-association. They would have felt awkward in promoting Quebec sovereignty, which they did not prefer themselves. They were more at ease in promoting Quebec exports, tourism, and culture in the United States.

Furthermore, after defeat of the referendum on sovereignty-association in 1980, members of the Lévesque government, without abandoning their long-term ideal, have become much more discreet in this regard in the United States. Particularly since the deepening economic malaise in Quebec and appointment of Deputy Prime Minister Jacques-Yvan Morin as Intergovernmental Affairs Minister in February 1982, Quebec has sought to convey an image of pragmatism. This development has been regarded with some surprise and scepticism in Quebec, particularly in light of that minister's reputation of tastes for elite European, particularly Parisian, culture and ideas. Moreover, the combination of intellectuals, people in the arts and education, labor leaders, and liberal professionals comprising the core of PQ activists outside the government have not been particularly interested in the United States; insofar as they had been internationally oriented, they too leaned to France. Furthermore, the Lévesque government during its initial years had continued to privilege traditional relationships with France. The Montreal anglophone and growing francophone business class, mostly federalists and PLQ supporters, has been much more oriented toward the United States.

Nonetheless, at least in the upper echelons of the Lévesque government the U.S. priority since early 1982 has been real. Premier Lévesque, new Minister of Intergovernmental Affairs Morin, and Minister of External Trade Landry have met (May 1983) repeatedly with groups in the states, including Republican senators, business people, intellectuals, and others across the country. Emphasis has focused on trade and investment, but in that domain Quebec officials continued to differentiate clearly Quebec's interests and policies from Canada's. They in effect aligned the government with U.S. corporate criticisms of the Foreign Investment Review Agency (FIRA), the National Energy Policy (NEP) announced in the fall of 1980, and other anglophone Canadian "nationalism." They stated that Quebec was open to U.S. investment under pragmatic conditions except in culturally sensitive and limited other spheres. They offered not only more active interest and collaboration, but also more expeditious handling in respect to investment proposals than at the federal level. Deputy Prime Minister and Intergovernmental Affairs Minister Morin even ventured Reagan-like attacks on federal "burearcrats:"

> Our trade exchanges with our various partners, including the United States, have made remarkable headway. Our vast energy resources can be a boon to our neighbors, both in Canada and to the south, if we combine our respective know-how and resources to serve our mutual interests.
>
> That sort of cooperation becomes difficult, if not downright impossible, when super-bureaucrats in Ottawa, who know little about Quebec, are empowered to make decisions that affect our very economic survival.[7]

These pro-U.S. investment arguments may prove profitable, at least in the relatively short run. Whether the Lévesque or a future government will remain so open to foreign investment with little restriction when and if the Quebec economy revives remains unclear. Moreover, bringing Quebec's conflicts with the federal government forcefully to U.S. attention may prove counterproductive over time. To believe that francophones can drive wedges between Americans and Anglo-Canadians and rally the support of the former against the latter is an old and persistent Quebec illusion. As early as the 1830s Patriot leader Louis-Joseph Papineau thought Americans would come to the rescue of his democratically inspired resistance against the British governor of Lower Canada (Quebec). Recently some have argued that Quebec independence would be more feasible in economic association with the United States than with Canada. Such was the essence of Minister Landry's proposal in early 1983, which elicited the U.S. State Department rebuke earlier noted.

The privileged natural affinities and traditional ties between Anglo-Canada and the United States are such that irritants and issues between the two are never apt to be severe enough to tempt the United States seriously to become aligned with Quebec better to counter Ottawa. If there is to be a loser in this triangle, Quebec is bound to lose. Quebec would be more effective in playing down its struggle with Ottawa and pressing its own objectives in positive terms, relatively autonomous of federal policies, than in bringing those conflicts to U.S. attention.

Further, while it is disagreeable and humbling to Quebec officials to be accompanied by Canadian diplomats as a criterion for meeting with U.S. officials, to refuse such opportunities is often counterproductive to Quebec interests and is misunderstood in the U.S. government. Quebec would thereby miss useful contacts and suffer negative judgments among influential Americans. The paucity of its means and access compared with those of the Canadian government suggests it would be self-wounding for Quebec to disassociate itself from such uses of Canadian diplomacy. Achievement of Quebec's ends south of the border requires that its officials be skillful enough to take optimal advantages of Ottawa's capabilities without becoming victims of them.

Cooperation with Other Provinces

Although wary of working through or in the presence of Canadian authorities, Quebec officials are much more inclined to cooperate with their counterparts in other Canadian provinces. Such collaboration is frequently essential to success in the United States. Thus, even though Quebec more often negotiates alone in the United States with both state and local governments and private interests, its active collaboration with other eastern Canadian provinces vis-à-vis the U.S. northeast and New England in particular has helped advance mutual interests.

Collaboration with anglophone provinces also reduces potential U.S. concerns about implicit francophone Quebec nationalist political objectives that might entail unwitting U.S. involvement in this enduring Canadian dispute. There is, moreover, an anglophilia particularly among North American elites and educated strata, including a natural and constant osmosis between U.S. and Anglo-Canadian cultures (see Chapter 11). Anglo-Canadians belong essentially to an American English-speaking universe. Francophones are not part of it and typically perceive much less difference between its Canadian and U.S. parts than Anglo-Canadians often allege.

English-speaking Quebeckers also have more rapport with Americans and should be brought more into Quebec policymaking and implementation in respect to the United States than has recently been evident, particularly under the PQ government, which owes very little to non-francophone support. (See also Chapter 11.)

Collaboration with other provinces in opposition to federal behavior regarding Americans can also reduce the risks for Quebec. U.S. interests would then be confronted with conflicting points of view between anglophone Canadians rather than between Ottawa and francophone Quebec alone. For example, Quebec and Alberta, like Quebec and the Maritimes, in collaboration could be more persuasive both in the United States and in conflict with Ottawa than could Quebec alone.

Such alliances of convenience may of course come apart as circumstances and interests change. Thus Quebec has serious conflicts with Newfoundland over pricing and transmission of Labrador hydropower which might reach the United States, but parallel interests in provincial control of energy and other resources. Quebec is sometimes in competition with other provinces, especially Ontario, for U.S. investments or markets. Ontario also favors more nationalist federal economic policies such as FIRA, often opposed to both U.S. and Quebec interests and policies. Quebec, due to lower economic development, higher unemployment, and less advanced and productive industries than Ontario's, and also due to a greater sense of insulation, through language differences, from U.S. cultural impacts, tends to be more open to U.S. investment. On the other hand, Quebec and Ontario are natural allies in protecting their soft-goods and branch-plant economies respectively from U.S. competition through tariffs and other barriers, against the self-interests of most other provinces.

Quebec's Other International Partners

Quebec's interests, purposes, and policies with respect to the United States contrast particularly with another vital focus of Quebec's foreign relations, with France and the rest of the French-speaking world.

Economics have always been and remain primary in relations with the United States, but they are rather minor with France. Of Quebec's exports in 1981, Can$ 10.366 billion, 65 percent of its shipments of goods outside Canada, went to the United States; only Can$ 267 million went to France. The ratio was thirty-nine to one in favor of the United States.[8] Moreover, Quebec's trade balance with the United States has been consistently positive, but with France consistently negative. Direct and indirect investment of the United States in Quebec is many times that of France. Of Quebec's professional personnel in its Paris delegation in 1982, fewer than ten of seventy-three had primarily economic functions or backgrounds. The budget of the Ministry of Intergovernmental Affairs for relations with France is, however, several multiples that for the United States (which was only Can$ 3.4 million in fiscal 1982–1983). Even when one adds those budgets of economic ministries related to their U.S.-connected functions—such as Agriculture, External Trade, and Industry, Commerce, and Tourism—the budgets for France, Belgium, African countries, and other francophone-related areas exceed those for the United States.[9]

Relations with francophone societies, especially France, are primarily cultural, symbolic, and in a broad sense political. Quebec as a small, long isolated francophone society—three thousand miles from any other important French-speaking country—seeks links with the most vibrant center of that culture to help counterbalance the massive cultural influence of 250 million adjacent anglophone North Americans. Quebec also wants the symbolic recognition and close cooperation of France and other French-speaking countries both to reinforce the cultural identity of its people and to raise Quebec's international visibility and status.

In contrast with the behavior of the U.S. government, successive senior French officials including presidents, prime ministers, and pertinent cabinet members and top civil servants have frequently met, often with much fanfare, with their Quebec counterparts both in France and in Quebec. Agreements have been signed, welcoming speeches and effusive hospitality offered. Even relatively minor meetings and agreements are covered prominently in the Quebec press since Premier Lesage opened Quebec's Paris delegation in 1961. Visits of the Quebec premier or his top ministers in Paris are widely noted in the French media, whereas their trips to the United States are accorded no such press coverage.

Understandably, conflicts with Ottawa over such symbolic, quasidiplomatic, inherently political relations are much more serious than are those over Quebec's relations with the United States. However, successive French governments since that of General DeGaulle have been increasingly wary of behavior toward Quebec officials that would be irritating to the Canadian federal government. The current Mitterrand regime has been especially prudent and correct in that regard.

Whatever Quebec's future role vis-à-vis the Canadian federal system, its relations with French-speaking countries will continue to receive priority, particularly in cultural domains. As Chapter 7 documents, needs to countervail massive North American cultural impacts are growing and are apt to continue to do so. Quebec, like Canada as a whole, will also continue to attempt to broaden its trade, sources of capital, and other economic cooperation beyond North America. However, its economic linkages with the French-speaking world are unlikely to increase greatly in proportion to those with the United States.

Moreover, as Quebec develops a greater sense of linguistic and cultural security and maturity, its identity is apt to become more intimately associated with economic growth out of its chronic state of relatively labor-intensive, little-competitive manufacturing with no growth or export potentials, highly cyclical resource-based exports, and related low wages and high unemployment. As Minister Jacques-Yvan Morin declared in May 1982: "I believe that in the context in which we are now, it is by a vigorous move on the economic level that we can best develop the distinct society which is modern Quebec."[10]

Such a "vigorous move on the economic level" requires closer economic relations with the United States in terms of export markets, capital, technology, and expertise. This new emphasis should be complementary rather than harmful to Quebec's other foreign relations. Within *francophonie*, the rest of Europe, and elsewhere, the genuine "Americanness" of Quebec may provide its trademark and unique attractiveness. A Quebec well informed on and in close rapport with both economic and political developments in the United States and well endowed with its technological and economic benefits could play growing and unique linkage roles for North America even in relation to France itself.

Interests and Policies

Domestic economic roots of Quebec's relations with the United States are described in Chapter 2. In a number of respects they parallel those of some other parts of Canada; in others they are rather different. As in the case of most other provinces, different Quebec economic interests with the United States often conflict with those of one or more other provinces.

Quebec's cultural identity and objectives at home are also a major factor in its relations with the United States, and in a number of respects are a more difficult sphere of its policies there. Those objectives relate to the dualist conception of a unique French-speaking society and culture based in Quebec, with the Quebec government as its primary representative, spokesman, and defender.

Quebec's Cultural Interests and the United States

Quebec's primary interest is to protect its very existence as a distinct cultural entity, to perpetuate it and develop as a society that is basically North American in character but francophone in speech and culture. But since perceptions among the North American majority society, and particularly among its elites, bear directly on Quebec's vital interests, its identity different from others surrounding it will be very fragile if the fundamental qualities of that identity are not understood. Quebec's identity will never be really assured as long as it is not so acknowledged and accepted by elites of its powerful neighbor to the south.

Certainly, the existence of "French-Canadians" is widely known in the United States. Many Americans also are aware that French-Canadians are concentrated in Quebec. But their existence and persistence are still perceived in many milieus, even among otherwise relatively well-informed elites, as rather folkloric, a sort of anachronism. French-Canadians are widely considered to be an ethnic minority, more or less like those in the United States who are immigrants or children or grandchildren of immigrants. That a Quebec based on such an ethnic minority claims to be a people and political entity of its own is often viewed as the futile, unrealistic, and incongruous dream of separatist romantics.

Consequently a major Quebec objective is to correct over time this pervasive U.S. image by communicating through multiple means pertinent information, especially among individuals and groups in the United States who may influence private or public policies and decisions and/or broader public opinion. In general, the U.S. public must be encouraged to understand that the Quebec government not only has much wider powers and autonomy than U.S. state governments, but that it is considered their "national government" by a majority of Quebeckers and that most of its general linguistic and cultural policies have the approval of a majority. Moreover, U.S. elites need to comprehend that though a majority rejected sovereignty-association, a clear majority also favors wider autonomy for Quebec within a more decentralized Canadian system.[11] In this regard the centralizing policies of the Trudeau government run counter to the preferences of most Quebeckers.

The central conceptions that not only the Lévesque, but likely successor governments, are apt to continue to try to communicate in one form or another are the following:

1. French-speaking Quebeckers have been a distinct people in North America for nearly four centuries. They have never ceased considering themselves as such, even during periods when they seemed relatively docile under British and thereafter Anglo-Canadian tutorship. They have as a group repeatedly rejected assimilation and will continue to do so. The United States tends to regard Canada first as a predominantly anglophone whole, and then to try to relate the francophone minority in Quebec to it from anglophone perspectives, largely derived from anglophone Canadian sources. (See Chapters 10 and 11.) This vision runs counter to basic Quebec history, psychology, interests, and cultural and

    political objectives, as reflected in a majority of Quebec francophones whatever their political and constitutional preferences. Quebeckers want to be seen by themselves, not always through the Canadian prism.

2.   Quebec has not been for at least twenty-five years what is usually considered a traditional society. The proportion of the population on farms now roughly corresponds with the U.S. average. Quebec society is a modern industrial society, and wants to become much more so with the aid of closer economic relations with the United States. Politics, education, social and health services, trade unions, and other aspects of life have for a generation been separated from control and major influence by the Catholic church. Religious practice, birthrates, and other convincing indicators document rapid transition to a basically secular society. Church and state are two distinct entities, more as in France than in Ireland. The average level of education among the younger generation approximates that across Canada and the United States. Moreover, educational emphases have been rapidly transformed from the humanities to engineering, business, and other applied fields of an industrial economy. Quebec wants the United States to perceive it as a dynamic, modern, francophone culture, society, and economy.

3.   French-speaking Quebeckers are not at all comparable to a U.S. ethnic group of relatively recent immigration. Their ancestors arrived in the New World contemporaneously with the Pilgrims in New England and the other British settlers to its south. Their origins and initial century and a half of experience were part of the history of one of the two world powers and civilizations that colonized most of North America. They have *always* used French as their daily language. They are not a minority in their own conception, but a growing majority in their home society, much as anglophones comprise majorities elsewhere on the continent, north of Mexico. They reject being thought of as an ethnic group by other North Americans, and are shocked or amused by such U.S. perceptions, such as comparisons with Mexican-Americans in the U.S. southwest, noted in Chapter 11.

4.   Quebec's *lingua franca* is not a patois "joual" incomprehensible to native European, African, and other francophones abroad. Regardless of a few Quebec authors who write in the once widespread patois of the little educated, today's relatively educated Quebeckers speak, read, and write international French. Their accents and expressions, even at the popular level, do not diverge

further from French spoken by educated Parisians than does the
English of U.S. masses from that of educated Londoners.

5. Though they are a distinctive people in linguistic and cultural
   respects, Quebeckers are at least as North American as are most
   other Americans. Like those North Americans whose ancestors
   arrived in the New World from Britain before the mid-eighteenth
   century, Quebeckers have over many generations adapted to a
   very different environment from Europe (the first of these groups
   from an English-speaking culture, the second from a French-
   speaking one). The pervasive North Americanness of Quebeckers
   is immediately obvious to any intelligent French-speaking European.

   Except for a small intellectual and cultural elite (and some of
   their students) around universities, the arts, and a few other
   intellectual and cultural institutions who are inclined toward left-
   of-center Paris elite culture, the dominant class shares most of
   the beliefs, tastes, and priorities of their Anglo–North American
   counterparts. And as Chapter 7 demonstrates, the masses are
   intimately linked to U.S. mass culture and values. Their attitudes
   toward the United States in regard to investment, trade, and most
   other relations either do not differ significantly from those of
   other Canadians, or they are somewhat more favorable.[12]

Even the pro-French, socialist-inclined intelligentsia just noted is a
small minority among Quebec elites and has little influence beyond its
numbers and its students, certainly not on policies of the PQ government
for which it voted overwhelmingly. Moreover, its relative numbers and
influence are likely to decline as the U.S.-oriented francophone business
class grows with economic development linked with the United States,
and as younger francophones increasingly pursue careers in export-
oriented enterprises.

Much of the foregoing realities have gradually become known among
a number of U.S. elites who follow Quebec developments since the
shock of the 1976 election of the PQ, generally unanticipated among
them. (See also Chapter 11.) A few scholars in U.S. universities, a
handful of French-speaking journalists, some well-informed investment
and other corporate elites, and a growing number in the U.S. Department
of State and other federal agencies and neighboring state governments
have become relatively familiar with *les faits* (the facts).

However, these relatively informed Americans are not many, even
among the elites whose views may influence others' actions and opinions
pertinent to Quebec. In the U.S. northeast, most of the U.S. foreign-
policy and relevant business communities seem still to hold many of

the anachronistic stereotypes that either really never applied, or that no longer apply. Because such misperceptions obstruct and confuse fruitful relations, the long-term objective of their gradual correction will remain an important priority of any likely future Quebec government.

Cultural and linguistic considerations also affect Quebec's economic purposes in regard to the United States (addressed in Chapter 2). The gradual growth in numbers particularly of younger francophones in management, technical, and professional career tracks in larger, more internationally competitive enterprises linked with the United States will increasingly result in their involvement with the U.S. private sector. However, as Chapter 2 also documents, francophones still comprise but a small minority in the decision-making levels of these dynamic enterprises with North America–wide (and often worldwide) involvements. It will be another decade or so before many francophones have direct personal rapport with U.S. business elites comparable to that of the Canadian anglophones who still control and manage most such enterprises.

Chapter 2 notes that inroads of francophone entrepreneurs are more widespread at decision-making levels in small and medium-sized enterprises (PME for *petites et moyennes entreprises*) than in the larger corporations. Many PMEs depend on U.S. markets for their viability and especially their growth. The Lévesque government is aiding them to develop exports, largely to the south. Whereas the larger corporations often have the capital, expertise, and contacts to fend for themselves south of the border, PMEs run mainly by francophones do not and thereby need the active assistance of the Ministries of External Trade and of Commerce, Industry, and Tourism, and that of Quebec delegations serving the regions of potential markets (and suppliers) in the United States.

Quebec francophone decision makers and those who influence their decisions tend to be less anxious about direct U.S. investments than their anglophone counterparts because they feel their different language, culture, and related identity provide more effective barriers, or cushions, to U.S. cultural influences. As Chapter 7 suggests, many francophones underestimate the already massive and still growing impacts of U.S. mass culture. U.S. presence via subsidiaries and other direct economic involvement often comprises a major transmitter of U.S. popular culture, even through the vernacular language. More effective integration of U.S.-controlled enterprises into Quebec's culture can reduce these cultural impacts, but unhealthy dependence is not easily eliminated.

Moreover, the processes of so integrating U.S. subsidiaries are often more costly and more complex because of cultural differences than they are in other parts of Canada, or especially in the United States. U.S.

investors need to be made aware of advantages of operations in Quebec in spite of such higher costs and cultural restraints. Quebeckers are paying an economic price to be different, which they must convince U.S. interests to share to a degree that will be modest contrasted with the projected advantages.

If the government succeeds in developing primarily higher-technology industries as envisaged in its major policy paper, *Technological Conversion*, published in 1981, it will further stimulate educational, cultural, and intellectual as well as economic linkages with the United States. Such innovative, research-and-development–based enterprises will require advanced training most readily available in top U.S. universities, research institutions, and corporate laboratories and management programs. The flow of highly trained, often culturally demanding, personnel in both directions will thereby increase. More educated francophones will become familiar with the many internationally renowned universities, museums, symphony orchestras, and other cultural and educational institutions within a day's drive from Quebec. U.S. elite culture is thereby apt to become increasingly familiar and attractive to dynamic younger francophones. Although its Paris counterparts will not lose appeal, their influence relative to that just across the border is likely to decline.

Except among the small anti-U.S. leftist elite mentioned earlier, this development would be welcomed. Quebeckers, because of their history, traditions, and the residues of an insular past, know much less about the United States than its crucial importance to their province requires. U.S. indifference to and misperception and ignorance of Quebec are more understandable than ignorance or misperception of the United States among Quebec francophones. There are, for instance, no interdisciplinary francophone centers in Quebec universities or other institutions for research and study of the U.S. economic realities, history, politics, foreign policy, society, literature, and arts. There are even few individual courses in francophone universities on these aspects of life in the United States. Attendance of Quebec francophones at U.S. universities and exchanges of professors and students with them are still of sharply lower proportions than for Anglo-Canada. Alleviating such omissions are but among the more obvious developments that should be actively encouraged by Quebec governments in pursuit of more fruitful long-term relations with the United States.

Policies to Achieve These Objectives

Although Canada is juridically a sovereign country of which Quebec is but a province, in a sense Quebec's relations with the United States are more akin to classical international bilateral relations than those of

Canada with its great southern neighbor. Tensions and conflicts between the latter two are sometimes major. But relations between them are more like domestic relations, and are certainly more transnational than those between francophone Quebec and the United States. (See Chapter 11.)

Thus, Canadian-U.S. actors at both governmental and private levels often know each other well, anticipate their mutual reactions, naturally abide by the same rules of the game,[13] and grow up and live in the same language and in related cultures that differ much less than do those of Quebec and the United States. Much more of the complex relations between anglophone Canada and the United States takes place in diverse transnational networks than is true between francophone Quebec and the United States.

Rapport and communality of thought and action between Quebec officials and private actors on the one hand, and U.S. groups with whom they should do business on the other, are much less developed. Both sides of these relationships, but particularly the Quebeckers, are quite conscious of their cultural differences, even when the Quebeckers speak fluent, but usually accented, English. It is much more difficult for most people from the United States, officials or private citizens, to put themselves into the shoes of a Quebec nationalist than to understand the basic motivations of anglophone Canadian nationalist counterparts.

Policies and actions to develop U.S. understanding of Quebec identity can be more serene, direct, clear-cut, and less defensive than those of their Anglo-Canadian counterparts, because Quebec's cultural differences from the United States are more readily observable. Thus a responsible Canadian official would be unlikely to argue before a U.S. audience, as did the Quebec Minister of Intergovernmental Affairs, that "a vigorous move on the economic level" and U.S. investment and other expanded economic relations with the United States would be the best way "to develop the distinct society."

Aggressive salesmanship in a broad sense, to include cultural as well as economic purposes, is central to Quebec policy in the United States. Quebec needs to help Quebec businessmen learn more about and avail themselves of U.S. market opportunities and promote Quebec products, which are culturally different and thereby interesting to the U.S. market. Moreover, cultural endeavors designed for Americans of Canadian francophone background (discussed in Chapters 8 and 9), and those with teachers and students of French, as well as with others of the U.S. public, may not only help develop markets for Quebec's cultural products, but also for other exports that are influenced by the culture but not primarily cultural in character. Visits of U.S. journalists, scholars, and other elites to Quebec, which expose visitors to diverse points of view, may likewise in the long run have economic as well as informational and cultural impacts.

Francophiles in the United States, most of whom read and some of whom speak French, should also be an important target audience. They should comprise a major source of at least latent interest in and favorable impressions of Quebec, and moreover are potential communicators to other individuals and groups. But many of them manifest anachronistic, snobbish, and otherwise negative prejudices that they often learned from contacts in France. In this connection, meetings such as that of the American Association of Teachers of French in Quebec City in 1980 and of the New England Modern Language Association in 1981—both devoted in part to Quebec—are prototypes for better communication.

The projection of a favorable image of Quebec cultural products and individuals in the United States constitutes of course a difficult, long-term problem. Given budgetary restraints and other problems, it is unlikely that Quebec will greatly expand the level of its current efforts. Effectiveness requires that these efforts be concentrated on a few priority publics such as those mentioned above. Microwave and satellite television transmissions to make Quebec programs available to cable systems beyond the near border areas where they are carried (in 1983) by some cable networks would seem a priority, to reach optimal numbers at modest cost. Once signals are available, cable companies must be convinced of the commercial viability of transmitting them in larger metropolitan areas, university communities, and other areas with sufficient potential audiences. Quebec delegations might gradually develop networks of universities and cultural institutions where there would be sufficient interest in receiving Quebec theater and musical performances and other cultural events to warrant periodic tours by recognized performing artists.

Penetration by appropriate Quebeckers into teaching French in the United States is apt to be more difficult in light of already fierce competition of trained U.S. teachers for scarce openings. But in the long run Quebeckers should become at least one-tenth as numerous as native French among French teachers in the United States—roughly the ratio of the population of Quebec to that of France. Given their North American heritage and geographical proximity to the United States, Quebeckers of comparable pedagogical talents should be more effective in certain aspects of teaching than Europeans.

Other Communications Structures and Target Audiences

Top decision makers in international affairs in the United States government—in the National Security Council, the Executive Office of the President, the Department of State, and other departments and agencies—are not apt to be reachable by Quebec. Moreover, their decisions are unlikely to be changed even if they could be reached. Nor do they exert more than very indirect influence over most matters of concern to Quebec. Even at the Canada "desk" in the Department of State, which is relatively well informed on Quebec (see also Chapter 11), changes of policy of interest to Quebec are not likely under prevailing circumstances. Hence, these officials are neither realistic nor priority audiences.

Congress is both more significant for Quebec interests and more likely to be interested, as Premier Lévesque's and Deputy Premier and Intergovernmental Minister Morin's meeting with Republican senators in 1982 suggests. There, in committee or on the floor of the House and Senate, issues of importance to Quebec are apt to be influenced especially by senators and congressmen from the northeast, where Quebec's contacts with state governments and private sectors and its economic interests are likewise greatest. Some of these legislators whose constituencies relate or might relate to Quebec are on committees with purviews pertinent to Quebec's interests. When busy legislators are not available, Quebec representatives could get their arguments across to their senior staffs who have more time and who often greatly influence their legislators.

Executive officials outside the Department of State who are in commercial, environmental, and other functional roles of little diplomatic or political sensitivity are also more accessible and in important respects more relevant to Quebec concerns. Nongovernmental actors—lobbies, lawyers, consultants, and others—in Washington are important potential sources of information and suggestions and often exert influence on congressional and executive processes.

The Canadian government would actively oppose expansion of Quebec official presence in Washington beyond the existing tourism office and would effectively discourage influential U.S. citizens from dealing with it. Given concerns among both governmental and other people in Washington when the tourist office was established in 1977 that its real purposes were more political than tourist, Quebec officials in residence charged with broader responsibilities might well find their roles counterproductive. Quebec might, however, further explore working through a competent and well regarded U.S. private agency, such as an appropriate law firm, which could provide useful information and expert advice and arrange optimal contacts for brief visits by Quebec officials.

As the Quebec government recognizes, ties with state governors and their senior aides are much more likely to bear fruit than frustrating efforts indirectly to convince diplomatically and politically sensitive federal executive decision makers. Ties with New England, New York, and several other state governments, where mutually profitable economic linkages are apt to be feasible, have been greatly expanded under the PQ regime.

The Conference of New England Governors and Eastern Canadian Premiers is apt to remain primarily a forum for discussion, once a year, of pragmatic economic and functional collaboration among these adjacent regions. It makes no decisions. Cooperation is necessarily limited to matters over which New England or other states have jurisdiction, considerably less than the jurisdiction enjoyed by provinces in the Canadian federal system. There are important conflicts of interest between Quebec, Newfoundland, and the Maritimes in respect to New England, as there are in respect to the United States in general. Governors of Massachusetts, the most important of the six states economically to Quebec, have been less active in the conference than most of the others, especially from the three states adjacent to Quebec. The conference's political influence is quite limited and largely indirect.[14]

Nevertheless, this annual conference has been a significant vehicle for Quebec, and its importance could well grow further. The six governors have a joint staff in Boston and the five premiers one in Halifax; the two staffs collaborate regularly over optimal agenda, background materials, and recommendations emanating from annual meetings and individual premiers and governors between meetings. Political leaders and their implementing staffs get to know one another and hold fruitful informal bilateral discussions between "on camera" sessions. Issues are thrashed out before and after meetings between respective staffs. The conference has become a launching pad and facilitator for future cooperation in such diverse spheres as acid rain, transportation, energy, tourism, and other aspects of trade and investment.

Quebec's role in this conference could become considerably more important in both absolute terms and relative to those of the other four provinces. Quebec has three times the gross provincial product and more than twice the population of the other four provinces combined. Although its current exports in merchandise to the adjoining U.S. region are of about the same value as those of the Atlantic Provinces, its potential, especially, but not only, in electricity, is far greater. For New England, Quebec is by far the more lucrative customer, by a ratio of nearly eight to one. Furthermore, whereas influential New England groups oppose the expansion of the Atlantic Provinces' major exports— especially fish, potatoes, and other foodstuffs—such protectionist interests are minor in respect to Quebec's principal exports.[15]

Comparable relationships have been developed with New York governors and their staffs, exemplified in agreements reached on hydropower and environmental research (discussed in Chapters 2 and 6). The relationships with the Louisiana government, still primarily in regard to bilingual education but from time to time related to tourism and other economic matters, are also regarded as fruitful. Although there may be some concerns in Ottawa about proliferation of Quebec's closer linkages with New England and certain other states, that development is regarded by the U.S. government as generally apolitical and benign.

In Washington particularly, but also in U.S. relations generally, Quebec should be discreet, patient, well organized, and focused in its efforts on carefully chosen priority publics whose influence is pertinent and whose members are accessible under appropriate circumstances.

The Future

These basic interests of Quebec and the means available to pursue them are unlikely to change substantially, at least not in the next decade or so. A different Quebec government might shift only somewhat the priorities of Quebec policies. A PLQ government, for example, would perhaps emphasize economic relations even more than the PQ, though no government could ignore cultural dimensions. For the PLQ, discussion of sovereignty-association and related conflicts with Ottawa would no longer be on the agenda within the United States. But major political conflicts with Ottawa would remain, pending its greater recognition of the concept of duality and related devolution of jurisdictions pertaining to language, communications, and culture to Quebec. And in one guise or another, Quebec-Ottawa controversies are likely to affect Quebec behavior toward the United States.

As noted earlier, evolution of the constitutional and political role of Quebec vis-à-vis the federal system is apt to relate in part to the latter's success in developing a more productive economy linked with the United States. Reciprocally, Quebec's relations with the United States will depend in important respects on the direction and details of that evolution.

Scenarios in sufficient detail to consider such interconnections systematically cannot be examined in the few pages remaining. Within each alternative scenario, sub-scenarios could also make considerable differences for relations with Quebec's southern neighbor.[16] The likely general implications for several of the more probable eventualities and one less probable one—Quebec independence—are as much as can be attempted here.

Major Constitutional, Political, or Economic Changes

A sovereign Quebec is at the lower end of eventualities in ascending order of probability, at least in the foreseeable future. Perhaps the least improbable scenario for that rather unlikely outcome would begin with the PQ campaigning during the next general provincial election, which must take place no later than 1986, as it has promised, on a platform requesting a clear majority mandate to proceed to independent political status. The PQ has stated that to implement that decision, it would need to win a majority not only of seats, but also of the total popular vote (which would include nonfrancophones). Even with such leverage, negotiations with Ottawa over the terms in respect to sharing assets and debts, and other thorny details, are likely to be long and painful.

Though the explicit proviso of economic association would probably not be included in the enabling electoral platform and in PQ vocabulary, the Quebec government would attempt to negotiate a customs union or common market in Quebec's economic interest, and probably a common currency as well. But outside of Ontario, other provinces would regard any form of sovereignty-association as contrary to some of their inportant interests and would not be amenable to much compromise with Quebec. They would not be apt to accord Quebec a veto or its equivalent in the intergovernmental agencies required to make critical decisions and run these common arrangements. Thus Quebec, if it were unwilling to proceed to independence without such economic arrangements, could gain little more control over important commercial, monetary, and related policies affecting its economy than it now has.

Independence without continued protected markets for Quebec's soft goods across Canada would result in major short-run increases in unemployment and in other economic dislocations. Unless and until Quebec's economy had achieved major progress toward the modernization objectives and U.S. markets envisaged by the current government—highly unlikely for at least a decade—the government's alternatives would be to go independent without protected Canadian markets and suffer the economic consequences, become politically independent without marginally greater control over economic decisions affecting its welfare, or else to use its leverage to win a compromise in the direction of the Pépin-Robarts and other devolutionist proposals.

During this process Washington would adopt an attentive, prudent, hands-off stance (as it did during the pre-referendum period of the first PQ government when the sovereignty issue was more active), but it would maintain close contacts with Ottawa and perhaps quietly urge the Canadian government to compromise sufficiently to head off Quebec's departure from the federation. In the ensuing arrangement Quebec would achieve official diplomatic relations with Washington. But unless it went completely independent rather than compromise its sovereignty to achieve a viable customs union, then Ottawa, with some input from the Quebec government, would probably continue de facto to have the predominant roles in determining most economic, defense, and security arrangements with the United States. In that eventuality only modest changes would occur in U.S.-Canadian relations, except that the Quebec government would represent Quebec through minority roles vis-à-vis Ottawa in determination of those relations. However, Quebec would deal alone with the United States in a few economic fields, particularly natural resources and hydropower, and in cultural affairs.

Under such circumstances Quebec would proceed with great caution on matters of concern to the United States so as not to alarm its elites in or out of government.

Somewhat less improbable than sovereignty, at the other extreme, would be major further centralization of authority in the federal government, taking advantage of popular political apathy and an unlikely decline of Quebec nationalism. Continued economic stagnation or, worse, further decline, would encourage that trend, as it did during the Great Depression. Similar to the post–Civil War historical trend in the United States, Canada would succeed, at least for a period, in integrating francophone Quebeckers into a single Canadian nation and would seek to reduce Quebec's international role to roughly that of one of the states of the United States.

Quebec's influence in external relations would thereby decline significantly. The federal government might, for example, limit Quebec's degree of freedom in energy matters. It might enforce its declared intention of expropriating a transmission corridor for Newfoundland electricity across Quebec to New England or New York, tax electricity exports, and/or require their sale to neighboring provinces instead, at lower prices. Political repercussions in Quebec would be pervasive. Quebec would take the dispute to the Supreme Court, but would probably fail to achieve reversal. However, unless Anglo-Canada should succeed in assimilating francophone Quebeckers, their nationalist feelings would be further augmented and the likelihood of later secession, under more favorable economic and political circumstances, would probably increase.

A third major trend might be slow, progressive liberalization of Canadian-U.S. trade beyond that projected through 1988 under GATT (General Agreement on Tariffs and Trade) agreements of 1979. Quebec would thereby be obliged to replace jobs in older, labor-intensive industries with alternatives in newer, more competitive ones. As suggested earlier, such a trend would reinforce north-south economic interdependencies and reduce Quebec's relative dependence on the Canadian economy, thereby also reducing francophone Quebeckers' hesitations to leave the federation; Quebec's bargaining power with Ottawa for expanded autonomy would rest on a much more credible threat of going independent. Economic association would thereby become less essential for Quebec. This seems to be the notion of the Lévesque government, reflected in Minister Landry's proposal in early 1983.

Lesser Changes

More likely than either of the first two scenarios above, at least over the next decade, is evolution toward greater autonomy for interested provinces including, but not limited to, Quebec. At the federal level, pressures are strong for Mr. Trudeau to resign (as he said he would do when he was returned to office in 1980) before the end of his present term in 1985. His successor would probably be an anglophone, who would have to do more than "favorite son" Trudeau to be acceptable to Quebeckers. The new Liberal leader would be likely to make more concessions to Quebec (perhaps reminiscent of the style of Prime Minister Pearson in the 1960s), particularly if he were to head a minority government. He would want to reduce controversy with the Quebec government both at home and abroad. Quebec might thus be freer to some extent to develop its U.S. relations. Its criticisms of the federal government therefore would probably decline.

Another eventuality is moderate success of the "National Party," an extension of the PQ at the federal level, which will present candidates in all Quebec ridings at the next federal election. This idea is favorably regarded by many voters; in October 1981, 58 percent of Quebec francophones favored the PQ naming federal candidates. In such an event, 35 percent said they would vote for these candidates, 22 percent would vote for Liberals, 8 percent for Conservatives, and 3 percent for NDP candidates; the rest were undecided.[17]

Although the PQ could hardly rally its traditional support at a level where many voters would consider the role of "independentists" as a contradiction (Quebeckers have a habit of electing strong federalists to the House of Commons and Quebec nationalists to the provincial National Assembly), the party could be successful in a dozen or even more ridings. A vigorous PQ campaign with attractive candidates in heavily francophone ridings would press Liberal opponents to compete by moderating their centralist stances to win nationalist votes. The spectrum of views in Quebec in federal-provincial relations would be more apparent in the House of Commons than under the prevailing Liberal monopoly (but for one Tory MP, Roch LaSalle). Particularly if enough Nationalist Party MPs should be elected to deny a majority of seats to both major parties, then the PQ could enhance Quebec's position vis-à-vis a centralist government in Ottawa.

A Progressive Conservative Party victory in the next general election could also modify federal behavior regarding Quebec. The new Conservative leader, Brian Mulroney, is regarded as having good chances to form the next government. As a fluently bilingual Quebecker, he may become as popular in Quebec as Pierre Elliot Trudeau. He has approved

Mr. Trudeau's constitutional policy and patriation move, which resulted in the 1982 Constitution. Hence there is no great expectation from him as regards a larger Quebec autonomy.

However, the Conservative Party's stances in recent years have been more favorable than Liberal ones toward provincial autonomy. During their brief minority government in 1979, no Ottawa policy was deemed antagonistic to Quebec's interests by most Quebec elites. Flexible federal-provincial policies and agreements evolved. Prime Minister Clark defined Canada as a "community of communities." If Senator Arthur Tremblay, who has been recognized by Mulroney, is still able to influence a Tory government's constitutional and political policies, some decentralization might result.

A minority Tory government motivated to avoid opposition by a dozen or more Nationalist Party MPs might likewise lead to a similar outcome. In either event, Quebec's degrees of freedom to be active with respect to the United States would improve. Furthermore, Canadian anglophone nationalist policies toward the United States under a Tory government or a Tory minority government would be less likely than under the Liberals. Confrontations regarding Canadian-U.S. relations between Quebec City and Ottawa would decline.

The next Quebec provincial election must be held before 1986. If the PQ maintains its commitment to run primarily on the sovereignty issue, demanding a clear mandate from 50 percent or more of the electorate as the criterion for pursuing that objective, only a virtual miracle would prevent the Liberals from winning that election and forming the next government. However, Lévesque and his governmental colleagues in mid-1983 were considering running on broader issues, but simultaneously conducting a separate referendum on pursuing independence without the requirement of economic association. In that case the referendum would probably fail, whereas the government might be reelected, especially if Lévesque would resign in favor of a younger minister like Pierre-Marc Johnson.

It is difficult to extrapolate a future provincial Liberal government's policies regarding the United States when former Premier Bourassa is again assuming leadership of the PLQ. It is clear, however, that no Liberal government would argue sovereignty at home or abroad, except to make sure that the idea is dead and buried. Tension with Ottawa in that regard in the United States would disappear. U.S. business and political leaders, the foreign-policy community, and most other elites would welcome that development. Their concerns of being caught in a crossfire between Quebec and Ottawa would be eliminated.

It is highly improbable that a Bourassa Liberal government would close any U.S. delegations or otherwise become less active in the United

States. It has merely been tactically useful for federalist Liberals in the National Assembly opposition to criticize alleged links of the PQ government's extended international relations with its campaign for sovereignty. Although these Liberal criticisms have pertained particularly to relations with France, they are also applied to relations with the United States. An important, virtually unconditionally federalist wing in the 1983 Liberal caucus argues for channeling most of Quebec's foreign relations through the Canadian government, reminiscent of pre–Quiet Revolution days. However, that Liberal minority is more representative of natural anti-PQ fervor and tactics than of a winning trend in the PLQ.

The PLQ, after all, when it was previously in power under Jean Lesage (1960–1966) and Robert Bourassa himself (1970–1976), fiercely argued Quebec's rights to and interests in active representation abroad. As noted above, the PLQ established the controversial Quebec presence in Paris, greatly expanded the role of its bureau in New York, and opened most of the succeeding Quebec offices in the United States and elsewhere abroad. Premier Bourassa, a convinced federalist who, however, spoke of cultural sovereignty and was in nearly continuous conflict with Prime Minister Trudeau over Quebec's role with respect to Ottawa, himself traveled regularly to the United States in search of trade and investment. Since his 1976 defeat he has taught, given speeches, and participated in many discussions in the United States. He has, for example, fervently promoted expanded hydroelectricity exports to the U.S. northeast. If he should preside over a future Liberal government, then that government would be even more active than the PQ one in promoting Quebec's economic interests south of the border. It might well press more effectively, for example, PQ Minister Landry's proposed move toward a free-trade area of Canada with the United States. A PLQ government would be free of all suspicion of its ultimate political goals as it pursued north-south policies dictated by concrete economic objectives understandable to people of the United States. Its inherent conflicts with Ottawa would not disappear, but its style would be less flamboyant. Quebec's identity and basic interests would remain, and its policies would be at least as aggressive as under the PQ, if not more aggressive.

Conclusions

Quebec's interests vis-à-vis the United States are fundamental to the province, not to a particular party in power in its government. These interests converge on close linkages with the United States for Quebec's economic and related cultural growth. Friendly relations with that country are essential to Quebec. Emphasis on those relations is a deliberate choice as well as a geographical necessity.

Hence there is a permanent Quebec policy toward the United States. Except in the relatively unlikely eventuality of independence, Quebec's margin of maneuver will remain limited. Ottawa does not always serve Quebec's best interests, but Quebec cannot serve them alone with its minimal instrumental resources. Ideally, Quebec needs to collaborate with the Canadian government to promote more effective federal representation of its interests and make optimal use of Ottawa's much wider contacts and greater resources and constitutional powers in dealing with the United States.

Although particular emphases, tones, styles, and details of Quebec policies toward its superpower neighbor may fluctuate over time with different governments and personalities, their underlying tenets are unlikely to change in any significant way.

Notes

1. Press release, the Department of State, Washington, D.C., February 2, 1983.
2. "Except for those who live close to the border, Americans have few if any complaints about Canada. When disputes reach the media, the average American tends to be pro-Canadian and critical of the U.S. government." Willis C. Armstrong et al., The Atlantic Council Working Group on the U.S. and Canada, *Canada and the United States, Dependence and Divergence* (Cambridge, Mass.: Ballinger Publishing Co., 1982), p. 3.
3. Of Canadian diplomatic personnel in the United States, no more than 5 percent in 1983 are francophone in background, for a country where 25 percent of the population is French speaking.
4. M. Jacques-Yvan Morin, Étude des cŕedits du ministère des affaires intergouvernementales, Commission permanente des affaires intergouvernementales, *Journal des Débats* 113 (May 26, 1982), Assemblée nationale, Quebec, Éditeur officiel du Québec, 1982, p. B-4919. (Author's translation.)
5. For brief empirical documentation, see Chapter 1, note 2. For more extensive discussion and documentation, see Alfred O. Hero, Jr., and Louis Balthazar, *The United States, Quebec, and Canada* (forthcoming), Chapters 1 and 2.
6. Lise Bissonnette, "La Vocation Tardive: Perceptions des milieux politiques québécois à l'égard des États Unis," unpublished paper for the colloquium of the Quebec Center for International Relations and the World Peace Foundation at the Harvard Faculty Club, Cambridge, Mass., September 1–3, 1982.
7. Address by the Vice Prime Minister of Quebec and Minister of Intergovernmental Affairs, Jacques-Yvan Morin, before the World Affairs Council of Northern California in San Francisco, June 3, 1982, at the Westin St. Francis Hotel.

248   *Louis Balthazar*

8. *Commerce international du Québec: 1981* (Quebec: Bureau Statistique du Québec, 1982). Moreover, whereas U.S. imports from Quebec had increased over 1980, those of France had decreased.

9. Bissonnette, "La Vocation Tardive."

10. Morin, *Étude des crédits du ministère des affaires intergouvernementales*, p. B-4909. (Author's translation.)

11. See Chapter 1, note 2, and Chapter 2, notes 6, 7, and 8.

12. See Chapter 1, notes 4 and 5, and Chapter 2, notes 6, 7, and 8.

13. "There is a comfortable informal quality about the Canadian-U.S. relationship. Officials of the two countries are frequently on a first-name basis and communicate easily. Differences of opinion or tough negotiating problems are usually put plainly on the table. Efforts to resolve issues tend to be characterized by fairness and mutual consideration. To most people in the United States, Canada is not really a foreign country. Most Canadians also feel themselves at home in the U.S.A." Armstrong et al., The Atlantic Council, *Canada and the United States*, p. 1.

14. See Lise Bissonnette, "Orthodoxie fédéraliste et relations régionales transfrontières, une ménace illusiore," *Études internationales* 12(4), December 1981, pp. 635–655.

15. This paragraph is derived from a forthcoming volume edited by William D. Shipman and reporting on a joint study of economic linkages, product by product, between New England, Quebec, and the Atlantic Provinces sponsored by the World Peace Foundation, the Atlantic Provinces Economic Council, and the Quebec Center for International Relations.

16. For more thoroughgoing discussion of implications of different scenarios, ranging from further federal centralization to Quebec independence, see Hero and Balthazar, *The United States, Quebec, and Canada*, Chapter 11.

17. Survey cited in *Le Devoir*, October 29, 1981.

13

American Perceptions of Quebec

Charles Doran
Brian Job

In brief, Quebec's most privileged links, aside from its most essential relationship with the Canadian partner, would be first with the United States—where there is no imaginable reason to frown on such a tardy but natural and healthy development.

—Premier René Lévesque
July 1976

The United States obviously follows with interest what is happening in your country. I . . . wanted to indicate clearly that we believe it is important that there be a united Canada but also to make clear that this is an internal matter, and we do not intend to interfere in the internal affairs of Canada.

—Secretary of State Cyrus Vance
January 1979

. . . diplomacy must include the Provinces and States. That does not mean that either Ottawa or Washington should attempt to contract business with the States or Provinces; that would violate the Constitutions. But each capital can and is developing its liaison with other governments in its own country. And informal contacts between the Provinces and the Canadian Embassy in Washington can prevent misunderstanding and expedite our affairs.

—Ambassador Thomas Enders
June 1979

This triad of quotations aptly sets the stage for discussion of U.S. interests and policy concerning Quebec.

U.S. policy starts from the simple premise that federal-provincial matters are internal political matters and that the United States has neither the intention nor the mandate to interfere in those matters. Second is the oft-expressed and diplomatically correct statement, and actual statement of preference, that Canada ought to remain united. But the United States will obviously accept any Canada that it finds. This position does not mean that the United States fails to take note of the differing attitudes toward U.S.-Canada relations expressed by the provinces. But these differences of viewpoint have no direct impact on the conduct of foreign relations until they become official policy and are implemented. And technically, in the majority of situations, only federal governments make foreign policy. Therefore there is little room for Washington to deal directly with the provinces, even though individual states may deal directly with them from time to time[1] and even though Washington takes the preferences of individual provinces into account, often at the urging of Ottawa itself, when formulating policy toward Canada.

But because Quebec places apparent singular emphasis on its relations to the south, Washington gives special attention to Quebec for this and other reasons, not in terms of formal ties or representation but in terms of the posited consequences of U.S. initiatives and policy toward Canada.[2] It is probably the case that inside the framework of overall policy toward Canada and despite the importance of an Ontario, an Alberta, or a British Columbia to U.S. interests, Quebec receives substantially more analytic time and attention from U.S. policymakers.

In seeking to understand the official U.S. attitude toward Quebec, this chapter begins with an exploration of some of the deeper historical and cultural factors that underlie U.S. preferences and policies. It also considers how these factors explain the U.S. perspective toward the internal Canadian debate regarding increased Quebec autonomy. This broad discussion on perceptions and images establishes the context in which Washington formulates U.S. national interests regarding Quebec and regarding Canada. The second section of the chapter provides an assessment of these interests, focusing particularly upon the U.S. preoccupation with security and on the linkages between political and economic actors in determining U.S. governmental policy. The record of U.S. policy, or lack of official policy, toward Quebec is then examined to detect any recent shifts of consequence in either substance or implementation. Finally, the chapter attempts to summarize, from the U.S. perspective, both outlook and policy toward Quebec in the 1980s.

American Perceptions and Attitudes Concerning Quebec

Statements about the "attitude" of one nation toward another must be made with care and viewed with caution. A picture of "political culture" has to be painted with very broad brush strokes. Although the result may be quite representative of general attitudes and policies over an extended time period, the precision of detail necessary to allow specific inferences about the actions taken by individual governments or forecasts about future policies will be missing. On the other hand, failure to understand the fundamental, if somewhat hidden, tenets of a nation's history and culture will also lead to mistaken assumptions and misguided actions. This is especially true when the national entities involved do not, as is the case with the United States and Quebec, share a common historical experience.

It is further necessary to make clear exactly whose perceptions and whose knowledge are considered relevant. Distinctions between the elite and the remainder of society are crucial. By and large, the public in the United States, as elsewhere, is uninterested and uninformed about international happenings and foreign policy.[3] Knowledge about Canada and about Quebec can be assumed to be minimal in these strata of the population. What are relevant are the elites within the United States, i.e., those groups of persons who by virtue of their positions in government, educational institutions, business, media, etc., conduct relations with Canada and Quebec and/or can influence official attitudes and policies.

Unfortunately, even among these narrow strata of the U.S. population, little information or thought is devoted to Canada and to Quebec. In a forthcoming volume on this topic, Alfred O. Hero, Jr., and Louis Balthazar convincingly demonstrate that (1) among the members of the internationally attentive public in the United States there are very few people who are concerned and interested in Canada, (2) of these, only a rather small fraction are informed and interested about Quebec, and (3) for those who do follow events in Quebec, their information and opinions are predominantly shaped by exposure to exclusively "Anglo" media.[4] (See also Chapter 10.)

U.S. Attitudes Toward Quebec Culture

It is not without note that perhaps the ablest critic in the history of U.S. mores and institutions, Alexis de Tocqueville, was French. He felt he had learned enough about the republic in a mere nine months to write about it with some abandon. De Tocqueville pondered why Americans showed so little sensitivity to culture in their own country and yet were so sensitive about their own culture abroad. His answer holds some meaning for how the U.S. public views French Canada.

The temper of the Americans is vindictive, like that of all serious and reflecting nations. They hardly ever forget an offense, but it is not easy to offend them; and their resentment is as slow to kindle as it is to abate.[5]

This explains, better than most other analyses, why people in the United States were so slow to discover the implications of the Canadian National Energy Program, and why they acted with such indignation upon the eventual discovery. For better or for worse, they are not very perceptive about their own culture and therefore can hardly be expected to be perceptive of that of others. But this very lack of cultural self-awareness can become a sore spot for other societies of a different ethos in dealing with the United States, for the temper of the U.S. public is earnest and "vindictive." There is a tendency toward caricature in U.S. society, especially of cultural unknowns, of which there are a great many. Hence the complexity of Quebec social and political values, for example, is likely to forever escape most Americans. The notion that Quebeckers could be "separatists against Trudeau and federalists against Lévesque" may have been hard for Mr. Parizeau to accept.[6] For most people in the United States, including members of the business and policy elites, it has proved almost impossible to understand.

In the absence of familiarity with a foreign people, the average person substitutes his own values for those actually held by the foreigners.[7] He substitutes his own priorities as well as his own uncertainties and fears. Most of all, he substitutes his own misconceptions. Since a people's image can be self-consciously created to some extent and projected onto the minds of others, Quebec may have an advantage in this regard because of comparative anonymity. But what kind of image would Quebec like to generate? (See Chapter 12.) In the absence of such image projection the U.S. public is likely to continue to perceive Quebec culture through its own cultural lens.

Many people of the United States have an affinity for things French. For them, the French language and culture connote luxury, an exciting life-style, romance, and the romantic.[8] For the more intellectual, the famed analytic prowess of the French mind is paramount. Derivatively, French-Canadians may benefit from this legacy of (largely uninformed) cultural thought in the United States. For the most part, Quebec is not singled out. Quebec is considered French and is associated with the essentially positive attributes of other French-speaking communities.

But at the same time this habit of thought in the United States contains pitfalls; the francophone must struggle to be taken seriously. It is quite possible to drown in affection. Quebec might be viewed as a nice place to visit, but not in which to do business. The Québécois may be viewed as an attractive people, but hardly equal to scientific and technological discussion. The same Americans that esteem the French language as a kind of badge of intellectual and cultural achievement to be displayed discriminately at cocktail parties and university colloquia feel it is irrelevant and a hindrance to the conduct of business and commerce. The problem for French culture in Quebec is that many Americans may enjoy it but may not have learned to respect it sufficiently or, at least, not on the terms that the Québécois would prefer and that ultimately count in the United States.

For Quebec, the problem of cultural authenticity and acceptance in the United States is masked by paradox. The Quebec personality—more than the French, English, or perhaps for that matter the English-Canadian—is wonderfully congruent to the American. Attributes of warmth, informality, equalitarianism, and sociability are appreciated in the United States. They identify with these characteristics, which, they assume, mean that the Québécois are "just like themselves." To be "easy to get along with" goes far in societies that are democratic, commercial, and subject to values learned on the frontier (where isolation had to be quickly overcome) and in the middle social strata (where personal differences were not to be allowed to interfere with mobility). These are the values that allow U.S. social and political institutions to cohere and to "work smoothly." These are also the values that Americans would like to see in others and that they think they see in the Québécois.

The paradox here is that while the Québécois may be liked as individuals, their culture escapes their admirers. The very empathy that Americans have for the Québécois as individuals interferes with a capacity to probe, to understand, and to accept differences between the two cultures. Equating individual personality with collective cultural outlook means that the Americans may never learn the difference between the culture of Quebec and their own, and therefore will not treat Quebec culture with the "American" earnestness it deserves. Moreover, misconceptions on the individual level, although positive, reinforce misconceptions at the societal level that may not be flattering and helpful to Quebec.

By and large, people in the United States are infatuated with an image of Quebec that the Québécois themselves are rapidly leaving behind. The danger is that modern Quebec will remain neglected and poorly understood. In thinking about Quebec, many of its neighbors to the south suffer from what might be described as a "voyageur mentality." The myth of the *coureur du bois* and the *voyageur,* like the pastoral myths of the Arab bedouin and the American cowboy, occupies the imagination of a largely sedentary, urban people in the United States.[9] Indulgence in nostalgia, however, threatens to obscure the more accurate image of a province and a nation now industrially sophisticated, urban and urbane, educated, and committed to many of the same social and political goals as those of the United States. When Quebec is better understood, the United States will become a more tolerant trade and commercial partner. When the United States acquires a better appreciation of all of French Canada, the voyageur mentality will no longer hinder respect for the spirit of entrepreneurship that encompasses Quebec today.

In reverse of the U.S. tendency to be indifferent to culture at home but hypersensitive abroad regarding how others perceive U.S. institutions and values, the Québécois are very confident of their own culture abroad but hypersensitive about it at home. How is this contrast to be explained? Surely each society's traditional myths about culture have a great deal to do with the way culture is perceived by each. But deeper explanations involve status and self-image. Americans feel isolated in cultural terms in a foreign country. Because they feel somewhat alienated in less informal, less equalitarian societies, they often overreact and overcompensate when outside the United States.[10] Abroad they discover, sometimes for the first time, that they are a minority. French-Canadians have no doubt that they are a minority in Canada. They are hypersensitive at home because they are on guard against transgressions of their cultural space. Francophone Quebeckers are all the more sensitive because of their awareness of being a numerical majority in the Province of Quebec although historically, in some ways, having occupied minority status. Hence the strange coincidence of hypersensitivity to culture felt by Americans in a foreign country and by French-Canadians at home is to be explained largely in terms of isolation, a sense of alienation, and perceived minority status. People from the states have to go abroad to discover this awareness, but Quebeckers, unless they go abroad, cannot escape this awareness.

But the Québécois may draw a fallacious conclusion from the congruence of personality and the apparent similarity of social and political attitudes between people in the United States and themselves. French-Canadians may falsely conclude that the U.S. people are more sympathetic to their objectives because of these similarities, and that U.S. culture presents less of a threat to the Quebec life-style and value orientation than that of anglophone Canadians.

At bottom U.S. culture is assimilationist.[11] The middle North Americans are not cultural imperialists; certainly they have no designs on Quebec. Yet far more than the comparatively aloof, more hierarchically structured anglophone society of Canada, English-speaking society in the United States is a potential threat to the integrity of French Canada. U.S. values and outlook are not so much likely to dominate Quebec culture as to undermine it. This outlook and value system is not foisted upon anyone. Instead, in spite of elite objections, Quebec masses seek out U.S. mass culture and devour it. Anglophone Canadians are on their guard, perhaps too much so, against cultural incursions from the south. Francophone Canadians seem to be more confident, secure behind the linguistic barrier that few from the United States cross. U.S. institutions, values, and life-style are much more of a challenge to French Canada than is English-speaking Canada. Because U.S. culture is not politically or self-consciously oppressive, it is more penetrating. It spreads through contact and imitation and it is unremittingly assimilationist. The Québécois will find cultural coexistence with English Canada far easier in the long term than with the United States, despite the fact (or because of it) that Americans and French-Canadians as individuals can be so sympatico apart from their language differences. It is a societal paradox emerging out of mutual admiration and consonance.

The U.S. Perspective Concerning Greater Quebec Autonomy

In thinking about Quebec most thinking Americans are torn between memories of two historic events: the American Revolution and the Civil War. In a sense, the Civil War was the only true revolution the United States ever experienced, because it transformed land tenure and social institutions in the South, paving the way for industrial development there. By contrast, the American Revolution was a civil war fought with Britain and accompanied by very little social or class change. These events are remembered in their mystical rather than their real form. The complexity of the events does hold significance for the ambivalence U.S. people feel toward massive social and economic change and therefore, potentially, for how they might view the emergence of a sovereign Quebec.

On the one hand, Americans tend to sympathize with an underdog or with what they interpret to be the victim of oppression. Despite the reality that American colonials in 1776 were paying next to nothing to the British on behalf of the colonies' defense, even this was argued to be excessive taxation, thus enabling the colonials to think of themselves in the underdog role opposing the imperial giant.[12] Similarly, their descendants today come easily to the view that because Quebec is smaller than the rest of Canada, Quebec is the underdog in the federal/provincial struggle. Quebec thus earns sympathy, not on the basis of sophisticated argumentation over the distribution of rights and obligations, or on the basis of culture, but essentially because Quebec is the minority participant in the Canadian federation.

On the other hand, for many Americans the historical memory of the Civil War is stark. They fear the disunity for themselves and others. Many have always felt that a sense of community in the Americas was necessary in order to oppose the degradations of nature or the threats presented by outside powers. Fear of subversion and disunity lies very near the surface of U.S. diplomatic thought. Hence, based upon this type of reasoning, some U.S. groups are ritualistically opposed to even the discussion of a more sovereign Quebec. A fragmentation of Canada appears like the awakening of the stresses of 1860 all over again. According to this view Quebec sovereignty appears not so much like the creation of a new nation as the destruction of an older one. The anxieties this view raises in the United States should by no means be disregarded when many of these anxieties are traceable to past U.S. historical and political experience. The people of the United States had to struggle very hard, first to generate, then to maintain, their own unity, and they therefore do not consider even for others that the matter of unity is to be treated lightly. It is symbolic that Americans decided to highlight, above all other values, the word "United" in the name they chose for their country.

In the United States small is not beautiful. Size is esteemed in office buildings, ranches, weddings, armored tanks, industrial plants, and until recently, automobiles. The United States has always championed inter-national integration even when it has meant more serious trade and commercial competition for themselves. The Rome Treaties of 1958 that established the European Economic Community (EEC) created an important economic rival for the United States. But the United States chose to think of the EEC instead as a strong and stable trading and alliance partner.[13] Despite the differing circumstances, both political and psychological, that prevail in North America and that negate the opportunity for the type of regional integration adopted in Europe, the United States continues to think in terms of large economic aggregates. For this reason the emergence of a sovereign Quebec of 6.5 million people looks like movement in the wrong direction to policymakers in Washington. They see small polities as dependent and vulnerable. Quebec, according to this view, would find itself subject to trade barriers and commercial limitations that it does not now face.[14] Most Americans have not thought very deeply about these matters, but the prospect of a balkanized series of countries to the North, if put in those terms, could strike them as inefficient and fractious. Some are worried, not about the consequences for Quebec, for Quebec may be able to care for itself quite nicely, but about the consequences for the other Canadian provinces physically severed from the rest of Canada.

Small size is not of itself objectionable to Americans; it is the expected international consequences of small size that Americans reject, some of which consequences are of a secondary and tertiary variety. In particular, most U.S. analysts are extremely skeptical that, given the decentralized and legally primitive international system, conflict between communities that cannot be regulated internally can more successfully be regulated externally (where the instruments of destruction are so much more available, but the instruments of management so much weaker). Hence one response to Quebec sovereignty heard widely in the United States questions whether the existence of two or more polities on the northern border of the United States would create a climate that is any more peaceful and stable than Canada presently is.

On the other hand, two other concepts involving some degree of structural change appear more plausible from a U.S. viewpoint. Given the current mood of lower profile for the federal government in Washington, the notion of further decentralization of power in Canada seems reasonable.[15] Of course, many U.S. observers are not aware of how powerful the provinces already are within the Canadian federal system, or of their role as representatives of critical regional and cultural interests in Canada. The First Ministers' Conference has virtually no parallel in the United States, for example. But the idea of less government at the center has a kind of Jeffersonian ring that many in the United States find appealing even if they are not fully aware of the complexity of the legal and cultural arguments that underlie the movement for change. The American public, however, would certainly express dismay at the discovery that a further shift of authority over taxation and services, for example, had undermined the capacity of Ottawa to function effectively as a federal government or to carry out its responsibilities as a member of the international community. From the U.S. perspective the purposes of a shift of power toward the provinces would be to make the Canadian federal system work more harmoniously, and to increase efficiency and equity, not to strengthen one or more provinces per se. If people in the United States thought that these objectives could not be fulfilled by some form of restructured Canadian federalism, most of them would oppose additional decentralization, insofar as their opinion was sought.

A second concept that would find some support in the United States, if other reforms failed, would be increased sovereignty for Quebec combined with tight economic association with Canada.[16] This would overcome some of the qualms regarding the anticipated impact of small size on economic growth and efficiency for Canada and for Quebec, assuming that the impact of separation on Canada did not involve additional political fragmentation. U.S. observers may be less skeptical than many Canadians that such a scheme of economic association could be made to work in a technical sense; however, they wonder whether the political atmosphere would be conducive in such circumstances to intricate negotiation. In the absence of far-reaching economic association between Canada and Quebec, many informed Americans would have strong reservations about increased Quebec sovereignty, especially if it were negotiated in a way that fostered recriminations.

Despite their general predilection in favor of supranational integration, federal and state policymakers in the United States are likely to react very cautiously to proposals for selective regional integration within North America. First, in narrow interest terms, it is somewhat difficult to see what economic benefits would accrue to the United States in terms of greater wealth or efficiency, because of the disparity in size of the integrating units. Of course this attitude would change if certain resources such as energy were to enter into the agreement. In the Quebec-New England context, accelerated development of hydropower, yielding off-peak surpluses for export and phased out over time so as to be available to Quebec as Quebec domestic needs grow, has attractions.[17] Without energy or resource development as an incentive, regional arrangements for integration are likely to have less appeal in the United States; and whenever such development is included in a proposal it is likely to have less appeal to Canadians. A plateau for the real price for world energy only strengthens these obstacles to regional energy agreement.

A second and more paramount hesitation in the United States about regional integration schemes of any substantial sort is the possible negative spillover on Canada-U.S. relations even in such limited instances in which such agreements can be concluded without the active participation of Ottawa, Washington, or both governments. Will regional integration schemes strain the fabric of Canadian unity in economic and political terms, or will they strengthen that unity? Constitutions permitting, New England or other states will enter such limited regional trade or commercial arrangements only if economic considerations can truly be divorced from questions of political impact on Canadian unity and sovereignty. This desire not to get involved in "politically motivated" regional initiatives is different from the U.S. federal attitude toward North American integration. Federally, the idea that economic integration would lead to closer political ties is not rejected, as the North American accord (although defunct) indicates. But regional integration schemes would only be acceptable to the U.S. government if they did not threaten the unity of political structures or institutions in either Canada or the United States. While some proponents might believe that the purpose of closer regional economic ties would be to eventually loosen the political bonds of federation, the predominant U.S. view is that regional economic ties must be their own justification and ought to lead to no further structural or institutional consequences for federation.

In short, the U.S. preoccupation with size may stem from historical experiences as much as from any realities of international relations or the global marketplace. There is little reason to believe that large polities necessarily cohere any better than small ones, but the ideal of "unity" is half the name of the United States. Because their country is heterogeneous in an ethnic and cultural sense and is founded on the twin notions of assimilation and unfettered internal mobility, size has always been important to Americans, and they have seen no reason to define "community" in any other than the largest of territorial terms. Manifest Destiny encompassed both a spatial and a temporal dimension. Unity and size reinforced the setting in which Manifest Destiny could thrive, and, until 1896, Manifest Destiny seemed to reinforce size and unity.[18] Even today notions of international economic integration are supported in the United States whenever integration reinforces the values of size and unity. But in the North American context these notions are severely constrained by the peculiarities of geography, culture, and nationalism. Hence only certain types of integration are feasible; even within these limits, from the U.S. perspective, the underlying societal values of size and unity must be respected.

U.S. Interests Regarding Quebec

In considering the specifics of U.S. relationships with Canada and with Quebec, two factors must not be forgotten: first, that U.S. interests with regard to the other actors in this hemisphere will be implicitly, if not explicitly, formulated within the context of the United States' perceived role as a global power; second, that the vast size, diversity, complexity, and transitional character of the U.S. government will mitigate against the emergence of clear-cut statements of U.S. interests and U.S. policies that appear coherently and consistently to advance these interests. With these caveats in mind, U.S. interests concerning Quebec may be broadly characterized as threefold.

Security Interests

From the Washington perspective, security interests are always primary or, put differently, all other interests are anchored in the security interest.[19] This perspective emerges not because the United States feels less secure than other polities or because its commercial, middle-class culture encourages militarism of any kind; the opposite is more likely the case. Because of the leadership position forced upon the United States in the post-1945 period, its security perspective emerges mostly out of the paramount responsibility it feels for conflict management and Western alliance defense.

What does this mean for Quebec? It means that by this set of priorities the parameters are established for what Quebec can expect of the United States and what, in turn, the United States expects of Canada and therefore indirectly of Quebec. The United States is happiest with peace and tranquility on its northern border. According to the logic of this security interest, whatever internal arrangement is most acceptable to Canadians and is most conducive to this stability is preferred by the United States. In the U.S. view stability is an end in itself, not a means to additional ends; nor is stability to be abridged in pursuit of larger or higher ends. In reflecting this latter priority, the U.S. interest is hardly different from that of Canada as a whole, or of Quebec.

Washington is also aware, however, of the twentieth-century differences among Canadians regarding how they view security. On the one hand there is awareness of the effectiveness with which Canadians, including French-Canadians, defended their national honor and security during the World Wars I and II.[20] On the other hand there is the memory of the two fights over conscription enmeshed in questions of authority, legality, alleged cultural discrimination, and divided support for the war effort.[21] Mindful of its own population's arguments over the nature of the voluntary army, Washington is uncertain of what lessons these historical experiences hold, if any, for contemporary Quebec attitudes toward a crisis serious enough to require a massive military commitment once again. Moreover, foreign-policy observers are puzzled by the apparent difference in francophone and anglophone attitudes toward defense expenditures, despite repeated official statements from Quebec City that under all forseeable circumstances Quebec will support NATO. (See Chapter 12.) Whether greater Quebec autonomy would strengthen commitments to NATO or would weaken those commitments is a continuing source of speculation among those U.S. policymakers responsible for considering security and alliance relationships.

Inasmuch as U.S. leaders in this period of history view their perceived security interests so seriously, a major concern for those on both sides of the border concerned with Quebec is that everything may take on a security coloration and that every statement from the government in Quebec City will be seen as having importance for the Atlantic Alliance or for some sort of new and therefore perhaps dangerous ideological departure. What Washington has yet to learn is that others, whose responsibilities for continental or hemispheric security are less direct, may value order and peace as strongly but may tolerate more ideological diversity in the process. The United States must struggle against the temptation to see international security implications in every nuance of domestic social behavior. Insofar as Quebec provides the United States with no stimuli to paranoia, the security of all concerned will receive a psychological boost.

Interests in Commerce and Trade

In matters of commerce and trade, the interests of Canada as a whole, of Quebec, and of the United States would at first glance seem closely parallel. This first view is not entirely correct. The United States is and has been for more than three decades in a phase of economic development in which the export of capital and the trade in commodities and semimanufactured goods from abroad is especially important to it. Until recently, Quebec on the other hand has been in a phase of rapid economic development, dependent upon large capital imports from abroad and upon markets that address its huge comparative advantage in minerals, pulp and paper production, hydroelectric power, electronics and transportation equipment, and certain areas of construction and engineering.[22] Thus the economies of Quebec and the rest of Canada have been roughly similar in structure and phase of development, and the economies of Quebec and the United States have been quite complementary. Trade and commercial interaction is spurred by complementarity. Where then is the possibility of a divergence of economic interest?

Without exaggerating the disparity of economic interests between the United States and Quebec, a possible divergence emerges not so much at the micro- as at the macro-level, i.e., not so much at the level of the firm but at the aggregate level. The United States favors as open a world economy as possible because, despite problems of lagging productivity in certain industries such as steel, the overall U.S. economy can compete quite well in international terms. Size, capital availability, technological innovativeness, and a skilled and stable (if high-cost) labor supply are the keys to this competitiveness. The United States would like to continue to export capital in the form of direct foreign investment and to benefit from the earnings of capital already invested abroad.[23]

By contrast, although Quebec remains interested in foreign investment as a source of capital supply, the province's needs and strategies in this regard are undergoing change.[24] Quebec would like to move away from the production of commodities and semimanufactured goods toward more of the technology-intensive leading sectors and, like Ottawa, is prepared to utilize relatively more government intervention and ownership than is the United States to achieve this objective. (See Chapter 2.) Quebec, like the rest of Canada, would prefer to own and control a larger fraction of its industry and is prepared to establish channels of low and high priority for foreign capital sources to observe. Furthermore, while provincial officials may chafe at various federal policies and institutions including the Foreign Investment Review Agency (FIRA) for restricting commercial activity and development, there is no evidence (1) that FIRA acts in a manner discriminatory vis-à-vis Quebec, or (2) that in the absence of FIRA, Quebec officials would not regulate foreign investment in much the same fashion. (See Chapter 2.) In one sense, the existence of FIRA as a federal agency is a convenience, allowing provincial officials to deflect criticism of foreign investment regulation to another officialdom. U.S. businessmen and policymakers appear quite cognizant of these circumstances.

Thus, given these differences of industrial phase, structure, and emphasis between the Quebec and U.S. economies, the natural complementarity between them that has fostered so much beneficial interdependence will periodically come under some strain. Such strains are not the result of ill will or bad intentions. They emerge for quite natural historical and structural reasons. It is in the interest of all parties involved to optimize economic benefits while managing conflicts with farsightedness and sensitivity.[25] In periods of recession such management is especially crucial because unilateral actions can harm the capacity of the economies to flourish in subsequent intervals of recovery.

Political and Cultural Interests

The United States has perhaps the only culture in the world that operates on the basis of the market. This is both the strength and the weakness of U.S. culture. In each case the contrasts with Quebec are marked. U.S. culture is mass-oriented and it sells, both at home and abroad. It is not very self-critical and always takes a second seat to the pride most U.S. citizens have in their political institutions. Thus the U.S. public is hardly equipped to understand what many Québécois hold most dear—the survival of a particular cultural-linguistic tradition that takes precedence over aspects of economics and even institutions.[26]

Given the American attitude toward political and cultural interests, the U.S. position on the border broadcasting issue is a characteristic response.[27] Random deletion of U.S. advertising from television signals beamed across the border from the United States into Canada is not looked upon as a deterrent designed to protect Canadians from cultural incursions from the south. The United States views the border broadcasting issue in strictly economic and political terms as a form of Canadian government–manipulated commercial discrimination and also perhaps as a form of government interference in communication.

Hence Quebec must contend with a society and government that for the most part is oblivious to the concepts and arguments underlying cultural content. The U.S. view of culture is that it is self-sustaining and is as vital as the citizenry want to make it. Government, in this view, has little relevance to the sustenance of culture in other than the most basic form of grants to support performances or the education of young artists. Thus the United States is not hostile to the cultural goals of Quebec, certainly not to the rich culture itself. But it perceives its own political and cultural interest in such a fashion that it may experience difficulty understanding what the struggle over culture is all about.[28] If mistakes are made, these mistakes may emerge as much out of ignorance and differing priorities as out of any actions involving greater calculation.

The Operational Aspects of the
Washington-Quebec Relationship

Federalism, American-style

Analogies cannot be carried very easily from the federal system of the United States to the federal system of Canada. Powers and responsibilities are not distributed in the same way among federal and provincial/state governments.[29] By and large, the U.S. states cannot regulate or legislate over the range and scope of sectors that fall within the authority of the Canadian provinces.

Several consequences result from this structural characteristic: First, federal-state/provincial relationships in the two countries are fundamentally different in substance *and* in procedure. Constitutional arguments regarding the foreign policies of U.S. states have already been settled, largely in favor of the federal government. U.S. state officials spend little effort attempting to enhance their "foreign presence" or to guard against encroachment on their authority by Washington. Obviously that situation is different in Canada. Second, U.S. state officials operate with Canadian provincial and federal officials within "functional" areas. Matters of "higher" policy import remain, by and large, to be dealt with by Washington.

Third, from an operational viewpoint, U.S. federal officials cannot presume that the state-federal relationship in the United States is a meaningful guide or parallel to the provincial-federal relationship in Canada. Canadian provincial officials, on the other hand, cannot expect that the U.S. federal government will react to the types of approaches, strategies, and ploys that are viable when dealing with Ottawa.

Thus, the tensions and sensitivities of an Ottawa official to a provincial initiative will not be mirrored by a Washington official, for whom direct provincial contacts or provincial-state contacts will engender little concern of being bypassed or losing authority. As a consequence, one can expect Washington not to inhibit increased functional cooperation between provinces and states, largely because U.S. federal officials feel confident that their interest and authority will not be challenged by such dealings. Nor will such arrangements have connotations of either greater recognition or foreign-relations capacity for their participants. Washington's effective control over these aspects of U.S. government is solidified and cannot be bypassed. Of equal import is the fact that U.S. state officials do not view themselves as being restrained by Washington, or in "competition" with federal authorities.

From the other point of view, officials in Washington find it difficult at times to cope with Quebec, i.e., a Canadian province that does not fit into the mold of a U.S. state (nor does it behave like the other Canadian provinces, for that matter). Washington's federal authorities are conditioned, both in mind set and in practice, to deal with Ottawa's federal authorities. The same persons charged with U.S.-Canadian affairs will almost always be the ones to handle U.S.-Quebec interests. There will be some difficulties as a result in sorting out priorities, in separating out what might be U.S. interests not coincident with, or subsumed by, the prior assessment of U.S. concerns regarding the Canadian federal government. Events in Canada could certainly force changes in Washington's perspective on federal-provincial matters, but it is unlikely that these would precede the events themselves.

A number of the operational aspects of the Washington-Quebec-Ottawa triangle are worth examining because they have indirect effects on the tone and direction of substantive policy.[30] First is the role and resources of the Department of State. Relations with Quebec are handled by the U.S. Consul General in Quebec City, the Consul General in Montreal, the U.S. Embassy in Ottawa, and the Office of Canadian Affairs in the Department of State in Washington. In this hierarchy, the latter two are charged with management of the Ottawa-Washington relationship. Here, in offices that are to say the least not overstaffed, provincial matters fall into the hands of persons with other major functional responsibilities. There is no single person, for instance, handling provincial matters in the Office of Canadian Affairs Bureau in Washington; soon, because of asserted budgetary constraints, there may no longer be a "state and local" officer in the U.S. embassy in Ottawa. All of these offices are organized around, and are attuned to, a U.S. federal–Canadian federal government perspective. As a result, U.S. relationships with Canadian provinces tend to be viewed by Washington bureaucrats from within a federal context. One of the major sticking points for a province wishing greater access and recognition in Washington is to break through this "federal mindset." However, as long as the structure and staffing limitations exist, the institutional environment itself will not foster any such reassessment of priorities.

One of the major complaints about the U.S. bureaucracy is the lack of continuity in administration and policy resulting from the constant regular turnover of personnel. This is particularly a phenomenon of the State Department; persons seldom stay more than several years in the Office of Canadian Affairs, for instance. As a result, lack of continuity and "institutional memory" is an abiding concern of officials in both countries. However, it should not be assumed that the U.S. government operates on a day-to-day basis in ignorance of Quebec in general or Quebec political affairs in particular. Maintenance of the Consulate General in Quebec City, manned by a particularly able political officer, has ensured that Washington is well attuned to happenings within the province and to their relevance to U.S. interests.

Congress and Foreign Policy

A Canadian province's efforts to deal with the U.S. Congress are constrained by two large factors: (1) the necessity of coordination with Ottawa even in situations where the federal and provincial interests may seem divergent; and (2) the size and apparent diffuseness of power within the U.S. Congress. In the simplest of terms, how can a provincial representative not based in Washington be expected to learn the idiosyncracies of Congress and establish useful contacts with the appropriate centers of power there? The answer is oblique, namely that provincial governments probably underestimate the difficulty of having much visibility or influence in Washington apart from that obtained by Ottawa itself. And yet the pathways to Congress may be smoother where a provincial government, including Quebec, is able to coordinate policies with other provinces on the one hand, and with the Canadian private sector on the other. (See Chapter 12.) In any case, relations with Congress must under no circumstances be allowed to embarrass either federal government, for the likely consequence is that such embarrassment will redound to the eventual disadvantage of the entity responsible. Especially for a foreign subnational unit, Congress is an easier place to gather information than to seek influence.

Government and Private Sector: Identical Interests?

In the U.S. governmental system, one sees to an extent not found elsewhere competition by private interests for access to and influence over legislation and regulations. Foreign and domestic critics are often led to the conclusion that government and private-sector interests are synonymous. Certainly there are examples in the short term, concerning specific policies or pieces of legislation, to support this conclusion. However, equating private and government interests in the longer term or assuming that access to the seats of power in one milieu translates to influence and access in the other are mistaken conceptions.

There are a variety of arguments to support such distinctions. First, U.S. officialdom has its own interests to protect and to promote through policy.[31] Second, U.S. policymakers have to evaluate U.S. interests on an overall and long-term basis. The interests of a single corporation or of competing industries are often inconsistent and will tend to change with economic conditions. Third, U.S. presidents may define the national interest on ideological principles that, in turn, may result in policies that are inflexible and run counter to the pragmatic and functional approaches adopted by the private sector in its foreign dealings. Fourth, the existence of extensive commercial ties with a foreign country has failed, on numerous occasions, to prevent the U.S. government from acting in a manner detrimental to those interests.

It is fair to assume, therefore, that the U.S. government will evaluate its interests toward Quebec and Canada cognizant of the aggregate level of financial commitments at stake. But only in exceptional instances will U.S. policy directly reflect the short-term interests of a single corporation, industry or state.[32] "Larger" U.S. interests in national security, stability, and political support on international issues will usually be dominant. Conversely, external actors seeking to gain influence in the U.S. governmental and private-sector communities should realize the limited extent to which these two overlap when it comes to establishing foreign policy. Influence in one community does not translate into influence in the other.[33] In normal times, Washington does not seek to alter substantially the perceptions and behavior of Wall Street, and vice versa. On the other hand, if circumstances appear to warrant policy change for political reasons, Washington does not appear to hesitate to act without consultation with, or without consideration of, the U.S. private sector. On matters of foreign-policy definition, therefore, access to and understanding of Washington is essential; it cannot be bypassed or substituted by influence in other arenas.

U.S. Policy Concerning Quebec: Official Statements and Protocol

Nowhere can one find record or copies of detailed analyses of U.S. interests concerning Canada and Quebec. Interviews suggest that a thorough policy review was conducted in the State Department in 1976–1977, and that no substantial or substantive review has been conducted since. However, the existence of a policy cannot be doubted. For example, on February 2, 1983, the State Department issued a position paper regarding the Quebec Minister's statement on a possible Quebec-U.S.-Canada common market; the statement underlined the "U.S. hope that Canada will remain strong and united."

In other respects the public statements of senior U.S. spokesmen, i.e., the president, the secretary of state, and assistant secretaries, come to represent the official record of U.S. policy concerning Quebec. Still, apart from the State Department position paper there is little else to report, so little, in fact, that one must turn to analyzing U.S.-Quebec interactions to see if they portray subtle shifts, either intended or inadvertent, in policy.

First, a look at the public record: In rather informal settings of a television interview and a news conference in early 1977, then-President Carter established the benchmarks of U.S. policy.[34] These were (1) his "personal preference" for a united Canada, (2) an official U.S. posture of neutrality, and (3) a policy of noninterference in Canadian internal affairs. On subsequent occasions, Cyrus Vance reiterated in 1978 and 1980 the president's stance, making clear that what was initially put in personal terms was in fact now U.S. government policy. There is as yet no public statement by President Reagan or a senior official of his administration on the Quebec issue. Privately, one is assured that there has been absolutely no change in U.S. policy. Even so, it remains somewhat surprising that even congressional testimony by State Department officials on Canadian-U.S. relations makes no mention of the Quebec situation.[35]

The apparent consistency of this series of statements has been interrupted only once, in a speech made by U.S. Ambassador Thomas Enders in May 1979. Within a statement of some length on Canadian-U.S. relations, Enders stated in that portion of his text discussing the evolution of the relationships:

> Yet clearly not only are the federal executives, the Parliament, and the Congress involved (in international relations) but increasingly the Provinces and States. . . .
>
> Our implication is that we have to conduct our relations far more openly than before, using the media as a means to inform and engage players on both sides. . . .
>
> Another implication is that diplomacy must now include the Provinces and States. That does not mean that either Ottawa or Washington should attempt to contract business with the States or Provinces; that would violate the Constitutions. But each capital can and is developing its liaison with other governments in its own country. And informal contacts between the Provinces and the U.S. Embassy in Ottawa and the States and the Canadian Embassy in Washington can prevent misunderstanding and expedite our affairs.[36]

As to whether Enders intended this statement to signal a shift in U.S. policy or simply to reflect the current state of affairs in intergovernmental contacts was, and remains, unclear. Speculation on this matter enters the discussion below. It is instructive to examine another official aspect of U.S. policy, namely, the protocol and procedures that supposedly guide U.S. officials when dealing with Quebec and other Canadian provinces. The U.S. government subscribes to the view, vigorously and jealously set forth by Ottawa, that provincial relations with the U.S. federal government should take place within the context of U.S.-Canadian relations. That is, the Canadian government wishes to be informed in advance, and to supervise, official contact by the provinces with the United States government. In the course of day-to-day relations this should result in (1) the Department of External Affairs (DEA) or the Canadian Embassy being informed and subsequently involved whenever the U.S. State Department is contacted concerning a visit in an official capacity by a senior Quebec delegation, (2) the DEA or embassy being notified by the State Department after it has been informed by another federal agency of contact with a province regarding policy matters, and (3) local Canadian consulates being notified and involved by U.S. state government officials whenever Quebec officials seek meetings or negotiations with policy implications. However, when a Canadian province engages in functional dealings with a state or local government in the United States, neither federal government sees a need to be notified or involved.

By design and inadvertence, both in subtle and direct ways, provincial actions occasionally avoid or violate these operational norms. This is true of all the provinces, but is perhaps felt most acutely in the DEA when Quebec is involved.

U.S. Behavior Toward Quebec

To all observers, whether in Washington, Ottawa, or Quebec, the general posture of U.S. relations with Quebec has been fairly reflected by the official statements. The United States has remained "neutral in favor of unity"—a stance not necessarily pleasing to Quebec, which would desire at least a more flexible attitude, nor always satisfying to Ottawa, which would prefer a stronger endorsement of its federal position.[37] There have, however, been some subtle shifts in U.S. behavior. In the wake of the 1976 Quebec election, the Carter administration, wishing to make apparent its preference for an undivided Canadian federal union and demonstrating the good relationship between Carter and Trudeau, invited the Canadian prime minister to address a joint session of Congress in 1977. This "symbolic gesture" gave important exposure to Trudeau, bestowing upon him prestige and publicity at a time when the new PQ government was capturing attention and was beginning to make its presence felt in the United States.

Since then, there have been no further symbolic gestures to the Canadian federal government. The U.S. official stance became, and has remained, slightly more aloof. In the 1978–1980 period, this reaction can be explained as a strategy on the part of Washington to avoid accusations of interference in Canadian affairs and to keep its options open in light of uncertainty concerning the future of Quebec. In the post-referendum period, U.S. officials appear to be taking the attitude that the Quebec issue is no longer as critical, that Ottawa and Quebec have reached a temporary hiatus in the struggle, that Quebec for various reasons is not as forward in its approaches to Washington, and, most importantly, that economic conditions and issues currently dominate U.S.-Canadian relations at all levels. U.S. officials, however, remain alert and cautious concerning the prospect of the Quebec sovereignty issue reemerging on their agenda.

Thomas Enders' statement appears to have signaled or caused no change in U.S. policy or attitudes toward the provinces. If the ambassador was attempting to stimulate new policy discussion, the ideas were lost in the transition of administrations or lacked support for other reasons. On the other hand, Enders may simply have been acknowledging in public the obvious; namely, that provincial relations, largely of a functional nature, especially with U.S. state governments, were increasing in number and importance. Although no exact monitoring of these ties has been documented recently, observers all confirm that the expansionary trends identified in Swanson's 1974 study have continued into the 1980s.[38] This trend is particularly true of Quebec's relationships with U.S. states. (See Chapter 12.)

The question then arises, of course, as to the possible consequences of such ties for U.S. policy toward Ottawa and the provinces. The answer appears to be "very few" insofar as they would lead Washington to reassess its general attitude as outlined earlier. Both federal governments officially encourage provincial-state cooperation. The U.S. government sees these relationships as functionally useful. They pose no problems (as yet) concerning federal authority; furthermore, with relationships at these levels, Washington avoids any entanglements in matters sensitive to Ottawa. The latter's perspective is somewhat more ambivalent. On the one hand, provincial-state relationships clearly are at the subfederal level, thus implicitly continuing Ottawa's desired status. On the other hand, in light of the constitutional distribution of powers and because of the provinces' increasingly aggressive posture in pursuing their own trade and industrial strategies, Ottawa is concerned that the provinces are extending themselves beyond functional relationships into policy arenas. But in the United States this risk does not appear to be an issue. State-provincial transactions appear to be of the sort that Washington does not care about or has ultimate control over, either legislative or regulatory. Such transactions are not a route that U.S. states or Canadian provinces can pursue with the anticipation of gaining a new voice or influencing foreign or economic policy formulation in Washington.

A recent development should be noted. Because the distribution of powers within the two federal systems is not symmetrical, and further because under certain conditions Canadian provinces can opt out of federal programs, the possibility is created for the necessity of official negotiations between Washington and a Canadian province. This possibility has recently been realized with Quebec, concerning reciprocity in handling social security payments. An agreement was hammered out between Ottawa and Washington and signed by Reagan during his visit to Canada in 1981. However, since the provinces can administer their own social security programs (in fact, only Quebec does so), the agreement provided for subsequent negotiations between Washington and the provinces to devise arrangements compatible within the provisions of the larger agreement. Officials from the U.S. Social Security Administration and the Quebec government, along with observers from Ottawa, worked to conclude the required arrangements. These arrangements will take the form of a "memorandum of understanding" between the Social Security administrations of Quebec and Washington. When finalized, the "memorandum" is to be exchanged without the necessity of an official signing to become protocol to the original Ottawa-Washington pact.

The details of these events are important because they make clear that Ottawa was very careful to maintain a continuing preeminent position in the Washington relationship. Nevertheless, the fact that Quebec and Washington had to engage directly in negotiations because their governments possessed equivalent jurisdiction over the matters at issue is significant as well. Observers do not see the social security dealings as precedent-setting, nor do they envisage any immediate likelihood of formal provincial-U.S. federal negotiations. However, the potential for recurrence remains in other areas, especially in matters such as environmental protection or regulation of the trucking industry, where there are needs for legislation and regulation to be coordinated on both sides of the border. Informal agreements, consultations, and previously utilized bilateral institutional mechanisms may no longer be acceptable to the province, thus forcing Washington to engage in relations with these governments.

It thus seems fair to conclude, as others have, that Washington, although having some contact with Quebec, neither has nor at this time desires a more articulated relationship with Quebec. Nor, finally, does it have a long-term strategy for dealing with Quebec.[39] Washington essentially pursues a "policy of having no policy." There is no evidence in recent years to suggest that the United States has ever initiated contacts in Quebec for any purpose other than to stay informed; nor is there any indication that the U.S. government has any interest in establishing a subnational foreign policy toward the province.

Conclusions

U.S. perceptions regarding Quebec are a mixture of ignorance, esteem, curiosity, and benevolence. A part of the U.S. public has elevated the French language and life-style to a kind of social pedestal. A larger number find French-Canadian personalities congruent in many respects with their own and for this reason enjoy the company and professional association of the Québécois.

Neither the premises of current U.S. policy toward Canada and Quebec nor the identification of U.S. interests is beset with much ambiguity. Reasoning first from a security perspective and next from the imperatives of commerce and trade, the United States encourages close contact between its states and seeks tranquility and continued political order. Officially the United States prefers not to get involved in the domestic affairs of Canada and approaches all matters involving Canadian political unity with the caution and circumspection born of a sense of national history and contemporary global political responsibility. The view from Washington in this regard does not seem appreciably to lead U.S. public opinion or to lag behind that opinion.

If more is implied in the term "subnational foreign policy" than staying abreast of events and remaining in contact with leading decision makers, there is little evidence that the U.S. government is practicing such a policy. The conscious lack of formal federal policy toward Quebec is nearer the mark than the calculated formulation of policy. In this hesitance to formalize policy, the United States has shown consistency since 1976. Indeed, the implicit rule of behavior (if such rules can be articulated) may be that the more Quebec attempts to dissociate its policies from Ottawa, the more Washington leans toward Ottawa; and the more Ottawa attempts to dissociate itself from Washington, the more Washington is likely to listen to Quebec City. Some have interpreted the 1977 invitation to Prime Minister Trudeau to address a joint session of Congress, and the August 1982 invitation to Premier Lévesque from Senator Jesse Helms to speak to a group of thirty-eight U.S. senators, in this light. But in this posturing one is speaking of nuance more than substance, and nuance is often overwhelmed by events or contravening influence either in terms of domestic politics or global foreign policy.[40]

Concerning perceptions of Quebec by the U.S. public, overinterpretation is probably more dangerous than underinterpretation, especially given the nascent awareness most of the public has of Quebec issues. The possiblity of misperception exists on both sides but for quite different reasons on each side. A higher intensity of dialogue across the border between university educators and between members of the press may help to offset some of this potential misperception. But in terms of substantive U.S. policy, because of the difference in the U.S. and Canadian federal systems, the political "buck" stops in Washington, not at the regional level. As is true for so much in Canadian-American relations outside the security field, the United States more frequently responds to initiatives from the North than it takes the initiative itself. Perceptions of Quebec are likely to be limited by this pattern. In matters involving Quebec the United States is less an "unmoved mover" than an interested but much-preoccupied observer.

Notes

1. An agreement such as that signed recently between Quebec and the state of New York to establish a computerized documentation center on acid precipitation in both Quebec City and Rochester, financed by a U.S.$100,000 grant from each government, is clearly the type of province-state interaction that can be mutually advantageous. See *Quebec Update* 5(23), August 2, 1982.

2. Highlights of the history of the Quebec-U.S. relations in the early post-1945 period are found in Jean-Louis Roy, "Les relations du Québec et des États-Unis (1945–1970)," in Paul Painchaud, ed., *Le Canada et le Québec sur la scène internationale* (Montreal: Les Presses de l'Université du Québec, 1977), pp. 497–514.

3. John E. Reilly, "American Opinion: Continuity, Not Reaganism," *Foreign Policy* 50, Spring 1983, pp. 86–104.

4. Alfred O. Hero, Jr., and Louis Balthazar, *The United States, Quebec, and Canada* (forthcoming), chapter 9.

5. Alexis de Tocqueville, *Democracy in America*, Richard D. Heffnes, ed., (New York: Mentor, 1956), p. 223.

6. See John Saywell, *The Rise of the Parti Québécois 1967–1976* (Toronto: University of Toronto Press, 1977), p. 26.

7. David M. Potter, "Canadian Views of the United States as a Reflex of Canadian Values: A Commentary," in S. F. Wise and Robert Craig Brown, eds., *Canada Views the United States: Nineteenth-Century Political Attitudes* (Toronto: Macmillan of Canada, 1967), pp. 121–130. See also Peter Burroughs, *British Attitudes Towards Canada, 1822–1849* (Scarborough, Ontario: Prentice-Hall of Canada, 1971).

8. Howard Mumford Jones, *America and French Culture, 1750–1848* (Montreal: Carrier, 1928); and Edward Fecteau, *French Contributions to America* (Methuen, MA: Soucy Press, 1945), published under the auspices of the Franco-American Historical Society.

9. Grace Lee Nute, *The Voyageur* (New York: Appleton, 1931); and Raymond Douville, "Jacques Largillier, dit le castor, coureur des bois et frère donné," in *Cahiers de Dix* 29, 1964, pp. 47–69.

10. John Holmes, *Life With Uncle* (Toronto: University of Toronto Press, 1981), p. 1. See especially his discussion of the disparity between ideals and behavior and impacts on policy.

11. John Higham, "Origins of Immigration Restriction, 1882–1897: A Social Anaylsis," *Mississippi Valley Historical Review* 39, June 1952, pp. 77–88; and Oscar Hardlin, *The Uprooted* (Boston: Little, Brown, 1951).

12. Lawrence Henry Gipson, "The American Revolution as an Aftermath of the Great War for the Empire, 1754–1765," *The Political Science Quarterly* 65, March 1950, pp. 86–104.

13. See, for example, Charles Kindleberger, "Optimal Economic Interdependence," in Charles Kindleberger and Andrew Schonfield, eds., *North American and Western European Economic Policies* (London: Macmillan, 1971).

14. For two quite different viewpoints on this matter see Jane Jacobs, *The Question of Separation: Quebec and the Struggle over Sovereignty* (New York: Random House, 1980), pp. 65–77, and Bernard Landry, "Quebec's Economic Prospects Within a North American Context," for the University Consortium for Research on North America, Harvard University, Cambridge and Boston, November 17, 1979.

15. Alfred O. Hero, Jr., "Quebec Trends vs. U.S. Interests and Policies," in the Atlantic Council Working Group on the United States and Canada, Willis C. Armstrong et al., eds., *Canada and the United States: Dependence and Divergence* (Cambridge, MA: Ballinger Publishing Co., 1982), page 298; and Robert Gilpin, "Le Québec dans un contexte économique transnational: Un commentaire américain," in Albert Legault and Alfred O. Hero, Jr., eds., *Le nationalisme québécois à la croisée des chemins* (Quebec: Centre Québécois des Relations Internationales, Choix 7, 1975), pp. 232–242.

16. "As soon as the relationship between Canada and Quebec has been redefined and democratically decided upon by Quebec, when both sides have reached an understanding in this connection, nothing will stand in the way of more positive cooperation between Quebec and Canada." Claude Morin, "Quebec's External Policy," Canadian Institute of International Affairs (Quebec Branch), March 7, 1978, pp. 12–13.

17. Frederick J. Nemergut, "Energy Exchanges: Quebec and New England," unpublished paper presented at Conference on Quebec-United States Relations, Carnegie Conference Center, New York, June 5, 1981; and Direction générale de l'énergie, *An Energy Policy for Quebec: Insurance for the Future* (Quebec: Government of Quebec, 1978), p. 50.

18. Frederick Merk, "The Demise of Continentalism," in *Manifest Destiny and Mission in American History* (New York: Vintage Books, 1963), pp. 215–227.

19. Charles F. Doran, *Forgotten Partnership? U.S.-Canada Relations Today* (Baltimore, MD: Johns Hopkins University Press, 1983), Chapter 5.

20. G. P. de T. Glazebrook, *A History of Canadian External Relations,* vols I and II (Toronto: McClelland and Stewart, 1966); and C. P. Stacey, *Canada and the Age of Conflict,* vol. I (Toronto: Macmillan of Canada, 1977), pp. 172–202.

21. A.M.J. Hyatt, "Sir Arthur Currie and Conscription: A Soldier's View," *Canadian Historical Review* 50(3), 1969, pp. 285–296; and J. L. Granatstein, *Canada's War: The Politics of the Mackenzie King Government 1939–1945* (Toronto: Oxford University Press, 1975), pp. 338–381.

22. L. Auer, *Regional Disparities of Productivity and Growth in Canada* (Economic Council of Canada, Supply and Services, 1979); and A. M. Pinchin, *The Regional Impact of the Canadian Tariff* (Economic Council of Canada, Supply and Services, 1982).

23. Robert B. Reich, "Making Industrial Policy," *Foreign Affairs* 60(4), Spring 1982, pp. 852–881.

24. Gerard Gaudet, "Quebec and the American Presence in Natural Resources Development," and Bernard Bonin, "American Investments in Quebec," both unpublished papers presented at the Conference on Quebec-United States Relations, Carnegie Conference Center, New York, June 5, 1981.

25. Jock A. Finlayson and Mark W. Zacher, "International Trade Institutions and the North-South Dialogue," *International Journal* 36(4), Autumn 1981, pp. 732–765.

26. Solange Chaput Rolland, "Reflections on Quebec's Cultural Nationalism," in Janice L. Murray, ed., *Canadian Cultural Nationalism* (New York: New York University Press, 1977), pp. 45–54.

27. *Report of the Royal Commission on National Devlopment in the Arts, Letters, and Sciences* (Ottawa: Government of Canada, 1951); Canadian Radio-Television and Telecommunications Commission, "CRTC Background Paper: The Economic Realities of Canadian Television Production," *Symposium on Television Violence* (Ottawa: Government of Canada, 1976); and Isaiah A. Litvak and Christopher J. Maule, "Canadian Multinational Media Firms and Canada-United States Relations," *Behind the Headlines* 39(5), 1982.

28. Seymour Martin Lipset, *The First New Nation: The United States in Historical and Comparative Perspective* (New York: Anchor Books, 1967), p. 118. In his interesting "The Ascendancy of the Ethnic Idea in North America," *Canadian Journal of Political Science* 14(2), June 1978, pp. 229–257, Allan Smith perhaps underestimates the degree to which the U.S. assimilationist outlook differs from that of Canada and therefore blocks a full appreciation of the Canadian notion of "two founding peoples."

29. Louis Henkin, *Foreign Affairs and the Constitution* (Mineola, NY: The Foundation Press, Inc., 1972), pp. 225–248; and Howard A. Leeson, "Foreign Relations and Quebec," in J. Peter Meekison, ed., *Canadian Federalism: Myth or Reality?* 3rd ed. (Toronto: Methuen, 1977), pp. 510–575.

30. Hero, "Quebec Trends vs. U.S. Interests and Policies," pp. 261–312.

31. Stephan Krasner, *Defending the National Interest: Raw Materials Investments and U.S. Foreign Policy* (Princeton: Princeton University Press, 1978).

32. The Bombardier case became highly politicized only because subsidized export financing was on the agenda of the Economic Summit at Versailles and because Washington was seeking a negotiated agreement within the OECD to reduce government export subsidies. See *The New York Times,* June 22, 1982, for a U.S. perspective.

33. Bruce M. Russett and Elizabeth C. Hanson, *Interest and Ideology: The Foreign Policy Beliefs of American Businessmen* (San Francisco: W. H. Freeman, 1975), pp. 263–265.

34. See President Carter's remarks as reported in *The New York Times,* February 22, 1977, p. 9, and in the *Department of State Bulletin,* March 21, 1977.

35. Lawrence S. Eagleburger, Assistant Secretary for European Affairs, "U.S. Policy Toward West Europe and Canada," statement before the Subcommittee on Europe and the Middle East of the House Foreign Affairs Committee, June 2, 1981.

36. Speech by Ambassador Thomas Enders at Stanford University, May 3, 1979, reprinted in the *Department of State Bulletin,* June 1979, p. 8.

37. As one Canadian federal official put it privately, "Canada expects the U.S. government not be evenhanded" but lean instead toward the position of the Canadian federal government.

38. Roger Swanson, *Intergovernmental Perspectives on the Canada-U.S. Relationship* (New York: New York University Press, 1978), pp. 221–270.

39. Lise Bissonnette, "The Evolution of Quebec-American Diplomacy," in Calvin Veltman, ed., *Contemporary Quebec* (Montreal: Université du Québec à Montreal, 1981); and Harold von Reikhoff, John H. Sigler, and Brian W. Tomlin, *Canada-U.S. Relations: Policy Environments, Issues, and Prospects* (Montreal: C. D. Howe Research Institute, 1979).

40. Consider for example, that the premier's visit was arranged a full nine months earlier and that the origin of the visit can as easily be explained in terms of Quebec's new drive for export markets. See Graham Fraser, "Quebec Turns to the U.S. in New-Look 'Foreign Policy': Jacques-Yvan Morin Has Shifted Emphasis from Relations with France to Promoting Trade with the United States," *The Gazette* (Montreal), July 10, 1982.

14
Conclusions and Recommendations

Alfred O. Hero, Jr.
Marcel Daneau

The preceding analyses examine underlying forces, issues, and trends and suggest opportunities in U.S.-Quebec relations that we believe should receive thoughtful attention by appropriate governments, nongovernmental institutions, and individual citizens on both sides of the border. Coping effectively with the problems outlined will require the imaginative efforts and energies of a variety of talents over decades.

Although the observations in the preceding material are those of individual authors, we are in accord with most of them. We shall not attempt to summarize the diverse findings, insights, speculations, and recommendations advanced by the authoritative specialists whose contributions appear in this volume. Instead, we shall speculate judiciously about potential trends bearing on how these bilateral phenomena might evolve and be dealt with on both sides over the intermediate and long-term futures. We shall close with some general recommendations about how private institutions, citizens, and governments can better cope with the implications of the observed or anticipated phenomena and of our own projections.

Canadian Evolution Toward Greater Provincial Autonomy

Like Louis Balthazar, we doubt that political sovereignty, in the generally understood meaning of that term, is a likely scenario for Quebec in the time frame of the next few years or the next decade, for the reasons he notes. As he suggests, even if the PQ or a successor government obtains a majority vote in an election or referendum for sovereignty, ensuing negotiations with Ottawa and other provincial governments would probably extend over some years before linkages with Canada were clarified.

We also doubt, as does Balthazar, that the recent trend under Pierre Elliott Trudeau toward further centralization in the federal government of decision making on issues of central concern to the francophone Quebec majority will continue much further. On the contrary, we believe this trend will eventually be reversed, toward devolution of responsibilities of particular interest not only to Quebec, but also to other provinces. Decentralization will probably not go so far as that suggested in the Pépin-Robarts report and similar recommendations. However, it will probably take that general direction, so that domains of particular interest to Quebec will be made available incrementally to all provinces, with the expectation that primarily Quebec will avail itself of these measures.

Projections over the next half-decade are necessarily uncertain. Some de facto devolution rather than either further centralization or the status quo seems likely under most potential successor federal leaders and governments, following Trudeau's departure. The longer he remains, the longer gradual decentralization to accommodate particularly Quebec's, but also other, provincial demands will be delayed. Once he leaves office, much will depend on which party, under what leader, will govern, whether that government will have a parliamentary majority, and the composition and leadership of the minority between the Liberals and Conservatives in the event neither of these two major parties has a majority.

Some potential Liberal anglophone replacements for Trudeau are apt to be more flexible than others toward demands for decentralization. Brian Mulroney, as leader of a Conservative government or coalition, would probably be less compromising toward Quebec than Joseph Clark. Significant dependence of a minority government on a dozen or more MPs elected by the new Quebec Nationalist Party with the active support of the PQ would, as Balthazar again notes, be conducive to compromise toward Quebec's position. Dependence on an NDP minority of equal or larger numbers would not be as conducive to such compromise.

Another potential development that could encourage devolution and that has not so far been mentioned would be adoption of even a relatively limited degree of proportional representation (P.R.) whereby a modest minority of House of Commons seats would be distributed by province to parties according to their proportion of votes above a specified minimum. Although perhaps not yet likely, neither is this eventuality unlikely, particularly if the number of seats so distributed were increased incrementally over several federal elections, and if the final number of seats so added (to the 282 House seats in the 1980 federal election) were no fewer than fifty and no more than a hundred as suggested by the Task Force on Canadian Unity and other thoughtful advocates.[1]

Trudeau, among other political leaders, has indicated that the idea has merits.

Vested political interests in both the Liberal and Conservative parties, particularly from areas where they heretofore have respectively and regularly won the great majority of seats with bare majorities or only pluralities of the total votes, are understandably opposed to this parliamentary reform. Others fear proliferations of parties and of weak minority governments. Supporters among strong federalists conceive of P.R. as a means of strengthening the center against Quebec and other provinces that demand wider powers, rather than enhancing their bargaining power. At least the Trudeau government is not likely to adopt P.R. if it feels the change would strengthen the provinces vis-à-vis Ottawa.

Nevertheless, even if the number of seats so allocated were but a modest minority of the House of Commons, the concentration of Liberal seats in Quebec and ridings with large populations of francophone heritage in Ontario and New Brunswick on the one hand, and of Conservative strength west of Ontario on the other, would be significantly reduced. More able Conservatives would run and win in Quebec and be available as ministers in case of a Tory majority or minority government. A PQ affiliated provincial party would be likely to win more seats than under the current system whereby pluralities in each riding choose all MPs. Liberals, to compete with popular, less centralist Tory, péquiste, and perhaps even NDP and other candidates across Quebec, would tend to compromise toward their opponents' positions regarding federal-Quebec relations.

Depending on the number of MPs chosen proportional to province-wide votes for each party that had achieved more than a specified minimum percentage of the total, coalition federal governments would be more frequent than heretofore. Candidates with a wider, more representative spectrum of views from Quebec would thus not only be elected and speak out in the House, but also exert influence especially on minority governments. Bargaining by Quebec MPs and ad hoc coalitions with those of devolutionist persuasion in other provinces would thereby be enhanced.

In Quebec itself, as we noted in our introduction, the majority "no" vote in the 1980 referendum is unlikely to comprise a final decision. Persistent majorities of francophone Quebeckers want either independence with or without economic association or real devolution toward Pépin-Robarts proposals, special Quebec status, de jure or de facto, or some combination thereof. So-minded majorities are larger among more highly educated, articulate, and influential Québécois, and among the young. Although the percentages will continue to fluctuate depending on economic cycles, personalities, parties in power, and other changing conditions, Quebec nationalism is the reflection of nearly four centuries of history and it is unlikely to decline over the long run.

The federal government and at least the anglophone elites across Canada who influence it will either eventually accept sufficient devolution to satisfy more moderate, conditional federalist Québécois nationalists, or the PQ or another party or coalition representative of the francophone majority is likely under more favorable conditions than today to win enough support to leave the federation. Quebec's role vis-à-vis the rest of Canada several decades from now is apt to be one or the other— independent or part of the federation but with significantly expanded powers in regard to language, communications, culture, and at least those economic domains more or less directly related thereto.

Meaningful compromise has not yet taken place, primarily because even the PQ government reelected by a francophone majority in 1981 has little leverage, after defeat of its 1980 referendum, to enable it to negotiate sovereignty-association; it has also been preoccupied in the early 1980s with economic problems during its worst economic crisis since the Great Depression. Because Quebec's threat to secede was, after May 1980, no longer credible in Ottawa or Canada generally, at least for the short run, why compromise?

However, short of permanent economic malaise and thus continuing dependence on protected Canadian markets for obsolete manufactures, major subsidies from richer provinces via equalization payments, DREE/ ITC (combined Department of Regional Economic Expansion and International Trade and Commerce) investment assistance, cheap oil and gas, and so on, the likely trend noted in Chapters 2, 3, and 12 are apt gradually to increase Quebec's leverage vis-à-vis the rest of Canada. Public support may be won for "going to" and even "over the brink" toward independence if compromise is consistently refused.

The substance, quality, and tone of Quebec's relations with the United States will markedly influence the outcome in Quebec, independent of any likely action by the United States government. Growing, mutually profitable economic relations with the United States, as persuasively argued by Mr. Bonin as well as a number of other qualified observers in academia or business, the senior civil service, PQ cabinet ministers, and their PLQ opponents, will lessen Quebec's relative economic dependence on Canada. The more successful the widely supported efforts to replace protected labor-intensive industries with more modern, internationally competitive ones based on exports, joint ventures, investment, transfers of technology, and other linkages particularly with the U.S. private sector, the less hesitant Québécois voters will be to risk independence if Ottawa remains insensitive to their demands.

Understandable economic concerns, combined with residual identities with Canada particularly among older, more traditional Québécois, prevented enough of the majority favorable to decentralization from voting "yes" in the referendum to overcome the "no" nonfrancophone vote. Many Québécois did not believe the rest of Canada, given its conflicting economic interests, would accept a customs union to assure protected markets to Quebec's manufactures, or that oil and gas would continue to flow from Alberta below world prices, once Quebec was no longer in the federation's parliament. Many envisaged further decline in their standards of living due to termination of Canadian equalization payments and other economic assistance. The passing of the older, strongly federalist generations more identified with Canada will reduce that inhibition. A more prosperous, confident Quebec economy, linked increasingly to North America as a whole, and less dependent on Canadian subsidies and markets, would be more willing to attempt independence.

The history and basically pragmatic character of most of anglophone Canada suggests that, when and if faced with the probability of Quebec independence, it will compromise. Whether the final outcome will preserve a viable federal government with the powers and revenues to deal effectively with economic policy, foreign policy, defense, and other issues facing the country as a whole will depend in considerable measure on what jurisdictions are decentralized, and other details. If compromise is refused until Quebec opinion and political leadership have evolved through escalating confrontations, rejections, and frustrations to a majority or near-majority favoring leaving the federation, the compromises required to head off that eventuality are apt to entail a severely weakened federal system that might not survive, or could do so only with the anglophone provinces without Quebec.

Before that potential point of no return is reached, the types of devolution required to meet objectives acceptable to a majority of Québécois and their respective elites need not result in an unmanageable federal system as argued by Trudeau and others. A viable arrangement could probably be achieved without formal constitutional amendment, difficult to achieve under procedures of the constitution patriated in 1982. Even change toward a more conciliatory style and tone by an anglophone prime minister could make a significant difference.

Domains thus devolved would necessarily include final recognition of the principle of duality of two founding cultures and societies integrally linked with the French and English languages, respectively, the former based primarily in Quebec, as argued by Balthazar and most other Québécois. Control of cable television, pressed by previous as well as PQ governments, must be among the devolved domains. Some compromise might even be negotiated for joint control of Radio-Canada in

French, perhaps through a governing board partially chosen by the Quebec government but also representative of the approximately one-tenth of the average total audience outside that province—largely Acadians in New Brunswick and people of Québécois ancestry in Ontario. More difficult politically would be achievement of a modus vivendi relative to Quebec's relations with francophone societies outside North America, mainly symbolic and cultural in content.

The immigration issue has been largely settled in fact, as noted by Lachapelle, by the agreement in 1978 between Ottawa and Quebec authorizing the latter to refuse entry from abroad of immigrants, refugees, temporary workers, and students. Although this agreement does not prevent immigrants from entering Quebec via Toronto or other parts of Canada, Law 101 should effectively discourage those who are unwilling to work in a French culture and send their children to French schools.

Law 101 even requires that children of bona fide anglophone Canadians, who themselves attended English schools elsewhere in Canada before moving to Quebec, attend French public primary and secondary schools. A final federal court decision opening English schools to these children under the new charter of rights, although symbolically and politically controversial, would affect only a small number and would not necessarily threaten the basic objective of Quebec's legislation. It would, moreover, broaden the pool of highly trained technological and professional talent that might be willing to move to Quebec to help modernize the economy. The clause in the 1982 constitution opening English schools to U.S., British, and other bona fide anglophone immigrants will apply to Quebec only if a future provincial government accepts it via a majority vote in the National Assembly. Quebec already largely controls and administers family allowances, social welfare, education, and most other programs entailing direct contacts with individuals—formerly controversial areas between it and Ottawa.

The most difficult federal-provincial issues to resolve—with other, resource-rich provinces as much or more than with Quebec—relate to economic decision making. Devolution should maintain sufficient federal powers to cope with national economic problems. Concessions could thus not be nearly as liberal as PQ elites (and some in Alberta and elsewhere) argue. Ottawa should likewise conserve the limited powers it now has to prevent escalation of provincial non-tariff barriers (NTBs), already major deterrents to flows of goods, manpower, and services. FIRA's powers would be curtailed de facto, if not de jure. Quebec, Alberta, and other energy producers would demand curtailment of the National Energy Board's authority to tax or prevent foreign energy exports. But Bonin notes that, in practice, FIRA has consulted closely with pertinent provincial authorities before rendering decisions. It has not refused investments favored by the PQ government. Decision making on economic issues of direct or indirect interest to U.S. nationals would devolve further to Quebec, as well as to other provinces, a trend already underway over the last decade or so.

Independentists, including articulate academicians, intellectuals, journalists, artists, politicians, students, and other activists, would argue against acceptance of such compromises, but their popular support is apt to be a limited minority. Such conciliation would gain the acceptance of a majority, including among elites. It should also be optimal for most U.S. as well as Quebec and Canadian long-term interests, always with provisos of a federal government remaining with sufficient powers and revenues to cope with national and international issues of concern to the United States, and to limit further growth of provincial barriers to a viable national economy.

Particular implications for both Quebec and the United States in relation to one another would depend on the details of federal-provincial arrangements as they unfolded. Quebeckers, like other Canadians, would finally be gradually relieved of their overriding domestic preoccupations. These preoccupations have diverted their energies, talents, and resources for a generation and longer from dealing effectively, and in their own terms unaffected by implications for Quebec-Ottawa relations, with the many other pressing problems facing them. Those problems have included relations with the United States.

Anglophone nationalist arguments that a number of U.S. economic interests would profit from decentralization of economic decision making are valid, though their speculations about active encouragement of that development by U.S. corporate and other elites are not. The latter overwhelmingly prefer an effective Canadian federation with Quebec inside it to "separatism," or to a loose confederation wherein the center had lost so much of its decision making and revenues to Quebec and/ or other provinces as to be unable to hold Canada together as a functioning unit. As among the U.S. foreign-policy community, the corporate elite's ultimate worry is Quebec leaving the federation and the rest of Canada thereafter coming apart into several "squabbling" provinces or several confederations of them, with projected dire multiple strategic, defense, foreign policy, political, and economic consequences.

Particularly for U.S. manufacturing subsidiaries on either side of Quebec-Canada borders dependent on Canada-wide markets, further increases in NTBs due to devolution of economic powers would become a major negative consideration. On the positive side for both Quebec and U.S. economic interests would be Ottawa's probable relinquishment of its authority to tax exports of hydropower, gas, and other resources, and to require that they be sold in Canada much below prices prevailing in the United States. Any new federal arrangement acceptable to Quebec would reduce federal powers to limit Quebec's freedom to negotiate trade and investment arrangements with the United States as the elected government deemed in Quebec's interest.

The currently expanding cross-border linkages in trade, investment, environmental dealings, talent exchanges, and other services based on specific comparative advantages would be further encouraged, especially between Quebec and the U.S. northeast and areas reachable along the Great Lakes by cheap St. Lawrence Seaway shipping. The governments of New York and of New England states would accelerate their growing collaboration with the government in Quebec City. Although the growing transborder interdependencies of provinces, particularly Quebec, with private interests and state governments in the adjoining U.S. regions are followed by Ottawa officials with some concern as potentially threatening centrifugal developments with political as well as economic consequences, Washington officials regard those developments with relative indifference or encourage them as likely net benefits rather than threats to overall U.S. interests.

Wider provincial differences between Quebec and some other provinces in economic policies of interest to Americans should evolve as the provinces compete with one another for U.S. markets, investments, tourists, and other desirables. U.S. economic sectors should have greater bargaining power than under a more centralized system. Relevant economic decision making in Quebec and other provinces should become simpler and quicker, involving fewer government officials on fewer levels. Positions of successive Quebec governments, like those of several other provinces, have often been closer and their climates more hospitable to U.S. business linkages than those of Ottawa.

Businessmen, regardless of their nationality, usually prefer to deal with more accessible officials, nearer to the phenomenon in question, more apt to accord it priority, more inclined to deal with proposals in terms of particular local and provincial needs and objectives, and less influenced by general considerations and precedents across such a diverse country as Canada. Anglophone economic nationalists would accordingly have less influence on U.S. investments in Quebec.

For example, Quebec under virtually any government would be more likely to export electricity under attractive terms to the U.S. northeast than would the National Energy Board. Quebec could make whatever arrangements it felt to its advantage with U.S. utilities and state governments. It would be more able, for example, to bargain hydropower exports not only for expanded generating capacity and transmission systems, but also for U.S. tariff and NTB, as well as state NTB, reductions on semifabricated aluminum, copper, zinc, asbestos, and forest products.

Electricity could become Quebec's strongest suit in its relations with the United States. If Quebec brought New Brunswick into a negotiating coalition and, particularly, reached a compromise with Newfoundland on transmissions to expand generation on the Lower Churchill, and brought that province into the discussions, its leverage in the adjoining region and thereby in the U.S. Congress would expand further.

Insofar as these developing relationships with the United States would enable Quebec gradually to phase out its protected softgoods industries in favor of higher-technology, higher-skill, export-competitive ones, both partners would benefit directly, as well as in less obvious ways. Quebec would thereby develop a more modern, generally competitive economy, higher quality labor, higher incomes, become less dependent on protected Canadian markets, and thereby increase both its economic and political bargaining power in Canada and to a lesser degree in the United States. Although ensuing reductions of Canadian protection in these sectors would particularly benefit newly industrializing countries' exports, they would also result in expanded U.S. synthetic textile and other exports to Canada.

Increased linguistic and cultural autonomy—the central focus of Quebec's demands—would probably only somewhat enhance its abilities to cope with already massive U.S. cultural impacts documented by Mr. Lamonde, which are apt to grow further with new communications technologies. Mass interests would preclude any Quebec government, even one completely independent of Canada, from implementing more than limited restrictions on access to popular American cultural products— films, television and radio programs, records, magazines, and so on. Expanded provincial communications roles, with some increases in funds, could perhaps result in more indigenous programs of wider public appeal to Québécois, thereby broadening somewhat attractive alternatives to American cultural products. Quebec might increase somewhat the minimum required proportion of such indigenous materials on television, cable, radio, and other media it controlled. But any Quebec government concerned about winning the next election could institute only marginally more restrictive policies on American cultural imports than it already has in its jurisdiction.

Quebec's extended cultural autonomy, combined with reduction of fears that the federal government or courts will strike down provisions of Law 101 applying to French as the predominant language of work and of education for immigrants and native francophones, should in the long run be a net plus for U.S. interests. Québécois elites could thereby devote more thoughtful attention, less encumbered with this pervasive preoccupation, to cultural and other relations with their giant southern neighbor. Feeling more culturally secure, Quebec could well become more interested in and open to higher quality, more sophisticated, cultural imports from the United States, including drama and other products in English. Quebec could likewise become more interesting to culturally sophisticated, influential U.S. tourists. A secure and vibrant Quebec culture should also be more attractive to at least those culturally aware Americans at home, including but not limited to the minorities who speak some French and/or are interested in that language and its related cultural aspects.

No Quebec government is apt to increase greatly its expenditures on cultural and educational programs in the United States, including those for Americans of francophone heritages, until and unless active interest in such endeavors grows demonstrably south of the border. However, a more dynamic Quebec culture would provide an improved base to profit optimally from any such opportunities, a wider range of means to cope with them, and growing talent and material resources to implement them.

Related further devolution of cultural and educational relations with *francophonie* to Quebec could likewise enhance cooperation with and efforts by Quebec itself in domains discussed by Messrs. Gold and Chartier. Less contention between Ottawa and Quebec over these largely symbolic political concerns, particularly if future governments in Paris, like the Mitterrand government, so behaved as not to encourage it, would likewise facilitate Quebec elites devoting more systematic attention to their more tangible and pervasive U.S. interests. The ensuing development of pragmatic rapport in continental Europe where French is spoken or understood and in francophone Africa and elsewhere, beyond politicians and government bureaucrats, but with a spectrum of potentially interested private institutions and individuals, could enhance Quebec's albeit modest role as go-between and interpreter of North America there and of the French-speaking world on this continent. Such expanded links should also over time enhance francophone Quebec's potential for developing markets for services as well as goods of North American origin other than Quebec itself among customers whose language is French.

The combined long-term direct and indirect effects of such expanded autonomy should also help mitigate the preponderant influences of Anglo-Canadian sources on U.S. perceptions of Quebec, as addressed in this volume by Banker and Lubin. A more vibrant Quebec culture, more effectively projected into the United States and more attractive to influential U.S. tourists, would gain wider U.S. press coverage and audiences. The already growing francophone business community in modern enterprises linked with the United States—largely American in training, business practices, tastes, and generally pro-American in attitudes—would grow faster in numbers, in contacts with the United States, and in influence both there and on Québécois public opinion and politics pertinent to the United States. As Québécois in other influential walks of life become more self-assured, less proccupied with Quebec's contentious relations with Ottawa and the rest of Canada, they too should develop less timid, more outgoing and mutually more rewarding relations with their U.S. counterparts.

Trends in U.S. Reactions

Knowledgeable Americans in and out of federal and state governments are often sceptical about the seriousness, breadth of public support, and future longevity of the Lévesque government's relatively recent emphases on relations with the United States.

A number of Americans who have dealt with the Quebec government even since its reelection in 1981 question its real priorities in contradistinction to the relative importance it says it accords to U.S. relations. Intergovernmental Affairs Minister Morin and other pertinent ministers and senior aides visit Europe, especially France, as frequently as the United States. The number of people, funds, and the general magnitude and prestige allocated to French activities remain considerably larger than those devoted to the United States by Mr. Morin's ministry. Even when funds and personnel devoted to relations with the United States in the Ministries of External Trade, Agriculture, Environment, and Commerce, Industry, and Tourism are included, those related to *francophonie* are greater. The post of delegate general in New York, by far Quebec's most important in the United States, remained vacant for six months in 1981–1982 and that in Boston, its second most important, for almost as long in 1982, hardly likely for their counterpart in Paris. Three different acting directors of the office charged with relations with the United States in the Ministry of Intergovernmental Affairs spanned the gap between departure of its incumbent in 1982 and appointment of his replacement over nine months later—likewise improbable for his counterpart charged with relations with France.

Even the Lévesque government's post-1981 public emphases on economic relations are not widely regarded as altogether convincing. As Bonin observes, the government's major post-election economic policy statement, *The Technological Conversion,* according priority to high technology, makes little reference to and suggests little prior empirical analysis of implications for relations with the United States. Nor does much systematic attention seem to have been devoted to such important linkages since. Although the Canadian government brought responsibility for foreign economic relations into its Department of External Affairs in 1982, the Quebec government seemed to interested Americans to do the reverse by concentrating foreign economic relations in a new, separate ministry. This reorganization denuded the Ministry of Intergovernmental Affairs of economic expertise and left it with primarily cultural and political responsibilities, much more important for relations with France than with the United States. Interested Americans remain to be convinced that the relevant participation of these two ministries, and of others such as Commerce, Industry, and Tourism, Environment, Agriculture, and Finance, will be effectively coordinated in respect to economic relations with the United States.

Tomlinson, Lubin, and Balthazar suggest that increasing numbers of interested U.S. corporate executives have developed relatively sophisticated judgments of Quebec developments. Nevertheless, many are still concerned about both the possibilities of "separatism" and a shift by the current or a later government back toward *dirigisme,* public corporations, and other policies and practices they regard as discouraging to private investment and initiative if and when the Quebec economy emerges from its malaise of the early 1980s. On several occasions since the Lévesque government, during its first mandate, raised personal income taxes to the highest in North America on well-paid talent it needs to develop its private sector, it has implied without implementation that taxes would be readjusted to levels competitive with Ontario and other Canadian provinces. As Banker and Lubin observe, many U.S. businessmen's perceptions of the Quebec business scene are further colored by contacts exclusively with Anglo-Canadian colleagues and/or by tones in the anglophone business presses of both countries.

U.S. business and financial elites, like most others, would adjust to whatever degrees and types of extended autonomy Quebec (and other provinces) might achieve. Although wider provincial economic jurisdictions would be to the net interest to most of these U.S. sources, they are not apt to change their preferences for a "united Canada," even though an independent Quebec would probably constitute a net plus in the long run for some important U.S. economic interests. However, most U.S. interests are concerned that an ensuing combination of political instability, economic difficulties and uncertainties, and increased barriers to flows of goods, services, and talents across Canada would more than negate gains from economic decision making concentrated in Quebec.

Balthazar is undoubtedly correct that many Québécois in the Canadian Foreign Service and elsewhere with expertise in international affairs would return to an independent Quebec if comparable careers were likely there. An independent government would be obliged to develop responsible foreign policies that provincial political elites in or out of government need not have considered seriously before. Quebec's vital dependence on smooth economic and other relations with the United States would motivate its government to accommodate its policies toward other international issues of concern to the United States.

The U.S. foreign-policy and defense communities, as Doran and Job suggest, doubt that an independent Quebec with many more immediately pressing budgetary demands at home would in practice maintain its share of the current Canadian military establishment, keep its share of troops in Western Europe, and remain as active in NATO, NORAD, and other multinational and bilateral arrangements when faced with the real expenses involved. They surmise that the PQ government's "conversion" has been more opportunist rhetoric to placate the United States than a derivative of serious consideration of all the substantive implications. They note the relative indifference to such issues not only among elites in the major provincial parties, but also in the intellectual and research communities, in French-language media, and in Québécois society in general. They also point to the history of francophone opposition to military conscription and active involvement in World Wars I and II, and to the isolationist, inward preoccupations of Quebeckers in their history and traditions.

Americans in the corporate, research, and other communities who deal with Quebec, and the larger number interested in U.S.-Canadian relations or in other pertinent domains, tend to be sceptical as well. Except for the growing francophone business community interested in economic relations with the United States, they note the relatively little or superficial interest and expertise in relations with the United States outside of the post-1981 PQ government mentioned by Balthazar. They point to the preoccupation with domestic Quebec issues, relations with Ottawa and the other provinces, and within international affairs, relations with France among political, civil service, intellectual, cultural, educational, and most other elites outside the business community. These educational, cultural, and political elites, along with trade union leaders, have comprised the more influential elements in the Parti Québécois; their efforts will be essential to its reelection. Furthermore, interested Americans have not been impressed that the degree and quality of interest in U.S. relations within the PLQ, aside from Bourassa and a few others, are much different.

As Doran and Job argue, Americans experience particular difficulties in understanding francophone nationalism and especially its cultural concerns. Little perceptive about their own culture, they cannot be expected to be so about the cultures of others. On the whole even more assimilationist than Anglo-Canadians, they do not readily comprehend a society that accords priority to linguistic and cultural over conflicting economic objectives. They furthermore feel no threat to their own taken-for-granted culture.

Few Americans are aware of, or even fewer yet care much about, the increasingly massive U.S. penetration of Quebec popular culture discussed by Lamonde. Many Americans regard Québécois concerns about their culture and language, like those in France, as a peculiarly francophone preoccupation. Outside of a limited minority of American francophiles and people of francophone Canadian heritage noted by Gold, Chartier, and Balthazar, few Americans have understood, or so far have shown much interest in understanding and relating to, the uniquely attractive aspects of Québécois culture. Even otherwise relatively informed and internationally interested Americans' perceptions of Quebec culture, as of Quebec in general, are derived primarily, directly or indirectly, from Anglo-Canadian sources for the mutually reinforcing reasons noted by Banker, Lubin, and Balthazar.

The editors, a native Louisianian of partly French heritage and a former Franco-American from Massachusetts, both of whom maintain frequent contacts with relatives and acquaintances among these two minorities, are less optimistic than either Gold or Chartier about the future maintenance of either the French language or its related cultures among both groups. Disappearance of use and fluency of French among descendants of French-speaking groups throughout the United States has much accelerated since World War II.[2] Short of basic changes in the underlying factors that have brought this assimilation about, only a small minority of mainly university educated young people atypically interested in the language and heritage of their ancestors is likely to continue French for another generation. We moreover doubt that much beyond nostalgic folklore of French culture will persist once the language disappears. Judicious assistance by Quebec, French, Belgian, and other francophone societies can slow down that process and provide significant encouragement and means for the interested minority to preserve and further develop their fluency and cultural involvements. However, the levels of such cultural assistance for which funding is apt to be politically acceptable are unlikely to be sufficient to reverse these basic trends.

Thus, since few Americans believe that Quebec will gain control of its defense, security, and foreign policies beyond cultural affairs, the interests and concerns of most U.S. elites focus primarily on economic and related issues, as they do for Canada as a whole.

Economics formerly comprised much of the very limited Quebec interest in U.S. university and other research and teaching communities, but some broader concerns and talents have developed, particularly since the unanticipated election of a PQ government in 1976. U.S. professors of French and comparative literature have increasingly included Quebec francophone literature in their courses. U.S. scholars and other analysts, especially in policy-related fields interested in U.S.-Canadian relations, have shown growing interest, some in Quebec itself, more in the implications of Quebec nationalism for Canada and the United States. The Association for Canadian Studies in the United States (ACSUS) reflects this increase in interest, particularly among its membership, but also to some degree in its meetings and the content of its quarterly, *The American Review of Canadian Studies.*[3]

A small core of academics, researchers, and others with serious interests in diverse fields who devote some part of their energies to Quebec has gradually evolved. In part because of the primarily Anglo-Canadian orientations of most of the leadership of ACSUS and with encouragement and some financial assistance from the Quebec government, this diverse group established an independent organization, The Northeast Council for Quebec Studies, in 1980. Its interdisciplinary annual, *Quebec Studies,* began publication in 1983.

Probably as, or maybe more, significant has been the bit-by-bit growth of albeit sporadic comparative attention to Quebec by especially able, internationally influential economists, political scientists, sociologists, and other scholars in their particular fields of expertise. Their widely read publications affect the thinking and stimulate the teaching and research interests of many others at more typical universities and other institutions across North America and overseas. They furthermore directly or indirectly influence the views of policymakers both in Washington and in many private elite institutions. Their number has grown from no more than three in the mid-1960s to a dozen or so two decades later. Under appropriate conditions (see below), they could become more numerous, more diverse, and of significantly wider influence on U.S. research, thought, teaching, and policy decisions pertinent to Quebec.

However, critical reinforcing difficulties remain to improvement of both the quality and diversity of systematic research, thought, and discussion of phenomena pertinent to Quebec. While many of the issues are sufficiently relevant to their priorities and research interests to attract the serious comparative attention of a considerably larger number of such influential scholars, the relatively low priorities ascribed to U.S.-Canadian relations in general combined with the much lower importance accorded to Quebec than to Anglo-Canada are overriding deterrents. Research on Canada in general, and especially on Quebec, enjoys little prestige, financial support, popularity among better non-Canadian students, or influence on relevant discussions in top U.S. universities, liberal arts colleges, research institutions, and foundations. Foundation and other sources of funds for serious research, graduate student fellowships, and publication of more imaginative and otherwise significant research are very few, and total resources available are much more limited than in other fields competing for the same talent.

Since the number of potential readers in university courses, governments, research institutions, and elsewhere is still small, publishing outlets are very limited short of subsidies. Even high quality book-length manuscripts by well regarded scholars whose works in other fields have been readily published by major commercial houses and received with praise by knowledgeable people experience such publishing difficulties. For the more promising, ambitious Ph.D. candidates and younger scholars, research on Quebec especially fails to provide the financial support, the likelihood of publication, the entry jobs, and the favorable career projections of competing possibilities.

These inhibiting factors are much reinforced by the difficulties able Americans interested or potentially interested in Quebec often experience in attempting to establish fruitful rapport and working relationships with their Québécois counterparts. Low prevalence of French fluency among the former, and hesitancy of many of the latter who read but do not fluently write and speak English to participate in meetings, collaborative research, and the like with such Americans are certainly important deterrents.

Americans encounter relatively few Québécois at meetings in the United States or Canada devoted to relations between the two. Americans also partially ascribe that experience to lack of acquaintance of both Americans and Anglo-Canadians with their francophone equivalents, and thus failure to invite them. But they also ascribe validity to complaints of Anglo-Canadians interested in relations with the United States that, even when invited, francophones often do not attend. Some Americans further ascribe the paucity of Québécois involvement not only to their difficulties of expressing themselves on complex issues in English, but also to awkward nuances of participating in endeavors that have been organized with Americans primarily by Anglo-Canadians; the francophones would be much outnumbered by the latter throughout the discussion. But many Americans have also concluded that their Québécois counterparts prefer to deliberate alone or among themselves rather than compare ideas and work with Americans on phenomena of mutual concern.

These impressions are unfortunately often deepened by frustrations in drawing able Québécois into collaborative enterprises—an experience of the relatively few Americans who have attempted to do so. To them the selection among able, research-oriented Québécois potentially interested in devoting significant time and energies to relations with the United States is small to virtually nonexistent in many fields that would seem important to Quebec's future. Many seem overly defensive, timid, or uninterested in dealing with Americans. They appear preoccupied with Quebec itself and with its relations with Ottawa, and to some extent with France and Europe, and little interested in developing more fruitful relations with their superpower neighbor either for themselves or for Quebec at large.

Authors of the the preceding chapters are among the growing, but still small, minority comprising notable exceptions. Because they are so few, the able exceptions are usually overworked, spread too thin over more domains than they can master, and unfortunately often under-appreciated among their Quebec-centric colleagues. Unless and until this relative handful of Québécois talent interested in the United States as it affects Quebec, and in working with appropriate Americans, manages to expand, attraction of many more Americans to such pursuits will also be more difficult.

Department of State officials involved in Canadian affairs also have broader interests than economic and security affairs. However, as Doran and Job argue, the policies they execute are unlikely to change from neutrality tilted toward Canadian "unity"—under any administration. There are not now, and are not apt to be, significant pressures from either within the government or the private sector favoring Canada's devolution of economic jurisdictions that might be in the interest of both particular U.S. private groups and the United States as a whole. However, U.S. federal officials and congressmen would not regard modest devolution as detrimental to U.S. interests, provided that Ottawa retained sufficient powers and revenues to cope with national economic, defense, foreign-policy, and other issues of U.S. concern. Although a Democratic administration less conservative than the current Republican admin-istration might shift the nuances of U.S. emphases from strategic and economic concerns, these concerns would remain priorities. Any con-ceivable administration or Congress is likely to view the eventuality of an independent Quebec as being contrary to U.S. interests.

U.S. policy will adjust to whatever role and interior changes Quebec institutes and works out for itself with the federal system, including independence. However, U.S. officials and most of the elites in and out of government with whose views these officials are in touch generally assume that U.S. abilities to influence the course of events in Quebec will be very limited under most conceivable circumstances. Officials will continue to avoid being caught in crossfires between Quebec and Ottawa and in any utterances or other behavior that might draw the United States into this controversy or result in its being blamed by one side for encouraging or supporting, directly or indirectly, the other, particularly Quebec independence.

Even should it appear in the course of events that a nationalist Quebec government had achieved majority support to leave the federation or gain a degree of autonomy apt to eventuate in a much enfeebled federal government, U.S. intervention beyond quietly reminding the respective parties of implications for U.S. interests, and urging them to work out a compromise to preserve a viable Canadian entity, is improbable.

Relations of U.S. state governments and private interests with the Quebec government and its fully owned or partially owned corporations would grow more rapidly under most likely devolutionist scenarios than under current arrangements, and probably more under a Conservative or a Conservative-minority federal government than under a Liberal one headed by Trudeau. But even should the latter continue as prime minister for another mandate, linkages between subfederal governments and private interests are apt to continue to develop, as they are currently developing with most other Canadian provincial governments as well.

U.S. state governments are generally much less equipped to deal with the Quebec government than is the latter to deal with them. Constitutionally, Canadian provinces have much wider jurisdictions than do states in the United States. Partly as a result, province-state financial and human resources are asymmetrical. Even the governments of larger, more affluent states such as New York and Massachusetts do not have the equivalents of Quebec ministries with similarly broad powers, funds, political visibility, and specialized personnel for transgovernmental relations. States likewise have much more limited roles in their respective economies and societies.

Thus U.S. state relations with Quebec will remain functional and apolitical. State officials, including those with large populations of francophone heritage in Louisiana and northern New England, will, like federal ones, resist being drawn into francophone Quebec disputes with either its nonfrancophone minorities or the Canadian government. As Gold and Chartier note, their Franco-American, Acadian, and Creole populations are also anxious to avoid such involvements. On the other hand, state officials will increasingly consider expansion of economic and other functional relations important to their electorate's interests. They would naturally be sympathetic to Quebec in case Canadian authorities intervened to inhibit any such arrangements that they might negotiate in the mutual interests of their states and individual Canadian provinces.

If relations develop along the lines of the apparent general consensus of most of the foregoing authors and ourselves, U.S. perceptions of Québécois and theirs of Americans should gradually become more realistic, knowledgeable, and mutually rewarding. Indeed, that trend has already proceeded considerably since the Quiet Revolution and particularly over the decade ending in 1983.

Nevertheless, both interested governments and private institutions could do considerably more than heretofore to facilitate and hasten that process. Quebeckers as much the more affected, dependent, and interested of the two partners in Quebec-U.S. relations need to provide most of the impetus and imagination in that regard. Without forthcoming efforts from Quebec, by private organizations and individuals as well as governmental agencies, Americans will generally remain indifferent, little informed, passive, and reactive. But unless pertinent U.S., particularly nongovernmental, institutions and elites manifest more openness, interest, and willingness to devote some of their talents and energies to encouraging and collaborating with Quebeckers, the process of developing understanding of one another in their mutual interests will be spotty, at times erratic and counterproductive, and likely to take much longer than potentially more fruitful relationships render desirable.

Some Recommendations for Private and Public Action

Our recommendations focus on two associated general, long-term objectives for Quebec and the United States in their relations:

The first is to develop more realistic perceptions on both sides of the frontier of the other side, particularly insofar as these perceptions may bear on more mutually rewarding future relations between the two. Especially U.S. elites who influence public policies, private actions, and wider publics in the diverse spheres discussed heretofore need to develop more balanced understanding of the objectives and thinking of their Quebec counterparts. Systematic biases toward Canadian anglophone perceptions and arguments, gleaned overwhelmingly from Anglo-Canadian sources, should be at least moderated by direct exposure to the range of francophone perceptions reflective of and influential on majority Québécois opinion about Quebec itself, its role in Canada, and its linkages with the United States. Comparable Québécois need to evolve a better understanding of the United States—in much greater depth than through their superficial experiences on vacations, their exposure to popular U.S. media including entertainment, the relatively sparse news coverage in their press (often written from non-Canadian frames of reference), and the specialized contacts a few of them have with Americans in their line of work.

The second objective is the development of networks of informal communications in the diverse spheres bearing on relations between the two societies, among those Americans and Québécois who make or influence pertinent decisions and their implementation. Although linguistic and cultural differences will probably prevent such direct contacts, rapport, and pragmatic working relationships from achieving the ease of exchange and mutual understanding that Americans have with their Anglo-Canadian counterparts, the existing paucity of U.S. elite communications with the francophone part of the "two solitudes" should and can be much improved.

Given the magnitude and complexity of problems of achieving these ends and the very modest resources in talent, institutions, and funds to do so, emphasis should be on pinpointing and working with and through influential minorities and promising younger people who may exert influences disproportionate to their numbers a decade and more hence. Larger publics, at least in Quebec, will over the longer term be influenced via these elites, in part as individuals, but more through their influences on media and institutions that do affect wider opinion and practical behavior.

Transborder relationships are further along and probably apt to progress more or less of their own accord in the growing francophone business community, in pursuits where dealing effectively with Americans is a sine qua non for success. Nevertheless, even these business contacts are usually within a specific, quite limited field. More needs to be done through joint efforts of francophone Quebec and anglophone U.S. business schools, Chambers of Commerce, and other institutions in which more thoughtful Québécois and U.S. businessmen have confidence, in order to cope via useful research and serious discussion with wider economic issues of mutual significance. The research and related discussions in 1981 in Quebec-U.S. economic relations sponsored by the School of Advanced Commercial Studies (*Ecole des hautes études commerciales*) associated with the University of Montreal and the World Peace Foundation, and those over 1977–1983 of triangular economic linkages and opportunities among Quebec, the Atlantic Provinces, and New England cosponsored by the Quebec Center for International Relations, the Atlantic Provinces Economic Council, the World Peace Foundation, the Greater Boston Fund for International Affairs, and the Greater Boston Chamber of Commerce, suggest constructive prototypes. Their experience might be applied in greater depth to promising bilateral sectors in such fields as higher technology, professional services, and specialized investment.

Quebec will probably never become the central interest, or for very long even one of several central interests, of more than two or three of the more intellectually able, widely influential scholars in each pertinent discipline in major U.S. research universities, "think tanks," and similar elite institutions. With more perceptive and systematic encouragement over a decade or so, Quebec could become one of several important comparative concerns for perhaps a score or more of such individuals across such fields as comparative politics, nationalism, public administration, urban studies, transportation, labor, sociology, cultural anthropology, trade and investment, mass communications, literature and drama, and so on. Only some of those scholars would continue active comparative research interest in Quebec. But most would retain throughout their influential careers an understanding in depth in their respective domains and would continue to influence students, scholarship of others, and through a network of contacts private and public action relevant to Quebec. And at least a significant fraction of these scholars would continue, or take up again later, their earlier intensity of interest under appropriate circumstances.

Funding and institutional support are not so critical to convincing such talented individuals to devote some of their comparative attention to Quebec as for stimulating a smaller number of top scholars to consider Quebec one of their several major interests throughout much of their careers. However, modest funds and related part-time encouragement are typically far from irrelevant.

The paucity of even small financial support for travel, research assistance, and other costs of the Quebec perspective in broader comparative endeavors deters these busy, much in demand, systematic scholars from needed work, when they can secure equivalent or larger resources more readily from a variety of sources for "more important" (or fashionable or exotic) comparative cases accorded higher priority by U.S. public and private funding institutions. Even very able analysts with extensive research experience and excellent reputations in their respective fields are generally frustrated by time-consuming, tedious efforts required to secure relatively small sums for work pertaining to Canada in general and Quebec in particular. Furthermore, they often fail to raise relatively minor sums after considerable effort.

Until this mutually reinforcing circle of lack of funds, lack of serious analyses and publications, and thereby lack of visibility and priority to stimulate more sources of support is broken, a combination of the Quebec government and one or two U.S. institutions—from among foundations, major universities, and other research institutions—should make such modest sums available. Moreover, these institutions should utilize a system of selection likely to favor the few proposals and individuals with real promise of excellence. Academic entrepreneurs with little serious interest in Quebec, who would dissipate modest funds to little productive outcome, are apt to be more the rule than the exception. Criteria must be carefully drawn to assure relevance as well as substantive quality, and individual choices should be decided by the most able peers of the talent being judged, who are themselves policy-concerned and seriously interested in Canadian-American and Quebec affairs.

Problems of funds and institutional contexts are more profound in regard to generating over the next few years a dozen or so top diverse social scientists and other analysts who become authorities on Quebec, and on U.S. relations with Quebec, in their respective fields. The funds needed are significantly greater, but the number of institutions with the required talented faculties, more able Ph.D. candidates, research libraries, and Canadian or Quebec interests are relatively few, not more than three or four in the more relevant disciplines and substantive fields, probably not more than a dozen altogether. Moreover, funds for individual Ph.D. studies at such institutions, by comparison with funds available in high-visibility, more prestigious and generally accepted competitive fields, would be modest, supporting probably no more than half a dozen Ph.D. candidates at any one time across the United States, in three or four different disciplines and institutions. The most able emerging from such intensive research under imaginative stimulation, critique, and supervision in these universities would gradually form a small pool from which would come future senior faculty at top institutions. They, in turn, would encourage colleagues and successive generations of better students, would write books and articles widely read in both academia and the practical foreign-policy community, and would generally raise the quality of thought about Quebec in North America (and elsewhere). The more nearly average of these generally able students would raise the quality and impact of courses dealing in part with Quebec at more typical U.S. educational institutions.

At more senior, but including younger scholar, levels, support for a few fellowships at such appropriate institutions should be moderately enhanced. Even these funds need not be large. Required selectivity among institutions and individual candidates would probably not result in more than two or three fellowships per semester or academic year. Some of the fellowships might require only partial support—moving and administrative expenses, partial salaries, and partial support for part-time research and typing assistance and overhead. Promising younger intellectuals, as well as their already proven seniors, could devote their talents intensively to Quebec for a significant block of time in their special areas of expertise, rather than focusing only on other phenomena for which supporting funds were available.

Until sufficient markets are generated across the country and in Canada by expansion of college courses, library demands, and growth of interest among foreign-policy and other elites to make publication of books dealing largely with Quebec commercially feasible, modest subsidies are needed for those manuscripts that meet the standards of relevance and quality of suitable judges (such as most anonymous readers for the better university presses). Again, the number of manuscripts written to these standards would comprise but several in any typical year. Able comparative studies for which Quebec provided one of several cases (provided the others were not also Canadian) would usually secure publishers without need of subsidies.

These recommendations are not to denigrate further encouragement of teaching about Quebec, or of cultural activities for interested publics, or of organizations, periodicals, and other publications that encourage larger numbers of individuals to become interested in Quebec. But improvement of the quality of thought about Quebec not only in such institutions, publications, and programs, but also among diverse elites who influence action and wider opinion, requires targeting modest sums on the most promising few in institutions where they are or to which they may be attracted.

On the Quebec side, the frustratingly small number and diversity of talented researchers and analysts interested in the United States as it impinges on Quebec must be expanded by several multiples over the next generation. Although graduate training at U.S. research universities has been one source of continuing interest in the United States and in working with U.S. counterparts, it has not been and need not be a necessary precondition. The fellowships recommended above should be open to and appropriately publicized for Quebeckers and other potential non-U.S. candidates. Quebeckers could thereby broaden their perspectives on their own interests in Quebec and Canada and deepen their understanding of the U.S. side of pertinent relationships through intensive daily contacts with the most able interested Americans.

The major Quebec francophone universities and research institutions should reciprocally develop post-doctoral opportunities, more advanced fellowships, visiting professorships, and other opportunities for interested, qualified Americans to study Quebec in situ and in the context of regular exchanges of perceptions with Québécois in their respective fields. U.S. direct involvement could also gradually improve the quality of research, teaching, and thought generally about the United States in Quebec. Americans who are apt to meet appropriate standards of quality and interest and who are sufficiently fluent in French are relatively few. But there now exist no such known opportunities comparable to those offered them at major Anglo-Canadian universities.

Probably as crucial to improving elite as mass understanding of one another's societies and of relations between the two are the limited coverage, and even more the unbalanced and biased coverage, by their respective media.

The problem of convincing U.S. media elites—owners, publishers, managers, editors, and their correspondents—is apt to be difficult and long-term in resolution, given the low priority, time, and space they accord to Canadian affairs generally and the prevailing Anglo-Canadian sources and biases in the little coverage they accord to Quebec itself and to its roles in respect to Canada and to the United States. At least the major wire services and larger and more serious dailies and magazines should and could send able correspondents to Quebec who both understand French and are determined to draw out the relevant spectrum of francophone views for brief periods, to produce more balanced and penetrating interpretations. They and even the less affluent media could search out qualified francophone bilingual "stringers" who would help counterbalance articles from Anglo-Canadians. Editors, editorialists, and other "home office" professionals need to become more alert to biases in materials from Anglo-Canadian sources and more solicitous of different input from francophones.

However, the relative paucity of coverage and the systematic biases of sources of even elite francophone Quebec media are the more surprising in light of the relative significance of the United States to Quebec. Even the daily *Le Devoir* and other periodicals read by university-trained Québécois devote rather little attention to the United States, considerably less than *The Globe and Mail*, published in Toronto, *The Gazette*, published in Montreal, and other influential Canadian papers in English. A 1982 study documented that francophone printed and electronic media in general allocated much less space and time to the United States (and to world affairs as a whole) than equivalent anglophone media. Other than *Radio-Canada*, no francophone media had a staff correspondent regularly posted anywhere in the United States, and only one, the monthly of *L'Actualité*, had as many as one part-time "stringer" there.[4]

Most francophone media coverage of the United States, as of the world outside Canada generally, is by *Agence France Presse* (AFP), which is easier and less expensive to use because its articles need not be translated as do UPI, AP, Reuters, *The New York Times* News Service, and other sources in English. More cosmopolitan readers supplement AFP articles in the Quebec press with others in such French periodicals as *Le Monde, Le Point,* and *Nouvel Observateur.* All of these are written primarily for European audiences, by Europeans, with European points of view and priorities. The phenomena chosen for coverage, aspects emphasized within them, tones of articles, and implications drawn are typically not those a Québécois or other North American would write. This content results both in interest well below Québécois potentials and in views and priorities biased toward those of francophone Europeans.

Quebec media elites argue that their readers are little interested in more extensive or more appropriate coverage of the United States and that their relatively small circulations and budgets do not warrant expense of staff correspondents or even "stringers" in the United States. The same considerations apparently argue against even balancing the views of European correspondents writing for Europeans by translating U.S. or Anglo-Canadian materials into French. Penetrating these resistances and modifying these habits must be among the more important objectives of those who would improve both elite and mass Québécois understanding of the United States.

Similarly concerted efforts over an extended period gradually to develop rapport between able Québécois and their U.S. counterparts should be exerted across other professional and interest groups in the two societies. Most of the impetus needs to come from the leaderships of these respective callings, especially those on the Quebec side of the frontier; among religious groups (especially Roman Catholic), the major professions, and the creative and performing arts, to mention only the more obvious. Unless and until Quebec elites in diverse relevant fields develop mutually rewarding rapport with their U.S. equivalents, gradually approaching that attained by their Anglo-Canadian counterparts, prognoses for improved mutual understanding among larger numbers of more typical members of Quebec and U.S. society are not hopeful.

Special attention should be accorded to promising younger people who are still flexible and adventurous enough to take part and to change their perceptions. They need to be engaged particularly at the senior high school-CEGEP, undergraduate university, and professional school levels in Quebec and in nearby regions of the United States. Recommendations above relative to cooperation between Québécois and U.S. academics would much advance that end. The existing (1983) student exchange programs between Quebec universities and certain New York and New England institutions should be expanded to include at least the central campuses of the major state universities there and in adjoining states of the U.S. northeast. In none of these are standards of entry or of performance so high as to exclude the typically better, more dynamic, Quebec university students who would want to spend a semester or academic year there. Nor are the U.S. students at these top state institutions, who might go to corresponding Quebec universities, more able on the average than those who might come from Quebec. Similar exchange arrangements could probably be developed between art and drama schools, conservatories of music and dance, and other educational bodies.

The few exchanges of Quebec and especially northeastern U.S. secondary school students could also be expanded considerably toward levels now prevailing between Quebec and Anglo-Canadian provinces and among the countries of Western Europe. Most current exchanges are with anglophone Canadian families and institutions. While only those U.S. youngsters particularly advanced in French might profitably attend Québécois schools with their host families' adolescents, many more who are interested in learning French and another culture could exchange visits over extended holidays and during summers.

Effective projection of more attractive Quebec cultural aspects into the United States beyond the potentially interested francophile and French-speaking minorities and the interested minority who have francophone Canadian origins likewise requires targeting on manageable numbers of relatively receptive Americans. University and even some private and public high school students in better secondary schools— necessarily via their teachers and interested administrators—could be more widely reached through attractive teaching materials with Quebec content, films, and opportunities several times per year to attend visiting performances of small drama companies, poetry readings, *chansonniers,* and the like. Some performances might be in English, some in French. Performers could tour a particular region over a week or so, performing in universities and larger metropolitan areas where audiences were sufficiently numerous to warrant costs.

Different audiences and larger numbers could be reached by combined means as suggested by Balthazar, Gold, and Chartier. Microwave trans-missions of Radio-Canada and perhaps Radio-Quebec beyond areas near the Quebec border, coupled with concerted efforts to convince cable operators to carry these transmissions on an experimental basis, could reach an extensive audience, including many who speak little or no French. Satellite transmission and other developing technologies will provide further opportunities.

More culturally sophisticated and influential Americans could prob-ably be attracted to Quebec at their own expense via quality tourism. Such Americans search out through word of mouth, sophisticated media, and certain tourist agencies small, authentic inns, restaurants, and other subtle experiences outside mass tourism elsewhere in the world. But since few of them are aware of the Quebec opportunities or have any sources of judgment they trust about them, they almost never discover the attractive Quebec settings. The cultural potential of tourism for discriminating Americans in the northeast, in a nearby, really different culture, could be judiciously explored. Economically, the numbers of tourists and the prospective profits are small, but the potential effects on perceptions among influential minorities, and thereby on others, are substantial.

Another approach that has often proven effective in Europe and that could be attempted between Quebec and the U.S. northeast is the pairing of communities of similar size and character. Mayors, business and professional people, secondary school students, and others develop contacts over time with one another and compare experiences, problems, and solutions. Many of the linkages between particular groups suggested above could thereby be initiated and deepened over extended periods.

Only the Quebec government is likely to have the overall continuing interests, priorities, organization, visibility, and financial resources to make possible effective trial and error and follow-up implementation of these, the foregoing, and other constructive proposals apt to make a difference over the coming generation. Quebec's resources in both money and talent are of course quite limited. However, if it is to carry out its declared emphases on long-term relations with the United States, it will need to reallocate some of the resources expended on less significant objectives. The increases required are small, provided that priorities are systematically thought through in terms of achievable long-run objectives, target minorities—largely elites and future elites—are chosen accordingly, and the most potentially effective means are designed and pursued over time, by successive governments. Much larger sums could be frittered away on ephemeral endeavors for larger numbers to little lasting effect.

The sophistication and the performance of the Quebec government in these respects have measurably improved, from a very low base, since the 1960s. Nevertheless, its priorities and performance require considerable further development and refinement if it is to progress toward its declared ends with the United States. It has not yet marshalled the breadth and depth of talent available to it in Quebec—and in advisory capacities from the United States—to realize its potentials for achievement of improved relations.

Part of its problem is political. The PQ's activist nationalist base includes relatively few outside the government who have been particularly experienced with or interested in the United States. Focus on the United States within and outside the government by its active supporters is a recent development, based on practical judgments and decisions of governmental leaders rather than pressures from supporters. Until its reelection and growing economic difficulties the Lévesque government was preoccupied with its struggle with Ottawa, its efforts to persuade a Quebec majority to support sovereignty-association, and its programs to stem assimilation into anglophone Montreal and to open private-sector careers to francophones. Its best talent, material resources, and energies were so allocated.

Conversely, the nongovernmental group in Quebec most interested and involved in the United States and the one with most potential is the business community. Its more U.S.-oriented elements generally vote PLQ; they oppose the PQ government's sovereignty *raison d'etre,* its more state interventionist and state corporation bent, and its tax policies, and feel little rapport with the leadership and cabinet of intellectuals, liberal professionals, and others of negligible business experience.

Similarly, the U.S. group most interested and influential with respect to Quebec and in contact with its counterparts there is the business and financial community. Inherently cautious and conservative, they are especially wary of uncertainty and political instability, which they perceive particularly in the PQ government's sovereignty objective and its likely economic implications. Like their Québécois associates, they would feel more comfortable with a federalist PLQ government more oriented toward economic development through private initiatives, and including more business people within the government.

The task of developing serious interest in and expertise on the United States in Quebec, outside the few who are now involved, will require a significant shift of priorities. The few economists, specialists in international management, and others who have paid serious attention to the United States need to be supplemented by others systematically to sort out pertinent phenomena, implications of alternative choices, and optimal ways to proceed in a variety of specific sectors and the considerations that cut across them. Able social scientists must be drawn into empirical analyses of multiple complex impacts of diverse U.S. cultural vehicles on different segments of Quebec society, so far the subject of much more questionable speculation and rhetoric than empirical analyses. Research and teaching about the United States must be upgraded across Quebec educational institutions, gradually to remedy the prevailing situation that Balthazar appropriately describes.

Given the persisting inward-looking proclivities of many Quebec intellectuals and of the society on which these proclivities are based, drawing these individuals constructively into such labors will be no mean task. It will require not only shifts in criteria for government allocation of research funds, but strong, credible, and consistent orchestration of forceful "carrots and sticks" for several decades.

Furthermore, the ministries and other parts of the government with the responsibilities and means of bringing such efforts about—for education, culture, communications, and science and technology—are domestically rather than internationally focused. The Ministry of Intergovernmental Affairs and other parts of the government responsible for U.S. relations will need the close cooperation, the active involvement, the political "muscle," and the funds of such ministries, and thus controversial cabinet decisions supported by the premier and the most influential ministers.

Although there is considerable talk in Quebec about reaching more influential elements in the United States, relatively little serious effort seems to have been devoted to sorting out who these individuals are, whom else they influence and in what domains, and what Quebec might hope to achieve with and through them and via what means. A combination of wishful thinking, naïveté, and amateurishness seems often to mark perceptions of how pertinent U.S. institutions and elites function, and thus mark programs supposedly designed to reach them, and evaluation of their results. Quebec can avoid bureaucratic pitfalls in many programs with the United States in which others, including the Canadian government, have often fallen, whereby numbers rather than talents attracted appear a more important criterion. The talents and likely influence of those who participate and the quality of the discussions that take place should comprise overriding criteria.

It is in the basic interest of the current and any successor government to organize and bring in personnel competent to deal much more effectively with able, truly influential Americans important to Quebec's long-term interests.

Notes

1. See, for example, Alan C. Cairns, "The Strong Case for Modest Electoral Reform in Canada," unpublished paper, University of British Columbia, 1980; William P. Irvine, *Does Canada Need a New Electoral System?* (Kingston, Ont.: Institute of Intergovernmental Relations, Queens University, 1979); and Task Force for Canadian Unity, *A Future Together* (Ottawa: Government of Canada, 1979), pp. 104–106.

2. Thus, in 1976, 92.4 percent of people of the French mother tongue in the three southern New England states, 77.1 percent in the northern New England states bordering on Quebec and New Brunswick, 72.9 percent in Louisiana, and 86.4 percent elsewhere in the United States had adopted English as their principal language of use, including use at home. Continuation of French speech in the United States was even more limited to older people than in Canada outside of Quebec and adjacent areas; in both parts of New England and in Louisiana those aged forty and older were three or more times as likely to speak French than those younger than twenty, and more than seven times as likely to do so as those younger than ten years old. Although the older group of francophone ancestry was more likely to speak French in Louisiana than elsewhere, those not yet twenty in Louisiana were no more likely to do so than their counterparts in northern New England adjacent to Quebec. If these trends continue without forceful contravention, Louisianans of French heritage, who maintained French longer than any other Americans, will have become unilingual

Americans in another generation with the exception of no more than one out of twenty children and adolescents of the mid-1970s at least one of whose parents, also as children, spoke and used French regularly at home. Only in British Columbia in Canada has assimilation of francophones taken place at comparable rates to those in these U.S. areas of concentration of persons of francophone Canadian ancestry. (Calvin J. Veltman, *The Retention of Minority Languages in the United States* [Washington, D.C.: U.S. Government Printing Office, 1980], pp. 4, 8, 9, 14, 20–27.) See also Peter Woolfson, "Le Franco-Américain compagnard dans l'état de Vermont," in Claire Quintal, ed., *L'Émigrant québécois vers les États-Unis: 1850–1920* (Quebec: Le Conseil de la vie française in Amérique, 1982), pp. 92–96.

3. A special issue, "Quebec Aujourd'hui/Today," appeared in the summer of 1983 as vol. 8, no. 2.

4. *L'Information internationale au Québec: Une enquête de la Fédération professionelle des journalistes du Québec* (Montreal: Federation professionelle des journalistes du Québec, 1982), pp. 5, 42, and 46; and the report on the meeting of the Quebec Federation of Professional Journalists over this study by Bernard Descôteaux, "L'Information internationale est negligée," *Le Devoir,* December 4, 1982. *La Presse,* the influential, large-circulation Montreal daily, maintained a staff correspondent in Washington for several years but closed its office there in 1981.

Abbreviations

ABC	American Broadcasting Company
ACA	*Association Canado-Américaine*
ACSUS	Association for Canadian Studies in the United States
ADL	Anti-Defamation League of B'nai Brith
AFA	Association of Franco-Americans
AFL	American Federation of Labor
AFP	*Agence France Presse*
AJC	American Jewish Congress
AP	Associated Press
BBC	British Broadcasting Corporation
BBM	Bureau of Broadcasting Management
BRAC	Brotherhood of Railway, Airline, and Steamship Clerks
BSCQ	*Bureau de surveillance du cinéma*
CALURA	Corporations and Labor Union Returns Act
CBC	Canadian Broadcasting Company
CBS	Columbia Broadcasting System
CCCW	Canadian Confederation of Catholic Workers
CDU	Central of Democratic Unions
CEGEP	*Collège d'enseignement général et professionnel*
CEQ	Central of Education of Quebec
CFL	Canadian Federation of Labor
CJC	Canadian Jewish Congress
CLC	Canadian Labor Congress
CNTU	Confederation of National Trade Unions
CODOFIL	Council on Development of French in Louisiana (*Le conseil pour le développement du française en Louisiane*)
COFI	*Centres d'orientation et de formation des immigrants*
CP	Canadian Press

CROP	*Centre de recherche sur l'opinion publique*
CRTC	Canadian Radio-television and Telecommunications Commission
CTV	Canadian national private television network
CSU	Canadian Seamen's Union
CUSEC	Canada-U.S. Environment Committee
CVFA	Council on French Life in America (*Conseil de la Vie Française en Amérique*)
DEA	Department of External Affairs
DREE/ITC	Department of Regional Economic Expansion and International Trade and Commerce
EEC	European Economic Community
F.A.R.O.G.	Franco-American Resource Opportunity Group
FDI	foreign direct investment
FIRA	Foreign Investment Review Act (and Agency)
FLQ	*Le Front de Libération du Québec*
GATT	General Agreement on Tariffs and Trade
IJC	International Joint Commission
LSU	Louisiana State University
MNC	multinational corporation
MP	member of parliament
NATO	North Atlantic Treaty Organization
NDP	New Democratic Party
NEP	National Energy Policy
NORAD	North American Aerospace Defense Command
NTB	non-tariff barrier
OCAW	Oil, Chemical, and Atomic Workers
OPEIU	Office and Professional Employees International Union
PBS	Public Broadcasting System
PLQ	Provincial Liberal Quebec political party
PME	small and medium-sized enterprises (*petites et moyennes entreprises*)
PQ	Parti Québécois
PR	proportional representation
QFL	Quebec Federation of Labor
REXFOR	*Société de récupération, d'exploitation et de développement forestier du Québec*
SIDBEC	*Sidérurgie du Québec*
SIU	Seafarers' International Union
SNA	*Société nationale de l'aminante*
SOQUEM	*Société québécoise d'exploration minière*
SOQUIP	*Société québécoise d'initiative pétrolière*

TLC	Trades and Labor Congress
TVA	*Télédiffuseurs Associés* (French-language commercial TV network)
UPC	United Press Canada
UPI	United Press International
USL	University of Southwestern Louisiana
WJC	World Jewish Congress
YMCA	Young Men's Christian Association
YMHA	Young Men's Hebrew Association

Index

ABC (network), 180
ACA. *See* Association Canado-Américaine
Acadians, 127, 129–132, 138, 139, 141
Acid rain, 95, 96–98, 100–101, 102, 272(n1)
ACSUS. *See* Association for Canadian Studies in the United States
ActFANE. *See* Action for Franco-Americans in the Northeast
Action for Franco-Americans in the Northeast (ActFANE), 158, 161, 163
Action française, L', 110
Actualité, L', 299
Adams, Roy J., 46
ADL. *See* Anti-Defamation League
AFA. *See* Association of Franco-Americans
AFL. *See* American Federation of Labor
AFP. *See* Agence France Presse
Agence France Presse (AFP), 5, 299
Air quality, 95, 102
Alliance libérale nationale, 111
Allophones, 186–187, 205–210, 216(n2)
    assimilation of, 191–192
    emigration of, 188(table), 189
    perceptions of U.S., 212–213
    polarization of, 200–201
Alpert, Jane, 171
American Federation of Labor (AFL), 46, 48, 50, 51

American Italian Congress, 207
Americanization, 109–112, 122. *See also* Cultural influences
American Press Association, 108
American Review of Canadian Studies, The, 290
Anderson, John, 170, 175
Anglophones, 7–8, 187, 217(n5,9)
    ascendancy of, 192–195
    "charter group," 193
    economy and, 198–199
    emigration of, 188(table), 189
    immigrants and, 67
    inter-provincial relations and, 228–229
    migration of, 192–193
    polarization of, 200–201
    unions and, 49
    U.S. and, 201–216
Anti-Defamation League (ADL), 208
AP. *See* Associated Press
Appel du Congrès aux Canadiens, L', 107
Aquin, Hubert, 203
Arkansas Gazette, The, 173
Arsenault, Bona, 132, 134
Asbestos, 42, 102
Assimilationism, 191–192, 274(n28)
Associated Press (AP), 178
Association Canado-Américaine (ACA), 153, 155, 157, 163, 164, 165
Association des francophones de la Louisiane, L', 146

310